EMPLOYMENT TRIBUNAL REMEDIES HANDBOOK

2023-24 Edition

General Editor

Benjamin Gray, Littleton Chambers

Forewords

The Honourable Mrs Justice Eady DBE
President of the Employment Appeal Tribunal

Judge Barry Clarke
President Employment Tribunals (England & Wales)

Judge Susan Walker
President Employment Tribunals (Scotland)

First edition: Published April 2014

Subsequent editions published 2015 and annually thereafter

Tenth edition published June 2023

ISBN 978-1-7393103-1-8

Text © Bath Publishing Limited

Typography © Bath Publishing Limited

Bath Publishing Limited
27 Charmouth Road
Bath
BA1 3LJ
Tel: 01225 577810

email: info@bathpublishing.co.uk
www.bathpublishing.co.uk

Bath Publishing Limited is a company registered in England: 5209173
Registered Office: As above

FOREWORD BY THE HON. MRS JUSTICE EADY DBE (2022/23 edition)

In the focus on winning on liability, issues relating to remedy in employment tribunal proceedings can often be forgotten. That might seem surprising given that most claimants will have brought their claim seeking some form of remedy. Moreover, a failure to properly address remedy issues is difficult to excuse when there are reliable resources to hand, such as this Handbook, that can steer the user through the challenges that can arise when attempting to quantify the various heads of claim.

This text, now in its tenth year, has been written by an experienced practitioner from a specialist employment law set, who demonstrates a ready familiarity with the full range of issues that can arise at the remedy stage of any employment tribunal claim. The handbook is an accessible and user-friendly guide which will appeal to a wide range of readers from seasoned representatives to those facing employment tribunal proceedings for the first time. Its accessibility lies in its clear presentation, where case law references are concise and manageable. Its user-friendliness lies in its alphabetic ordering of topics and (in the e-version) its hyperlinked cross-references. The handbook also provides worked examples, based on scenarios that are drawn from real world experience. There is also a substantial section on costs awards in the employment tribunal, the risks of which are sometimes underestimated in what is intended to be a predominantly costs-free jurisdiction.

A significant proportion of appeals heard in the employment appeal tribunal are based on, or include, remedy issues. That no doubt reflects the fact that issues relating to remedy are often the most difficult aspect of any employment claim. It is therefore a great relief for an adviser, whether at first instance or on appeal, to have to hand a reliable handbook to guide them through the maze of regulatory provisions and cases to provide an accurate idea of what the remedy should be or, at least, the range within which the remedy should lie.

The handbook is a valuable contribution to this complex and rapidly developing area of law and will no doubt continue to be for many editions to come.

The Hon. Mrs Justice Eady DBE

President

Employment Appeal Tribunal

July 2022

FOREWORD BY JUDGE BARRY CLARKE (2022/23 edition)

It is a pleasure to contribute this foreword to the latest edition of the Employment Tribunal Remedies Handbook. Employment law practice and procedure has transformed during the Covid-19 pandemic and its aftermath, but the need for clear guidance on matters relating to remedy has not diminished in any way.

All litigants must apply their minds to the remedy they seek. Litigation can be a long journey, so it must be right, before setting off, to identify the destination.

There are many reasons why people bring claims before the Employment Tribunals. They might include some of the following: the chance to have "my day in court"; vindication; a desire to restore a reputation or minimise the damage to it; the wish to "be listened to"; to make sure "no one goes through what I have been through"; and the wish to be seen "not to give in easily" or to "set a precedent". However, except where making recommendations in discrimination cases, Employment Tribunal litigation is principally about the provision of financial compensation to those who win their cases. Sooner rather than later, therefore, opposing parties to an Employment Tribunal dispute must address their minds to the value of a case. In simple terms, the question "will this claim succeed?" must be accompanied by "what is this claim worth?"

To the many lawyers and litigants who will read this handbook, I respectfully suggest that the answer is not "To be confirmed", whether it is written on the ET1 or on a subsequent schedule of loss. That answer is given surprisingly often. Perhaps that is because people fear arithmetic, or worry that the answer might be complex. What if the claimant only wins part of the claim? What types of loss might result in compensation? How far into the future might loss be awarded? How should an award for injury to feelings be calculated? What effect does interest, taxation or recoupment have on the award? How might pension loss be compensated? Will any costs be recovered?

While an editor's work is never truly done in this fast-moving field, Mr Gray's commendable work gets as close as any, and this handbook benefits from its user-friendly design and the sophisticated companion online toolkit. Together, they can give parties and practitioners considerable confidence that they have accounted for all types of financial remedy and the variables that might inflate or deflate them. They can also give judges confidence that the remedy has been calculated as fairly and as accurately as possible.

Judge Barry Clarke

President

Employment Tribunals (England & Wales)

July 2022

FOREWORD BY JUDGE SUSAN WALKER

It is easy to assume that because, in Great Britain, the power to make primary and secondary employment legislation resides almost entirely with the UK Government and Parliament, employment law must therefore be uniform in that territorial area. Whilst employment law is indeed largely the same in England, Wales and Scotland, those who make the assumption that it is exactly so fall into a trap, set for those who fail to undertake the legal research that should be done by those operating their legal practice on a cross border basis. Nowhere is that trap more dangerous than in the law governing remedies in Employment Tribunals.

By way of example, those practising on a cross border basis need to know that the discount rate to be taken into account when future loss is being calculated differs as between England and Wales (currently -0.25%) and Scotland (-0.75%). Similarly, income tax rates are different. Furthermore, although the interest rate on damages is currently the same both sides of the border that has not always been the position nor will it necessarily be so in the future as the rates used are those which apply in the respective civil courts systems: these are fixed by different mechanisms.

When it comes to quantification of damages generally, Employment Tribunals in Scotland will apply principles of Scots law. Further discussion about why this is so can be found at *https://www.judiciary.uk/wp-content/uploads/2017/07/vento-consultation-response-20170904.pdf*. This means, of course, that a degree of care requires to be taken when making submissions about principles which can be derived from case law. Citing Court of Appeal decisions on quantification of damages to a Scottish Employment Tribunal may lead to some embarrassment if the principle in question forms no part of Scots law.

Those concerned with trying to ensure there are assets available to pay any award made by an Employment Tribunal, where those assets are located in Scotland, will want to be aware also of the way in which the law of diligence (including diligence on the dependence) operates in Scotland and of the possibility of a parallel application being made to the Sheriff Court for a warrant for inhibition and arrestment on the dependence of an Employment Tribunal claim. Those with an appetite to know more can find that in the decision of the Supreme Court in the case of *Anwar v Advocate General for Scotland (representing the Sec of State for BEIS)* [2021] UKSC 44.

Help, though, is at hand when navigating this difficult terrain in the form of the Employment Tribunal Remedies Handbook 2023-24. Care has been taken by the General Editor to ensure that these cross border differences are drawn to the attention of the reader, making this a reference work which will be of considerable assistance, irrespective of whether those consulting it are pleading their case before an Employment Tribunal in England and Wales, on the one hand, or in Scotland, on the other.

Judge Susan Walker

President

Employment Tribunals (Scotland)

June 2023

INTRODUCTION

Welcome to the new edition of the Employment Tribunal Remedies Handbook which once again is packed with information about the calculation of remedy in employment claims. Now into its 10th year, the Handbook is rapidly gaining a reputation as the 'go-to' resource when calculating remedy and has even been relied on by the EAT.

The handbook is an invaluable tool for potential claimants and respondents from before proceedings have been brought through to all stages of later litigation. It is as important as ever that potential claimants understand what their claims might be worth before embarking on employment tribunal litigation. It is also useful for respondents to a potential claim to know, for example, what their liabilities could be before undertaking disciplinary proceedings or a redundancy exercise. And with Early Conciliation now compulsory, both parties benefit from having the key remedy information available to enable them to reach a compromise.

All of this means that the information contained in the Employment Tribunal Remedies Handbook is essential at any stage of a dispute where the assessment and valuation of remedies is a possibility.

Each employment right that can be enforced in an employment tribunal is summarised, followed by the principles that will be applied to any remedies. For example, the common claims of unfair dismissal, discrimination and detriment are covered, and also all the numerous less litigated rights such as time off for study and training and the right of a TUPE transferee to be notified of employee liability information. For each such entry, the nature of any award is set out, such as the route to calculate a basic award or the principles that will be applied to calculate a compensatory award.

There are also separate entries for each element of a remedy and the principles used in its calculation, such as mitigation, loss of chance, tax and termination payments, grossing up, order of adjustments, recoupment, the definition of a week's pay, and many other elements of a remedy calculation. Each entry is cross-referenced to others, so it is possible to start anywhere in the book when a specific issue arises, not just at the particular right that is being enforced.

The text is supported by worked examples, to show clearly how the law is applied. 39 essential tables are included with up to date information on caps, limitation periods, Ogden tables, National Minimum Wage rates and much more, so that the information needed is always to hand.

What's new in the 2023-24 edition?

The book has been updated to include the latest limits and caps, changes in legislation and recent case law. Apart from the new figures, the main changes are set out below:

- **Covid**: As with last year, much in the way of Covid-specific employment legislation no longer applies, the effect of the backlog of tribunal litigation is that disputes involving its application may be with us for some time, with some proceedings issued during the key phases of the pandemic only starting to come to trial. Consequently, the parts of the Handbook that deal with this have been retained, but caution needs to be exercised as these parts may no longer be an up-to-date statement of the law.

- **Statutory Cap**: Two new cases have addressed the interaction between the statutory cap for unfair dismissal claims, and reinstatement and re-engagement orders. In *Dafiaghor-Olomu v Community Integrated Care* [2022] EAT 84, the EAT has confirmed that payments on account, including sums paid pursuant to a reinstatement order where an employee was not reinstated, are to be deducted before the statutory cap is applied. *University of Huddersfield v Duxbury* [2023] EAT 72 has restated and applied the principle that the cap can be lifted to ensure that the payment remains no worse for the employee than the aggregate of the compensatory and additional award.

- **Wrongful Dismissal**: A recent challenge to the "least burdensome performance" rule in wrongful dismissal claims – namely that the measure of damages for wrongful dismissal will be what would have happened had the employer taken the least burdensome (to him) approach consistent with proper performance of the contract – has failed. The rule remains good law.

- **Holiday Pay**: There is no major change to report as such (which is the first time I think I have been able to say that since I started editing this Handbook), but a section is now included to draw attention to the current Government consultation on overturning the Supreme Court's decision in *Harpur v Brazel Trust* [2022] UKSC 21. *Connor v Chief Constable of The South Yorkshire Police* [2023] EAT 42 also confirms that any agreement to calculate a payment for accrued but unused leave on termination must result in a payment equal to or greater than the formula set out in the WTRs.

- **Johnson Exclusion Zone**: Not a reference to the recent decision of the Privileges Committee, but a High Court case that helps delineate the boundaries of this concept – *Parris v Ajayi* [2021] EWHC 285 (QB). The principles extend beyond Employment Tribunal litigation but are clearly relevant to breach of contract claims that could be brought in the Employment Tribunal, so are referred to there.

- **Mitigation of Loss**: Two recent cases that are more incremental evolution than significant change, but still worth noting. *Edward v Tavistock and Portman NHS Foundation Trust* [2023] EAT 33 confirms that the correct approach to a failure to mitigate is usually to identify when the employee would have started earning, and how much they would have earnt, had they taken reasonable steps to mitigate their losses. Whilst the door is not shut on the possibility of a percentage approach in a suitable case, this is likely to be the exception and whether it is available will have to be tested on appeal. In *Hilco Capital Ltd v Harrington* [2022] EAT 156, the EAT gave a useful reminder that whilst the burden of proving an unreasonable failure to mitigate is on the employer, it is enough to discharge that burden (at least initially) if the employee has failed to look for any jobs at all. It is then for the employee to explain why such a failure was reasonable. If the explanation is said to be stigma, that will need to be supported by evidence rather than assertion or assumption.

As always, any comments or suggestions for improvement or additions for subsequent editions are most welcome. Please forward any comments to the publishers at info@bathpublishing.co.uk.

Benjamin Gray

Littleton Chambers

June 2023

Benjamin Gray is a barrister at Littleton Chambers. He advises and represents both employees and employers in all stages of employment litigation and dispute resolution across the full spectrum of employment law. Benjamin was appointed a Deputy District Judge in September 2021 and a Recorder in January 2022, sitting on the South Eastern Circuit. He is also a co-editor of Bloomsbury's *Termination of Employment*.

Contents

Contents

Table of Cases

Table of Statutes

Table of Statutes

Table of Statutory Instruments

ACAS (The Advisory, Conciliation and Arbitration Service)

(see also *Adjustments and order of adjustments***)**

An award for compensation can be increased or reduced, by up to 25%, if the employer/employee (but not worker – see *Local Government Yorkshire & Humber v Shah* UKEAT/0587/11/ZT) has unreasonably failed to comply with a relevant code of practice relating to the resolution of disputes (see s207(A) TULRC(A) 1992). A relevant code of practice will have been issued either by ACAS or the Secretary of State under ss199 to 206 TULR(C)A. At present ACAS *Code of Practice 1: Disciplinary and Grievance Procedures* (2015) is the only relevant code of practice.

The ACAS Code is not engaged unless a grievance is raised in writing and therefore the ACAS uplift is not available if a grievance is raised orally (see *The Cadogan Hotel Partners Ltd v Ozog* UKEAT/0001/14/DM, paragraph 52). 'Grievance' is defined by the Code as *'concerns, problems or complaints that employees raise with their employers'*, and appears to be construed broadly (*Ikejiaku v British Institute of Technology Ltd* UKEAT/0243/19).

Tribunals are concerned with substantive compliance with the requirements of the Code. Pretending to apply an appropriate procedure will not amount to compliance – *Rentplus v Coulson* [2022] EAT 81.

The award has both compensatory and punitive elements – *Slade v Biggs* [2021] EA-2019-00687-VP; *Secretary of State for Justice v Plaistow* [2021] UKEAT/0016/20.

The full list of tribunal jurisdictions to which s207A applies is detailed in Schedule A2 of TULR(C)A:

- s120 and s127 EA 2010 (discrimination etc in work cases);
- s145A TULR(C)A 1992 (inducements relating to union membership or activities);
- s145B TULR(C)A 1992 (inducements relating to collective bargaining);
- s146 TULR(C)A 1992 (detriment in relation to union membership and activities);
- Paragraph 156 of Schedule A1 TULR(C)A 1992 (detriment in relation to union recognition rights);
- s23 ERA 1996 (unauthorised deductions and payments);
- s48 ERA 1996 (detriment in employment);
- s111 ERA 1996 (unfair dismissal, but see below);
- s163 ERA 1996 (redundancy payments);
- s24 NMWA 1998 (detriment in relation to national minimum wage);
- The Employment Tribunals Extension of Jurisdiction (England and Wales) Order 1994 (SI 1994/1623) (breach of employment contract and termination);
- The Employment Tribunals Extension of Jurisdiction (Scotland) Order 1994 (SI 1994/1624) (corresponding provision for Scotland);
- Regulation 30 of the Working Time Regulations 1998 (SI 1998/1833) (breach of regulations);
- Regulation 32 of the Transnational Information and Consultation of Employees Regulations 1999 (SI 1999/3323) (detriment relating to European Works Councils);
- Regulation 45 of the European Public Limited-Liability Company Regulations 2004 (SI 2004/2326) (detriment in employment);
- Regulation 33 of the Information and Consultation of Employees Regulations 2004 (SI 2004/3426) (detriment in employment);
- Paragraph 8 of the Schedule to the Occupational and Personal Pension Schemes (Consultation by Employers and Miscellaneous Amendment) Regulations 2006 (SI 2006/349) (detriment in employment);
- Regulation 34 of the European Cooperative Society (Involvement of Employees) Regulations 2006 (SI 2006/2059) (detriment in relation to involvement in a European Cooperative Society);
- Regulation 17 of the Cross-border Railway Services (Working Time) Regulations 2008 (SI 2008/1660) (breach of regulations);
- Regulation 9 of the Employment Relations Act 1999 (Blacklists) Regulations 2010 (SI 2010/493) (detriment connected with prohibited list).

Where part of a claim succeeds, but the unfair dismissal claim fails, an uplift for unreasonable breaches of the ACAS Code still needs to be considered – *Brown v Veolia* [2021] UKEAT/0041/20.

Ill health capability dismissals

The ACAS Code's disciplinary provisions only apply in cases where there is *'culpable conduct'* or performance correction or punishment (*Holmes v Qinetiq Ltd* UKEAT/0206/15). In *Holmes,* the claimant was dismissed because of ill-health. No disciplinary procedure was invoked because, apart from the effects of his illness, the claimant was able to perform the job of security guard and there was no suggestion that his conduct or performance gave rise to a disciplinary situation or involved culpable conduct. That meant the employer was not required to follow the ACAS Code of

Practice on Disciplinary and Grievance Procedures and the uplift under s207A(2) was not available.

The Code does not apply to a capability dismissal arising from ill-health or sickness absence *'and nothing more'*. It does, however, apply to capability cases involving poor performance. These were confirmed in *Rentplus v Coulson* [2022] EAT 81 to amount to disciplinary situations.

Dismissal for Some Other Substantial Reason (SOSR)

In *Phoenix House Ltd v Stockman & Anor* UKEAT/0264/15/DM the EAT held that the disciplinary section of the ACAS Code, and therefore the ACAS uplift, does not apply to dismissals for some other substantial reason where *'misconduct is not alleged and capacity is not in issue'*. Mitting J rejected the provisional view expressed by Laing J in *Hussain v Jury's Inn Group Ltd* UKEAT/0283/15/JOJ said that there were *'pointers in both directions'* on this issue, holding that *'clear words in the Code'* were needed for the ACAS adjustment to apply, and this was not the case in dismissals for Some Other Substantial Reason.

However, in *Rentplus v Coulson* [2022] EAT 81, the EAT said *obiter* that it considered that the Code *was* likely to apply to SOSR dismissals where a breakdown in working relationships results from the response of the Claimant's fellow employees to their alleged misconduct or poor performance. The EAT stressed, however, that this was only a provisional view.

Absolute value

When making an adjustment under these provisions, a tribunal must take account of the absolute value of a given uplift, rather than just the percentage value. Failure to do so when the award yields *'a significantly large amount in absolute terms'* is an error of law (*Acetrip Ltd v Dogra* UKEAT/0238/18/BA). Although *Dogra* was concerned with uplifts, it seems logical that the same principle will also apply to a reduction in compensation.

Even so, the fact that the absolute value will be large does not preclude the making of a 25% award in an appropriate case. In *Slade v Biggs* [2021] EA-2019-000687-VP, Griffiths J observed that those who pay large sums in compensation should not be given the benefit of a non-statutory ceiling. There must be cases where the maximum award of 25% applied, and whilst these will only be the most serious of cases, there is no requirement that they be exceptional.

In *Secretary of State for Justice v Plaistow* [2021] UKEAT/0016/20, the EAT suggested the following approach in high-value cases:

1) Identify the amount of the award to which the uplift is applied;

2) Determine the appropriate level of uplift, assessing

the employer's level of culpability and any harm to the employee;

3) Consider what that award would mean in monetary terms, assessing this against both the totality of the award if the uplift is applied, and the proportionality of the uplift itself;

4) If necessary, adjust the percentage in light of the actual sums involved.

Approach to take

In addition to the approach outlined above in *Plaistow*, the EAT offered guidance on the approach to take to calculating ACAS uplifts in *Coulson* and *Biggs* (both citations above). Both were offered as suggestions rather than a binding test, and they are as follows:

Coulson:

1) Is the claim one which raises a matter to which the ACAS Code applies?

2) Has there been a failure to comply with the ACAS Code in relation to that matter?

3) Was the failure to comply with the ACAS Code unreasonable?

4) Is it just and equitable to award an uplift because of the failure to comply with the CASC Code and, if so, by what percentage, up to 25%?

Biggs:

1) Is the case such to make it just and equitable to award any ACAS uplift?

2) If so, what does the ET consider a just and equitable percentage, not exceeding although possibly equalling, 25%?

3) Does the uplift overlap, or potentially overlap, with other general awards, such as injury to feelings and, if so, what in the ET's judgment is the appropriate adjustment, if any, to the percentage of those awards in order to avoid double-counting?

4) Applying a final sense-check, is the sum of money represented by the application of the percentage uplift arrived at by the ET disproportionate in absolute terms and, if so, what further adjustment needs to be made?

Order of Adjustments: Where a compensatory award for unfair dismissal falls to be adjusted for unreasonable failure to comply with a relevant code of practice, the adjustment is applied immediately before any reduction for contributory conduct (s123(6)) or reduction due to the receipt of an enhanced redundancy payment in excess of the basic award (s123(7)) (see s124A(a) and *Basic award, Compensatory award, Contributory conduct, Redundancy*).

Example 1

An ex-employee is awarded a basic award of £2,000, a compensatory award of £3,000 and damages for breach of contract of £500. The employer is found to have unreasonably failed to comply with a relevant code of practice and an uplift of 25% is applied to the applicable awards. The calculation would be as follows:

The basic award remains as £2,000 because the uplift does not apply to this award.

The compensatory award is now £3,000 x 1.25 = £3,750

The damages for wrongful dismissal are now £500 x 1.25 = £625

Example 2

An ex-employee would be awarded a basic award of £2,000, a compensatory award of £3,000 and damages for breach of contract of £500. However, he received an enhanced redundancy payment of £2,500. The employee is found to have unreasonably failed to comply with a relevant code of practice and a deduction of 25% is applied to the applicable awards. The calculation would be as follows:

The basic award is reduced to zero because of the enhanced redundancy payment, but there remains £500 of enhanced redundancy payment to put into the calculation of the compensatory award: £2,500 - £2,000 = £500

The compensatory award is now (£3,000 x 0.75) - £500 = £1,750

The damages for wrongful dismissal are now £500 x 0.75 = £375

Statutory authorities: ERA 1996 *s123(6), 123(7)* and *s124A(a)*; TULR(C)A *Schedule A2*

Relevant case law: *Acetrip Ltd v Dogra* UKEAT/0238/18/BA; *Brown v Veolia* [2021] UKEAT/0041/20; *Holmes v Qinetiq Ltd* UKEAT/0206/15/BA; *Local Government Yorkshire & Humber v Shah* UKEAT/0587/11/ZT; *Phoenix House Ltd v Stockman & Anor* UKEAT/0264/15/DM; *Rentplus v Coulson* [2022] EAT 81; *Secretary of State for Justice v Plaistow* [2021] UKEAT/0016/20; *Slade v Biggs* [2021] EA-2019-00687-VP

Accelerated/decelerated receipt

(see also *Adjustments and order of adjustments;* ***Table 38*****)**

Accelerated receipt

If an award is made to a claimant to compensate for future losses, they are in fact receiving the money before they would have received it if they had not been dismissed. The idea behind the discount for accelerated receipt, therefore, is to take into account any interest that might in fact be earned on this money if it were invested as a lump sum, when it would not ordinarily have been available to the claimant to do so.

A discount for accelerated receipt can be made on awards for future loss, including the compensatory award and an award for financial losses in a discrimination claim. The reduction will only apply to future losses, such as future income and benefits.

No discount will need to be applied if the award for future loss is relatively small, as will often be the case (see *Les Ambassadeurs Club v Bainda* [1982] IRLR 5).

There is no established route to calculate the appropriate reduction. Tribunals sometimes merely apply a single percentage adjustment to recognise accelerated receipt. However, in *Bentwood Bros (Manchester) Ltd v Shepherd* [2003] IRLR 364 the Court of Appeal overturned a decision to make a single 5% reduction for an award that covered 10 years' loss. It will always be necessary for a tribunal to set out the method it has used and its reasons for using it.

Decelerated receipt

Melia v Magna Kansei Ltd [2005] EWCA Civ 1547 holds that in principle an uplift can be applied for decelerated, or delayed, receipt to ensure that past and future losses are treated consistently.

Such awards are rare in practice, and *Francois v Castle Rock Properties Ltd (t/a Electric Ballroom)* EAT/0260/10 observes that it is not the routine practice of tribunals to make such awards. The logic underlying decelerated receipt adjustments is unlikely to apply in discrimination cases, where there are already specific provisions for interest.

It is an open question whether such an adjustment should be applied in cases where there is no future loss: the principle of *Melia* is to treat the past and future losses consistently, an issue that does not arise where only one of the two awards is made.

A tribunal may choose to use a similar approach to that used for accelerated receipt (but in the opposite direction) to calculate the interest due on an award paid after the loss has been incurred.

In *Francois* the EAT observed that when considering an adjustment for decelerated receipt, the tribunal is considering '*the loss of the use of the money which the recipient should have had earlier. Interest may be a measure of that loss. Other measures may also be appropriate.*'

Adjustments: The discount/increase for accelerated/decelerated receipt should be made within the first stage of any calculation, namely calculating the loss suffered by the individual. Any adjustments will be made afterwards (see also *Adjustments and order of adjustments*).

Statutory authorities: None

Relevant case law: *Benchmark Dental Laboratories Group v Perfitt* EAT/0304/04; *Bentwood Bros (Manchester) Ltd v Shepherd* [2003] EWCA Civ 380; *Francois v Castle Rock Properties Ltd (t/a Electric Ballroom)* EAT/0260/10; *Les Ambassadeurs Club v Bainda* [1982] IRLR 5; *Melia v Magna Kansei Ltd* [2005] EWCA Civ 1547; *York Trailer Co Ltd v Sparkes* [1973] IRLR 348

Accompaniment to a disciplinary, grievance or flexible working meeting

A worker has the right to be accompanied at a grievance or disciplinary meeting (s10 and s11 ERelA 1999), at a meeting to discuss their right to flexible working meeting (Reg 14 and Reg 15 FW(PR) Regs 2002) or at a meeting to discuss their right to make a request in relation to study or training (ss63D to 63K ERA 1996) (Reg 16 and Reg 17 EST(PR) Regs 2010) and a worker is allowed to have time off to accompany the other worker to the meeting. The worker is allowed to postpone the meeting in certain circumstances.

Remedy: Where a tribunal finds a complaint of a failure to comply well founded, it may make an award of up to 2 weeks' pay.

Gross or net: Gross. A week's pay as defined in ss220 to 229 ERA 1996 applies (see *Week's pay*).

Limit on a week's pay: £643 (see *Table 1* for historical rates).

Limit on number of weeks: 2

Any maximum or minimum: Maximum = £1,286; No minimum

Adjustments: None

Tax: The tax treatment relating to non-termination payments is not clear. If the claimant was claiming this head of loss alongside unfair or wrongful dismissal, it is arguable that any award under this head would be included in the compensatory award and therefore taxable under s401 ITEPA 2003. If the claimant's employment has not been terminated however, it could be argued that no tax is payable - the award is not 'earnings', nor is it an award on termination of employment, or change of duties or earnings (see *Tax and termination payments*).

Recoupment: N/A

Statutory authorities: ERelA 1999 *ss10* and *11*; ERA

1996 *s63D* to *63K*; EST(PR) Regs 2010 (SI 2010/155) Regs *16* and *17*; FW(PR) Regs 2002 (SI 2002/3207) Regs *14* and *15*

Additional award

(see also *Arrears of pay (reinstatement/re-engagement); Re-engagement and reinstatement***)**

An additional award may be made where an employer has failed to comply with an order for reinstatement or re-engagement made under s113 ERA 1996, following a finding of unfair dismissal, and has failed to establish that it was not practicable for them to comply. See also s166 TULR(C)A 1992.

Remedy: The award differs according to whether there has been partial or total non-compliance. Only where there has been total non-compliance with the order will the additional award be made. In both cases, a separate award of compensation to cover financial losses will be made, subject to a statutory cap (see below).

Partial compliance: An employer will be ordered to pay compensation to an employee if an employee is reinstated or re-engaged pursuant to such an order, but the employer does not fully comply with the terms of that order (s117(1) ERA 1996).

The tribunal will award the amount it thinks fit having regard to the loss sustained by the employee in consequence of that failure to comply, but there is no power to order an additional award for partial compliance.

Total non-compliance: If an order for reinstatement or re-engagement is made, but the employee is not reinstated or re-engaged, a compensatory award will be made under s124 ERA 1996 and an additional award of compensation of between 26 and 52 weeks' pay will be made (s117(3)).

The additional award will not be made, however, if the employer satisfies the tribunal that it was not practicable to comply with the order. The hiring of a permanent replacement will not satisfy this condition unless it was not practicable to arrange for the employee's work to be done without hiring a permanent replacement (s117(4) and s117(7)).

Calculation: Additional award = number of weeks x gross weekly pay

Gross or net: Gross. A week's pay as defined in ss220 to 229 ERA 1996 applies (see *Week's pay*).

Limit on a week's pay: £643 (see *Table 1* for historical rates).

Limit on number of weeks: Minimum is 26; Maximum is 52

Any maximum or minimum: Minimum depends

on employee's gross weekly pay (but see *National Minimum Wage*); Maximum is £33,436

Adjustments: The following applies to compensation (but not the additional award itself): where the claimant has unreasonably prevented an order for reinstatement or re-engagement from being complied with, and where the tribunal makes an award of compensation for losses suffered (see above) the tribunal will take that conduct into account as a failure on the part of the claimant to mitigate his loss.

Cap: The statutory cap applies to an award under s117(1) and (2) and s123 ERA 1996. The statutory cap is currently the lower of £105,707 or 52 weeks' gross pay (as defined in ss220 to 229 ERA 1996) (see s124 ERA 1996). It should be noted that the cap will be lifted to the extent necessary to compensate for arrears of pay and any additional award:

- in the case of compensation awarded under s117(1) (where there has been partial compliance) the cap can be exceeded to the extent necessary to enable the award fully to reflect the amount specified as payable under s114(2)(a) or s115(2)(d) (see *Arrears of pay (reinstatement/re-engagement)*). In other words, the employee is entitled to receive at least their arrears of pay, even if those arrears exceed the cap;

- in the case of an award under s117(3) (where the employer has not complied at all) the cap may be exceeded to the extent necessary to allow the aggregate of the compensatory and additional awards fully to reflect the amount specified as payable under s114(2)(a) or s115(2)(d) (see *National Westminster Bank Plc v Parry* [2004] EWCA Civ 1563 and *University of Huddersfield v Duxbury* [2023] EAT 72).

This means that, in the case of partial compliance:

- if the arrears of pay exceed the cap on their own, the individual will receive the total amount of arrears;

- if the arrears of pay do not exceed the cap on their own they will be offset against the compensatory award.

In the case of complete non-compliance:

- if the arrears of pay exceed the aggregate of the capped compensation award and the additional award, the individual will receive the total amount of arrears;

- if the arrears do not exceed the sum of the capped compensation award and the additional award, the arrears will be offset against this aggregate.

Mitigation: The additional award is not expressly related to an employee's losses, or to mitigation, however a tribunal may well take into account an employee's losses and attempts to mitigate them in reaching the amount of the award, particularly perhaps if the statutory cap prevents full recovery of the employee's losses.

Tax: The additional award will be taxed under s401 ITEPA 2003 and can be taken into account within the £30,000 tax free amount at termination (see also *Grossing up*).

Recoupment: Recoupment does not apply to the additional award but it does apply to any compensation awarded under s123 as a result of non-compliance with s113 and to arrears of pay which may have been ordered by ss114 or 115.

Statutory authorities: ERA 1996 *ss113 to 118*

Relevant case law: *National Westminster Bank Plc v Parry* [2004] EWCA Civ 1563; *Selfridges Ltd v Malek* [1998] ICR 268

Example 1

Basic award = £3,000

Financial losses = maximum available for this employee (52 weeks) = £25,000

Additional award = £15,000

Arrears of pay = £5,000 (The arrears of pay are included within the compensatory award with the remaining losses capped at £25,000 - £5,000 = £20,000)

Award = £3,000 + £25,000 + £15,000 = £43,000

Example 2

Basic award = £3,000

Financial losses = zero

Statutory cap for this employee is £25,000 (52 weeks' pay)

Additional award = zero (reinstatement or re-engagement order was partially complied with)

Arrears of pay = £28,000

Award = £3,000 + £28,000 = £31,000

Example 3

Basic award = £3,000

Financial losses = maximum available for this employee (52 weeks) = £30,000

Additional award = £25,000

Arrears of pay = £60,000

Aggregate of financial losses and additional award = £55,000, which is lower than the arrears of pay (£60,000) so replace the lower figure with £60,000.

Total Award = £3,000 + £60,000 = £63,000

Adjustments and order of adjustments

(see also *ACAS (The Advisory, Conciliation and Arbitration Service)*; *Accelerated/decelerated receipt*; *Contributory conduct*; *Interest*; *Polkey*; *Protected disclosure*)

It is important that adjustments are applied to awards in the correct order since this can significantly affect the final figure.

This can be seen in *Digital Equipment Co Ltd v Clements* [1997] EWCA Civ 2899; [1998] ICR 258. Mr Clements argued that the redundancy payment of £20,685 should be deducted from the compensatory award of £43,136, leaving a balance of £22,451; which should then be reduced by 50% (*Polkey*) giving a compensatory award of £11,275. This would result in the then-maximum of £11,000 being payable. Digital argued that the tribunal should give full credit for the enhanced redundancy payment and first reduce the loss by 50%, leaving a compensatory award of £21,568 from which the tribunal should then deduct the £20,685, leaving a balance of £883. The tribunal ruled in favour of the claimant, but the decision was overturned by the EAT and the Court of Appeal, leaving the claimant with £883.

Different adjustments apply to the different types of award - these adjustments, and the correct order in which they should be applied, are listed below.

Adjustments to the compensatory award

1) Calculate the total losses suffered by the claimant;

2) Deduct any amounts received from the employer such as payment in lieu of notice or a payment which is made to the employee as compensation for the dismissal (*Digital Equipment Co Ltd v Clements* [1997] EWCA Civ 289; *Dafiaghor-Olomu v Community Integrated Care* [2022] EAT 84). This must exclude any enhanced redundancy payment above the basic award;

3) Deduct earnings which have mitigated the claimant's loss or a sum which reflects any failure by the claimant to mitigate his or her loss (s123(4) ERA 1996) (see also *Mitigation*);

4) A '*Polkey*' deduction to reflect the chance that the claimant would have been dismissed in any event had the employer acted fairly (*Polkey v AE Dayton Services Ltd* [1987] IRLR 50 (HL)) (see also *Polkey*);

5) Decrease/increase for accelerated/decelerated receipt of compensation in respect of future/past loss (*Bentwood Bros (Manchester) Ltd v Shepherd* [2003] EWCA Civ 380) (see also *Accelerated/ decelerated receipt*);

6) Percentage increase or reduction up to a maximum of 25% to reflect an unreasonable failure by the employer or employee to comply with the ACAS disciplinary code (s207A TULR(C)A) (see *ACAS (The Advisory, Conciliation and Arbitration Service)*);

7) A percentage reduction, up to a maximum of 25%, if a protected disclosure was not made in good faith (see also *Protected disclosure*);

8) Any extra award for a failure by the employer to provide written particulars of employment (s38 EA 2002) (see also *Written statement of particulars*);

9) Percentage reduction for any contributory conduct on the part of the employee (s123(6) ERA 1996). Note that this percentage does not have to be same as any such deduction to the basic award (see also *Contributory conduct*);

10) Deduction for any enhanced redundancy payment to the extent that it exceeds the basic award (s123(7) ERA 1996) (see also *Redundancy*);

11) Interest on past losses, if available (see also *Interest*);

12) Gross up (see *Grossing up*);

13) Apply the statutory cap if relevant (see *Statutory cap*).

Adjustments to the basic award

The basic award can be reduced in the following situations:

- By an amount that the tribunal considers to be just and equitable where the employee has unreasonably refused an offer of reinstatement (s122(1) ERA 1996);

- By an amount to reflect contributory conduct (s122(2) ERA 1996). Note though that s122(2) does not apply in redundancy cases except as provided for in s122(3) (see *Basic award* and *Basic award, minimum* below). This percentage reduction does not have to be the same as that for the compensatory award. Note the case of *Granchester Construction (Eastern) Ltd v Attrill* UKEAT/0327/12/LA, where a 50% *Polkey* deduction was made to the compensatory award, and both the basic and compensatory awards were also reduced by 10%. The EAT said '*Whereas it may be appropriate to moderate what would otherwise be the degree of contributory conduct that would reduce an award because there have been matters of conduct taken into account in assessing the chances of a fair dismissal, so that it might be in effect double counting to impose upon the claimant a further reduction by way of contributory conduct, that reasoning cannot apply to that part of the award to which the*

Polkey principle itself does not apply' (i.e. the basic award);

- By any redundancy payment paid on termination for a genuine redundancy or as ordered by the tribunal (but see also *Redundancy*) (s122(4) ERA 1996). This must be a redundancy in fact, rather than one incorrectly labelled as such by the employer, even if the employee accepted the label at the time (see *Bowyer v Siemens plc* UKEAT/0021/05/SM). Any excess goes towards reducing the compensatory award (see *Boorman v Allmakes* [1995] IRLR 553);

- By an amount that the tribunal considers to be just and equitable where the claimant has been awarded an amount under a designated dismissal procedures agreement (s122(3A));

- Where the dismissal is unfair by virtue of s104F (blacklists) the basic award will be reduced (or further reduced) by the amount of any basic award paid in respect of the same dismissal under s156 TULR(C)A (minimum basic award in case of dismissal on grounds related to trade union membership or activities).

The basic award cannot be:

- increased or decreased for the failure by the employer/employee to comply with the ACAS Code of Practice (see s124A and s118(1)(b) ERA 1996);

- increased following a failure to provide the employee with a written statement of terms and conditions of employment, as that increase is applied within the compensatory award (s38 EA 2002 and s124A and s118(1)(b) ERA 1996);

- reduced on account of the employee's failure to mitigate their loss;

- reduced under *Polkey* (unless it is an *'exceptionally rare case where such a (fair) dismissal might have taken place virtually contemporaneously with the unfair dismissal which actually occurred'* - see again *Granchester Construction (Eastern) Ltd v Attrill* UKEAT/0327/12/LA, paragraph 19).

Minimum basic award under s120 ERA 1996

If the minimum award of £7,836 has been made because the principal reason for a redundancy dismissal was one of the reasons set out in s120(1) the figure may still be reduced for contributory conduct, but the percentage reduction is applied to the difference between what the claimant would have received under the standard case and the minimum £7,836. For example, if the claimant would only have received £2,000 but does in fact qualify for the minimum £7,836, any contributory conduct will be applied to the difference, i.e. £5,836.

Adjustments to a discrimination award

1) Possibly contributory conduct (but see *Discrimination* for further information);

2) Failure to comply with the ACAS Code of Practice;

3) Interest can be added to the awards for injury to feelings, personal injury, aggravated damages and the award for financial loss (see *Interest*);

4) Where a dismissal is both discriminatory and unfair, the tribunal should make the award for compensation under the discrimination legislation, but may also make a basic award (see *D'Souza v London Borough of Lambeth* [1997] IRLR 677).

Adjustments to damages for wrongful dismissal

Damages for wrongful dismissal can be adjusted in 3 ways:

1) An increase/decrease for the failure by the employer/employee to comply with the ACAS Code of Practice (see s207A and Schedule A2 of TULR(C)A);

2) A deduction for any contingencies and any accelerated payment of damages, which is only likely to arise where the (unexpired) period of notice under the contract is substantial;

3) Interest may be awarded from the date of the cause of action to the date of the hearing but only in the County Court, High Court and Court of Appeal. The ET does not have jurisdiction to award interest on a breach of contract.

Grossing up and the statutory cap

Grossing up is applied after all the adjustments have been applied (see also *Grossing up*).

The statutory cap is applied after the grossing up calculation (see also *Statutory cap*).

Example 1

Awards
Basic award = £3,000

Financial loss = £10,000

Adjustments
Contributory conduct (basic and compensatory awards) = 10%

ACAS uplift = 25%

Calculation
Total award = (£3,000 x 0.9) + (£10,000 x 0.9 x 1.25 but see note below) = £2,700 (basic award) + £11,250 (compensatory award) = £13,950

Remember that adjustments are **multiplied** cumulatively. In other words, don't add/subtract the adjustment percentages to get the overall change (i.e. an increase of 25% and a decrease of 10% does **not**

7

translate into an increase of 15%). The actual overall increase is 12.5% (because 1.25 x 0.9 = 1.125, where the .125 represents the 12.5%)

Example 2
Awards
Basic award = £3,000

Financial loss = £10,000

Award for lack of written particulars = 2 weeks' pay = £600

Credits
Ex gratia payment = £500

Earnings = £750

Adjustments
Contributory conduct (basic and compensatory awards) = 10%

Polkey deduction = 30%

Calculation
Basic award = £3,000 x 0.9 = £2,700 (*Polkey* does not apply to the basic award).

The order of adjustments for the compensatory award must be carefully considered because we have a mixture of multiplication (contributory conduct) and addition/subtraction (lack of written particulars, *ex gratia* payment and earnings). It is important that the order given on the previous page is followed.

The financial loss is first reduced by £500 and £750 and then the *Polkey* deduction is applied = (£10,000 - £500 - £750) x 0.7 = £6,125

Next, add the failure to provide written particulars = £6,125 + £600 = £6,725

Then apply the contributory conduct adjustment = £6,725 x 0.9 = £6,052.50

Total award = £2,700 (basic award) + £6,052.50 (compensatory award) = £8,752.50

Example 3
Awards
Basic award = £3,000

Financial loss = £10,000

Award for lack of written particulars = 2 weeks' pay = £600

Credits
Ex gratia payment = £500

Earnings = £750

Redundancy payment made on termination = £5,000

Adjustments
Contributory conduct (compensatory award only) = 10%

Polkey deduction = 30%

ACAS uplift = 15%

Calculation
First reduce the Basic Award by any redundancy pay received. The redundancy pay here exceeds the basic award, so this element is zero. The remainder (£5,000 - £3,000 = £2,000) goes towards reducing the compensatory award, but only at the end of the calculation.

The financial loss is first reduced by £500 and £750 and then the *Polkey* deduction and the ACAS uplift are applied = (£10,000 - £500 - £750) x 0.7 x 1.15 = £7,043.75

Next, the failure to provide written particulars is added = £7,043.75 + £600 = £7,643.75

Then contributory conduct has to be applied = £7,643.75 x 0.9 = £6,879.38

Finally, the remainder of the redundancy pay is deducted to the extent of the excess beyond the basic award = £6,879.38 - (£5,000 - £3,000) = £4,879.38

Total Award = £4,879.38

Example 4
This is identical to example 3 apart from the fact that the basic award also has contributory conduct applied to it.

Awards
Basic award = £3,000

Financial loss = £10,000

Award for lack of written particulars = 2 weeks' pay = £600

Credits
Ex gratia payment = £500

Earnings = £750

Redundancy pay paid on termination = £5,000

Adjustments
Contributory conduct (basic **and** compensatory awards) = 10%

Polkey deduction = 30%

ACAS uplift = 15%

Calculation
First the basic award needs to be reduced for contributory conduct = £3,000 x 0.9 = £2,700 Next it is reduced by any redundancy pay received. The redundancy pay exceeds the reduced basic award so the reduced basic award is zero. The remainder (£5,000 - £2,700 = £2,300) goes towards reducing the compensatory award, but only at the end of the calculation.

The financial loss is first reduced by £500 and £750 and

the *Polkey* deduction and the ACAS uplift are applied = (£10,000 - £500 - £750) x 0.7 x 1.15 = £7,043.75

Next, the failure to provide written particulars is added = £7,043.75 + £600 = £7,643.75

Then contributory conduct is applied = £7,643.75 x 0.9 = £6,879.38

Finally, the remainder of the redundancy pay should be deducted to the extent of the excess of the **reduced** basic award = £6,879.38 - £2,300 = £4,579.38

Total Award = £4,579.38

Statutory authorities: EA 2002 *s38*; ERA 1996 *ss118(1)(b), 120, 122(1) & (2), 123(4), (6) & (7)* and 124A; *The Industrial Tribunals (Interest on Awards in Discrimination Cases) Regulations 1996*; TULR(C)A *s207A & Schedule A2*

Relevant case law: *Bentwood Bros (Manchester) Ltd v Shepherd* [2003] EWCA Civ 380; *Dafiaghor-Olomu v Community Integrated Care* [2022] EAT 84; *Digital Equipment Co Ltd v Clements* [1997] EWCA Civ 2899; *Granchester Construction (Eastern) Ltd v Attrill* UKEAT/0327/12/LA; *Hardie Grant London Ltd v Aspden* [2012] I.C.R. D6 (EAT); *Polkey v AE Dayton Services Ltd* [1987] IRLR 50 (HL)

Adoption leave: see *Detriment*; *Unfair dismissal*; *Table 16*

Age discrimination: see *Discrimination*

Agency workers

Regulations 5, 12, 13 and 17(2) of the Agency Workers Regulations 2010/93 give agency workers a variety of rights, including the rights 'to the same basic working and employment conditions' as if they had been employed directly by those hiring them, where they have been working in the same role for the same hirer for 12 continuous calendar weeks (Regulation 5).

If a complaint to an Employment Tribunal in respect of a breach of the Regulations is held to be well-founded, regulation 18(8) directs the tribunal to take such of the following steps as it considers just and equitable:

1) Making a declaration as to the rights of the complainant in relation to the matters to which the complaint relates;

2) Ordering the respondent to pay compensation to the complainant;

3) Recommending that the respondent take, within a specified period, action appearing to the tribunal to be reasonable, in all the circumstances of the case, for the purpose of obviating or reducing the adverse effect on the complainant of any matter to which the complaint relates.

Any such compensation is to be 'such as the tribunal considers just and equitable in all the circumstances having regard to (a) the infringement or breach to which the complaint relates; and (b) any loss which is attributable to the infringement'. This loss is to be taken to include 'any expenses reasonably incurred by the complainant in consequence of the infringement or breach; and loss of any benefit which the complainant might reasonably be expected to have had but for the infringement or breach.'

This sum must not be less than 2 weeks' pay where the complaint is an infringement of Regulations 5 and 10, unless such a sum would not be a just and equitable amount 'taking into account the conduct of the claimant and the respondent', in which case a lower sum may be awarded.

An additional award may be granted where the agency or hirer is considered to have structured its assignments 'to prevent the agency worker from being entitled to, or from continuing to be entitled to, the rights conferred by Regulation 5', and but for that structure the agency worker would, or would continue to, be entitled to rights under Regulation 5. Such an award is not to be more than £5,000.

Alternatively, the tribunal may order the respondent to pay a penalty to the Secretary of State under s12A Employment Tribunals Act 1996.

If there is more than one respondent, the amount of compensation payable by either respondent is to be 'such as may be found by the tribunal to be just and equitable having regard to the extent of each respondent's responsibility for the infringement to which the complaint relates'. If an additional award is made, this is also to be apportioned on a 'just and equitable' basis 'having regard to the extent to which [the tribunal] considers each to have been responsible for the fact that' the assignments have been structured to avoid conferring Regulation 5 rights.

Failure to comply with any recommendation made by the tribunal, without reasonable justification, gives the tribunal the discretion (if it considers it just and equitable to do so) to increase the amount of any compensation ordered, or award compensation if it has not already done so.

The correct approach to compensation has been considered by the Court of Appeal in *London Underground Ltd v Amissah and Others* [2019] EWCA Civ 125:

1) The tribunal must identify the infringement – this is not simply a right to the same terms and conditions, but a right to actually receive the benefits in question.

2) The tribunal must then identify the loss attributable to the infringement – this is ordinarily the amount necessary *'to compensate the claimant for the pecuniary loss suffered as a result of the infringement'*. The reference to compensation being *'just and equitable'* is said to mean that tribunals have a degree of flexibility in the approach to proof of loss.

3) Where more than one respondent has been found liable, the tribunal must decide the question of apportionment as a percentage, based on the extent of the parties' relative responsibility for the breach. This consists of two elements:

   (i) Causation: the extent to which each wrongdoer contributed to the occurrence of the breach; and

   (ii) Culpability: their degree of relative fault.

4) Although it is open to tribunals to award less than the amount of the claimant's loss, or for a respondent to be ordered to pay the claimant less than the amount for which it is "responsible", such occasions are described respectively as *'extremely uncommon'* and *'exceptional'*. The Court of Appeal suggested their possible application in cases of fraud or *'serious misconduct'* by the claimant.

In assessing the loss, the tribunal should ask itself what would have happened but for the infringement for which the relevant party was responsible.

Injury to feelings is excluded for claims under Regulations 5, 12, 13, 10(1)(a) to (d) (see Reg 18(15)) but it does appear to apply to unfair dismissal claims under the regulations.

Gross or net: The compensation is calculated according to a week's pay, which is a gross figure.

A week's pay is defined as the higher of:

- the average weekly pay received by the agency worker in the previous 4 weeks in relation to the assignment to which the claim relates; and

- the average weekly pay that the agency worker should have received in the previous 4 weeks in relation to the assignment to which the claim relates.

Only payments in respect of basic pay whether by way of annual salary, payments for actual time worked or by reference to output or otherwise should be taken into account.

Limit on a week's pay: None

Any maximum or minimum: Minimum is 2 week's pay, unless 2 week's pay is not a just and equitable amount of compensation, in which case the tribunal can reduce the amount as it considers appropriate; There is no maximum.

Additional award: No minimum; Maximum is £5,000

Adjustments: The award can be reduced for contributory conduct (Reg 18(17)).

Mitigation: The tribunal may reduce the amount if it considers that the claimant has failed to mitigate their loss (Reg 18(16)).

Tax: The tax treatment is not clear. To the extent that any sum awarded is compensation for lost earnings, it is likely to be taxed under s62 ITEPA 2003.

Statutory authorities: Agency Workers Regulations 2010/93; Employment Tribunals Act 1996 s12A

Relevant case law: *London Underground Ltd v Amissah and Others* [2019] EWCA Civ 125

Aggravated damages

Aggravated damages are available in discrimination claims in England and Wales, but not in Scotland. They are an aspect of injury to feelings, and are awarded only on the basis, and to the extent that the aggravating features have increased the impact of the discriminatory act on the claimant and thus the injury to his or her feelings. They are compensatory, not punitive. The appropriate acts include:

- ***Where the act is done in an exceptionally upsetting way***: Underhill P in *Commissioner of Police of the Metropolis v Shaw* UKEAT/0125/11/ZT cites the phrase *'high-handed, malicious, insulting or oppressive'* behaviour;

- ***Motive***: discriminatory conduct that is evidently based on prejudice or animosity or which is spiteful or vindictive or intended to wound is likely to cause more distress than if done without such a motive – for example as a result of ignorance or insensitivity. Naturally, the claimant has to be aware of the motive in question; and

- ***Subsequent conduct***: for example, conducting the trial in an unnecessarily oppressive manner, failing to apologise, or failing to treat the complaint with the requisite seriousness. (*Bungay & Anor v Saini & Ors* UKEAT/0331/10 and *Zaiwalla & Co v Walia* [2002] UKEAT/451/00).

Tribunals must beware the risk of double recovery, and consider whether the overall award of injury to feelings and aggravated damages is proportionate to the totality of the suffering caused to the claimant.

If a tribunal makes an award of aggravated damages *'it is incumbent upon [it]... to explain why the amount of the basic award that it has made is insufficient to compensate the claimant and the extent to which the conduct giving rise to the award of aggravated damages has increased the impact of the discriminatory act on the claimant'* (*Wilson Barca LLP and others v Shirin* [2020] UKEAT/0276/19). 'Basic award' here should be taken to mean the amount awarded in respect of injury to feelings absent any increase for aggravated damages.

It is good practice to formulate aggravated damages as a sub-heading of injury to feelings – i.e. *'injury to feelings in the sum of £x, incorporating aggravated damages in the sum of £y'.*

Remedy: There is no specific calculation but it would appear from the decided cases that £20,000 is the top end of the bracket for aggravated damages. The award is compensatory, not punitive. There is no minimum award.

Double Recovery: Where an award of aggravated damages is made in respect of conduct that also results in an ACAS uplift (see *ACAS (The Advisory, Conciliation and Arbitration Service)*), the tribunal must avoid awarding twice in respect of the same loss (*Base Childrenswear Ltd v Otshudi* [2019] UKEAT/0267/18).

Adjustments: Interest can be applied (see also *Interest*) but no other adjustments are applicable.

Mitigation: N/A

Tax: The award is likely to be treated in the same way as an award for injury to feelings (see also *Injury to feelings* and *Tax and termination payments*).

Recoupment: N/A

Relevant case law: *Base Childrenswear Ltd v Otshudi* UKEAT/0267/18; *Bungay & Anor v Saini & Ors* UKEAT/0331/10; *Commissioner of Police of the Metropolis v Shaw* UKEAT/0125/11/ZT; *Ministry of Defence v Fletcher* [2009] UKEAT/0044/09; *Singh v University Hospital NHS Trust* EAT/1409/01; 1409/01; Zaiwalla & Co v Walia [2002] UKEAT/451/00; *Wilson Barca LLP and others v Shirin* [2020] UKEAT/0276/19; *Zaiwalla & Co v Walia* [2002] UKEAT/451/00

Ante-natal: see *Time off for ante-natal care*

Apprentices: see *National Minimum Wage*

Arrears of pay (reinstatement/re-engagement)

(see also *Additional award***)**

Where a tribunal makes an order for reinstatement or re-engagement, the claimant is entitled to arrears of pay from the date of dismissal to the date of reinstatement/re-engagement in respect of any benefit

that the employee might reasonably be expected to have had but for the dismissal. In the case of *National Westminster Bank Plc v Parry* [2004] EWCA Civ 1563 the court stated: *'Plainly that envisages a sum which will be payable whether or not the order for reinstatement is obeyed.'*

Reinstatement: if the claimant would have benefited from an improvement in his terms and conditions of employment had he not been dismissed, an order for reinstatement shall require him to be treated as if he had benefited from that improvement from the date on which he would have done so but for being dismissed. This could also include accrued holiday pay (s114 ERA 1996).

Re-engagement: again, the claimant is entitled to full back pay plus any accrued holiday pay. Arrears are normally calculated on the basis of the claimant's pay prior to dismissal, even if the new job on re-engagement is paid at a lower rate.

Remedy: The award will be the sum of any pay and benefits between the date of dismissal and reinstatement/re-engagement. Any payment in lieu, *ex gratia* payments paid by the employer, and any wages the employee has earned since dismissal should be deducted as well as any other benefits the tribunal thinks appropriate (see s114(4) and s115(3)).

Where an employer reinstates or re-engages an employee but fails fully to comply with the order, the loss suffered by the employee can be compensated for under s117(1), including any arrears of pay and benefits.

Where an employer fails to reinstate or re-engage a claimant, the losses suffered, including any unpaid arrears of pay and benefits, will fall to be compensated under the compensatory award (see s117(3)(a)).

Gross or net: Calculated on gross pay.

Adjustments: None

Cap: The statutory cap applies to an award under s117(1) and (2) ERA and s123. The statutory cap is currently the lower of £105,707 or 52 weeks' pay (as defined in ss220 to 229 ERA 1996) (see s124 ERA 1996). It should be noted that the cap will be lifted to the extent necessary to compensate for arrears of pay and any additional award:

- in the case of compensation awarded under s117(1) where the order for reinstatement or re-engagement has been partially complied with, the cap can be exceeded to the extent necessary to enable the award fully to reflect the amount specified as payable under s114(2)(a) or s115(2)(d). In other words, the employee is entitled to receive at least their arrears of pay, even if those arrears exceed the cap;

- in the case of an award under s117(3) (i.e. an award where the employer has not complied at all with an order for reinstatement or re-engagement) the statutory cap may be exceeded to the extent necessary to enable the aggregate of the compensatory and additional awards fully to reflect the amount specified as payable under s114(2)(a) or s115(2)(d) (see *National Westminster Bank Plc v Parry* [2004] EWCA Civ 1563).

This means that, in the case of partial compliance:

- if the arrears of pay exceed the cap on their own, the individual will receive the total amount of arrears;

- if the arrears of pay do not exceed the cap on their own they will be offset against the compensatory award.

In the case of complete non-compliance:

- if the arrears of pay exceed the aggregate of the capped compensation award and the additional award, the individual will receive the total amount of arrears;

- if the arrears do not exceed the sum of the capped compensation award and the additional award, the arrears will be offset against this aggregate.

In other words, the arrears of pay award is not freestanding - the arrears of pay, which by itself does not exceed the cap, should not be disregarded when applying the statutory cap (see *National Westminster Bank Plc v Parry* [2004] EWCA Civ 1563).

Mitigation: Any actual mitigation will be taken into account in identifying the loss suffered (s114(4) and s115(3)).

Tax: The arrears of pay sum is compensation for unfair dismissal and so is taxable only under s401 ITEPA 2003. The employer is expected to operate PAYE where the aggregate payments within that section exceed £30,000 (see *EIM12960*). If, unusually, there is as a matter of fact continuous employment between the dates of dismissal and reinstatement or re-engagement ordered by the tribunal, any payment for that period is taxable as earnings under s62 ITEPA 2003.

Recoupment: Arrears of pay up until the tribunal hearing will form part of the prescribed element for recoupment purposes.

Statutory authorities: ERA 1996 *ss114 to 117* and *s124*

Relevant case law: *National Westminster Bank Plc v Parry* [2004] EWCA Civ 1563

Basic award

(see also *Basic award, maximum*; *Basic award, minimum***)**

The basic award is a sum awarded to a claimant who has been unfairly dismissed and calculated on the same basis as statutory redundancy pay according to age and the number of complete years' continuous service.

There are circumstances where a maximum or minimum basic award can be paid - see the separate entries for more details.

Calculation of remedy: The total basic award is calculated as follows:

- 1 ½ weeks' gross pay for each year of employment in which they were not below the age of 41;

- 1 week's gross pay for each year of employment in which they were below the age of 41 but not below the age of 22; and

- ½ a week's gross pay for each year of employment in which they were below the age of 22.

Where an individual's continuous service straddles an age of 41 or 22, the individual only receives the higher rate for the complete years of service that have been worked after that age has been reached. In other words, an employee must have already reached their 42nd birthday for that year to qualify at the higher rate of 1 ½ weeks.

The maximum amount of a week's gross pay is currently £643. The definition of a week's pay (see *Week's pay*) can be found at ERA 1996 Part XIV Ch II.

The maximum number of years that can be taken into account is 20.

Thus, the current maximum basic award is 20 x 1.5 x £643 = £19,290.

Gross or net: Gross. A week's pay as defined in ss220 to 229 ERA 1996 applies (see *Week's pay*).

Limit on a week's pay: Currently £643 (see *Table 1* for historical rates).

Limit on number of weeks: The limit depends on the age of the employee during his period of employment, and the maximum is the equivalent of 30 weeks, corresponding to 20 years' service all at the age of 41 or greater (1 ½ weeks for every year's service).

Any maximum or minimum: Maximum = £19,290; No minimum except in certain circumstances (see *Basic award, maximum* and *Basic award, minimum*).

Adjustments: The basic award can be reduced for contributory conduct (s122(2)) or for unreasonable refusal by the employee to accept an offer of reinstatement (s122(1)). This reduction will be the amount the tribunal considers is 'just and equitable', which is broader than the contributory conduct provision for the compensatory award and can take into account conduct which was not known to the employer at the time (see *Optikinetics Ltd v Whooley* EAT/1275/97 and *Parker Foundary Ltd v Slack* [1992] IRLR 11).

The award will not be reduced for contributory conduct in a redundancy dismissal, except where such a dismissal is for one of a number of specified reasons requiring a minimum basic award, when special statutory rules limit the ability to reduce the basic award (see s122(3) ERA 1996). If the minimum award of £7,836 has been made because the principal reason for a redundancy dismissal was one of those set out in s120(1) the figure may still be reduced for contributory conduct, but the percentage reduction is applied to the difference between what the claimant would have received under the standard case and the minimum £7,836. For example, if the claimant would otherwise have received £2,000 but does in fact qualify for the minimum £7,836, any contributory conduct will be applied to the difference, i.e. £5,836.

The basic award can be reduced by an amount that the tribunal considers to be just and equitable where the claimant has been awarded an amount under a designated dismissal procedures agreement (s122(3A)).

Where the dismissal is unfair by virtue of s104F (blacklists) the basic award will be reduced (or further reduced) by the amount of any basic award paid in respect of the same dismissal under s156 TULR(C)A (minimum basic award in case of dismissal on grounds related to trade union membership or activities).

Any redundancy payment that has been made to the employee must be deducted from the basic award first (see *Allmakes Ltd v Boorman* [1993] UKEAT/695/92). If, on the other hand the tribunal finds that the real reason for dismissal was not redundancy the claimant may be entitled to both payments. So if, for example, the employer mistakenly makes a redundancy payment in circumstances where the dismissal is automatically unfair under TUPE, then the employee will be entitled to recover a basic award despite having received a redundancy payment.

The basic award is not subject to any other adjustments such as for failure to mitigate loss, a failure to comply with a code of practice, or the chance of a future fair dismissal (see *Polkey*).

Mitigation: The award cannot be reduced for a failure to mitigate loss.

Tax: The basic award will be taxed under s401 ITEPA 2003 and goes to reduce the tax free amount at termination of £30,000 (see also *Grossing up*).

Recoupment: Recoupment does not apply to the basic award.

Statutory authorities: ERA 1996 ss119 to 122; TULR(C)A 1992 s156

Relevant case law: *Allmakes Ltd v Boorman* [1993] UKEAT/695/92; *Optikinetics Ltd v Whooley* [1998] UKEAT/1257/97/1006; *Parker Foundary Ltd v Slack* [1992] IRLR 11

Example 1

An employee was 56 at EDT and had 20 years' continuous service, being paid £650 gross per week at an EDT of 10/04/2023. His basic award would be calculated as follows:

Number of years' service at or over the age of 41 = 56 - 41 = 15

Each of these years count for 1 ½ weeks' pay = 15 x 1.5 = 22.5

The other 5 years of service, i.e. 20 - 15, count for 1 week's pay = 5 x 1 = 5

The total number of weeks = 22.5 + 5 = 27.5

The total basic award is then 27.5 x £643 (the maximum gross weekly pay allowed as at 10/04/2023) = £17,682.50.

Example 2

An employee was 35 at EDT and had 15 years' continuous service, being paid £330 gross per week at an EDT of 10/04/2023. His basic award would be calculated as follows:

Number of years' service at or over the age of 22 = 35 - 22 = 13

Each of these years count for 1 week's pay = 13 x 1 = 13

The other 2 years of service, i.e. 15 - 13, count for ½ a week's pay = 2 x 0.5 = 1

The total number of weeks = 13 + 1 = 14

The total basic award is then 14 x £330 = £4,620

Example 3

An employee was 55 at EDT and had 25 years' continuous service, being paid £600 per week at an EDT of 10/04/2023. His basic award would be calculated as follows:

Number of years' service over the age of 41 = 55 - 41 = 14

Each of these years count for 1 ½ week's pay = 14 x 1.5 = 21

The other 11 years of service, i.e. 25 - 14, are limited to 6 years, because the maximum number of years that can be taken into account is 20. These 6 years each count for 1 week's pay = 6 x 1 = 6

The total number of weeks = 21 + 6 = 27

The total basic award is then 27 x £643 (the weekly limit as at 10/04/2023) = £17,361

See also the Statutory redundancy table, *Table 13*.

Basic award, maximum

(see also *Basic award***)**

The statutory maximum where the reason for dismissal is redundancy but the employee is not entitled to a redundancy payment because they have unreasonably refused an offer of suitable alternative employment, or have had their contract renewed so that there is no dismissal, is 2 weeks' gross pay (s121 ERA 1996).

Gross or net: Gross

Limit on a week's pay: £643 (see *Table 1* for historical rates).

Limit on number of weeks: 2

Any maximum or minimum: Maximum is £1,286

Adjustments: Contributory conduct reduction applies (s122 ERA 1996).

Mitigation: The basic award cannot be reduced for failure to mitigate loss.

Tax: The basic award will be taxed under s401 ITEPA 2003 and goes to reduce the tax free amount at termination of £30,000 (see *Grossing up*).

Recoupment: Recoupment does not apply to the basic award.

Statutory authorities: ERA 1996 *ss121 and 122*

Basic award, minimum

(see also *Basic award***)**

There is a statutory minimum basic award where dismissal is unfair by virtue of:

- s100(1)(a) and (b) ERA 1996 (health and safety cases);
- s101A(d) (employee representative in working time cases);
- s102(1) (trustee of a relevant pension scheme);
- s103 (employee representatives);
- s104F (union blacklist); or
- s152(1) or s153 of TULR(C)A (union membership).

The minimum is currently £7,836 (s120(1) ERA 1996 and s156 TULR(C)A 1992), except for the s104F (blacklisting) dismissal, where the minimum is £5,000 (s120(1C) ERA 1996). The statutory minimum is ignored if the basic award exceeds this figure when calculated in the normal way.

Adjustments: Contributory conduct reduction applies. However, the percentage reduction is applied only to so much of the basic award as is payable because of s120 (s122(3) ERA 1996) or s156, i.e. the deduction only applies to the difference between what the claimant would have received under the standard case and the minimum £7,836 (or £5,000 in a blacklisting case). For example, if the claimant would only have received £2,000 but does in fact qualify for the minimum £7,836, any contributory conduct should be applied to the difference, i.e. £5,836.

Mitigation: The basic award cannot be reduced for failure to mitigate loss.

Tax: The basic award will be taxed under s401 ITEPA 2003 and goes to reduce the tax free amount at termination of £30,000 (see also *Grossing up*).

Recoupment: Recoupment does not apply to the basic award.

Statutory authorities: ERA 1996 *ss120 and 122*; TULR(C)A 1992 *s156*

Benefits: see *Financial losses*

Bonuses

Loss of earnings within an unfair dismissal award can include any commission, bonus or other benefit that the employee reasonably expected to receive had they remained in the employment (s123(2)(b) ERA 1996). The sums do not need to be contractual, provided that the reasonable expectation can be established. The same approach will apply in discrimination awards.

Where the value of a bonus is sought under the unlawful deduction from wages jurisdiction or for breach of contract, specific considerations apply (see *Unlawful deductions from wages*).

Gross or net: Such sums should be paid net of tax and NI and grossed up where appropriate.

Adjustments: Any bonus will be included in the compensatory award and adjusted alongside.

Mitigation: The mitigation rules applicable to the compensatory award apply to bonuses.

Tax: The compensatory award, which includes loss of benefits, is taxable and will fall to be grossed up under s401 if the award overall exceeds £30,000 (see also *Grossing up*).

Recoupment: The recoupment regulations state that 'any amount ordered to be paid and calculated under s123 [of the ERA 1996] in respect of compensation for **loss of wages** for a period before the conclusion of the tribunal proceedings' form part of the prescribed element. It is unclear whether a bonus would be defined as 'wages' but it is likely that any bonus payment awarded would be subject to the recoupment regulations.

Statutory authorities: ERA 1996) *s123(2)(b)*

Relevant case law: York Trailer Co Ltd v Sparkes [1973] IRLR 348

Breach of contract

The Employment Tribunal has a jurisdiction to hear breach of contract claims in certain limited circumstances (Employment Tribunals Extension of Jurisdiction (England and Wales) Order 1994 SI 1994/1623). Claims may be brought by employees where the claim *"arises or is outstanding on the termination of the employee's employment"* (Reg 3). A counterclaim (but not a claim) may be brought by an employer similarly where it *"arises or is outstanding on the termination of the employment of the employee against whom it is made"* (Reg 4). Claims on certain contractual terms are excluded by Reg 5, including terms as to living accommodation, intellectual property, an obligation of confidence and a restrictive covenant.

A claim for constructive dismissal will rely on conduct that amounts to a repudiatory breach of contract by the employer, but an unfair dismissal claim will be brought under that jurisdiction without invoking the breach of contract jurisdiction, unless the individual chooses to bring such a claim in addition.

Claims based on the manner of dismissal are generally not recoverable, in line with the decisions in *Johnson v Unisys Ltd* [2001] UKHL 13 and *Eastwood v Magnox Electric Plc* [2004] UKHL 35. However, if a cause of action arises prior to, and is independent of, an employee's dismissal, it may be claimable: *Parris v Ajayi* [2021] EWHC 285 (QB).

Remedy: The remedy will be damages caused by the breach of contract. Typically, such claims are for unpaid notice pay and the value of discretionary bonuses.

Adjustments: Any failure to comply with the ACAS code of practice applies.

Limit: £25,000.

Calculation date: see *Interest*; *Week's pay*; *Table 5*

Cap on a week's pay

(see also *Week's pay*; *Table 1*)

For several awards referable to a definition of a 'week's pay' in ss220 to 229 ERA 1996, a cap on the gross weekly pay is used in the calculations (see s186 and s227 ERA 1996). The current cap, as at 06/04/2023, is £643. The weekly pay cap applies to the following awards:

- Statutory redundancy pay (s162 ERA 1996);
- Basic award (ss119 to 122 ERA 1996);
- Right to written particulars of employment (s38 EA 2002);
- Right to be accompanied at a disciplinary hearing (s11 ERelA 1999);
- Right to request flexible working (s80I(1)(b) ERA 1996);
- Right to be accompanied at a flexible working meeting (Reg 15 FW(PR) Regs 2002);
- Insolvency provisions (s186 ERA 1996);
- Additional award (s117(3)(b) ERA 1996).

Cap on wrongful dismissal damages

The cap on wrongful dismissal damages is £25,000 if the claim is brought in the ET (Reg 10 Industrial Tribunals Extension of Jurisdiction (England and Wales) Order 1994). There is no cap if the claim is brought in the County Court or High Court.

Child care costs: see *Financial losses*

Commission: see *Bonuses*

Company cars: see *Financial losses*

Compensatory award

(see also *Adjustments and order of adjustments*; *Immediate loss of earnings*; *Future loss of earnings*; *Concurrent unfair and wrongful dismissal*; *Grossing up*; *Tax and termination payments*; *Recoupment*; *Protected disclosure*; *Unfair dismissal*)

s123 of the ERA 1996 provides that the compensatory award shall be:

> '...such amount as the tribunal considers just and equitable in all the circumstances having regard to the loss sustained by the complainant in

consequence of the dismissal insofar as that loss is attributable to action taken by the employer'.

Compensation for unfair dismissal should be awarded to *'compensate and compensate fully, but not to award a bonus'* according to Sir John Donaldson in *Norton Tool Co Ltd v Tewson* [1973] All ER 183. The object of the compensatory award is to compensate the employee for their financial losses as if they had not been unfairly dismissed - it is not designed to punish the employer for their wrongdoing.

Calculation of remedy: The calculation falls under two headings:

Immediate loss of earnings
This is the loss suffered between the EDT to the date of the remedies hearing. Loss of earnings will be calculated on the basis of net take home pay (that is, after deduction of tax and national insurance). The compensatory award can take into account any pay increase which would have been awarded in the previous employment up to the date of the hearing, including a back-dated pay rise. Conversely, if the claimant would probably have been paid less than their net earnings at the EDT in this period if they had not been dismissed (for example because of the financial constraints on the respondent at the time), the amount of loss of earnings can be correspondingly reduced.

The employer's liability will normally cease before the date of the remedies hearing if the employee has (or ought to have) got a new permanent job paying at least as much as the old job as there will no longer be a loss arising from the dismissal.

For claims relating solely to unfair dismissal the period of immediate loss is the number of weeks between the EDT and the remedies hearing, or the date of a new equivalent job, or the date by which the claimant should have found a new job, whichever is the soonest.

If a claim for wrongful dismissal has also been made, the number of weeks for the unfair dismissal immediate loss of earnings should be calculated from the date at which the wrongful dismissal damages period ends through to the date of the hearing, new job or expectation of a new job (see also *Damages for wrongful dismissal*).

Future loss of earnings
An employee may have on-going future losses if by the date of the remedies hearing they have not secured a new job or have obtained a job but with salary and benefits that are less valuable than their previous employment.

The future loss figure is based on the number of weeks for which it is calculated the particular loss will continue, and it may be that pay rises in the future will reduce the loss suffered in each of those years. The tribunal should take into account the personal characteristics of the employee such as age and health. They also need to take into account contingencies such as whether and for how long the employee would have remained in the original employment, whether there would have been a possibility of promotion and whether the level of earnings would have remained the same. A broad brush approach will be used, with Ogden tables usually used only where there is career long loss, in order to calculate loss based on various statistical contingencies.

The assessment of loss of earnings is traditionally done on a "loss of a chance" basis (see *Loss of chance*).

Gross or net: Losses will be calculated on a basis net of tax and NIC and grossed up where appropriate (see *Grossing up*).

Limit on a week's pay: There is no limit - the award is based on actual net value of pay and benefits.

Limit on number of weeks: For dismissals occurring on or after 6 April 2023 the statutory cap (where it applies) is calculated as the lower of £105,707 or 52 weeks' gross pay (see *Statutory cap*).

Adjustments: (see also *Adjustments and order of adjustments*, *Contributory conduct*, *Mitigation*)

> ***Ex gratia payment:*** see *Ex gratia payment*

> ***Earnings:*** A deduction of earnings which have mitigated the claimant's loss or a sum which reflects any failure by the claimant's failure to mitigate his/her loss. It is important to maintain a consistent approach to mitigation and loss of earnings, for example ensuring that only net earnings in mitigation are deducted from net losses of earnings (*Davies v DL Insurance Services Ltd* UKEAT/0148/19/RN).

> ***Early payment of compensation:*** Any compensation paid to the employee before the tribunal hearing should be deducted from the compensatory award (see *Ex gratia payment*).

> ***Insurance:*** Payments under an insurance policy are deductible in full if the employer alone has paid for the policy. However, where an employee has paid or contributed to such a policy *'directly or indirectly'*, deduction in full is not appropriate.

> It appears that where, as in *Colt Technology Services Ltd v Brown* UKEAT/0023/17/BA, there is a combination of employer and employee contributions, the deduction should only reflect the level of insurance that would have been obtained absent the employee's contribution.

> ***Polkey:*** A '*Polkey*' deduction (see also *Polkey*) to represent the chance the claimant may have been fairly dismissed in any event.

> ***ACAS:*** A percentage increase or reduction up to a maximum of 25% to reflect an unreasonable failure

by the employer or employee to comply with the ACAS code of practice on disciplinary and grievance procedures (see *ACAS (The Advisory, Conciliation and Arbitration Service)*).

Protected disclosure not in good faith: Deduction, up to a maximum of 25%, if the award is under a s103A claim but the disclosure was not made in good faith (see *Protected disclosure*).

Written particulars: An increase for any failure by the employer to provide written particulars of employment (see also *Written statement of particulars*).

Contributory conduct: A percentage reduction for any contributory conduct on the part of the employee (see *Contributory conduct*).

Enhanced redundancy: A deduction of any enhanced redundancy payment to the extent that it exceeds the basic award (see *Redundancy*).

Accelerated payment: A deduction for accelerated payment of compensation in respect of future loss (see *Accelerated/decelerated receipt*).

Interest: Any interest on the losses suffered (see also *Interest*).

Statutory cap: The cap, currently the lower of £105,707 or 52 weeks' gross pay, does not apply in all circumstances. If the reason for dismissal is on the grounds of discrimination (s13, s15, s16, s18, s19, s21, s26, s27 EA 2010), uncapped compensation will be awarded under that statute, and if the dismissal is because of health and safety reasons or whistleblowing by virtue of sections 100 and 103A respectively (see s105(3) and s105(6A)) the cap will not apply.

The cap is applied **after** the grossing up calculation is applied (see *Hardie Grant London Ltd v Aspden* UKEAT/0242/11/RN).

If an additional award and arrears of pay are being claimed the statutory cap can be exceeded in certain circumstances (see *Arrears of pay (reinstatement/re-engagement)* and *Additional award*).

Mitigation: The employee is under a duty to mitigate their loss and a deduction in compensation can be made if they have not fully done so.

Tax: If the combined sum of any basic and compensatory award is greater than £30,000 then the excess figure will be subject to tax (see *Grossing up*).

This is so even if the reason for termination is discriminatory (see *Tax and termination payments*).

Recoupment: Recoupment will apply to immediate loss of earnings only (see *Recoupment*). Note that the recoupment regulations do not apply if an award has been made under the Equality Act 2010.

Statutory authorities: EA 2010 ss13, 15, 16, 18, 19, 21, 26 and 27; ERA 1996 ss100, 103A, 105(3), 105(6A) and ss123 to 126

Relevant case law: *Davies v DL Insurance Services Ltd* UKEAT/0148/19/RN; *Hardie Grant London Ltd v Aspden* UKEAT/0242/11/RN; *Norton Tool Co Ltd v Tewson* [1973] 1 All ER 183 [1973] 1 All ER 183

Note on calculating with dates: There is a useful website called *www.timeanddate.com*, which calculates the number of days, weeks or months between two given dates. The calculator will also add a number of days, weeks or months to a fixed date.

Concurrent unfair and wrongful dismissal

(see also *Compensatory award*; *Unfair dismissal***)**

It is often the case that unfair and wrongful dismissal claims are brought concurrently before an ET, for example where an employee has been summarily dismissed for gross misconduct. The wrongful dismissal claim falls within the tribunal's breach of contract jurisdiction which has a separate £25,000 cap.

However, it is important that awards are not double counted. In other words, damages for wrongful dismissal cannot be awarded for the same loss for which compensation for unfair dismissal is also awarded. As a corollary, where an individual's losses may be capped it is possible to take the losses during the notice period out of the (capped) compensatory award to maximise the value of the claims (or to take some of the (capped) wrongful dismissal losses into the compensatory award).

Where losses are compensated for under an award for damages the recoupment regulations will not apply, whereas they will apply to the compensatory award. Also, damages for breach of contract will not be reduced for contributory conduct or 'Polkey'.

Two matters should be addressed when considering bringing both claims in the tribunal (rather than reserving the breach of contract claim for the High Court/County Court):

- It is not possible to top up the £25,000 award from a tribunal by bringing a second claim in the civil courts as there will be no remaining cause of action (see *Fraser v HLMAD Ltd* [2006] EWCA Civ 738); and

- If a breach of contract claim has been started at a tribunal, it can be complicated to then withdraw it and bring it instead in the ordinary civil courts. Claimants should consider in which forum they wish to issue their claim at the outset, and if appropriate state explicitly in any ET1 that they *do not* intend to bring any breach of contract claim in the ET.

Calculation

There are two ways in which concurrent claims can be calculated and double counting avoided:

Either:

Calculate the damages for wrongful dismissal and then deduct this figure from the compensation awarded for unfair dismissal

Example

Damages = £5,000
Compensatory award = £6,000

The claimant would receive the damages figure of £5,000 plus (£6,000 - £5,000) = £6,000

Or:

Award the damages for wrongful dismissal, and then start the unfair dismissal period from the day after the damages period ended

Ordinarily both methods will produce the same outcome, but there will be different results where adjustments such as *Polkey*, contributory conduct, or an ACAS Code adjustment have to be applied. There are two potential advantages with the second method:

- there is no danger of the recoupment regulations being applied to the damages figure (see *Damages for wrongful dismissal* and *Recoupment*) because the two awards have been calculated completely separately;

- if the compensatory award has to be adjusted, for example for contributory conduct, it is much easier to determine the figure that should be used in the calculation. Damages for wrongful dismissal are not subject to adjustment for contributory conduct or '*Polkey*'.

The EAT in *Shifferaw v Hudson Music Co Ltd* UKEAT/0294/15 cited a previous edition of this Handbook with approval and held that Employment Tribunals have a discretion over which of the above two methods it wishes to use.

Continuous employment: see *Basic award*; *Effective date of termination*; *Qualifying period*

Contractual notice period

(see also *Damages for wrongful dismissal*; *Effective date of termination*; *Statutory notice period*)

An employee is entitled to be given notice of his dismissal in accordance with the terms of his contract, unless he has committed gross misconduct in which case dismissal can usually be effected summarily (subject to unfair dismissal and discrimination rights). Where a claimant has been dismissed without the appropriate contractual notice, the claimant is entitled to claim the damages which are equivalent to the wages which he would have earned between the time of the actual termination and the time at which the contract might lawfully have been terminated (by due notice), together with the value of any contractual fringe benefits which the employee would have received during the same period.

The damages are calculated by reference to the greater of the minimum period implied by s86 ERA and "reasonable notice". The calculation of a period of reasonable notice takes account of all the circumstances of the case including the nature of the employment, the seniority and responsibilities of the employee. The minimum periods under s86 ERA 1996 apply where a person who has been continuously employed for one month or more and are:

- one week's notice if his period of continuous employment is less than two years;

- one week's notice for each year of continuous employment if his period of continuous employment is two years or more but less than 12 years; and

- 12 weeks' notice if his period of continuous employment is twelve years or more.

Any provision for shorter notice in any contract of employment with a person who has been continuously employed for one month or more has effect subject to these provisions but they do not prevent the employee from waiving his right to notice on any occasion or from accepting a payment in lieu of notice (see *Damages for wrongful dismissal* and *Statutory notice period*).

Contributory conduct

(see also *Adjustments and order of adjustments*; *Basic award*)

A number of awards available to the tribunal may be reduced due to the contributory conduct of the employee (also called '*contributory fault*'). The size of the reduction will be that which the tribunal considers to be just and equitable.

The wording of the test differs between that for the basic award and other awards. The basic award may be reduced where the tribunal '*considers that any conduct of the complainant before the dismissal (or, where the dismissal was with notice, before the notice was given) was such as it would be just and equitable to reduce or reduce further the amount of the award to any extent...*'. In respect of other awards '*where the tribunal finds that the [act] was to any extent caused or contributed to by any action of the complainant, [the tribunal] shall reduce the amount of the compensatory award by such proportion as it considers just and equitable...'.*

For the basic award (but not other awards), conduct which was not known to the employer and cannot have caused or contributed to the dismissal can still be taken into account (see *Optikinetics Ltd v Whooley* [1999] ICR 984, *Parker Foundary Ltd v Slack* [1992] IRLR 11 and *Renewi UK Services Ltd v Pamment* [2021] UKEAT 2021-000584). For other awards the reduction will be a proportion (expressible as a percentage), whereas the reduction for the basic award may also be calculated to be a particular sum.

These different methods of calculation mean that the figure for contributory conduct can be different for the basic award and the compensatory award (see s122(2) and s123(6) ERA 1996). See in particular the cases of *Montracon Ltd v Hardcastle* UKEAT/0307/12/JO; *Optikinetics Ltd v Whooley* [1999] ICR 984; *Compass Group v Baldwin* UKEAT/0447/05/DM; *Rao v CAA* [1994] ICR 495. However, other than in the situation outlined above, an ET will need a good reason to adopt a different approach to the two types of award (*Pamment*, above).

To fall into this category, the claimant's conduct must be *'culpable or blameworthy'*. Save in respect of the basic award, such conduct must cause or contribute to the claimant's dismissal, rather than its fairness or unfairness. Such conduct need not amount to gross misconduct (*Jagex Ltd v McCambridge* UKEAT/0041/19). It is also possible to make a reduction for contributory conduct even if, had the employer acted fairly, a dismissal would not have occurred at all (*Wilkinson v DVSA* [2022] EAT 23).

Where there is a significant overlap between the factors taken into account when making a *Polkey* deduction and when making a deduction for contributory conduct, the ET should consider expressly, whether, in the light of that overlap, it is just and equitable to make a finding of contributory conduct, and if so, what its amount should be. This is to avoid the risk of a claimant being penalised twice for the same conduct (see *Lenlyn UK Ltd v Kular* UKEAT/0108/16/DM).

In assessing contribution the tribunal should in turn:

1) Identify the relevant conduct;

2) Assess whether it is objectively culpable or blameworthy;

3) Consider whether it caused or contributed to the claimant's dismissal; and

4) If so, determine to what extent it is just and equitable to reduce any award.

(See *Steen v ASP Packaging Ltd* UKEAT/0023/13/1707).

Reductions for contributory conduct apply to the following awards:

- Basic award (s122(2) ERA 1996) (but not in redundancy cases unless the reason for selecting the employee for dismissal was one of those specified in ss100(1)(a) and (b), 101A(d), 102(1) or 103, in which case the contributory conduct reduction applies only to the difference between the statutory minimum and the basic award that would otherwise have been received) (see *Basic award* and *Basic award, minimum*);

- Compensatory award (s123(6) ERA 1996);

- Award in respect of detriment (s49(5) ERA 1996, s149(6) TULR(C)A 1992 (but see s145E(6) and Paragraph 159(5) Schedule A1 TULR(C)A 1992);

- Right not to be unjustifiably disciplined (s67(7) TULR(C)A 1992);

- Right not to be expelled or excluded from a union (s176(5) TULR(C)A 1992);

- Part time worker discrimination (Reg 8(13) PTW(PLFT) Regs 2000);

- Fixed term employee discrimination (Reg 7(12) FTE(PLFT) Regs 2002).

Grossing up should take place after all adjustments have been made (see also *Grossing up*).

The statutory cap will be applied after any grossing up has been applied.

Example

Basic award = £4,500

Financial loss = £8,000

Financial loss after contributory fault assessed as 25% on the compensatory award only = £8,000 x 0.75 = £6,000

Award = £4,500 + £6,000 = £10,500

Statutory authorities: ERA 1996 *ss49(5), 100(1)(a) and (b), 101A(d), 102(1), 103, 120, 122(2)* and *123(6)*; PTW(PLFT) Regs 2000 *Reg 8(13)*; TULR(C)A 1992 *Paragraph 159(5) Schedule A1* and *ss67(7), 149(6)* and *176(5)*

Relevant case law: *Compass Group v Baldwin* UKEAT/0447/05/DM; *Jagex Ltd v McCambridge* UKEAT/0041/19; *Lenlyn UK Ltd v Kular* UKEAT/0108/16/DM; *Montracon Ltd v Hardcastle* UKEAT/0307/12/JO; *Optikinetics Ltd v Whooley* [1999] ICR 984; *Parker Foundary Ltd v Slack* [1992] IRLR 11; *Rao v CAA* [1994] ICR 495; *Renewi UK Services Ltd v Pamment* [2021] UKEAT 2021-000584; *Steen v ASP Packaging Ltd* UKEAT/0023/13/1707; *Wilkinson v DVSA* [2022] EAT 23

Costs and wasted costs

The *Employment Tribunals (Constitution and Rules of Procedure) Regulations 2013, Schedule 1, Rules 74 to 84* set out the tribunal's approach and powers to award costs incurred by a party to a tribunal claim. Unlike in the ordinary civil courts, the successful party's costs are not as a matter of course ordered to be paid by the losing party. The costs of one party will only be borne by another party in specified circumstances.

Discretionary orders

By Rule 76(1) a tribunal may make a costs order or a preparation time order, and shall consider whether to do so, where it considers that:

a) a party (or that party's representative) has acted vexatiously, abusively, disruptively or otherwise unreasonably in either the bringing of the proceedings (or part) or the way that the proceedings (or part) have been conducted; or

b) any claim or response had no reasonable prospect of success.

In assessing whether a party's conduct was unreasonable, the tribunal should adopt a "range of reasonable responses" approach rather than substituting its own view (*Solomon v University of Hertfordshire* UKEAT/0258/18).

A tribunal may also make a costs order or a preparation time order where a party has been in breach of any order or practice direction or where a hearing has been postponed or adjourned on the application of a party (Rule 76(2)). Tribunals are obliged to consider the imposition of a costs order or a preparation time order against a party that is granted a late postponement, i.e. one which is applied for less than seven days before the hearing. A party does not have to prove unreasonable behaviour to obtain a cost order in respect of a postponement (although the reasonableness of such behaviour may be relevant to whether the tribunal exercises its discretion in favour of granting such an order).

Costs that have been incurred in respect of the work undertaken by in-house lawyers are recoverable (see *Ladak v DRC Locums Ltd* UKEAT/0488/13/LA).

A tribunal may make an order that a party pay the expenses incurred by a witness in attending, and this order may be made at the request of the witness (Rule 76(5)).

In assessing costs, tribunals are to take a three-stage approach:

a) Consider whether a ground for considering costs has been made out;

b) Consider separately whether to exercise its discretion to make an award of costs; and

c) If so, decide the amount of costs to award.

Mandatory orders

A tribunal must make a costs order against the respondent where at a final hearing for unfair dismissal a claimant has given the respondent 7 days' notice that he wishes to be reinstated or re-engaged, but the hearing is postponed or adjourned because the employer has not provided reasonable evidence of the availability of the claimant's job without a special reason (Rule 76(3)).

Where a party has been subject to a deposit order due to a specific allegation or argument in the claim or response having little reasonable prospect of success (of up to £1,000) and the tribunal decides that issue against the paying party for substantially the reasons set out in the deposit order, the paying party is presumed to have acted unreasonably in pursuing that allegation, unless he shows the contrary, and the deposit will be paid to the other party (this sum will count towards any other costs award).

Costs orders

Rule 74 defines costs as fees, charges, disbursements or expenses incurred by or on behalf of the receiving party.

Costs can be awarded for work done while legally represented even before the proceedings have begun (e.g. where the employer engages in a sham dismissal. See *Sunuva Ltd v Martin* UKEAT/0174/17/JOJ).

Limit: The amount of a costs order where the amount costs is determined by the tribunal under its basic jurisdiction is limited to £20,000. However, the tribunal can order that the amount of costs be determined by way of detailed assessment at the County Court, or by an Employment Judge applying the same principles, (and the equivalent in Scotland). In such cases there is no cap on the overall amount of costs that can be awarded unless the tribunal chooses to impose one whilst ordering detailed assessment (*Kuwait Oil Company v Al-Tarkait* [2020] EWCA Civ 1752). The limit of £20,000 can also be exceeded if the tribunal orders the payment of witness expenses reasonably incurred or if both parties agree to a figure which is higher.

Where the costs are that of a lay representative, the maximum hourly available rate is the figure used for preparation time awards (currently £42) (Rule 78(2)).

Preparation time orders

Preparation time orders award an amount to a party to reflect their preparation time whilst not legally represented. A preparation time order and a costs order cannot both be awarded in favour of the same party in the same proceedings, though a party may apply for both, pending the tribunal's determination of entitlement (Rule 75(3) and also see *Duhoe v Support*

Services Group Ltd - In Liquidation UKEAT/0102/15/MC). The number of hours in respect of which a preparation time order can be made will be determined by the ET according to the actual time spent and the tribunal's own assessment of what it considers to be a reasonable and proportionate amount of time to spend on such preparatory work (Rule 79).

Hourly rate: The hourly rate is £43 (as at 6 April 2023) and increases by £1 on 6 April each year.

Calculation: Amount of preparation time order = number of hours assessed by the ET x 43

Wasted costs orders

Wasted costs orders require a party's representative rather than a party itself to pay an amount of costs. A tribunal may make a wasted costs order against a representative in favour of any party ('the receiving party') where that party has either:

a)   incurred costs as a result of any improper, unreasonable or negligent act or omission on the part of the representative; or

b)   incurred costs which, in the light of any such act or omission occurring after they were incurred, the tribunal considers it unreasonable to expect the receiving party to pay.

An award can be made against a representative in favour of his own client.

In considering this, tribunals must adopt the 3-stage test in *Ridehalgh v Horsefield* [1994] Ch 205. Simler P has provided a gloss on this approach in *Wentworth-Wood v Maritime Transport Ltd* UKEAT/0184/17 that emphasises the exceptional nature of such an award and the need to consider what specific conduct is said to be improper, unreasonable or negligent, and whether that *particular* conduct caused the receiving party to incur unnecessary costs. She set out the approach to be adopted by tribunals as:

1)   *to recognise that wasted costs is an exceptional jurisdiction to be exercised with great care adopting a staged approach, and requiring consideration of what specific conduct is said to be improper, unreasonable or negligent;*

2)   *to consider whether the particular conduct caused the opposing party unnecessary costs; [and]*

3)   *to consider whether in all the circumstances it is just to order the legal representative to compensate the receiving party for the whole or any part of those costs.*

In assessing part 3, Simler P emphasised the importance of '*the constitutional position of the lawyer and the fact that from his point of view the jurisdiction is penal.*' The benefit of the doubt may need to be afforded to lawyers where issues of privilege might

restrict the defence to the application, and tribunals must remember the obligation of a lawyer to argue a case even if they consider it to be hopeless.

Allowances

Where a tribunal has made any of the above orders, it may order the paying party to reimburse the Secretary of State for any allowances paid for example witness attendance (see Rule 84).

Ability to pay

In deciding whether to make a costs, preparation time, or wasted costs order, and if so in what amount, the tribunal may have regard to the paying party's (or, where a wasted costs order is made, the representative's) ability to pay (Rule 84). Any insurance policy that may have been taken out by the recipient of a costs award however is not a relevant consideration, nor is the fact that the paying party is a volunteer or trustee (see *Mardner v Gardner & Ors* UKEAT/0483/13/DA).

VAT

In *Raggett v John Lewis Plc* UKEAT/0082/12/RN it was confirmed that, if the receiver can claim back the VAT element of any costs incurred as input tax, then those costs should be calculated net of VAT because the receiver will otherwise receive a windfall. On the other hand, if the receiver is not VAT registered, the costs award should be calculated gross (see also Paragraph 5.3 of the Costs Practice Direction which supplements part 43 and Rule 38(3) of The Employment Tribunals (Constitution and Rules of Procedure) Regulations 2004).

Time limit

A party may apply for a costs order or preparation time order at any stage up to 28 days from which the judgment finally determining the proceedings in respect of that party was sent to the parties (Rule 77).

Damages for wrongful dismissal

(see also *Adjustments and order of adjustments*; *Contractual notice period*; *Concurrent unfair and wrongful dismissal*)

Damages can be awarded if the employee has been dismissed without the appropriate length of notice.

Calculation of remedy: The damages will cover the lost remuneration and benefits that would have been received during the full notice period. For the position in respect of Fixed Term Contracts see *Fixed term contract.*

Damages for wrongful dismissal are assessed applying the "least burdensome performance" rule, namely that the Tribunal will assess them on the basis that the employer would have terminated the contract in the least burdensome method permitted under its terms. This usually means dismissal on the contractual minimum notice period, or pay in lieu of notice. This principle was recently reaffirmed by the Court of Appeal in *MacKenzie v AA Ltd* [2022] EWCA Civ 901.

Damages are only awarded for payments and benefits to which the claimant is contractually entitled. Where the contractual entitlement is discretionary, damages for the loss of that benefit will be assessed on the basis that the discretion would have been exercised rationally and in good faith (see *Cantor Fitzgerald International v Horkulak* [2004] EWCA Civ 1287).

Gross or net: Net

Limit on a week's pay: There is no limit on a week's pay, and the statutory definition of a week's pay does not apply.

Any maximum or minimum: None

Adjustments: Damages can be reduced for mitigation or failure to mitigate, reduced/increased for accelerated/decelerated receipt (see *Accelerated/ decelerated receipt*), and for failure by the employer/ employee to comply with the ACAS code of practice (TULR(C)A 1992 s207A and Schedule A2). Interest may be awarded in the County Court and High Court, but not in the Employment Tribunal.

Cap on award: £25,000 if the claim is brought to the ET, no cap if brought in the County Court or High Court.

Mitigation: The employee has a duty to take reasonable steps to mitigate their loss.

Tax: The award for damages for wrongful dismissal is taxable under s401 ITEPA 2003 and will fall to be grossed up to the extent it causes the £30,000 allowance to be exceeded.

Recoupment: Recoupment does not apply to damages for wrongful dismissal.

Statutory authorities: ERA 1996 s86; TULR(C)A s207A and Schedule A2

Relevant case law: *Cantor Fitzgerald International v Horkulak* [2004] EWCA Civ 1287

Damages period: see *Damages for wrongful dismissal*

Day's pay

In certain situations, such as the withholding of wages for strike action, it may be necessary to calculate an employee's salary in days rather than weeks or months. Where a contract contains an express daily salary, this will be easy, but frequently this is not the case.

In such situations, section 2 of the Apportionment Act 1870 will apply to apportion salary into equal daily amounts, unless the contract clearly stipulates otherwise or is clearly inconsistent with such an approach being taken.

How that daily amount will be calculated will depend on the particular contract and the type of work involved. In *Hartley & Ors v King Edward VI College* [2017] UKSC 39, the Supreme Court apportioned daily salary as 1/365 of annual salary, as opposed to the 1/260 figure contended for by the employer. The claimants were on annual contracts and regularly carried out work outside normal working hours; on evenings, weekends and days of annual leave. The position may well be different where the contract is not annual, or the work is clearly confined to particular dates and times.

Decelerated receipt: see *Accelerated/ decelerated receipt*

Deductions: see *Adjustments and order of adjustments*

Deductions from wages: see *Unlawful deductions from wages*

Deferred pension: see *Pension loss*

Defined benefit pension scheme: see *Pension loss*

Defined contribution pension scheme: see *Pension loss*

Deposit order: see *Costs and wasted costs*

Detriment

There are a large number of employment rights which can themselves be enforced by bringing a direct claim, including the right not to be unfairly dismissed. In addition to this type of right, there are rights protecting employees from suffering detriment because of certain protected behaviour and rights to protection from dismissal because of certain protected behaviour (see *Unfair dismissal*). This section deals with the statutory protections from detriment - some rights apply only to employees; some also apply to the broader class of workers.

An **employee** has the right not to be subjected to a detriment because of them:

- having to attend jury service (s43M ERA 1996);

- acting as a health and safety representative (s44);

- refusing to work on Sundays (s45) or refusing to work additional hours on a Sunday (s45ZA), if the employee is a shop or betting worker;

- being a pension scheme trustee (s46);

- being an employee representative (s47);

- exercising right to time off work for education, study or training (s47A and s47AA);

- exercising their right to take leave for family or domestic reasons including pregnancy, childbirth or maternity; time off under section 57ZE; time off under section 57ZJ or 57ZL; ordinary, compulsory or additional maternity leave; ordinary or additional adoption leave; shared parental leave; parental leave; paternity leave; parental bereavement leave; or time off under section 57A (s47C);

- exercising rights in connection with tax credits (s47D);

- exercising rights under the flexible working regulations (s47E);

- exercising rights to request study and training (s47F);

- exercising the right to be accompanied or to accompany someone else to a disciplinary or grievance meeting (ERelA 1999 s12);

- exercising rights in relation to part-time workers (Reg 7(2) PTW(PLFT) Regs 2000).

A **worker** (which includes an employee) has the right not to be subjected to a detriment because of them:

- exercising working time rights (s45A);

- making a protected disclosure (s47B);

- exercising rights in relation to fixed-term employees (FTE(PLFT) Regs 2002);

- exercising rights related to trade union membership (s146 TULR(C)A 1992); or

- exercising rights related to trade union recognition (Paragraph 156 to Schedule A1 TULR(C)A 1992);

- exercising rights under the Exclusivity Terms in Zero Hours Contracts (Redress) Regulations 2015 (Reg 2) (see *Zero-hours contracts*);

- exercising rights under the Agency Workers Regulations 2010 (see *Agency workers*).

Remedy: If a claim is well founded the tribunal must make a declaration and may make an award of such an amount as it considers is just and equitable having regard to:

1) the infringement to which the complaint relates;

2) any loss which is attributable to the act, or failure to act, which infringed the claimant's right (s49(2) ERA 1996, s149(2) and Paragraph 159(2) to Schedule A1, TULR(C)A 1992).

The loss shall be taken to include: any expenses reasonably incurred by the claimant in consequence of the act, or failure to act, to which the complaint relates; and loss of any benefit which the claimant might reasonably be expected to have had but for the act or failure to act (s49(3) ERA 1996, s149(3) and Paragraph 159(3) to Schedule A1, TULR(C)A 1992).

The award may also include compensation for injury to feelings. Where a worker has brought the claim under s45A, 47B or 47D and the detriment is termination of the contract, which is akin to a claim for unfair dismissal of an employee, it is arguable that injury to feelings may be awarded, but only up to the amount of a basic award (see *Injury to feelings*).

In determining the amount of compensation to be awarded in relation to detriment for exercising rights related to trade union membership, no account can be taken of any pressure which was exercised on the employer by calling, organising, procuring or financing a strike or other industrial action, or by threatening to do so. The question must be determined as if no such pressure had been exercised (s149(5) TULR(C)A 1992).

Any maximum or minimum:

- For claims under ss43M, 44, 45, 46, 47, 47A, 47C, 47E, and 47F ERA 1996, and for s12 ERelA 1999, the compensation is unlimited;

- For a claim under s45A ERA 1996, if a worker has brought the claim and detriment is termination of the contract, the cap relevant to being dismissed under s101A (currently none) will apply;

- For a claim under s47B ERA 1996, if a worker has brought the claim and detriment is termination of the contract, the cap relevant to being dismissed under s103A (currently none) will apply;

- For a claim under s47D ERA 1996, if a worker has brought the claim and detriment is termination of the contract, the cap relevant to being dismissed under s104B (currently none) will apply;

- For a claim under the zero-hours contracts regulations, any award is limited to the sum of a basic award and compensatory award which would have been awarded if the worker had been an employee and had been dismissed (Reg 4(6) Exclusivity Terms in Zero Hours Contracts (Redress) Regulations 2015);

- For a claim under the Agency Workers Regulations 2010, the minimum award is 2 weeks' pay (Reg 18(12)) and an additional sum of £5,000 where Reg 9 applies (Reg 18(14)).

Adjustments: Contributory conduct (s49(5) ERA 1996, s149(6) and Paragraph 159(5) to Schedule A1, TULR(C)A 1992) and a failure to comply with the ACAS code of practice apply (see TULR(C)A s207A and Schedule A2). Also, the tribunal can reduce any award by up to 25% if a protected disclosure has been made but not in good faith (s49(6A) ERA 1996) (see *Adjustments and order of adjustments*).

Mitigation: The tribunal may reduce the award if the claimant has failed to mitigate their loss (s49(4) ERA 1996, s149(4) and Paragraph 159(4) to Schedule A1 TULR(C)A 1992).

Tax: The tax treatment will depend on the nature of the loss awarded (see *Tax and termination payments*).

Personal liability and dismissal: Under section 47B(1A) Employment Rights Act 1996 it is open to a claimant to bring a claim against an individual worker for subjecting them to a detriment for making a protected disclosure. Such a detriment can include dismissal, and it is in turn possible to bring a claim against the employer for vicarious liability for that act. Similarly, it is open to a claimant to recover losses flowing from a dismissal where their claim is based on a distinct prior detriment that results in the claimant's dismissal (*Timis & Anor v Osipov & Anor* [2018] EWCA Civ 2321).

Recoupment: N/A

Statutory authorities: Agency Workers Regulations 2010 Reg 18(12) and 18(14); ERA 1996 *ss43M, 44, 45, 46, 47, 47A, 47C, 47E, 47F, 49(4)*; ERelA 1999 *s12*; Exclusivity Terms in Zero Hours Contracts (Redress) Regulations 2015 Reg 4(6); TULR(C)A 1992 *s149(5)* and Paragraph 159 to *Schedule A1*

Relevant case law: *Santos Gomez v Higher Level Care Ltd* [2018] EWCA Civ 418; *Timis & Anor v Osipov & Anor* [2018] EWCA Civ 2321

Direct discrimination: see

Discrimination

Discrimination

(see also *Aggravated damages*; *Compensatory award*; *Contributory conduct*; *Exemplary damages*; *Financial losses*; *Injury to feelings*; *Physical and psychiatric injury*; *Sex Equality Clause***)**

The Equality Act 2010 creates the right not to be discriminated against where the reason for the discrimination is one of a number of protected characteristics. These are: age; disability; gender reassignment; marriage and civil partnership; pregnancy and maternity; race; religion or belief; sex; and sexual orientation (s4 and ss5 to 12 EA 2010).

Discrimination may take different forms, and the types of conduct prohibited by the Equality Act 2010 are:

- direct discrimination (s13 EA 2010);
- discrimination arising from disability (s15);
- gender reassignment discrimination in cases of absence from work (s16);
- pregnancy and maternity discrimination (s18);
- indirect discrimination (s19);
- failure to comply with the duty to make reasonable adjustments (ss20 and 21);
- harassment (s26); and
- victimisation (s27).

The Equality Act 2010 consolidated a number of different strands of discrimination found in SDA 1975 (sex), RRA 1976 (race), DDA 1995 (disability), EE(RB)R 2003 (religion or belief), EE(SO)R 2003 (sexual orientation) and EE(Age)R 2006 (age). Many of the authorities relevant to discrimination under EA 2010 relate to the earlier statutory provisions.

The right to equality of terms, formerly called equal pay, is contained in the EA 2010 (ss64 to 80 and ss127 to 135). The remedies for breach of the right to equality of terms is addressed in the *Sex Equality Clause* entry.

There are other employment rights that protect individuals against less favourable or detrimental treatment on the grounds of the individual having certain characteristics or satisfying certain conditions. These are not strictly speaking prohibitions on 'discrimination', though the prohibitions may take similar forms and the remedies may be calculated in similar ways, for example, the protections against suffering detriment in Part V ERA 1996, the Fixed-Term Employees (Prevention of Less Favourable Treatment) Regulations 2002 and the Part-Time Workers (Prevention of Less Favourable Treatment) Regulations 2000 which both give an employee a right not to be treated 'less favourably' than a comparator employee. Further, the remedy for breach of the right not to be subjected to a detriment under ERA 1996 s47B, and probably other similar protections in Part V ERA 1996 may include not just compensation for financial loss but also an award for injury to feelings.

Remedy: If a tribunal finds that an employer has discriminated against an employee, there are three types of remedy available (s124 EA 2010). The tribunal may:

a) make a declaration as to the rights of the complainant and the respondent in relation to the matters to which the proceedings relate;

b) order the respondent to pay compensation to the complainant;

c) make a recommendation that the respondent take specified steps for the purpose of obviating or reducing the adverse effect of any matter to which the proceedings relate on the complainant or any other person.

Each of the remedies is discretionary, and though it is highly unusual for a remedy not to be awarded, under previous statutory provisions the motive and intention of the discriminator was relevant to the issue of remedy, in particular the value of any injury to feelings award (though not to the issue of whether discrimination had occurred) (see *O'Neill v Governors of St Thomas More Roman Catholic Voluntary Aided Upper School* [1997] ICR 33 and *Chief Constable of Manchester v Hope* [1999] ICR 338). It is, however, unlikely that tribunals can apply a similar approach under EA 2010.

Where the tribunal has found indirect discrimination under s19 EA 2010, and where the tribunal is satisfied that the provision, criteria or practice was not applied with the intention of discriminating against the claimant, the tribunal must consider making either a declaration or a recommendation before it awards compensation (see s124(4) and (5) EA 2010). The Court of Appeal has explained that this is simply the order in which the three remedies should be considered: it does not prioritise or emphasise one over the other, and it does not restrict or otherwise act as an obstacle to granting compensation in cases of unintentional discrimination. Where loss has occurred as a result of the discrimination, tribunals are expected to award compensation that is both adequate to compensate for the loss and proportionate to it (*Wisbey v Commissioner of the City of London Police* [2021] EWCA Civ 650).

The remedy most frequently obtained by claimants is compensation and the principles to be applied are outlined below, with detailed analysis set out elsewhere under the specific headings where appropriate.

Failure to comply with recommendation: Where the tribunal has made a recommendation under s124(2)(c) EA 2010, but so far as it relates to the claimant it has without reasonable excuse failed to comply with the recommendation, the tribunal may increase any award for compensation or make an award of compensation where it has not already done so (see s124(7) EA 2010).

Compensation: Any award of compensation will be assessed under the same principles as apply to torts (see s124(6) and s119(2)). The central aim is to put the claimant in the position, so far as is reasonable, that he or she would have been had the tort not occurred

(*Ministry of Defence v Wheeler* [1998] IRLR 23 and *Chagger v Abbey National plc* [2010] IRLR 47). The sum is not determined by what the tribunal considers just and equitable in the circumstances as it would do in an unfair dismissal award (*Hurley v Mustoe (No 2)* [1983] ICR 422), though the two approaches will often generate the same result. One impact is that certain items for which credit must be given by an employee are treated differently under the two awards, such as earnings from a new job during a notice period.

Causation and remoteness limit the damages available to a claimant; only those losses caused by the unlawful act will be recoverable, so for example where an individual would have lost their job at some point in any event, and if the discriminatory dismissal they have suffered has not altered their job prospects, the losses suffered after the date when the individual would have been dismissed anyway have not been caused by the discriminatory dismissal. Further, in the general law of tort losses that are too remote and unforeseeable will not be recoverable. However, in *Essa v Laing Ltd* [2004] ICR 746 the Court of Appeal held that this principle does not apply to all statutory torts including discriminatory harassment, such that any loss proved to flow directly from the discriminatory act will be recoverable. It may be that the principle applies to other forms of discrimination.

Awards may be made not just against employers, but also against individual respondents where these have been named in the ET1 (see *Individual respondents*).

Non-financial losses are also recoverable (see *Aggravated damages; Exemplary damages; Injury to feelings; Physical and psychiatric injury*).

The types of financial loss that are recoverable are in general the same as for an unfair dismissal compensatory award, and will include the value of lost earnings and benefits. The calculation of the financial losses the claimant has suffered will also be broadly similar to awards for unfair dismissal (see *Financial losses*).

The central matters the tribunal will need to determine are the 'old job' facts and the 'new job' facts. It will need to compare the financial benefits had the claimant not been treated unlawfully with the financial benefits the claimant has been able to obtain or will be able to in the future (see *Chagger v Abbey National plc* [2010] IRLR 47). Factors that will be considered include whether the employment would have terminated anyway, whether the individual would have been promoted or received a pay rise, what employment has been or will be obtained, what the financial rewards will be and whether these will increase to meet the losses currently being suffered at some point in the future.

The tribunal can take into account the chance of the

original employment not continuing, and the chance of any particular employment arising in the future (see *Loss of chance* and *Polkey*).

Gross or net: Net for the compensatory element.

Limit on a week's pay: There is no limit on a week's pay - the claimant's actual net pay will be used in the calculation of loss.

Limit on number of weeks: There is no statutory limit to the number of weeks' loss that can be awarded.

Any maximum or minimum: None

Adjustments:

Contributory conduct: Discrimination is a statutory tort and awards may be reduced for contributory fault, though this is unusual (see *Contributory conduct*).

ACAS: An adjustment for failure by the employer/ employee to comply with the ACAS Code of Practice for Grievance and Disciplinary Procedures can also be made (Schedule A2 TULR(C)A).

Failure to comply with recommendation: Where the tribunal has made a recommendation under s124(2)(c) EA 2010, but so far as it relates to the claimant the respondent has without reasonable excuse failed to comply with the recommendation, the tribunal may increase any award for compensation or make an award of compensation where it has not already done so (see s124(7) EA 2010).

Grossing up: Where an award will attract a tax liability on the claimant who receives the award, the award will be increased to reflect the net sum the claimant ought to receive (see *Grossing up*).

Interest: Interest can also be added to the sum awarded (see *Interest*).

Cap: There is no statutory cap on compensation for discrimination.

Mitigation: The claimant is under the usual duty to mitigate their loss (see *Mitigation*).

Tax: s401 ITEPA 2003 will apply to the compensatory element of the award if there has been a discriminatory dismissal but an award of injury to feelings will generally not be taxed unless, possibly, it is in connection to termination (see in particular *Injury to feelings; Tax and termination payments*).

Recoupment: Recoupment does not apply to compensation for discrimination.

Statutory authorities: Equality Act 2010 *ss15 to 27, s119* and *s124*

Relevant case law: *Carmelli Bakeries Ltd v Benali_* UKEAT/0616/12/RN; *Chagger v Abbey National Plc*

& Anor [2009] EWCA Civ 1202; *Way & Anor v Crouch* UKEAT/0614/04/CK

Early conciliation

Before a claimant can bring certain claims in the tribunal (set out at s18(1) Employment Tribunals Act 1996), they must contact ACAS and provide them with basic information to see if it is possible to resolve the claim without litigation.

Although the requirement to contact ACAS is mandatory, the scheme itself is voluntary. Upon conclusion of the early conciliation process (either through unsuccessful negotiations or a lack of desire to participate), ACAS issues a certificate containing a start date and an end date.

Time Limits

In calculating time limits for any claim, time spent on Early Conciliation (defined as running from the day after contacting ACAS to the date of the claimant receiving an Early Conciliation certificate) 'is not to be counted' (s207B(3) Employment Rights Act 1996).

Any time spent in Early Conciliation prior to the start of a time limit (e.g. prior to the Effective Date of Termination in an unfair dismissal claim) does not operate to extend time limits: the scheme is a 'stop the clock' provision, rather than a general extension of time. It cannot stop a time limit clock that has not started (*HMRC v Garau* UKEAT/0348/16).

Where, however, a time limit would expire during the period from the beginning of Early Conciliation to one month after receipt of the Early Conciliation certificate, the time limit is then extended to expire a further month after the receipt of the certificate.

Early payment of compensation: see *Ex gratia payment*

Effective date of termination

(see also *Basic award; Cap on a week's pay; Compensatory award; Statutory cap***)**

The 'effective date of termination' (see s97 ERA 1996) or 'EDT' is a statutory concept necessary for the following calculations:

1) identifying the number of years of continuous service necessary to bring a claim (claims of normal unfair dismissal and claims for a redundancy payment can only be brought after 2 years of continuous service (subject to the exceptions listed in s108(3)) (see s108 ERA 1996);

2) determining whether a claim for unfair dismissal has been brought within the time limit (the claim must be presented to the tribunal before the end of the period of 3 months beginning with the EDT unless the time limit is extended by the tribunal: for example, if the EDT is 5 July, the claim must be brought by 4 October) (see s111 ERA 1996); and

3) calculating the basic award, since this is based on the number of continuous years of service (see s119).

Often the EDT is the actual date of termination of the employment contract, and there is extensive case law surrounding exactly when the termination of employment takes place (for example where an employee is dismissed during a heated argument but the employer quickly attempts to withdraw the dismissal, or where the dismissal is communicated by a third party and only on a later date communicated directly by the employer). This is often critical to determine whether a claim has been brought in time, but can also be relevant to establishing an employee's length of service (for example because the right to bring a claim of unfair dismissal, and the amount of any basic award or redundancy payment, depends on the number of *complete* years' service).

Usually, where notice of termination of employment has been given either by the employee or the employer, the EDT will be the date on which notice expires. If the notice given is greater than that required by s86 ERA 1996, the former date is the EDT.

However, there are two situations where an EDT is 'deemed' to be a particular date. If the employer gives no notice or less than the minimum guaranteed by s86 ERA 1996, the EDT will be the date on which statutory notice would have expired if it had been given (see s97(1) to (3)). If the employee resigns where he is not already under notice, the EDT will be the date the employment terminates, but if that notice period is less than the employer would have had to give the employee under s86 ERA 1996, then the EDT will be the date of the expiry of that notional notice. By s86(6) there is no statutory minimum notice period where either party terminates the contract for repudiatory breach by the other party. The EDT will therefore not be extended where the tribunal considers that the claimant was guilty of gross misconduct (*Lancaster & Duke Ltd v Wileman* UKEAT/0256/17/LA).

The period of notice begins on the day after the day on which notice was given unless the contract provides otherwise (see *Wang v University of Keele* [2011] IRLR 542 and *West v Kneels Ltd* [1986] IRLR 430).

Where an employee is dismissed by written notice, that notice does not take effect until the employee has read, or had a reasonable opportunity to read, the notice (*Newcastle upon Tyne Hospitals NHS Foundation Trust*

v Haywood [2018] UKSC 22). The same is true in cases of summary dismissal (*Gisda Cyf v Barratt* [2010] UKSC 41).

Some examples

The claimant is given notice and it is worked out in full
The EDT is the date of expiry of the contractual notice period, or the statutory notice period, whichever is the later (s97(1)(a) ERA 1996).

Contractual notice has been given, the claimant is working during the notice period and then is summarily dismissed before the expiry of the contractual notice period, but after the statutory notice period would have expired
The EDT is the date of dismissal, and not the date when contractual notice would have ended. Relevant authorities dealing with a range of such factual circumstances include: *M-Choice UK Ltd v A* UKEAT/0227/11/DA, *Harper v Virgin Net Ltd* [2004] EWCA Civ 271 and *Parker Rhodes Hickmott Solicitors v Harvey* UKEAT/0455/11/SM.

The claimant is summarily dismissed, but the employer was not entitled to do so and the claimant is entitled to statutory notice under s86
The EDT is the date that the statutory notice would have ended (s97(2) ERA 1996). **Note**: the EDT is only extended by the statutory notice period, not any contractual notice period.

The claimant is summarily dismissed and the employer was entitled to do so due to the conduct of the employee
The EDT is the date on which termination takes effect (s97(1)(b) ERA 1996).

The claimant has been put on garden leave
The EDT is the date the notice period expires.

The claimant is dismissed with a payment in lieu of notice
The contract ends when the PILON clause is successfully put into effect, with the EDT being the date of termination of the contract (see *Société Générale, London Branch v Geys* [2013] IRLR 122).

The employee resigns in response to a repudiatory breach by the employer
The EDT will normally be the date of expiry of the statutory notice period which the employer would have had to give if they had given the employee notice of termination on the day the employee resigned.

The claimant resigns on notice following which there is correspondence/ discussions between the parties
The EDT is the date on which the notice period expires. The claimant's unequivocal notice of resignation is unaffected by subsequent discussions/ correspondence between the parties and the claimant cannot subsequently unilaterally withdraw or extend the notice

period (see *Wallace v Ladbrokes Betting and Gaming Limited* UKEAT/0168/15/JOJ).

The employer and employee agree on a date when the employment will terminate

The EDT will be the date of the agreed termination, even if the employee had already received notice but then later agreed to an earlier termination date (*Palfrey v Transco Plc* [2004] IRLR 916).

The employer summarily dismisses an employee but on appeal varies the date of dismissal to a later date

The EDT will be the later date as varied by the appeal decision (see *Hawes & Curtis Ltd v Arfan & Anor* UKEAT/0229/12/JOJ; [2012] ICR 1244).

The dismissal was without notice but the employer pays PILON

The EDT is the date of the summary dismissal (see *Rabess v London Fire & Emergency Planning Authority* UKEAT/0029/14/JOJ). The EDT is not extended by the PILON.

Termination of fixed term contract which is not renewed

The EDT is the last day of the fixed term.

Statutory authorities: *ss86, 97, 108* and *119* ERA 1996

Relevant case law: *Gisda Cyf v Barratt* [2010] UKSC 41; *Harper v Virgin Net Ltd* [2004] EWCA Civ 271; *Hawes & Curtis Ltd v Arfan & Anor* UKEAT/0229/12/JOJ; *Lancaster & Duke Ltd v Wileman* UKEAT/0256/17/LA *M-Choice UK Ltd v A* UKEAT/0227/11/DA; *Martin v Yeoman Aggregates Limited* [1983] ICR 314; *Newcastle upon Tyne Hospitals NHS Foundation Trust v Haywood* [2018] UKSC 22; *Palfrey v Transco Plc* [2004] IRLR 916; *Parker Rhodes Hickmott Solicitors v Harvey* UKEAT/0455/11/SM; *Rabess v London Fire & Emergency Planning Authority* UKEAT/0029/14/JOJ; *Robinson v Bowskill & Ors Practising as Fairhill Medical Practice* UKEAT/0313/12/JOJ; *Société Générale, London Branch v Geys* [2013] IRLR 122; *The Governing Body of Wishmorecross School v Balado* UKEAT/0199/11/CEA; *The Secretary of State for Justice v Hibbert* UKEAT/0289/13/GE; *Wallace v Ladbrokes Betting and Gaming Limited* UKEAT/0168/15/JOJ; *Wang v University Of Keele (Jurisdictional Points: Claim in time and effective date of termination)* [2010] UKEAT/0223/10; *West v Kneels Ltd* [1986] IRLR 430

Employment and Support Allowance (ESA)

(see also *Housing benefit*; *Recoupment*)

Employment and Support Allowance may be paid if the individual cannot work because they are ill or disabled.

Damages for wrongful dismissal

Credit must be given for the receipt of state benefits during the damages period. However, some state benefits are excluded. It is not clear whether ESA will always be deducted since it will depend on the facts of the case and how remote or otherwise the benefit is. It could also be argued that state benefits received during the statutory notice period should not be deducted in full (see *Westwood v Secretary of State for Employment* [1984] 1 All ER 874 where the employee was dismissed without the statutory notice period or payment in lieu) because the employee would exhaust their entitlement to state benefits earlier than they would have done if they had been given the statutory notice.

Compensatory award

ESA can be deducted from the compensatory award if, but for the dismissal, the benefit would not have been obtained. *Morgans v Alpha Plus Security Ltd* [2005] ICR 525 confirms this position, where the claimant was dismissed and then was unable to work because of his psychological state attributable to the respondent's action in dismissing him. The EAT held that there is no jurisdiction to disregard receipts, or to claim and recover a sum in excess of the actual loss. Where a claimant has suffered a lesser loss by virtue of his receipt of benefits, which would not have been paid had they remained employed, credit must be given for them.

However, credit need not be given for benefits that are too remote. Often, the decision as to whether the benefits are deductible or not is up for argument.

Relevant case law: *Morgans v Alpha Plus Security Ltd* [2005] ICR 525; *Westwood v Secretary of State for Employment* [1984] 1 All ER 874

Enhanced redundancy: see *Redundancy*

Enhancement of accrued pension rights: see *Pension loss*

Equal pay: see *Sex Equality Clause*

Equality of terms: see *Sex Equality Clause*

Ex gratia payment

(see also *Adjustments and order of adjustments*; *Tax and termination payments*)

An employee may receive an *ex gratia* payment from his employer following his dismissal. There are various reasons why any such payment may be made, and the sum may be viewed as compensation for the losses suffered, advance payment of any liability caused by the dismissal, or as a payment unrelated to the dismissal. An *ex gratia* payment is made where there is no legal obligation to do so.

The claimant will normally be required to give credit for the *ex gratia* payment (see *Digital Equipment Co Ltd v Clements (No 2)* [1998] IRLR 134 (CA)).

The particular reason for the payment dictates how it is factored into the tribunal's calculation of the sum to be paid by the ex-employer. If the payment is taken to reduce the loss suffered by the claimant flowing from the dismissal, credit will be given before the application of any adjustments such as contributory conduct. However, if the payment is treated as reducing the ultimate liability of the employer, then the credit will apply to the award before the cap has been imposed. The employee will likely benefit if the former approach is applied, and the employer if the latter approach is applied. Full benefit to the employer will only occur if the award is less than the statutory cap. The following principles apply:

- Payment made under a legal obligation, such as pay in lieu of notice, will be taken to reduce the loss sustained (see *Heggie v Uniroyal Ltd* [1999] IRLR 802);

- Payment of a contractual enhanced redundancy payment is dealt with by s123(7) ERA 1996 (see *Adjustments and order of adjustments*);

- *Ex gratia* payments will usually be taken to reduce the loss suffered (see *Horizon Holiday Ltd v Grassi* [1987] IRLR 371 and *Babcock FATA Ltd v Addison* [1987] IRLR 173);

- Payments made by mistake will usually be taken to reduce the loss suffered (see *Boorman v Allmakes* [1995] IRLR 553);

- Where the payment is expressly made by reference to liability for compensation for an unfair dismissal, it may be set off against any basic award and compensatory award (see *Chelsea Football Club & Athletic Co Ltd v Heath* [1981] IRLR 73);

- Where the employee receives an *ex gratia* payment that he would have received had he not been unfairly dismissed it will not factor into reducing the losses suffered by the claimant (see *Babcock FATA Ltd v Addison* [1987] IRLR 173 and *Roadchef v Hastings* [1988] IRLR 142).

Adjustments: The *ex gratia* payment, where it is taken to reduce the losses suffered by the claimant, should be deducted before any reduction/increase for contributory conduct, *Polkey*, ACAS, interest and accelerated payment (see *Digital Equipment Co Ltd v Clements (No 2)* [1997] IRLR 140 (EAT)). Credit for the *ex gratia* payment will be made before the statutory cap

is applied (see *McCarthy v British Insulated Callenders Cables Plc* [1985] IRLR 94).

Tax: Assuming that the *ex gratia* payment has been deducted from the calculation of financial loss, any sums awarded exceeding £30,000 will be taxed under ITEPA 2003 s401. Whether or not the employer should have taxed the *ex gratia* payment when it was made will depend on the nature of the payment - see HMRC NIM02510 for further information, although this point would not be an issue for the tribunal to decide.

Relevant case law: *Babcock FATA Ltd v Addison* [1987] IRLR 173; *Boorman v Allmakes* [1995] IRLR 553; *Chelsea Football Club & Athletic Co Ltd v Heath* [1981] IRLR 73; *Digital Equipment Co Ltd v Clements (No 2)* [1997] IRLR 140; *Heggie v Uniroyal Ltd* [1999] IRLR 802; *Horizon Holiday Ltd v Grassi* [1987] IRLR 371; *McCarthy v British Insulated Callenders Cables Plc* [1985] IRLR 94; *Publicis Consultants UK Ltd v O'Farrell* UKEAT/0430/10; *Roadchef v Hastings* [1988] IRLR 142

Exemplary damages

Exemplary damages are available in discrimination claims but are very rarely awarded. In contrast to the usual awards made by tribunals, exemplary damages are punitive not compensatory. They will only be awarded if compensation is insufficient to punish the wrongdoer and if the conduct is either:

- oppressive, arbitrary or unconstitutional action by the agents of government; or

- where the defendant's conduct has been calculated to make a profit which may well exceed the compensation payable to the claimant.

The EAT in *MOD v Fletcher* [2010] IRLR 25 has stated that exemplary cases are reserved for the worst cases of the oppressive use of power by public authorities, where the wrongdoing was '*conscious and contumelious*'.

Remedy: Damages. There is no formulaic calculation.

Any maximum or minimum: None. However, in *MOD v Fletcher*, the EAT held that an award of £50,000 was excessive, it reflected the type of award for false imprisonment, and that had an award been appropriate a sum of £7,500 would have been awarded by the EAT. Such a figure would have reflected the level of award in other torts.

Adjustments: None

Tax: It is unlikely that such an award will be taxable, due to its punitive rather than compensatory nature.

Recoupment: N/A

Relevant case law: *Kuddus v Chief Constable of Leicestershire Constabulary* [2002] 2 AC 122, HL; *London*

Borough of Hackney v Sivanandan and Ors [2001] IRLR 740; *MOD v Fletcher* [2010] IRLR 25; UKEAT/0044/09

Expenses

(see also *Compensatory award***)**

Expenses incurred as a result of being unfairly dismissed or discriminated against can be claimed as part of the financial losses suffered. These may include the following costs: looking for alternative work; starting up a new business; extra child or dependant care; accommodation; medical expenses etc. In all cases, the expenses should have been reasonably incurred as a result of the dismissal/discrimination/detriment and the sums claimed should be reasonable. Any such expenses will have to be proved by evidence in the usual way.

Final salary pension scheme: see
Pension loss

Financial losses

Financial losses suffered from unfair dismissal and discrimination that an employee can claim will generally include loss of any benefits that have a monetary value as well as loss of actual income. Such benefits could include: bonus; commission; holiday pay for lost holiday leave; stock options and profit related pay; enhanced redundancy pay; company car allowance; accommodation; company loan; food allowance; travel allowance; free telephone; private medical insurance; childcare benefits; share ownership; pensions (see also *Pension loss*).

Calculation: The calculation of the value of lost benefits will often take a broad brush approach unless, for example with a company car, it can easily be ascertained exactly the value of the benefit the employee has lost. Such losses have to represent the *personal* loss to the employee, rather than just the value of the benefit generally.

> **Bonuses and commission:** financial losses can include loss of bonus and commission, and it is not necessary to show that the employee had a contractual right to them. s123(1) ERA 1996 states that: *'the amount of the compensatory award shall be such amount as the tribunal considers just and equitable in all the circumstances having regard to the loss sustained by the complainant in consequence of the dismissal in so far as that loss is attributable to action taken by the employer.'* s123(2) ERA 1996 states that the amount may include: *'loss of any benefit which he might reasonably be expected to have had but for the dismissal.'* The claimant needs to show on the

balance of probabilities that he had an expectation of receiving the payment and that that expectation was reasonable. It may be difficult to quantify a bonus where it is discretionary, and tribunals may make an award for the loss of a chance of a particular level of bonus, following from the approach taken in *Allied Maples Group Ltd v Simmons & Simmons* [1995] WLR 1602.

> **Loss of holiday pay:** If the claimant obtains another job with less generous holiday benefits, he may seek compensation for the value of those benefits.

> **Stock options and profit related pay:** Such schemes are common for senior staff and may take a number of forms. The valuation of the lost benefits will depend on the terms of the scheme. One simple way in which to value the lost options is to calculate the value of the shares to the employee at the date of termination, and then to calculate the profit, if any, that the employee might have made if they remained part of the scheme. In addition, if the employee is forced to sell their shares as a result of the dismissal and the share price rises, they may be able to claim the difference in valuation between dismissal and a future date. The valuation of share options can be difficult and tribunals will generally base their assessment on an estimate of what appears just and equitable in the circumstances.

> **Enhanced Redundancy Payments:** Compensation for the loss of any redundancy payment in excess of the statutory redundancy can be claimed (see s123(3)), whether contractual or whether the employee would merely have an expectation of such payment. Arguably there is a loss that can be claimed where the employee might have been dismissed as redundant during the period covered by the compensatory award.

> **Company car:** Compensation can only be awarded for the private use of a company car and also any loss of free fuel, insurance etc.

Several methods are available to calculate the loss as follows:

- Consider the AA or RAC estimates for the weekly running costs of a particular car (see *http://www. theaa.com/motoring_advice/running_costs/index. html* for more information). Then the cost should be adjusted to take into account the proportion of private use as opposed to business use, and again reduced if the employee had to contribute to the running of the car. If the employer has a different method of valuing the company car benefit, this may be used instead;

- HMRC have an online calculator which can be used to calculate the value of company cars (see *https://www.gov.uk/expenses-and-benefits-company-cars/work-out-the-value*). This is HMRC's method of valuing the company car benefit for tax purposes but this may not be an appropriate way to value the actual benefit lost by the claimant;

- Calculate the cost of buying a car or the hire of a car and claim a proportion of the cost from the employer;
- For cars bought on hire purchase in the employee's name and where the employer paid part or all of the repayments the tribunal could award the employee a proportion of the outstanding amount.

Accommodation: one method to assess the value of free or subsidised accommodation is to find evidence of the open-market value of similar accommodation. Alternatively, if the employee has found somewhere else similar to live, the loss could be calculated as the difference between what he would have been paying to the employer and what he is paying now. If the employee had bought their new accommodation, the loss could be calculated on the basis of a proportion of the interest paid on a mortgage (but not the capital).

Company loans: the value of such a benefit can be calculated as the difference between the cost to the employee whilst still in employment and the comparable market rate.

Free food: the loss may be calculated by finding out the value of the food and drink to which the employee was entitled.

Travel allowances: the loss is the value of the travel allowance.

Telephone: the loss is again the value of the telephone, including line rental and actual call charges.

Medical insurance: this can be calculated by finding out the equivalent cost to the employee of obtaining private medical insurance.

Childcare benefits: the loss can be calculated by working out the cost of equivalent child care that was provided by, or subsidised by, the employer. In the case of a subsidy, the difference between the costs can be claimed.

Pensions: the employee may be able to claim for the value of their lost occupational pension (either defined benefit or defined contribution) as well as loss of enhancement of accrued pension rights.

Consequential losses: In *Timbulas v The Construction Workers Guild Ltd* UKEAT/0325/13/GE, the claimant won his claim of unpaid holiday pay and also argued that, because his holiday pay was not paid at the date it should have been, he was unable to take advantage of an offer from his mortgage company to pay off his mortgage without

incurring a penalty. In consequence, he paid interest on the outstanding mortgage which would not have been payable if he had paid the mortgage off in full. The ET ruled that interest at 5% above base should be added to the holiday pay award.

Gross or net: Any tax deductible benefits should be calculated net of tax and NI.

Adjustments: Any benefits will be included within the compensatory award and adjusted in the normal way (see *Compensatory award*).

Cap: The loss of benefits will be included in the compensatory award and the statutory cap (where applicable) will be applied to the total.

Mitigation: Normal mitigation expectations apply.

Tax: The compensatory award, including benefits, is taxable above £30,000 and will fall to be grossed up under s401 ITEPA 2003 if the award overall exceeds this figure (see also *Grossing up*).

Recoupment: Loss of benefits are not subject to the recoupment regulations. Recoupment applies only to immediate loss of earnings, so loss of benefits during the time between dismissal and the hearing should not be included in the calculation.

Statutory authorities: ERA 1996 *s123*

Financial penalties on employers

(see also *Interest*)

There are two financial penalties that can be imposed on employers.

Breach of worker's rights with aggravating features

Employment tribunals have a discretionary power to impose a financial penalty on a losing employer if they find the employer has breached a worker's rights and the employer's behaviour has '*one or more aggravating features*' (see *s12A* ETA 1996).

A penalty may be ordered even if no financial award is made to the claimant, e.g. where the tribunal makes a declaration. The payment is made from the employer to the Secretary of State, not to the claimant.

Calculation: The penalty is calculated as a fixed 50% of the compensation awarded with a 50% discount where the employer pays within 21 days of the tribunal's decision. Only one penalty will be imposed where there are two or more claims in respect of the same act and worker, e.g. overlapping claims of wrongful and unfair dismissal.

Any maximum or minimum: Minimum is £200 (but if

the award is less than £200, the penalty will be £100); Maximum is £20,000.

Financial penalty for failure to pay sums ordered by the ET

Part 2A of the Employment Tribunals Act 1996 allows for financial penalties to be imposed on employers who do not pay workers the award that the ET has ordered (or awards ordered on a relevant appeal) including costs and sums to cover preparation time as awarded by an ET. Employers who do not pay costs awarded against them to cover a worker's ET fee can also be required to pay a penalty under the new provisions, as can employers who fail to pay sums due under ACAS conciliated settlements (sections 37A to 37D in Part 2A ETA 1996). The financial penalty regime will be operated by enforcement officers appointed or authorised by the Secretary of State (s37M).

Penalties will be payable to the Secretary of State not to the employee.

Calculation: The amount of the penalty will be based on the total amount that remains unpaid to the worker, including interest on the award payable on the last date for responding to the warning notice, as well as any amount the employer has been told to pay in respect to employment tribunal fees: it will be 50% of the sum owed. In cases where an employer has defaulted on an agreement to pay by instalments, the penalty will be based on the whole unpaid amount. The penalty can be reduced by 50% if both the penalty and the whole unpaid amount are paid within 14 days of the penalty notice.

Any maximum or minimum: Minimum is £200 (but if the award is less than £200, the penalty will be £100); Maximum is £20,000.

Statutory authorities: Employment Tribunals Act 1996 s12A; The Employment Rights (Miscellaneous Amendments) Regulations 2019 (SI 2019/731)

Fixed term contract

(see also *Damages for wrongful dismissal*)

When determining damages for wrongful dismissal, it is important first to identify whether the claimant was employed on a permanent or fixed term contract since the period of loss as calculated depends on the period of notice (see *Damages for wrongful dismissal*).

If the contract is for a fixed term and there is no right to terminate on notice, the earliest date at which the employer can end the contract is at the end of the term. If the contract is terminable by notice, the earliest date at which the contract can be brought to an end is the end of the notice period. No notice is required for

a fixed-term contract to come to its natural end (*DWP v Webley* [2005] IRLR 288).

If a fixed term contract contains a provision entitling an employee to resign on notice in the event of a repudiatory breach by the employer, this is unlikely to alter the above analysis: *Hall v London Lions Basketball Club (UK) Ltd* UKEAT/0273/19/OO. Such a clause is unlikely to exclude the common law right to resign and claim damages for the duration of the contractual period without clear wording to that effect. It is unclear, in the light of *Hall*, whether this would also be the case if the employee expressly resigns under such a notice clause.

Fixed-term employee protection

An employee working under a fixed-term contract has the right not to be treated by his employer less favourably than the employer treats a comparable permanent employee for the following reasons (see Reg 3 FTE(PLFT) Regs 2002 SI 2002/2034):

- as regards the terms of his contract; or
- by being subjected to any other detriment by any act, or deliberate failure to act, of his employer.

Particular reference is made in the FTE(PLFT) Regs 2002 to less favourable treatment in relation to qualification for benefits on the basis of periods of service, the opportunity to receive training and the opportunity to secure a permanent position (including being informed of any vacancies).

Less favourable treatment will be permitted where it can be objectively justified (Reg 3(3)(b) and Reg 4).

The employee has a right to written reasons for his treatment from his employer (see Reg 5).

The employee has the right to not be unfairly dismissed or be subject to detrimental treatment in relation to exercising the rights of a fixed term employee (see Reg 6).

Remedy: Where a tribunal finds that an employee has been subject to less favourable treatment or detriment as set out above, the tribunal (Reg 7(7)):

"shall take such of the following steps as it considers just and equitable:

(a) making a declaration as to the rights of the complainant and the employer in relation to the matters to which the complaint relates;

(b) ordering the employer to pay compensation to the complainant;

(c) recommending that the employer take, in all the circumstances of the case, for the purposes of obviating or reducing the adverse effect on the complainant of any matter to which the complaint relates."

There are specific provisions providing for the calculation of compensation awarded under Reg 7 and 7(b) (see Regs 7(8) to (12)):

- The amount of compensation awarded shall be such as the tribunal considers just and equitable in all the circumstances (this phrase is used in the assessment of the compensatory award for unfair dismissal and similar principles will apply);

- The tribunal will have regard to the infringement to which the complaint relates and any loss which is attributable to the infringement;

- The loss will include any expenses reasonably incurred by the claimant as a consequence of the infringement and any loss of any benefit he has suffered as a result;

- Compensation for infringement of the right not to be less favourably treated under Reg 3 will not include an award to injury to feelings (although an award for detriment under Reg 6 may include such an award – see *Detriment* and *Injury to feelings*); and

- Where there has been contributory fault by the claimant, the amount of compensation will be reduced by such proportion as the tribunal considers just and equitable having regard to that failing.

Failure to comply with recommendation: Where the tribunal has made a recommendation under Reg 7(c), but the employer has without reasonable excuse failed to comply with the recommendation, the tribunal may increase any award for compensation under Reg 7(7)(b) or make an award of compensation where it has not already done so (see Reg 7(13)).

Gross or net: This will depend on whether the sums paid are treated as suppressed wages, an award for discrimination or injury to feelings (see *Tax* below, within this entry). Where a sum is paid to represent a net loss it will be calculated on the net figure and grossed up where appropriate to make the final award. Where the sum is viewed as suppressed wages the award will be calculated on gross earnings, with the employer deducting tax and NI.

Any maximum or minimum: No, the award is unlimited.

Adjustments: A percentage deduction for contributory conduct can be applied (Reg 7(12)). Also, if the employer fails to comply with a tribunal's recommendation, the award can be increased to a level that the tribunal considers is just and equitable (Reg 7(13)).

Mitigation: The usual rules on mitigation apply.

Tax: Any payment to compensate for an employee's reduced wages or benefits would probably be classed as arrears of pay and taxed under s62 ITEPA 2003 in the normal way (see EIM02550 and EIM02530, HMRC). The tax to be paid should be calculated according to the tax year in which the pay was withheld, not the tax year in which the repayment is made.

However, EIM12965 of the Employment Income Manual states that payments of compensation for discrimination which occurs before termination is not employment income for the purposes of s401 and that they are therefore not taxable. It is therefore arguable that the award for infringement of Reg 3 or Reg 6 FTE(PLFT) would not be subject to tax as they are compensation for discrimination (in its broadest sense).

Injury to feelings awards arising other than from dismissal are not taxable.

Statutory authorities: FTE(PLFT) Regs 2002 (SI 2002/2034) Regs *3*, *6* and *7*

Flexible working

Every employee has the statutory right to request a change in their terms and conditions of employment (s80F ERA 1996) to enable flexible working after 26 weeks' employment service.

Section 80G identifies procedural and substantive rules for how an employer must deal with a request.

Remedy: Where an employee succeeds in a complaint that the employer has failed to comply with the requirements of s80G ERA 1996, or that a decision to reject the application was based on incorrect facts, the tribunal must make a declaration to that effect, may make an order for reconsideration of the application and may make an order that compensation be paid (s80I ERA 1996).

The amount of compensation is the sum the tribunal considers just and equitable, up to the permitted maximum (s80I(2)).

The maximum award is 8 weeks' pay, currently capped at £643 per week (see Reg 7 FW(ECR) Regs 2002/3236 and s227(za) ERA 1996).

Gross or net: The maximum is calculated according to a week's pay, which is a gross figure.

A week's pay as defined in ss220 to 229 ERA 1996 applies (see *Week's pay*).

Limit on a week's pay: £643 (see *Table 1* for historical rates).

Limit on number of weeks: 8

Any maximum or minimum: No minimum; Maximum is 8 x a week's pay (capped at £643 per week) = £5,144.

Adjustments: None, although any compensation ordered will be the sum which the tribunal considers just and equitable. This will include considerations such as the loss actually suffered and attempts to mitigate.

Mitigation: Within the tribunal's consideration of what sum is just and equitable to award.

Tax: The tax treatment is not clear. To the extent that any sum awarded is compensation for lost earnings, it is likely to be taxed under s62 ITEPA 2003 (see *Tax and termination payments*).

Recoupment: N/A

Statutory authorities: ERA 1996 *s80G to 80I* and *ss220-229; FW(ECR) Regs 2002/3236*

Future loss of earnings

(see also *Compensatory award*; *Financial losses*; *Mitigation*)

Where the remedy available to a claimant includes compensation for losses suffered as a result of the unlawful conduct, the losses may still be continuing at the date of the tribunal hearing. A frequently occurring example is an individual found to have been unfairly dismissed who has not obtained employment at the same level of pay as their old job. The tribunal must assess the losses that the employee will suffer in the future, and the period over which these will continue.

The tribunal will compare the financial circumstances of the claimant, had the unlawful act not occurred, with the circumstances in which they continue to find themselves. Both require the tribunal to assess uncertain scenarios: would the claimant have remained employed or would he have been dismissed in any event; if so would he have found equivalent employment or would he have suffered the same difficulties as he is currently experiencing, or might he have been promoted and received higher pay; when will the claimant obtain equivalent remuneration, or when ought he to? The tribunal will take into account the personal characteristics of the employee such as age and health.

The tribunal's assessment will be based on findings of fact, and will then go on *'to assess the loss flowing from the dismissal, using its common sense, experience and sense of justice'* (see *Software 2000 Ltd v Andrews* [2007] IRLR 568, per Elias P). As HHJ Hand QC said in *Stroud Rugby Football Club v Monkman* UKEAT/0143/13/SM, the assessment of future loss is a *'rough and ready matter. It always has been and it always will be'*.

However, in order to make a judgement of the extent of future loss, the tribunal must have any relevant information that will help it to make its decision. This includes disclosure of information relating to the claimant's pension entitlement from other sources since this would be clearly relevant to an assessment of the chance that the claimant would have remained in employment until a future date (see *Essex County Council v Jarrett* UKEAT/0087/15/MC).

The tribunal will also assess the relevant weekly loss figure for the purpose of the loss of earnings calculation. This may not be the same as the weekly loss at the date of dismissal (for example, if the claimant would only have been paid sick pay as a result of a condition unrelated to the dismissal - see *The Royal Bank of Scotland v O'Doherty* UKEAT/0307/14/RN).

Whole career loss

In exceptional cases a tribunal may be able to award whole career loss. Such cases are rare and only suitable where there is no real prospect of an employee ever obtaining an equivalent job. Otherwise, a tribunal should stick to the usual approach, suitable for the vast majority of cases, of assessing when it is likely that an employee will get an equivalent job (*Wardle v Credit Agricole* [2011] EWCA Civ 545; *Lennon-Knight v Yakira Group Ltd* UKEAT/0186/16).

If a tribunal makes such an award, it must *'take account of the more general uncertainties of life that might impact on the length of a person's working life or even just the length of their working day'* (*Secretary of State for Justice v Plaistow* [2021] UKEAT/0016/20). Tribunals need to consider not only the prospect that the employee might have retired before pension age, but also:

1) The possibility that over the course of a career the employee might have sought to work shorter hours than they did at the time of the wrong complained of;

2) *'The more general vicissitudes of life: the possibility, that all of us must accept, of a working life cut short by reason of early death, disability or other unforeseen circumstance.'*

Plaistow did not offer further guidance on how to make this assessment, but remitted the question to the tribunal.

Garden leave

(see also *Effective date of termination*; *Tax and termination payments*)

The employment contract of an employee who possesses or has access to the employer's confidential information and/or through whom the employer's customer connections are maintained and developed may well have a "garden leave" or "gardening leave" clause which empowers the employer to withdraw all or some of the employee's duties during the period of notice given by either party to the other. Such a power may be implied but this runs up against arguments that the employee has a countervailing (implied) right to work during the period of the contract. During a period of garden leave the employee's express or implied duties of fidelity, and in particular constraints on working for other employers, will continue to apply and may be enforced by an injunction. Frequently employees will contend that their employer has repudiated the employment contract, entitling them to be discharged from compliance with its terms (including as to garden leave and any restrictive covenants).

A case considering the extent to which the public policy against clauses in restraint of trade applies to garden leave is *JM Finn & Co Ltd v Holliday* [2013] EWHC 3450 (QB), [2014] IRLR 102.

Workers on garden leave are not entitled to payment in lieu of any accrued holiday they could have taken when on such leave, save when they are unable to use up that entitlement due to illness (*Maschek v Magistratsdirektion der Statdt Wien – Personalstelle Wiener Stadtwerke* [2016] EUECJ C-341/15; [2016] IRLR 801).

Gourley principle

(see also *Tax and termination payments***)**

The *Gourley* principle is that damages awarded for loss suffered to the claimant should put him in the same position as he would have been in if he had not suffered the unlawful conduct. Where his remuneration would have been subject to tax and NI, the award will be based on his net loss.

The *Gourley* principle was established in the case of *British Transport Commission v Gourley* [1955] UKHL 4 where a civil engineer was awarded damages by the British Transport Commission in respect of a railway accident. The award included an amount for loss of earnings. The question was whether the amount of damages should be paid to the recipient gross or net of deductions that would have been suffered by the individual had he remained in employment.

The court held that '*the broad general principle which should govern the assessment of damage in cases such as this is that the tribunal should award the injured party such a sum of money as will put him in the same position as he would have been in if he had not sustained the injuries … to ignore the tax element at the present day would be to act in a manner which is out of touch with reality*'. The significance of the *Gourley* principle is that damages will be calculated on the basis of the loss suffered after tax and NI had been deducted from his earnings.

However, where the claimant will have to pay tax on

the award, or where the employer will have to deduct tax and NI, the tribunal must 'gross up' the award to ensure that the claimant's net loss is compensated for by an equivalent net sum (see also *Grossing up*). For example, where an award for unfair dismissal exceeds the tax free £30,000, the tribunal will calculate the net loss suffered by the claimant and increase the sum awarded to reflect any tax that the claimant will have to pay on receipt of the award. The two incidences of tax are set off against each other - see *Parsons v BNM Laboratories Ltd* [1963] 2 All ER 658, and *Shove v Downs Surgical Plc* [1984] 1 All ER 7.

Grievance procedure

(see also *ACAS (The Advisory, Conciliation and Arbitration Service)***;** *Adjustments and order of adjustments***)**

Employers will often have written procedures for considering grievances raised by employees. The core principles upon which a grievance should be considered have been set out by ACAS in the ACAS *Code of Practice 1: Code of Practice on Disciplinary and Grievance Procedures*. This code provides basic practical guidance to employers, employees and their representatives and sets out principles for handling disciplinary and grievance situations in the workplace. The Code is issued under *s199 of the Trade Union and Labour Relations (Consolidation) Act 1992* and came into effect on 11 March 2015. In a number of types of tribunal claims, if an employee or employer has unreasonably failed to follow the guidance set out in the code relating to the grievance procedure a tribunal may reduce or increase any award they have made by up to 25% (see *ACAS (The Advisory, Conciliation and Arbitration Service)*).

Gross weekly pay

(see also *Week's pay***)**

This is to be contrasted with net weekly pay. Gross weekly pay is the total sum payable under the contract of employment before the deduction of tax, NI or pension contributions. Where this is calculated as the sum 'payable under the contract' (e.g. unfair dismissal cap; Protective awards; or under ss220 to 228 ERA 1996), it can also include employer pension contributions (see *University of Sunderland v Drossou* UKEAT/0341/16/RN).

Gross weekly pay is used in the calculation of the following claims:

- Additional award;
- Basic award;
- Guarantee pay;

- Insolvency;

- Protective award;

- Suspension;

- Right for union member not to be unjustifiably disciplined/expelled;

- Time off for looking for work/training after redundancy; antenatal care; employee representatives; pension trustees; union duties, activities and union learning reps; study or training; young person for study or training; members of a European Council;

- TUPE claims;

- Right to be accompanied;

- Flexible working;

- Written reasons for dismissal;

- Redundancy payments.

Gross weekly pensionable pay: see *Pension loss*

Grossing up

(see also *Gourley principle*; *Marginal tax rate*; *Tax and termination payments*)

Awards will be 'grossed up' by a tribunal where the sum to be received by the claimant will be taxed. The purpose is to place in the claimant's hands the sum he would have held had he not been treated unlawfully, i.e. to compensate for the true net loss.

It is the responsibility of the claimant or their representative to raise the question of grossing up at the ET. If they do not, the point may not be raised at the EAT (see *Bethnal Green & Shoreditch Education Trust v Dippenaar* UKEAT/0064/15/JOJ).

Where the award will be taxed by the employer before payment is made to the claimant, such as where the award is for unpaid wages, the tribunal will award the true gross sum. Grossing up therefore applies to awards where s401 ITEPA 2003 operates to tax the sum in the claimant's hands.

Section 401 applies to payments and other benefits which are received directly or indirectly in consideration or in consequence of, or otherwise in connection with:

a) the termination of a person's employment;

b) a change in the duties of a person's employment; or

c) a change in the earnings from a person's employment, by the person, or the person's spouse, blood relative, dependant or personal representatives.

In this case the recipient enjoys a tax free amount of £30,000 in any particular tax year and will then pay tax on sums in excess of this figure. Neither the tax free sum nor the excess is subject to employee national insurance, but, from 6 April 2020, employer national insurance is payable at a rate of 13.8% on any amount above the £30,000 threshold.

To avoid disadvantage to the claimant, the tribunal should 'gross up' any award it makes over £30,000. This requires the tribunal to estimate the tax the claimant will have to pay on receipt of the award and add a sum for that tax back on to the award, thus cancelling out the tax burden to the claimant. In other words, where the tribunal has determined the sum a claimant is to be awarded, the tribunal will consider the likely tax consequences and increase the award to ensure that the claimant retains the sum to which the tribunal has determined he is entitled. The relevant tax year for grossing up is the year the award is received by the claimant. Any adjustment to the award in subsequent tax years (e.g. upon reconsideration of a judgment) should be grossed up by reference to that subsequent tax year (*PA Finlay & Co Ltd v Finlay* UKEAT/0260/14).

Gross or net figures to be used in the calculation?

It is not necessarily an error of law to use gross figures when calculating loss of earnings, and then not perform any further grossing up (see *Acetrip Ltd v Dogra* UKEAT/0238/18/BA). However, if the award exceeds £30,000, it will be an error of law if the tribunal fails to take into account that the first £30,000 of its award would be tax free. By working entirely on gross figures, the claimant will be over-compensated. EJ Auerbach in *Acetrip* said:

> "... it is, in my view, better, wherever possible, to start with net figures and perform a grossing up calculation, but particularly so where the first £30,000 will be tax free, as the tribunal may otherwise run into further difficulties if it attempts to mix and match, starting with gross figures, but still having to take on board the tax free element."

Determination of aggregated total

Before the £30,000 threshold (see *EIM13505*) is applied to an award, it is necessary to add together all the payments and benefits within s401 ITEPA 2003 that are made to, or are in respect of, the same person in connection with:

- the same office or employment; and

- different offices or employments with the same employer; and

- different offices or employments with associated employers (see EIM13540).

The threshold is then applied to the total. This ensures that all sums fall within just the one £30,000 threshold.

For example, a director is dismissed from two separate employments with associated employers within the same tax year, receiving payments and benefits worth £25,000 in each case which all fall within s401 ITEPA 2003. He also receives a tribunal award of £40,000 for unfair dismissal. The aggregated total received in connection with the terminated employments is £90,000 and only one £30,000 threshold is available against that total.

The tribunal will gross up the sum in excess of £30,000 taking into account the employee's personal allowance and tax banding (*Shove v Downs Surgical Plc* [1984] 1 All ER 7). This tax rate that should be applied is called the claimant's marginal tax rate and may be difficult to ascertain. Further, different marginal tax rates may be applied to different elements of the award (see *Yorkshire Housing Ltd v Cuerden* UKEAT/0397/09).

Awards to be grossed up

The only awards that should be grossed up are those that are calculated using net weekly pay and which will be taxed in the recipient's hands i.e.:

- Compensatory award;

- Damages for wrongful dismissal;

- Financial losses suffered as a result of unlawful discrimination.

The following heads of loss will not be grossed up:

- any awards that have been calculated as a gross figure and tax will be deducted either before the claimant receives the payment (for example, accrued holiday pay and the claimant is still employed); or on the claimant's self-assessment (if they are no longer employed);

- any other awards calculated as a gross figure (such as the basic award or additional award);

- awards which will not be taxed (for example *Physical and psychiatric injury*).

An award for pension loss also falls to be grossed up – see *Yorkshire Housing Ltd v Cuerden* UKEAT/0397/09. The pension loss figure should therefore be the *net* loss (see *Chief Constable of Northumbria Police v Erichsen* UKEAT/0027/15/BA).

In what order should grossing up be applied?

Calculations should be performed in the following order:

1) Adjustments, including the addition of interest (see *Adjustments and order of adjustments*);

2) Grossing up;

3) Statutory cap applied (see *Hardie Grant London Ltd v Aspden* UKEAT/0242/11/RN).

Recoupment: There is no information to explain

whether the prescribed element should be calculated before grossing up or after. However, it is likely that the sums involved would render the distinction of no relevance.

Relevant case law: *Bethnal Green & Shoreditch Education Trust v Dippenaar* UKEAT/0064/15/JOJ; *Chief Constable of Northumbria Police v Erichsen* UKEAT/0027/15/BA; *Hall v Durham County Council & Ors* UKEAT/0256/14/MC; *Hardie Grant London Ltd v Aspden* UKEAT/0242/11/RN; *Shove v Downs Surgical Plc* [1984] 1 All ER 7; *Yorkshire Housing Ltd v Cuerden* UKEAT/0397/09/SM

Examples

Single marginal tax rate

It is important to understand that the percentage by which the claimant will be taxed should **not** just be 'added back' to the award (see *Hall v Durham County Council & Ors* UKEAT/0256/14/MC). The following examples demonstrate how the calculation should be performed.

All examples assume that the claimant's marginal tax rate is 20% and the maximum statutory cap on an unfair dismissal award as at 6 April 2023, which is £105,707. The calculation for grossing up the award is:

(Grossed up sum) x (1 – marginal tax rate) = true net loss

Therefore:

Grossed up sum = (true net loss) / (1 – marginal tax rate)

Example 1

Basic award = £11,000 (Taxable)

Compensatory award = £100,000 (Taxable)

Tax free element = £30,000

Calculation

Amount of compensation up to the £30,000 tax free element = £30,000 - £11,000 = £19,000

Amount of compensation award that should be taxed = £100,000 - £19,000 = £81,000

The grossed up compensation of £81,000 = £81,000 ÷ 0.8 = £101,250

Total compensation = £19,000 + £101,250 = £120,250

Compensation cap = £105,707

Total award = £11,000 (basic) + £105,707 (statutory cap) = £116,707

Example 2 (discrimination case where EDT is after 6 April 2018)

Basic award = £11,000 (Taxable)

Injury to feelings = £25,000 (Taxable)

Compensation for financial loss = £100,000 (Taxable)

Tax free element = £30,000

Calculation

Basic award = £11,000

Amount of compensation up to the £30,000 tax free element = £30,000 - £11,000 = £19,000

Amount of compensation award that should be taxed = £100,000 - £19,000 = £81,000

The grossed up compensation of £81,000 = £81,000 ÷ 0.8 = £101,250

Total compensation = £19,000 + £101,250 = £120,250 (the statutory cap does not apply to awards for discrimination).

Injury to feelings = £25,000 and must be grossed up because it is taxable (EDT after 6 April 2018) = £25,000 ÷ 0.8 = £31,250.

Total award = £11,000 (basic) + £31,250 (grossed up injury to feelings award) + £120,250 (uncapped compensation) = £162,500

Example 3

Basic award = £11,000 (Taxable)

Detriment award = £25,000 (Taxable)

Compensation award = £10,000 (Taxable)

Tax free element = £30,000

Calculation

Basic award = £11,000

Detriment award = £19,000 plus £6,000, of which £6,000 should be grossed up

Grossed up detriment award = £6,000 ÷ 0.8 = £7,500

Compensation award = £10,000 which will be taxed in full

Grossed up compensation = £10,000 ÷ 0.8 = £12,500

Total award = £11,000 (basic) + £19,000 (untaxed detriment award) + £7,500 (grossed up detriment award) + £12,500 (grossed up compensation) = £50,000

Example 4

Basic award = £11,000 (Taxable)

Compensation award = £40,000 (Taxable)

Tax free element = £30,000

Calculation

Compensation award exceeding the tax free element = £40,000 − (£30,000 - £11,000) = £21,000

Grossed up compensation = £21,000 ÷ 0.8 = £26,250

Total award = £11,000 (basic) + £19,000 (compensation up to tax free limit) + £26,250 (grossed up compensation) = £56,250

Differential tax rates

Different tax rates may apply to different elements of the award (see *Yorkshire Housing Ltd v Cuerden* [2010] UKEAT/0397/09) and therefore different elements of the award may need to be grossed up by different percentages. However, the calculations are not straightforward and there is the added complication of a tapering personal allowance for earnings/tribunal awards between £100,000 and £125,140 (for the 2023/24 tax year - unchanged from previous year).

It is important to work with **net** figures when calculating how much of the salary/tribunal award falls within each tax band. The balancing net figure then needs to be grossed up according to the tax band it falls into.

Personal allowance

The full personal allowance (PA) for the tax year 2023/24 is £12,570. This can be reduced by HMRC if the employee receives certain benefits; additionally, the PA will be tapered where earnings exceed £100,000. For every £2 earned above £100,000 the PA is reduced by £1 which means that the PA will be reduced to zero once the employee earns £125,140. This has implications for the grossing up of a tribunal award since until the grossing up calculation has been done, the final tribunal award will not be known; but the grossing up calculation cannot be done until any reduction in the PA has been obtained. The solution to this problem is explained fully below.

The following examples explain how the grossing up should be done when the employee has received/will receive a salary and a tribunal award in the tax year of payment.

Example 1 (PA remains intact)

Tax year: 2023/24

Personal allowance (PA) = £12,570 (gross)

Basic rate (BR) = 20% on the next £37,700 (gross) leaving £30,160 (net)

Higher rate (HR) = 40% on the next £99,730 (gross) leaving £59,838 (net)

Additional rate (AR) = 45% on anything over £150,000 (not applicable in this example)

Salary received = £27,000 (gross)

Tribunal award = £60,000 (net, of which £30,000 will be tax free)

The first £12,570 of the £27,000 salary would be free of tax. The next £14,430 (i.e. £27,000 - £12,570) would be taxable at the rate of 20% leaving a net figure of £11,544. It is then necessary to deduct £11,544 from the **net tax band figure** of £30,160 to find the amount of the tribunal award that falls within the BR tax band. This is £30,160 - £11,544 = £18,616.

The £18,616 now needs to be grossed up by 20% to get £23,270 (i.e. £18,616 ÷ 0.8).

Remember that the employee requires £30,000 (plus the £30,000 tax free sum) in their hand, so the net balance required is now £30,000 - £18,616 = £11,384 which now needs to be grossed up by 40% to get a gross figure of £18,973 (i.e. £11,384 ÷ 0.6).

The table below summarises the calculations.

	Earnings			Tribunal Award		
Band	**Gross**	**Tax**	**Net**	**Gross**	**Tax**	**Net**
PA	12,570	0	12,570	0	0	0
BR	14,430	2,886	11,544	23,270	4,654	18,616
HR	0	0	0	18,973	7,589	11,384
Total	27,000	2,886	24,114	42,243	12,243	30,000

The gross amount that should be awarded by the tribunal is therefore £42,243 + £30,000 tax free amount = £72,243.

Example 2 (PA reduced to zero)

Tax year: 2023/24

Personal allowance (PA) = 0

Basic rate (BR) = 20% on the next £37,700 (gross) leaving £30,160 (net)

Higher rate (HR) = 40% on the next £112,300 (gross) leaving £67,380 (net). (Note that the HR tax band has effectively been widened because the PA is now zero. The HR tax band now stretches between £37,700 and £150,000).

Additional rate (AR) = 45% on anything over £150,000

Salary received = £27,000 (gross)

Tribunal award = £130,000 (net, of which £30,000 will be tax free)

First, the entire salary figure falls within the basic rate tax band. Next, the net salary figure of £21,600 (i.e. £27,000 x 0.8) should be subtracted from the net basic rate figure of £30,160 to obtain the net amount of the tribunal award that falls within this tax band. This is £8,560.

The £8,560 should be grossed up by 20% to get £10,700 (i.e. £8,560 ÷ 0.8).

The next £67,380 net (or £112,300 gross) will fall within the HR tax band. Remember that the claimant requires £100,000 (plus £30,000 tax free sum) in their hand, leaving £24,060 net (i.e. £100,000 - £8,560 - £67,380) in the AR tax band to be grossed up by 45%. This comes to £43,745 (i.e. £24,060 ÷ 0.55).

The table below summarises the calculations.

	Earnings			Tribunal Award		
Band	**Gross**	**Tax**	**Net**	**Gross**	**Tax**	**Net**
PA	0	0	0	0	0	0
BR	27,000	5,400	21,600	10,700	2,140	8,560
HR	0	0	0	112,300	44,920	67,380
AR	0	0	0	43,745	19,685	24,060
Total	27,000	5,400	21,600	166,745	66,745	100,000

The gross amount that should be awarded by the tribunal is therefore £166,745 + £30,000 tax free amount = £196,745.

Tapering of the personal allowance

The calculations for anyone receiving a gross sum of between £100,000 and £125,140 are more complicated. The reduction in the PA for earnings between £100,000 and £125,140 effectively means that some (or all) of the current PA of £12,570 moves into the HR tax band so is taxed at 40%. In reality this will actually be 20% because the PA is only reduced by £1 for every £2 of earnings between £100,000 and £125,140. However, the earnings between these 2 amounts are taxed at 40% too – so creating a 'new' tax band between £100,000 and £125,140 of 60%, and keeping the PA intact, will take care of any tapering problems. The following worked example illustrates the calculations that should be performed.

Example 3 (Tapering PA)

Tax year: 2023/24

Personal allowance (PA) = 12,570 (this has been obtained by looking at the claimant's last payslip)

Basic rate (BR) = 20% on the next £37,700 (gross) leaving £30,160 (net)

Higher rate (HR) = 40% on the next £49,730 (gross) leaving £29,838 (net). Remember that once the combined earnings/taxable tribunal award exceed £100,000, the PA is reduced. Therefore, it is important to identify the portion of the HR tax band that is below £100,000 which, in this case, is £100,000 - £12,570 - £37,700 = £49,730

Higher rate plus (HR+) = 60% on anything between £100,000 and £125,140

Salary received = £30,000 (gross)

Tribunal award = £80,000 (net, of which £30,000 will be tax free)

The first £12,570 of the £30,000 salary would be free of tax. The next £17,430 (i.e. £30,000 - £12,570) would be taxable at the rate of 20% leaving a net figure of £13,944. It is then necessary to deduct £13,944 from the net tax band figure of £30,160 to find the amount of the tribunal award that falls within the BR tax band. This is £30,160 - £13,944 = £16,216.

The £16,216 now needs to be grossed up by 20% to get £20,270 (i.e. £16,216 ÷ 0.8).

Remember that the employee requires £50,000 (plus the £30,000 tax free sum) in their hand, so the net balance required is now £50,000 - £16,216 = £33,784 of which £29,838 falls within the HR tax band. Grossing up this figure by 40% comes to £49,730 (i.e. £29,838 ÷ 0.6).

The balancing net figure of £3,946 (i.e. £33,784 - £29,838) should now be grossed up by our new tax rate of 60% to give £9,865 (i.e. £3,946 ÷ 0.4).

The table below summarises the calculations.

Band	Earnings			Tribunal Award		
	Gross	Tax	Net	Gross	Tax	Net
PA	12,570	0	12,570	0	0	0
BR	17,430	3,486	13,944	20,270	4,054	16,216
HR	0	0	0	49,730	19,892	29,838
HR+				9,865	5,919	3,946
Total	30,000	3,486	26,514	79,865	29,865	50,000

The gross amount that should be awarded by the tribunal is therefore £79,865 + £30,000 tax free amount = £109,865.

Guarantee payment

(see also Week's pay; Table 3**)**

Employees are entitled to be paid a minimum amount where throughout a day during any part of which an employee would normally be required to work in accordance with his contract of employment the employee is not provided with work by his employer, and the reason is:

a)   a diminution in the requirements of the employer's business for work of the kind which the employee is employed to do; or

b)   any other occurrence affecting the normal working of the employer's business in relation to work of the kind which the employee is employed to do.

That minimum sum is called a guarantee payment (s28 ERA 1996).

An employee may bring a complaint to a tribunal that his employer has failed to pay the whole or any part of a guarantee payment to which he is entitled (s34 ERA 1996).

Remedy: The remedy is an order from the tribunal that the employer must pay to the employee the amount of guarantee payment that the tribunal has found to be due.

Calculation of remedy: Guarantee pay for a particular day = normal working hours on that day x guaranteed hourly rate

where:

Guaranteed hourly rate = 1 week's pay ÷ number of normal working hours in a week for that employee when employed under the contract of employment in force on the particular day (s30(1) ERA 1996).

If the number of hours the employee works differs from week to week, the number of normal working hours is calculated by taking the total number of the employee's normal working hours during the period of 12 weeks ending with the last complete week before the day in respect of which the guarantee payment is payable, and dividing that by 12. Where the employee has not been employed for a sufficient period to enable the calculation to be made, a number which fairly represents the number of normal working hours in a week will be used (s30(3) and (4) ERA 1996).

Gross or net: Gross. Any guarantee pay, either paid by the employer or awarded by the tribunal, should be added to other gross pay in that period and PAYE and NI deducted in the normal way.

Limit on guarantee payment: The limit on the guarantee payment for a particular day is £35 from 06/04/2023 (s31(1) ERA 1996).

Limit on number of days: A tribunal can order a guarantee payment to be paid for a maximum of 5 days in any 3 month period (s31(2) and (3) ERA 1996).

Any maximum or minimum: No minimum; Maximum will be £175 in any 3 month period.

Adjustments: None

Mitigation: N/A

Tax: Taxed under s62 ITEPA 2003 (see EIM02550, HMRC)

Recoupment: Any amount found to be due to the employee and ordered to be paid under s34(3) for a period before the conclusion of the tribunal proceedings will form part of the prescribed element.

Statutory authorities: ERA 1996 ss28 to 35; ITEPA 2003 s62; EP(RJAIS) Regs 1996

Harassment: see Discrimination

Holiday pay

(see also *Insolvency*; *Table 6*; *APPENDIX 3*)

The Working Time Regulations 1998 provide workers with a minimum entitlement to paid leave. The minimum entitlement, subject to certain exclusions, is 5.6 weeks paid holiday per year subject to a cap of 28 days. The 5.6 weeks are made up of 4 weeks basic annual leave under Reg 13 and 1.6 weeks additional leave under Reg 13A. 28 days corresponds to 5.6 weeks for a worker working 5 days per week, but if a working week is longer, the statutory minimum remains capped at 28 days even though the full 5.6 weeks of holiday will thereby not be guaranteed. Workers may in addition to the guaranteed minimum holiday be entitled under their contractual terms to enhanced holiday entitlement.

Reg 13 was amended by the Working Time (Coronavirus) (Amendment) Regulations 2020 to allow workers to carry over any basic annual leave that it was not reasonably practicable for them to take due to the effects of coronavirus for the subsequent two leave years. Any employer may not prevent a worker from taking such leave except where there is *'good reason to do so.'* This amendment remains in force at the time of editing. The Government has published guidance on what should be considered when assessing whether it was reasonably practicable to take the leave in the relevant year: *Holiday entitlement and pay during coronavirus (COVID-19)*.

For a typical worker calculating holiday entitlement and the corresponding holiday pay may not be straightforward. Difficulties can arise for example where workers start, or leave, part way through a holiday year, where workers seek to carry over leave from one year to another, or where a worker's working time is non-standard. Special rules apply to calculating statutory holiday entitlement for part time workers, workers working atypical days and hours, and workers absent on sick leave or family related leave.

Where a part time worker's hours are increased there is no retrospective recalculation of the amount of holiday that has accrued (*Greenfield v The Care Bureau* [2016] IRLR 62).

Holiday and holiday pay claims may arise in a number of circumstances including where:

- the worker has been denied the right to take holiday;
- the worker has not been paid for the holiday they have taken;
- the worker has left their employment without having taken the leave to which they were entitled and seeks pay in lieu of that holiday; or
- the worker may have been subject to a detriment or dismissed for conduct relating to seeking to take holiday or enforce the right to paid holiday.

Claims for unpaid statutory holiday pay may be made under Reg 30 WTR 1998 and, where the right is contractual, under s13 ERA 1996 (see *Revenue and Customs Commissioners v Stringer* [2009] ICR 985). Where the right is contractual, a claim for unpaid holiday pay may be made under s13 ERA 1996. It is also possible to bring such a contractual claim in the ordinary civil courts, or where the contract has been terminated, in the employment tribunal under its limited contractual jurisdiction (ETEJ Order).

The rights not to suffer detriment or be dismissed for seeking to enforce rights to holiday pay flow from s45A, 101A and 104 ERA 1996 (see *Detriment* and *Unfair dismissal*).

Remedy: Reg 16(1) WTR 1998 provides that *'A worker is entitled to be paid in respect of any period of annual leave to which he is entitled under regulation 13, at the rate of a week's pay in respect of each week of leave'*. A week's pay is calculated according to ss221 to 224 ERA 1996 subject to slight technical modifications and the removal of the limit on a week's pay (see *Week's pay*).

Section 224 applies to both full time and part time employees, and is not to be pro-rated for the latter, even if this produces anomalous results. The plain wording of the legislation should be applied (*Harpur Trust v Brazel* [2022] UKSC 21). The Department for Business and Trade (DBT) are consulting on introducing legislation to reverse or alter the decision in *Harpur*, potentially allowing for pro-rating. The Government has yet to publish its response and for now *Harpur* remains the law.

Where a worker is seeking pay in lieu of holiday on termination, Reg 14 states that this shall be calculated either according to the terms of a 'relevant agreement', or a formula set out in Reg 14(3)(b). Any 'relevant agreement' must pay as much or more than the statutory formula (*Connor v Chief Constable of The South Yorkshire Police* [2023] EAT 42).

Calculating annual leave for people working variable hours or for variable pay

The Employment Rights (Employment Particulars and Paid Annual Leave) (Amendment) Regulations 2018 amended Regulation 16 of the Working Time Regulations 1998 and came into force on 6 April 2020. The amendments have the effect of changing the reference period for calculating annual leave pay from 12 to 52 weeks for workers whose pay varies because either: (a) they have no normal working hours; or (b) they have normal working hours but the amount of work or days or times they work each week varies.

Where the worker has been employed for less than 52

weeks, the reference period is reduced to the number of weeks of employment.

Weeks preceding the period of 104 weeks before the beginning of the leave shall not be taken into account. Where this yields fewer than 52 weeks to take into account, the reference period is reduced to the number of weeks which can be taken into account, i.e. in which remuneration was payable.

Where applying sections 221 to 224 gives no weeks to take into account (either because the worker is at the beginning of their employment, or because they have no weeks in the reference period in which remuneration was payable) a week's pay is not calculated by applying those sections. Instead, it is the amount which fairly represents a week's pay, having regard to the considerations specified at section 228(3) (which include, for example, the remuneration received by other persons engaged in relevant comparable employment with the same employer).

Note: the operation of ss221 to 224 has been the subject of extensive litigation in the last few years. The legislation often fails to take into account pay a worker would in fact receive during a pay period. The Working Time Regulations implement the Working Time Directive and ss221 to 224 in many respects fail to provide workers with the full entitlement to pay required by EU law (see *British Airways plc v Williams* [2012] IRLR 1014 and *Z.J.R. Lock v British Gas Trading Ltd and Others* [2014] ICR 813 (CJEU)). The Working Time Directive only provides for 4 weeks' leave, so the existing ERA 1996 provisions continue to apply unmodified to the additional statutory 1.6 weeks' leave available to employees unmodified.

It is now clear that the calculation of a week's pay in the ERA 1996 should not be followed blindly, but where possible should be interpreted in accordance with the Working Time Directive. The precise consequences of this have yet to be fully determined. Two key cases are:

- *Bear Scotland & Ors v Fulton & Ors* UKEATS/0047/13/BI; [2015] ICR 221: the EAT held that sums paid for non-guaranteed overtime (i.e. overtime that was offered at the employer's discretion, but not guaranteed, but which the employees were obliged to perform) should be included in the calculation of holiday pay. It modified regulation 16(3)(d) of the WTR to read:

    "as if the references to sections 227 and 228 did not apply and, in the case of the entitlement under regulation 13, sections 223(3) and 234 do not apply".

- *Lock v British* Gas: On 22 May 2014, the Court of Justice of the European Union (CJEU) handed down their decision in this case. The claimant successfully argued that his paid annual leave

should include commission payments if these were part of his normal pay. On remission of the case to the Leicester Employment Tribunal in February 2015, the tribunal interpreted the WTR to achieve this result by inserting new words into regulation 16(3) of the Working Time Regulations 1998 as follows:

> *"(e) as if, in the case of the entitlement under regulation 13, a worker with normal working hours whose remuneration includes commission or similar payment shall be deemed to have remuneration which varies with the amount of work done for the purpose of section 221 ."*

On 22 February 2016, the EAT dismissed the employer's appeal against this decision. The EAT saw no reason to depart from its earlier decision in *Bear Scotland*. The Court of Appeal also dismissed the appeal. The WTR have to be interpreted in conformity with the Directive, and holiday pay should be calculated by reference to an employee's normal remuneration.

The proposed wording above, however, was amended by the Court of Appeal because it was considered too wide insofar as it applied to all types of commission rather than just contractual 'results-based' commission. The judgment did not, however, state what form this amendment took.

Voluntary overtime should be included in any calculation of holiday pay where the pattern of work is sufficiently regular and settled for payments made in respect of it to amount to normal remuneration (*Dudley Metropolitan Borough Council v Willetts & Ors* UKEAT/0334/16, *Flowers & Ors v East of England Ambulance Trust* UKEAT/0235/17/JOJ and *East of England Ambulance Service NHS Trust v Flowers and others* [2019] EWCA Civ 947).

Where the worker relies not upon the statutory minimum entitlement to holiday, but a contractual term, the calculation of holiday pay will be in accordance with the provisions of the contract.

The CJEU has held in *King v The Sash Window Workshop Ltd* EUECJ C-214/16 that Article 7 of the Working Time Directive precludes national provisions or practices that prevent workers from accumulating untaken annual leave throughout the whole period of their employment, where such accumulation has happened because the employer has refused to pay for the leave. *King* has been considered by the Court of Appeal in *Smith v Pimlico Plumbers Ltd* [2022] EWCA Civ 70, which held (overturning the EAT):

- Paid annual leave is a *'single composite right'*. Unpaid annual leave does not satisfy the requirements of that right. Providing unpaid annual leave is to be treated as the same as if no annual leave were provided at all.

- If an employer fails to provide an employee with paid annual leave in a given leave year, that right does not lapse, but accumulates until the termination of the working relationship.

- Regulations 13 and 14 WTRs should be re-read as set out in an Appendix to the Court of Appeal's judgment.

Gross or net: Any order for the payment of accrued holiday pay should use gross figures, and the sum will be taxed by the employer.

Adjustments: Accrued holiday pay may be claimed as an unlawful deduction from wages, in which case the ACAS uplift could apply where there has been a failure in any grievance process.

Cap: Accrued holiday pay is not included in the award for financial losses arising from an unfair dismissal, so it falls outside the statutory cap.

Mitigation: N/A

Tax: Tax should be paid either by the employer through payroll or by the employee under Self-Assessment where this has not been done.

Recoupment: Recoupment will not apply to accrued holiday pay if the employee has been dismissed.

Statutory authorities: ERA 1996 *s13*; WTR 1998 Regs *13, 14, 16* and *30*

Relevant case law: *Bear Scotland & Ors v Fulton & Ors* UKEATS/0047/13/BI; *British Airways plc v Williams* [2012] IRLR 1014; *Dudley Metropolitan Borough Council v Willetts & Ors* UKEAT/0334/16; *East of England Ambulance Service NHS Trust v Flowers and others* [2019] EWCA Civ 947; *Flowers & Ors v East of England Ambulance Trust* UKEAT/0235/17/JOJ; *Harpur Trust v Brazel* [2022] UKSC 21; *King v The Sash Window Workshop Ltd* EUECJ C-214/16; *Smith v Pimlico Plumbers Ltd* [2022] EWCA Civ 70; *Z.J.R. Lock v British Gas Trading Ltd and Others* [2014] ICR 813 (CJEU)

Housing benefit

(see also *Recoupment*)

In the case of *Savage v Saxena* [1998] UKEAT/605/97 the EAT held that housing benefit the claimant had received since her dismissal should not be deducted from the compensatory award, as it would not be just or equitable to allow a defaulting employer to retain the benefits and to place an unfairly dismissed employee at the disadvantage of possibly having to pay the benefit back once her situation had been reassessed. Housing benefit is not a recoupable benefit so the employer would not have to pay its value to the Secretary of State if it were deducted from the claimant's award. If a claimant's entitlement was reassessed and the benefit did not have to be paid

back, the claimant would appear to recover from the employer a greater sum than his losses.

This view was confirmed by the EAT in *Olayemi v Athena Medical Centre & Anor* UKEAT/0140/15, and applies to both unfair dismissal and discrimination awards.

Immediate loss of earnings

(**see also** *Compensatory award*; *Future loss of earnings*)

Immediate (sometimes called 'past') loss of earnings is the phrase used to describe the loss of earnings up until the tribunal hearing where remedy is determined. It is to be contrasted with future loss of earnings which are those losses suffered after the hearing. Immediate loss of earnings will often be simpler to assess than future loss, as the requirement to predict what will happen in the future is absent.

The tribunal will compare the financial circumstances of the claimant, had the unlawful act not occurred, with the circumstances in which they now find themselves. Both require the tribunal to assess uncertain scenarios: would the claimant have remained employed or would they have been dismissed in any event, if so would they have found equivalent employment or would they have suffered the same difficulties as they have experienced, or might they have been promoted and received higher pay; when did the claimant obtain equivalent remuneration, or when ought they to have done so? The tribunal will take into account the personal characteristics of the employee such as age and health.

The tribunal's assessment will be based on findings of fact, and then 'to assess the loss flowing from the dismissal, using its common sense, experience and sense of justice' (see *Software 2000 Ltd v Andrews* [2007] IRLR 568, per Elias P).

Incapacity benefit: see *Employment and Support Allowance (ESA)*

Income support

(**see also** *Job seekers allowance*; *Recoupment*)

Income Support is paid to those on a low income or none at all, who are working less than 16 hours a week and have not signed on as unemployed.

Income support is not deducted from an award of compensation but instead is subject to the recoupment regulations (see *Savage v Saxena* [1998] ICR 357).

If the tribunal is satisfied that in respect of each day falling within the period to which the prescribed element relates the employee has neither received nor claimed jobseeker's allowance or income support the recoupment regulations will not apply.

Statutory cap: If the statutory cap has been applied the prescribed element should be adjusted by the same proportion (see also *Recoupment*).

Statutory authorities: The *Employment Protection (Recoupment of jobseekers allowance and income support) Regulations 1996*

Relevant case law: *Savage v Saxena* [1998] ICR 357

Indirect discrimination: see *Discrimination*

Individual respondents

(see also *Detriment*; *Discrimination***)**

An individual employee may be a respondent to a discrimination claim, and it is often the case that claims will be brought against an employer and one or more individual employees responsible for the acts complained of (see s110 EA 2010).

Where a claim against an individual is upheld by the tribunal the tribunal may make individual awards against any particular respondent or make all respondents jointly and severally liable for the award. It is not possible to apportion an award between contributing respondents under the Civil Liability (Contribution) Act 1978 (see *London Borough of Hackney v Sivanandan* [2013] EWCA Civ 22).

Section 47B(1A) Employment Rights Act 1996 allows for claims against individual workers for subjecting a claimant to a detriment for making a protected disclosure. Such a detriment can include dismissal, and it is in turn possible to bring a claim against the employer for vicarious liability for that act. Similarly, it is open to a claimant to recover losses flowing from a dismissal where their claim is based on a distinct prior detriment that results in the claimant's dismissal (*Timis & Anor v Osipov & Anor* [2018] EWCA Civ 2321).

Industrial action

Sections 237 to 239 TULR(C)A 1992 make specific provision governing the availability of the right to claim unfair dismissal under s111 ERA 1996 where the dismissal is related to having taken industrial action. Industrial action may take the form of strikes or action less than a strike. Dismissals related to official industrial action, where the action has the support of a trade union's ballot of its members, are treated differently from dismissals related to unofficial industrial action. In general terms, the right to claim unfair dismissal is restricted in some circumstances and a dismissal will be automatically unfair if other conditions are satisfied. The qualifying period and the time limit for bringing certain industrial action unfair dismissal claims are also altered.

Remedy: The unfair dismissal jurisdiction, and the principles that apply to the remedy available, are those for unfair dismissal generally (see *Unfair dismissal*).

Adjustments: The House of Lords in *Crosville Wales Ltd v Tracey* [1997] IRLR 691 held that tribunals should not reduce an award for contributory fault where an employee has been unfairly dismissed for taking industrial action under s238 TULR(C)A 1992. It is likely that where an employee is dismissed for threatening to take such industrial action a reduction for contributory fault will also be denied (see *Adapters and Eliminators v Paterson* EAT 21 April 1983 unreported). It may be possible to reduce an award for contributory fault where the actions of the employee have gone beyond mere participation in industrial action, for example if the individual has acted in an inflammatory or intimidatory manner (see also *Courtaulds Northern Spinning Ltd v Moosa* [1984] IRLR 43).

Statutory authorities: TULR(C)A 1992 *ss237 to 239*

Relevant case law: Adapters and Eliminators v Paterson EAT 21 April 1983 unreported; *Courtaulds Northern Spinning Ltd v Moosa* [1984] IRLR 43; *Crosville Wales Ltd v Tracey* [1997] IRLR 691

Injury to feelings

(see also *Discrimination***)**

Injury to feelings awards compensate for non-pecuniary loss. Injury to feelings awards are available where a tribunal has upheld a complaint of discrimination (see s119(4) EA 2010) or unlawful detriment, but are not available for unfair dismissal (see *Dunnachie v Kingston upon Hull City Council* [2004] UKHL 36), or claims under the Working Time Regulations 'akin to breach of contract', such as those under Part 2 of the Regulations (see *Gomes v Higher Level Care Ltd* [2018] EWCA Civ 418). Claims for injury to health, however, have been held to be recoverable in such cases (*Grange v Abellio London Ltd* UKEAT/0304/17/JOJ).

Subject to the following caveat, such an award is also not available where a worker has suffered the detriment of termination of his or her contract for making a protected disclosure or for reasons related to working time protections (see s49(5A) and (6) ERA 1996), since compensation is limited to that available for unfair dismissal. The caveat is that since both injury to feelings and a basic award compensate for non-pecuniary loss, it would appear that an injury to feelings award may be made, up to the level of an appropriate basic award had in fact the claim been brought as unfair dismissal. This approach would ensure that the availability of an injury to feelings award is not unnecessarily limited where a basic award for equivalent unfair dismissal is not available.

There are other heads of non-economic loss that may be compensated for by a tribunal (see *Aggravated damages; Exemplary damages; Physical and psychiatric injury*).

Remedy: The award of injury to feelings is intended to compensate the claimant for the anger, distress and upset caused by the unlawful treatment they have received. It is compensatory, not punitive. Tribunals have a broad discretion about what level of award to make, which can only be overturned on appeal if the figure chosen is obviously wrong. This will only occur very rarely.

The focus is on the actual injury suffered by the claimant and not the gravity of the acts of the respondent (see *Komeng v Creative Support Ltd* UKEAT/0275/18/JOJ).

General principles

The general principles that apply to assessing an appropriate injury to feelings award have been set out by the EAT in *Prison Service v Johnson* [1997] IRLR 162, para 27:

- Injury to feelings awards are compensatory and should be just to both parties. They should compensate fully without punishing the discriminator. Feelings of indignation at the discriminator's conduct should not be allowed to inflate the award;

- Awards should not be too low, as that would diminish respect for the policy of the anti-discrimination legislation. Society has condemned discrimination and awards must ensure that it is seen to be wrong. On the other hand, awards should be restrained, as excessive awards could be seen as the way to untaxed riches;

- Awards should bear some broad general similarity to the range of awards in personal injury cases – not to any particular type of personal injury but to the whole range of such awards;

- Tribunals should take into account the value in everyday life of the sum they have in mind, by reference to purchasing power or by reference to earnings;

- Tribunals should bear in mind the need for public respect for the level of awards made.

The matters compensated for by an injury to feelings award encompass subjective feelings of upset, frustration, worry, anxiety, mental distress, fear, grief, anguish, humiliation, unhappiness, stress and depression (see *Vento v Chief Constable of West Yorkshire Police (No2)* [2003] IRLR 102).

Bands of compensation

In *Vento* the Court of Appeal identified three broad bands of compensation for injury to feelings and gave the following guidance (however, see below for revised figures):

1) The top band should normally be between £15,000 and £25,000. Sums in this range should be awarded in the most serious cases, such as where there has been a lengthy campaign of discriminatory harassment on the ground of sex or race. Only in the most exceptional case should an award of compensation for injury to feelings exceed £25,000;

2) The middle band of between £5,000 and £15,000 should be used for serious cases, which do not merit an award in the highest band;

3) Awards of between £500 and £5,000 are appropriate for less serious cases, such as where the act of discrimination is an isolated or one-off occurrence. In general, awards of less than £500 are to be avoided altogether, as they risk being regarded as so low as not to be a proper recognition of injury to feelings.

Within each band there is considerable flexibility, allowing tribunals to fix what is considered to be fair, reasonable and just compensation in the particular circumstances of the case.

The boundaries of the bands have been revised in several subsequent cases, culminating in the decision in *De Souza v Vinci Construction (UK) Ltd* [2017] EWCA Civ 879, which held that the 10% uplift in *Simmons v Castle* [2012] EWCA Civ 1288 should apply to awards for injury to feelings.

Following this, the Presidents of the Employment Tribunals in England & Wales and Scotland issued '*Presidential Guidance: Employment Tribunal Awards for Injury to Feelings and Psychiatric Injury Following De Souza v Vinci Construction (UK) Ltd*'. This Guidance, the *sixth addendum* of which was released on 24 March 2023 taking into account changes in the RPI All Items Index released on 22 March 2023, updated the bands as follows for any claims on or after 6 April 2023:

- Upper Band: £33,700 to £56,200 (the most serious cases);

- Middle Band: £11,200 to £33,700 (cases that do not merit an award in the upper band); and

- Lower Band: £1,100 to £11,200 (less serious cases).

The '*most exceptional cases*' are capable of exceeding the maximum of £56,200.

Note that these bands take account of the 10% *Simmons v Castle* uplift.

The original Guidance, which was released in September 2017, also included a formula for claims presented before 11 September 2017 which should be uprated by applying the formula:

$$\left(\left(\frac{x}{178.5}\right) \times z\right) \times 1.1$$

where:

x = the relevant boundary of the relevant band in the original *Vento* decision; and

z = the appropriate value from the RPI All Items Index for the month and year closest to the date of presentation of the claim.

The "x 1.1" multiplication applies the *Simmons v Castle* uplift.

The Presidential Guidance is something towards which tribunals must have regard, but it is not binding. The tribunal has the power to update the figures themselves, and it is open to parties to contend for a different calculation.

The law in Scotland

The calculation of ET awards for injury to feelings is essentially the same in Scotland as in England and Wales. However, since injury to feelings awards relate to quantification of damages which is a matter of Scots law, Employment Tribunals in Scotland, unlike those in England and Wales, are not legally bound by the decision of the Court of Appeal in *De Souza*. The President of the Employment Tribunals (Scotland) has said that the relevant awards in Scotland should be uprated in line with *De Souza* but employment judges in Scotland would be entitled to come to a different view on the matter and to quantify awards accordingly. Employment Judges should, if they decline to apply the *Simmons v Castle* uplift, set out their reasons for so doing.

Other relevant factors

Proof of injury: It is not inevitable that a tribunal will award an injury to feelings award where it is permitted to, though it is very unusual for no such award to be made. It is necessary for the individual to prove the nature of the injury to feelings and its extent, though this could be at its simplest the fact that a claimant has stated he was upset by his dismissal (see *Murray v Powertech (Scotland) Ltd* [1992] IRLR 257 and *Ministry of Defence v Cannock* [1994] ICR 918). The evidence a claimant will want to produce is the material which shows the impact of the discrimination on any subjective feelings of upset, frustration, worry, anxiety, mental distress, fear, grief, anguish, humiliation,

unhappiness, stress and depression. For example, this might include evidence about the impact the discrimination has had on relationships with colleagues, friends and family and any particular difficulties caused by the discrimination. Such evidence might include medical evidence, but where the injury to feelings amounts to a mental illness such as depression, the claimant might well consider seeking an award for personal injury in addition to injury to feelings.

Double recovery: Where an individual is awarded sums both for injury to feelings and personal injury (e.g. depression) caused by the discrimination, the injury to feelings and personal injury awards must compensate for different injuries and not overlap. The consequence is that for example where discrimination has caused a period of depression, either the injury to feelings award or the personal injuries award will be less than would be appropriate if only one of the awards had been made.

In *Slade v Biggs* [2021] EA-2019-000687, the EAT observed that awards for injury to feelings, aggravated damages and the ACAS uplift do not necessarily overlap: '*the three awards are assessing different things and may do so in different ways.*' It is possible, however, for there to be some element of double-counting if on the facts of a particular case the award for injury to feelings is a consequence of a breach of the ACAS Code. If so, an adjustment should be made, but there is no requirement for a rigorous definition of territory between the awards.

Claimant's knowledge: It is not necessary for an injury to feelings award to be made that the claimant's injured feelings are caused by his knowledge that he has been discriminated against, contrary to the interpretation given to *Skyrail Oceanic Ltd v Coleman* [1981] IRLR 398. The EAT in *Taylor v XLN Telecom Ltd* [2010] IRLR 49 held that the calculation of the remedy for discrimination is the same as in other torts, and that knowledge of the discriminator's motives was not necessary for recovery of injury to feelings. The EAT nevertheless observed that the distress and humiliation suffered by a claimant will generally be greater where the discrimination has been overt or the claimant appreciates at the time that the motivation was discriminatory.

Separate awards for separate grounds of discrimination: Where an individual has suffered a number of acts of discrimination, some caused by one protected ground, e.g. race, others by another protected ground, e.g. disability, the tribunal should make separate awards for each protected ground, as each is a separate wrong giving a right to damages (see *Al Jumard v Clywd Leisure Ltd* [2008] IRLR 345). However, where the discriminatory acts overlap as they arise from the same set of facts, such as where a dismissal is on grounds of both race and disability, a tribunal will not be expected to separate the injury to feelings and attribute parts to each form of discrimination. This may not necessarily result in an increased award compared to the situation where all the acts of discrimination are caused by one protected characteristic, as the tribunal must always have regard to the proportionality of the overall figure awarded for injury to feelings.

Future contingencies: Where the discriminatory act, such as a dismissal, would have occurred at some point in the future for legitimate reasons in any event, it is not appropriate to reduce the injury to feelings award to reflect that future possibility. The award reflects the injury to feelings caused by the knowledge that the reason for the act was discrimination, which cannot be offset by the fact that a lawful dismissal may have been carried out in any event (see *O'Donoghue v Redcar and Cleveland Borough Council* [2001] IRLR 615).

Adjustments: Interest can be awarded on the sum for injury to feelings (see *Interest*). Tribunals are required to consider interest whether or not an application has been made by a party (see *Komeng v Creative Support Ltd* UKEAT/0275/18/JOJ).

Reg 6(1)(a) of the Industrial Tribunals (Interest on Awards in Discrimination Cases) Regulations 1996 provides that the period over which interest accrues begins with the date of the discrimination and ends on the date the tribunal calculates compensation.

A percentage increase or reduction up to a maximum of 25% can be applied to reflect a failure by the employer or employee to comply with the ACAS disciplinary code of practice (see *ACAS*).

A *Polkey*-type deduction should not be applied to the award, even if the claimant would have been fairly dismissed at a date soon afterwards (*O'Donoghue v Redcar and Cleveland Borough Council* [2001] IRLR 615).

Tax: Awards for injury to feelings unrelated to termination of employment are tax-free, as are such awards related to the termination of employment prior to 6 April 2018 (*Moorthy v HMRC* [2018] EWCA Civ 847). However, from 6 April 2018, any compensation for injury to feelings in a termination payment will be taxable to the extent that the £30,000 'allowance' has been exceeded, following an amendment to s406 ITEPA 2003, except where the compensation is for a psychiatric injury.

Section 401 ITEPA 2003 applies to all payments *'received directly or indirectly in consideration or in consequence of, or otherwise in connection with the termination of a person's employment'*. This is broader than just damages for dismissal (*Slade v Biggs* [2021] EA-2019-000687).

Recoupment: N/A

Relevant case law: *A v HM Revenue & Customs* [2009]; *Al Jumard v Clywd Leisure Ltd* [2008] IRLR 345; *De Souza v Vinci Construction UK Limited* UKEAT/0328/14/DXA; *De Souza v Vinci Construction (UK) Ltd* [2017] EWCA Civ 879; *Dunnachie v Kingston upon Hull City Council* [2004] UKHL 36; *Ministry of Defence v Cannock* [1994] ICR 918; *Moorthy v The Commissioners for Her Majesty's Revenue & Customs* [2014] UKFTT 834 (TC); *Moorthy v Revenue & Customs* [2016] UKUT 13 (TCC); *Moorthy v HMRC* [2018] EWCA Civ 847; *Murray v Powertech (Scotland) Ltd* [1992] IRLR 257; *O'Donoghue v Redcar and Cleveland Borough Council* [2001] IRLR 615; *Prison Service v Johnson* [1997] IRLR 162; *Gomes v Higher Level Care Ltd* [2018] EWCA Civ 418; *Grange v Abellio London Ltd* UKEAT/0304/17/JOJ; *Komeng v Creative Support Ltd* UKEAT/0275/18/JOJ; *Skyrail Oceanic Ltd v Coleman* [1981] IRLR 398; *Slade v Biggs* [2021] EA-2019-000687; *Taylor v XLN Telecom Ltd* [2010] IRLR 49; *Vento v Chief Constable of West Yorkshire Police* [2002] EWCA Civ 1871; *Voith Turbo Ltd v Stowe* [2005] IRLR 228

Insolvency

The Redundancy Payments Service ("RPS") operates a scheme whereby the National Insurance Fund ("NIF") will make certain payments to ex-employees of an insolvent employer where certain conditions are satisfied (see ss182 to 190 ERA 1996). The ex-employee must make a claim to the RPS, who may make payments for a limited amount of the debts of the employer to the ex-employee. The debts covered are (s184):

- any arrears of pay in respect of one or more weeks, capped at 8 weeks (this includes Equal Pay claims);

- statutory notice pay;

- up to 6 weeks holiday pay accruing over the 12 months before 'the appropriate date';

- any basic award for unfair dismissal; and

- any reasonable sum by way of reimbursement of the whole or part of any fee or premium paid by an apprentice or articled clerk.

Unpaid maternity pay, paternity pay or sick pay cannot be claimed from the RPS under the insolvency rules. Maternity pay should be claimed from HMRC and sick pay from the DWP.

Sections 184(2) to 184(6) define what may amount to arrears of pay (which includes amongst other matters a guarantee payment and a protective award), what amounts to holiday pay and what may amount to 'a reasonable sum'.

Sums due under a Sex Equality Clause (i.e. an Equal Pay claim) amount to 'arrears of pay' within the meaning of ss182 and 184 (*Graysons Restaurants Ltd v Jones and Ors* [2019] EWCA Civ 725).

The debts must have been due on 'the appropriate date' which is defined in s185, and depending on the nature of the debt may be the date of the formal insolvency of the employer, the date of termination of employment or the date on which the award was made (for example if the debt is the basic award or an unpaid protective award).

Where an individual has applied to the Redundancy Payments Service for payment, but it has not been made, or payment has not been made in full he can make a claim to the employment tribunal (s188 ERA 1996).

Under s124 Pension Schemes Act 1993 there is a comparable scheme for requesting (and enforcing) payment from the NIF for unpaid pension contributions.

Remedy: Where a tribunal upholds a claim for payment, the tribunal will make a declaration to that effect stating the amount that ought to be paid to the ex-employee from the NIF.

Calculation of remedy

Various limits apply to the entitlement of the ex-employee to be paid certain debts:

- Arrears of pay are limited to 8 weeks, with each week capped at £643 (or an appropriate proportion of that if the debt arises from part of a week) (ss184 and 186 ERA 1996);

- Statutory notice pay is anyway capped at 12 weeks, and each week is capped at £643 (or an appropriate proportion of that if the debt arises from part of a week) (ss184 and 186 ERA 1996);

- Holiday pay is limited to 6 weeks, with each week capped at £643 (or an appropriate proportion of that if the debt arises from part of a week) (ss184 and s186 ERA 1996).

Gross or net: Gross. A week's pay as defined in ss220 to 229 ERA 1996 applies (see *Week's pay*).

Limit on a week's pay: £643 (see *Table 1* for historical rates).

Limit on number of weeks: See individual limits above.

Any maximum or minimum: Maximum = £5,144 (arrears) + £7,716 (notice pay) + £19,290 (basic award/redundancy) + £3,858 (holiday pay) = £36,008; No minimum

Adjustments: None

Mitigation: The nature of the underlying debt will determine whether the duty to mitigate applies. For example, the ex-employee is under a duty to mitigate their loss for failure to pay wages for the length of the statutory notice period, but there is no duty to mitigate loss in relation to a protective award or a basic award (see *Mitigation* and *Protective award*).

Any state benefits that have been received, or could have been claimed, will be deducted (see the Government's webpage on '*Your rights if your employer is insolvent*').

Tax: Any arrears of pay/protective award and accrued holiday pay will have income tax and national insurance deducted at the basic rate. 'Notional' tax, equivalent to the basic rate, will be deducted from compensation for failure to give statutory notice (this tax is not actually paid to HMRC but may be claimed back by the employee if their total income for the year is less than their personal allowance). The basic award will not be taxed at all unless it exceeds £30,000, which will in practice never happen because of the statutory limit.

Recoupment: Recoupment does not apply. Any state benefits received will be deducted from the award.

Statutory authorities: ERA 1996 *ss182 to 190*; Pension Schemes Act 1993 *s124*; TULR(C)A 1992 *s188*

Relevant case law: *Graysons Restaurants Ltd v Jones and Ors* [2019] EWCA Civ 725

Insurance

Under the Third Parties (Rights Against Insurers) Act 2010, where a person has insurance cover against a particular liability, or becomes insolvent, the rights under that insurance contract covering that liability transfer to the relevant claimant. That claimant can then bring a claim against the insurer directly before having established the liability in question (but will have to establish the liability before the right itself can be enforced). The EAT has held in *Watson v Hemingway Design Ltd (in liquidation) and others* [2019] UKEAT/0007/19 that Employment Tribunals have jurisdiction to hear such proceedings.

Interest

(see also *Discrimination*; *Financial penalties on employers*; *Injury to feelings*; *Table 12***)**

There are two different situations in which interest is available on a tribunal award. First, where a tribunal award has not been paid interest accrues on the unpaid sum (see *Interest on unpaid compensation*). Secondly, a tribunal is able to award interest in discrimination claims brought under the EA 2010 as part of its award of compensation, to compensate for the fact that compensation has been awarded after the loss compensated for has been suffered (see *Interest on discrimination awards*).

Interest on discrimination awards

A tribunal is able to award interest on awards of compensation made in discrimination claims brought under s124(2)(b) EA 2010, to compensate for the fact that compensation has been awarded after the relevant loss has been suffered (see s139 EA 2010, EA 2010 (Commencement No 4 etc) Order SI 2010/2317 and IT(IADC) Regs 1996).

The tribunal may award interest to the following types of discrimination award:

- Past financial loss;

- Injury to feelings;

- Aggravated and exemplary damages; and

- Physical and psychiatric injury.

Since a tribunal cannot award interest on past loss within a compensatory award for unfair dismissal, where an unfair dismissal is also a discriminatory dismissal, tribunals will often compensate such losses under the discrimination legislation.

Calculation: Interest is calculated as simple interest accruing from day to day (Reg 3(1)).

Interest rate: Until 29 July 2013 the interest rate to be applied in England and Wales was that prescribed for the special investment account under rule 27(1) of the Court Funds Rules 1987. The interest rate until 29 July 2013 was 0.5%. For claims presented on or after 29 July 2013 the relevant interest rate is that specified in s17 of the Judgments Act 1838 (see The Employment Tribunals (Interest on Awards in Discrimination Cases) (Amendment) Regulations 2013).

The interest rate now to be applied is 8% (see *Table 12* for a list of interest rates). It is important to note that, although the interest rate is currently the same in England and Wales and in Scotland, that has not always been the position nor will it necessarily be so in the future.

If the rate of interest changes during the period over which interest is calculated, the tribunal may use such median or average of those rates as seems to it appropriate, in the interests of simplicity (see The Industrial Tribunals (Interest on Awards in Discrimination Cases) Regulations 1996 Reg 3(3)).

Period of calculation, injury to feelings: interest is awarded on injury to feelings awards from the date of the act of discrimination complained of until the date on which the tribunal calculates the compensation (see Reg 6(1)(a) IT(IADC) Regs 1996).

Period of calculation, all other sums: interest is awarded on all sums other than injury to feelings awards from the mid-point of the date of the act of discrimination complained of and the date the tribunal calculates the award (Reg 6(1)(b) IT(IADC) Regs 1996). The mid-point date is the date half way through the period between the date of the discrimination complained of and the date the tribunal calculates the award (Reg 4 IT(IADC) Regs 1996).

Period of calculation, early payment: where payment of any of the sums attracting interest has already been made by the respondent, the date of payment is taken as the date of calculation of the award for those particular sums (Reg 6(2) IT(IADC) Regs 1996).

Period of calculation, serious injustice discretion: where a tribunal considers that serious injustice would be caused if interest were to be calculated according to the approaches above, it can calculate interest on such different periods as it considers appropriate (Reg 6(3) IT(IADC) Regs 1996). See *Ministry of Defence v Cannock* [1994] IRLR 509, where interest was awarded over a longer period than provided for by the regulations due to the long period since the loss was incurred.

Interest cannot be awarded in respect of future loss or loss arising before the discrimination complained of (Reg 5 IT(IADC) Regs 1996). This reflects the broad principle behind the award of interest which is that it is compensation to the successful claimant for the loss they have suffered by virtue of not having received payment of the award at the date of the loss suffered.

Worked examples

Interest on past loss
Interest runs from the 'mid-point' date to the date of calculation. The mid-point is calculated as the date halfway between the date of the discriminatory act and ending on the calculation date (usually the judgment date). Interest accrues from day to day and is simple rather than compound.

Interest = (number of days from discriminatory act date to calculation date x 1/2 x interest rate x 1/100 x 1/365 x compensatory award (after all adjustments have been made - see *Adjustments and order of adjustments*).

Example 1

Compensation award = £20,000

Discriminatory date = 01/04/2021

Calculation date = 05/02/2023

Interest rate = 8%

Number of days between discriminatory date and calculation date = 676 inclusive

Interest = 676 ÷ 2 x 0.08 x 1/365 x 20,000 = £1,481.64 (the number of days have been divided by 2 because of the mid-point rule)

Interest on Injury to feelings
Interest runs from the date of the discriminatory act to the date of calculation. Interest accrues from day to day and is simple rather than compound.

Example 2

Injury to feelings award = £5,000

Discriminatory date = 01/04/2021

Calculation date = 05/02/2023

Interest rate = 8%

Number of days = 676 inclusive

Interest = 676 x 0.08 x 1/365 x 5,000 = £740.82

Interest on Physical and psychiatric injury and Aggravated damages

Interest on physical and psychiatric injury runs from the 'mid-point' date to the date of calculation. The mid-point date is calculated as the date half way between the discriminatory act and the calculation date (usually the judgment date). Interest accrues from day to day and is simple rather than compound.

The calculation works in exactly the same way as that for interest on past loss.

Any maximum or minimum: There is no minimum, and interest does not have to be awarded if the tribunal considers it would be unjust to do so (Reg 2). The maximum would be determined by the interest rate in force during the relevant period.

Adjustments: Interest is calculated after the final adjustments have been made to the award and after enhanced redundancy has been deducted (see *Adjustments and order of adjustments*).

Tax: Interest is awarded on the net loss suffered by the individual, see *Bentwood Bros (Manchester) Ltd v Shepherd* [2003] IRLR 364. Any grossing up, if required, will apply after interest has been calculated (see *Grossing up*).

Recoupment: The recoupment regulations do not apply to discrimination claims and hence they will not apply to any interest awarded.

Statutory authorities: *Court Funds Rules 1987 r27(1); Judgments Act 1838 s17; The Employment Tribunals (Interest on Awards in Discrimination Cases) (Amendment) Regulations 2013; The Industrial Tribunals (Interest on Awards in Discrimination Cases) Regulations 1996 Reg 3(3)*

Interest on unpaid compensation

If the employer fails to pay the compensation that has been awarded to the claimant within a certain prescribed time period, interest will accrue on unpaid sums. Interest is calculated as simple interest accruing from day to day.

In both discriminatory and non-discriminatory cases interest will start accruing from the date of the judgment but no interest will be payable if the award is paid within 14 days of the judgment.

Any sums withheld on account of the recoupment regulations will not accrue interest.

Interest is not payable on a sum due under a re-engagement order where the employer declines to re-engage the employee (*Fotheringhame v Barclays Services Ltd* UKEAT/0208/19/BA). It is likely that the same principle applies to an order for reinstatement.

Interim relief

Where a claim for unfair dismissal is brought, and where it is alleged that the reason or principal reason for the dismissal was for one of a number of protected reasons, the claimant may claim interim relief. Specific procedural rules apply, including that the claim must be brought within 7 days of the effective date of termination (see ss161 to 163 TULR(C)A 1992 and ss128 to 129 ERA 1996). The protected reasons are:

- Relating to enforcement of rights given to shop and betting shop workers, s100(1)(a) and (b) (see s128(1)(a)(i));

- Relating to acting as a representative under the WTR 1998, s101A(d) (see s128(1)(a)(i));

- Relating to performing the functions of a pensions trustee, s102(1) (see s128(1)(a)(i));

- Performing the functions of an employee representative, s103 (see s128(1)(a)(i));

- Making a protected disclosure, s103A (see s128(1)(a)(i));

- Relating to action over trade union recognition, para 161(2) Sch 1A TULR(C)A 1992 (see s128(1)(a)(ii));

- Relating to blacklisting, s104F(1) (see s128(1)(b));

- Membership of a trade union, participating in its activities, or making use of trade union services, s152(1)(a), (b) and (c) TULR(C)A 1992 (see s161(1) TULR(C)A 1992);

- Refusing to accept an offer to give up membership or collective bargaining rights, s152(bb) TULR(C)A 1992 (see s161(1) TULR(C)A 1992).

Interim relief does not apply to claims for unlawful discrimination: *Steer v Stormsure Ltd* [2021] EWCA Civ 887.

Remedy: If at the hearing of an application for interim relief it appears to the tribunal that the claim for unfair dismissal is likely to succeed (defined as a '"*pretty good" chance of succeeding*' in *Taplin v C Shippam Ltd*

[1978] ICR 1068), the tribunal will announce its findings and explain to the parties its powers and how it can exercise them.

The tribunal must be persuaded that *all* elements of an automatic unfair dismissal claim are likely to succeed before granting interim relief. This includes, for example, any issue of employee status or whether there was a dismissal at all (see *Hancock v Ter-Berg and another* UKEAT/0138/19/BA).

If the employer is willing, pending the final determination of the unfair dismissal complaint, the tribunal can order that the employee be reinstated or re-engaged. Otherwise, the tribunal will make an order that the contract of employment is continued. Such an order has the effect that, until the unfair dismissal complaint is determined, the contract of employment continues for the purposes of pay, seniority, pension rights and similar matters, and for continuity of employment.

Either party may apply to the tribunal for the revocation or variation of such an order on the grounds that there has been a relevant change in circumstances (see s165 TULR(C)A 1992 and s131 ERA 1992).

If a claimant makes a complaint, and the tribunal finds, that the employer has failed to comply with an order for reinstatement or re-engagement, the tribunal will make an order for the continuation of the contract of employment and such compensation as it considers just and equitable in all the circumstances having regard to the infringement of the order and the loss suffered as a consequence.

If a claimant makes a complaint, and the tribunal finds, that the employer has failed to comply with an order for the continuation of the contract of employment, it will make an order for such compensation as it considers just and equitable in all the circumstances having regard to the infringement of the order and the loss suffered as a consequence (see s166 TULR(C)A or s132 ERA 1996).

If an ET makes an order for the continuation of the contract of employment at an interim relief hearing, and subsequently at the full hearing the claimant loses and the respondent is successful, it is unlikely that the claimant will have to repay the interim relief payments (see *Initial Textile Services v Rendell* [1991] UKEAT 383/91/230).

Gross or net: The award of any unpaid salary will be made gross under the continuing contract of employment and subject to PAYE (but see *Tax* below).

Tax: Payments under an interim relief order are taxable as payments in connection with termination of employment under s401 **not** in full as earnings under s62 ITEPA (see also *Tax and termination payments*). See *Turullols v HMRC* where the First Tier Tribunal held

that the claimant, who was found to have been unfairly dismissed, could claim back the tax that had been paid on the salary payments made under the interim relief order because they were payments in connection with the termination of her employment and therefore should have been tax-free up to £30,000. This would also have been the case even if the ET had ruled that the dismissal was fair.

Cap: There is no statutory cap, and this award falls outside the compensatory award (see s166 TULR(C)A 1992 and s132 ERA 196).

Statutory authorities: ERA 1996 *ss128 to 132*; TULR(C)A 1992 *ss161 to 166*

Relevant case law: *Hancock v Ter-Berg and another UKEAT/0138/19/BA; Initial Textile Services v Rendell* [1991] UKEAT 383/91/230; *Steer v Stormsure Ltd* [2021] EWCA Civ 887; *Taplin v C Shippam Ltd* [1978] ICR 1068; *Turullols v Revenue & Customs* [2014] UKFTT 672 (TC)

Itemised pay statement

A worker has the right to be given by his employer, at or before the time at which any payment of wages or salary is made to him, a written itemised pay statement (s8 ERA 1996). Where an employer does not give a worker a statement as required (either because the employer gives the worker no statement or because the statement the employer gives does not comply with what is required), the worker may require a reference to be made to an employment tribunal to determine what particulars ought to have been included or referred to in a statement so as to comply with the requirements of the section concerned.

Calculation: Where the tribunal finds that an itemised pay statement has not been given to the worker and further that any unnotified deductions have been made from the pay of the worker during the period of 13 weeks immediately preceding the date of the application for the reference (whether or not the deductions were made in breach of the contract of employment), the tribunal may order the employer to pay the worker a sum not exceeding the aggregate of the unnotified deductions so made (s12(4) ERA 1996).

Gross or net: Gross

Limit on a week's pay: None

Limit on number of weeks: 13

Any maximum or minimum: None

Adjustments: N/A

Tax: The employer will deduct tax and national insurance as normal if the worker is still employed. However, if the worker is no longer in employment, the worker will be responsible for declaring this income on their self-assessment.

Statutory authorities: ERA 1996 *ss8* and *12(4)*

Job seekers allowance

(see also *Recoupment***)**

There are 3 types of job seekers allowance (JSA):

- Contribution-based where the claimant has paid enough national insurance contributions during their employment;

- 'New style' JSA, also based on NI contributions;

- Income-based, where the claimant has not paid enough national contributions as an employee but was on a low wage. Universal Credit has replaced income-based JSA for most people.

Receipt of job seeker's allowance should be treated in 2 different ways, depending on whether the claim is for damages for wrongful dismissal or compensation for unfair dismissal.

Damages

Credit should be given for any job seekers allowance received during the damages period and during the statutory notice period. However, as with other state benefits, it could be argued that full credit should not be given if the employee did not receive their statutory notice period or payment in lieu, because they would exhaust their entitlement to state benefits sooner than they would have done if they had received their statutory notice.

Compensatory award

Job seekers allowance is not deducted from the compensatory award but is instead subject to the recoupment regulations (see *Recoupment*).

Adjustments: See *Recoupment* (Prescribed element)

Cap: See *Recoupment* (Prescribed element)

Recoupment: Only for compensation for unfair dismissal. Recoupment does not apply to wrongful dismissal.

Statutory authorities: The Employment Protection (Recoupment of Jobseeker's Allowance and Income Support) Regulations 1996

Judicial assessment and mediation

These two forms of Alternative Dispute Resolution are offered by tribunals in appropriate cases, and expressly considered at case management Preliminary Hearings.

Judicial Assessment

The principles and protocol are set out in the *Presidential Guidance – Rule 3 – Protocol on Judicial Assessment*.

Assessment is to take place at the first case management preliminary hearing, only after the identification of the issues and the making of case management orders. It is considered suitable for most cases and parties are encouraged to inform the tribunal in advance of their wish to undergo this procedure. Both parties must consent, and the process is strictly confidential. It is also free.

The assessment consists of a provisional Early Neutral Evaluation of the merits of liability and/or remedy by an Employment Judge.

Although Judicial Assessment has been around for some time, it does not appear to be used much in practice. At the first case management preliminary hearing there is usually a substantial gap between the parties on the facts, and the tribunal will either not have a copy of the documents that might shed light on the dispute, or not be able to adjudicate a dispute of oral evidence. The decision has to be made by a time-pressed judge who is unlikely to have all relevant factual material to hand. The risk of such a process is that an erroneous judicial assessment may render a dispute more intractable by locking the parties into an erroneous assessment of their cases.

From a remedy perspective, Judicial Assessment may be suitable where one party has unrealistic views of the quantum of their case that are easily identifiable without the need to resolve complex questions of fact or significant conflicts of evidence.

Judicial Mediation

This is a free service conducted by an Employment Judge over the course of a single day at the Employment Tribunal. Following an initial opening session, the parties sit in separate rooms and a Judge conducts 'shuttle diplomacy' between them.

Judicial Mediators tend to be facilitative rather than evaluative, focusing on relaying each party's position to the other side, and testing the realism of each party's position. The aim is to help each side understand the other's position, identify common ground and seek agreement.

The mediation is conducted on a Without Prejudice basis with the Judicial Mediator having no further involvement in the case following the mediation.

Although there are no formal criteria for Judicial Mediation, it tends to be offered in cases lasting more than 3 days and/or where there is a continuing employment relationship between the parties (these requirements were relaxed during the Covid-19 pandemic). The tribunal has to be satisfied that the mediation has a real prospect of success.

Leave for family and domestic reasons, maternity, paternity, adoption, shared parental: see *Detriment*; *Parental bereavement leave*; *Time off (various)*

Limitation period

This is the maximum period allowed between the act complained of and when the claim should be lodged at the ET (see *Table 18*).

Loss of chance

Once a tribunal has upheld a complaint of unlawful treatment such as discrimination or unfair dismissal, it is necessary for it to assess the remedy available to the claimant. Where the remedy includes an award to compensate for financial loss, it will be necessary to identify the sums the claimant would have received had the unlawful conduct not taken place. For a dismissal, in a straightforward case this will be the salary that would have been earned by the claimant.

In assessing the loss suffered by the claimant, the tribunal will take into account the chance of events having occurred following the unlawful act, and determine the award on the basis of the loss of that chance. For example, if there was a 25% chance that an individual would have been dismissed fairly in any event 6 months after their unlawful dismissal, the tribunal will calculate the losses suffered after that date as 75% of salary etc. that would have been earned had the individual remained in employment after that event.

Another example would be an individual who had, say, a 50% chance of being promoted shortly after their unlawful dismissal, where the tribunal could award future losses based on 50% of the increased salary to reflect the chance of it having been obtained (see *O'Donoghue v Redcar and Cleveland Borough Council* [2001] IRLR 615 and *Ministry of Defence v Wheeler* [1998] IRLR 23).

Where the chance of a future event is very high, or very low, the tribunal may well treat the chance as 100% or 0% as appropriate (see *Timothy James Consulting Ltd v Wilton* UKEAT/0082/14/DXA. A tribunal should only limit compensation to a particular period, or refuse compensation entirely, if it is 100% confident that the claimant would have been dismissed or resigned on the cut-off date in question (*Shittu v South London & Maudsley NHS Foundation Trust* [2022] EAT 18).

The *Polkey* reduction is an example of this approach in the unfair dismissal context (see *Polkey*), but in considering the future actions of the employer the tribunal will take account of the actions of a reasonable employer (see *Abbey National v Formso* [1999] ICR 222). In discrimination cases the tribunal will seek to determine the future conduct of the actual employer. It will require evidence to demonstrate the chances of future events occurring (see *Wardle v Credit Agricole Corporate & Investment Bank* [2011] IRLR 604 and *Chagger v Abbey National plc & Anor* [2010] IRLR 47). Statistical evidence may well be relevant and admissible (see *Vento v Chief Constable of West Yorkshire Police* [2003] ICR 318).

Marginal tax rate

(see also *Grossing up***)**

The marginal tax rate is a single tax rate that could be applied to a claimant's award when grossing up (see *Grossing up*). When deciding on the marginal tax rate, account should be taken of the claimant's personal tax free allowance (which can be found from their tax code at the date of dismissal), earnings already received in that tax year (including since dismissal), the relevant tax thresholds (see *Table 7*, *Table 8* and *Table 9*) and any other income the claimant may earn in the remainder of that tax year. The calculations are straightforward if a single tax rate is used but this is not always the appropriate approach.

Differential tax rates

Different tax rates may apply to different elements of the award (see *Yorkshire Housing Ltd v Cuerden* [2010] UKEAT/0397/09). However, the calculations are not straightforward and there is the added complication of a tapering personal allowance for earnings/tribunal awards between £100,000 and £125,140 (for the tax year 2023/24). See *Grossing up* for worked examples where differential tax rates are used.

Tax year

The relevant tax year for grossing up is the year the award is received by the claimant. Any adjustment to the award in subsequent tax years (e.g. upon reconsideration of a judgment) should be grossed up by reference to that subsequent tax year (*PA Finlay & Co Ltd v Finlay* UKEAT/0260/14).

Maternity Equality Clause

Women on maternity leave must receive any increases in pay due to them at the time they would have received them, had they not been on maternity leave and their pay, when they return, must reflect the increases they would have had, had they not been absent. The Maternity Equality Clause (s73 EA 2010) modifies the woman's contract so that her maternity related pay is increased in line with any actual increase in pay, or any increase that she would have been paid had she not been on maternity leave.

The tribunal has jurisdiction to determine a complaint relating to breach of an equality clause under s127 EA 2010.

Remedy: Arrears of up to 6 years' actual pay may be ordered (s132 EA 2010).

Gross or net: Gross

Limit on a week's pay: None

Limit on number of years: 6

Any maximum or minimum: None

Tax: Taxable under s62 ITEPA 2003.

Statutory authorities: EA 2010 ss73, 127 and 132

Maternity: see *Detriment*; *Maternity Equality Clause*; *Unfair dismissal*; *Table 16*

Maximum compensatory award: see *Statutory cap*

Minimum wage: see *National Minimum Wage*

Misconduct: see *Contributory conduct*

Money purchase pension scheme: see *Pension loss*

Mitigation

It is a fundamental principle that any claimant will be expected to mitigate the losses they suffer as a result of an unlawful act by giving credit, for example for earnings in a new job (mitigation in fact), and that the tribunal will not make an award to cover losses that could reasonably have been avoided (mitigation in law). For example, an unfairly dismissed employee is expected to search for other work, and will not recover losses beyond a date by which the tribunal concludes the individual ought reasonably to have been able to find new employment at a similar rate of pay. Such an individual may be awarded the difference between the salary of a lower paid new job, and their previous salary, for a period until the tribunal concludes they could reasonably have found similarly well paid work.

The claimant is expected to take reasonable steps to minimise the losses suffered as a consequence of the unlawful act. The burden of proving a failure to mitigate

is on the respondent (*Fyfe v Scientific Furnishing Ltd* [1989] IRLR 331). It is insufficient for a respondent merely to show that the claimant failed to take a step that it was reasonable for them to take: rather, the respondent has to prove that the claimant acted unreasonably. There is a difference between acting reasonably and not acting unreasonably. If the claimant has failed to take a reasonable step, the respondent has to show that any such failure was *unreasonable* (*Wright v Silverline Car Caledonia Ltd* UKEATS/0008/16). The tribunal will consider:

1) what steps the claimant should have taken to mitigate his or her losses;

2) whether it was *un*reasonable for the claimant to have failed to take any such steps; and

3) if so, the date from which an alternative income would have been obtained, and the amount of that income.

The possibility of applying a percentage reduction to compensation as an alternative was raised *obiter* in *Hakim v The Scottish Trade Unions Congress* UKEATS/0047/19/SS, but only 'where the facts are so uncertain' that it is a more logical approach than applying an end date. There, the EAT said that a Tribunal that adopts this method 'should be in a position to justify the adoption of a crude approach', and risks being overturned on appeal. This approach was challenged recently in *Edward v Tavistock and Portman NHS Foundation Trust* [2023] EAT 33 without finally determining the point. It appears to be unlikely to apply save in exceptional cases. Tribunals are encouraged to avoid striving 'for a false appearance of precision; the tribunal is entitled to use its judgment to fix a suitable point in time.'

A summary of the relevant principles can be found in *Cooper Contracting Ltd v Lindsey* UKEAT/0184/15/JOJ at paragraph 16.

The duty arises only after dismissal, so a failure to take up an alternative job offer made before that date will not constitute a failure to mitigate. It may be reasonable to attempt to mitigate loss by setting up a new business or becoming self-employed (see *Cooper Contracting Ltd v Lindsey* UKEAT/0184/15/JOJ and *Gardiner-Hill v Roland Berger Technics Ltd* [1982] IRLR 498) or by retraining (see *Sealy v Avon Aluminium Co Ltd* UKEAT/515/78, *Holroyd v Gravure Cylinders Ltd* [1984] IRLR 259 and *Orthet Ltd v Vince-Cain* [2004] IRLR 857).

The question of reasonableness is to be determined by the tribunal itself, with the claimant's wishes and views simply one of the factors in its analysis. Tribunals are encouraged not to apply too demanding a standard of the claimant.

'*Where [an] employee has simply made no job*

applications at all, the employer is entitled to assert, at least as a starting point, that by failing to do so, she has acted unreasonably, subject to the tribunal being satisfied as to the explanation.' An employee failing to look for any jobs at all is likely to be sufficient to discharge the employer's burden of proof. It is then for the Claimant to explain why such a failure was reasonable (*Hilco Capital Ltd v Harrington* [2022] EAT 156).

If an employee seeks to justify an apparent failure to mitigate due to stigma, there must be evidence to support such a claim – assertion or assumption is insufficient (*Harrington*, above).

Mitigation and 'good industrial relations practice'

An unfairly dismissed employee will not need to give credit for earnings received from a new job during the notice period where good industrial relations practice would have required payment in lieu of notice to the employee (see *Norton Tool Co Ltd v Tewson* [1973] All ER 183 and *Voith Turbo Ltd v Stowe* [2005] IRLR 228). However, the principle does not apply to constructive dismissal (*Stuart Peters Ltd v Bell* [2009] IRLR 941).

Dismissal from subsequent employment

Dismissal from a new job does not automatically break the chain of causation. Where, for example, a new job only partially mitigates an employee's loss of earnings, dismissal from that job may not sever the causal link between the respondent's act and the difference in earnings. A tribunal may therefore continue to award the difference in earnings between the old job and the new job after the claimant has left the new job (provided he or she is not earning more elsewhere): *Hakim v The Scottish Trade Unions Congress* UKEATS/0047/19/SS.

Mitigation and receipt of pension

In *Knapton v ECC Card Clothing Ltd* [2006] IRLR 756 the EAT held that credit does not need to be given for the early receipt of pension following dismissal, as it is deferred wages not a sum analogous to incapacity benefit which would be brought into account. However, if an individual is dismissed after the date when the pension can be drawn and there is no reduction in the value of the pension by being drawn at dismissal, it may be that a failure to draw the pension would be seen as a failure to mitigate a loss, and a sum for which the ex-employer should receive credit.

National Insurance Contributions

An unemployed person may receive Class 1 National Insurance credits to fill any gaps in their national insurance contributions (these contributions are automatically made if the person claims JSA). However, Reg 7(1) of The Social Security (Unemployment, Sickness and Invalidity Benefit) Regulations 1983 SI 1983/1598 states that if the person has received compensation for unfair dismissal, they are not entitled to receive national insurance contributions for the same period. If the person is unemployed for a long time, this could affect their entitlement to a state pension and other state benefits. The loss of NI contributions can therefore be claimed from the employer as a head of loss. The amount of compensation is fixed by reference to the weekly Class 3 NIC rate which is currently £17.45 per week (tax year 2023/24).

Remedy: Compensation per week = weekly Class 3 NIC rate.

Limit on a week's pay: The Class 3 NIC rate

Limit on number of weeks: None

Any maximum or minimum: None

Adjustments: Loss of NIC will form part of the compensatory award or damages and thus will be adjusted along with these awards.

Recoupment: Recoupment does not apply to this head of loss.

Statutory authorities: Social Security (Unemployment, Sickness and Invalidity Benefit) Regulations 1983 (SI 1983/1598) *Reg 7(1)*

National Living Wage: see *National Minimum Wage*

National Minimum Wage

(see also *Unlawful deductions from wages*; *Table 15***)**

A broad range of workers are entitled to receive the national minimum wage. The rate depends upon the age of the worker and whether they qualify for an apprentice rate or, if an agricultural worker, the agricultural minimum wage (see *Table 15*). Calculating the pay received for the purposes of assessing whether the national minimum wage has been paid may in some cases be complex. An employer must keep sufficient records to show that workers who qualify have been paid the national minimum wage (Reg 38(1) NMWR 1999 and s9 and s31 NMWA 1998), and a worker is entitled to inspect those records (s10 NMWA).

There are four main routes by which an individual may enforce NMW rights:

1) A worker may bring a claim to the ET for unlawful deductions from wages (s17 NMWA 1998) (see *Unlawful deductions from wages*);

2) It is automatically unfair to dismiss a worker because he has asserted his right to the NMW or might qualify for the NMW (s104A ERA 1996) (see *Unfair dismissal*);

3) Under s23(1) NMWA 1998, a worker has the right not to be subjected to any detriment by any act or failure to act for specified reasons relating to the NMW (see *Detriment*);

4) A worker may bring a claim to the ET that his or her employer has refused access to records in accordance with s10 NMWA 1998 (s11 NMWA 1998).

Living accommodation

When an employer charges a worker for living accommodation the charge must be taken into account by comparing it to the worker's accommodation offset calculated using the accommodation offset rate (currently £9.10 per day or £63.70 per week, 2023/24 tax year). If the charge is higher than the accommodation offset, then any excess amount above the accommodation offset will reduce the worker's national minimum wage pay.

If the accommodation charge is at or below the offset rate, it does not have an effect on the worker's pay.

If the accommodation is free, the offset rate is added to the worker's pay.

Although the EAT in *HMRC v Ant Marketing Ltd* UKEAT/0051/19/OO concluded that accommodation provided by a separate company was not provided by 'the employer', and therefore not subject to this offset, Choudhury P went on to hold that this conclusion was the result of the '*narrow basis*' upon which the appeal was brought. He went on to conclude, in *obiter* remarks that are likely to be highly persuasive, that '*had the issue in this appeal been whether or not an employer could be said to be a provider of accommodation, even though it is not the owner or landlord in such accommodation, I would have unhesitatingly answered in the affirmative.*'

No other kind of company benefit (e.g. food, a car, childcare vouchers) count towards the National Minimum Wage.

Penalty for not paying NMW

HMRC can impose a penalty on employers if they are found not to have paid the NMW. Penalties for non-payment were doubled from 1 April 2016, from 100% of arrears owed to 200%, although these will be halved if paid within 14 days. The maximum penalty is £20,000 per worker.

Remedy for failing to pay the NMW

If a worker who is entitled to be paid the NMW is paid less than the NMW, the worker is entitled to be paid the difference between the relevant remuneration received by the worker for the pay reference period; and the relevant remuneration which the worker would have received for that period had he been remunerated by the employer at a rate equal to the NMW (s17 NMWA 1998).

Living accommodation provided by the employer should be taken into account when assessing the employer's liability (see Regs 30(d) and 36(1) NMWR 1999 and *Eastern Eye (Plymouth) Ltd v Hassan & Anor* UKEAT/0383/14/DA).

Remedy for refusal to permit access to records

Where a tribunal finds a complaint under s11 well founded, it will make a declaration to that effect and will make an award of 80 times the hourly minimum wage in force at the date when the award is made (s11(2) NMWA 1998).

If the claimant's employment is transferred under the Transfer of Undertakings (Protection of Employment) Regulations 2006, the obligation to maintain records under the NMWA transfers to the transferee (see *Mears Homecare Ltd v Bradburn and others* UKEAT/0170/18/JOJ).

Gross or net: Gross

Limit on number of years: 2 years for any claim presented on or after 8 January 2015, otherwise none. Although *Coletta v Bath Hill Court (Bournemouth) Property Management Ltd* UKEAT/0200/17/RN has held that there is no temporal cap on the recovery of a series of deductions of wages, the Deductions from Wages (Limitation) Regulations 2014 (SI 2014/3322) (which came into force after the events in *Coletta*) place a 2-year limit on claims for unlawful deductions from wages involving pay.

Tax: It is likely that this award will not be subject to tax, and should be characterised as a punishment or fine, not earnings or a payment connected to termination.

Statutory authorities: *NMWA 1998 ss10 and 11; NMWR 1999 Regs 30(d), 36(1) and 38(1)*

Relevant case law: *Coletta v Bath Hill Court (Bournemouth) Property Management Ltd UKEAT/0200/17/RN; Eastern Eye (Plymouth) Ltd v Hassan & Anor UKEAT/0383/14/DA; HMRC v Ant Marketing Ltd UKEAT/0051/19/OO; Mears Homecare Ltd v Bradburn and others UKEAT/0170/18/JOJ*

Net weekly pay

(see also *Gourley principle*; *Gross weekly pay*; *Week's pay*)

This is the figure used to calculate the actual net loss to the claimant in a number of awards. This will often be the gross weekly pay less tax and NI, and may also be less employer's pension contributions and other benefits if the value of the loss of those benefits is calculated separately, which is often the approach used. Some awards are calculated on gross weekly pay, for example where an employer is ordered to pay unpaid remuneration (where tax will be deducted at source upon payment in the usual way). The following awards use net weekly pay as the basis of the loss:

- Compensatory award;
- Damages for wrongful dismissal;
- Financial losses suffered as a result of unlawful discrimination.

Non-recoupable state benefits

(see also *Recoupment*)

The state benefits of job seekers allowance and income support, income-related employment support allowance and universal credit are subject to recoupment under the *Employment Protection (Recoupment of Jobseeker's Allowance and Income Support) Regulations 1996* (SI 1996/2349). The Regulations provide that, where a monetary award is made by the tribunal, it must identify any part of that award that constitutes the prescribed element (past loss of earnings) and the period to which it relates.

Other benefits, benefits awarded outside of the 'prescribed period', or benefits received in relation to awards that do not fall within the recoupment provisions are non-recoupable benefits.

Housing benefit, which can also be the subject of claw-back provisions, should not be deducted from any award for loss of earnings (*Olayemi v Athena Medical Centre and Anor* UKEAT/0140/15).

Normal working hours: see *Week's pay*

Notice pay

(see also *Breach of contract*; *Contractual notice period*; *Effective date of termination*; *Garden leave*; *Statutory notice period*; *Table 14*)

If an employee gives or is given notice of termination of their employment, they will usually be entitled to their normal pay during this period of notice. Four general approaches can be taken to whether the individual works their notice period and how they are paid:

1) The employee works their notice and gets paid their normal wage;

2) The employee is placed on garden leave, in which case they do not actually work during their notice but the employment contract is still in force and they get paid as normal;

3) The employee does not work their notice period, the contract is terminated earlier, and instead receives a payment equivalent to what would have been earned during this period (payment in lieu of notice or PILON);

4) The employee does not work during the notice period, and does not get paid all or some of their normal wage for the notice period.

In the fourth example, the employee may be entitled to compensation for breach of the obligation to be paid under the contract.

Occupational pension scheme: see *Pension loss*

Order of adjustments: see *Adjustments and order of adjustments*

Overtime: see *Compensatory award*; *Holiday pay*; *Week's pay*; *APPENDIX 3*

Parental bereavement leave

The *Parental Bereavement Leave Regulations 2020* implemented a statutory entitlement under the *Parental Bereavement (Leave and Pay) Act 2018* to Parental Bereavement Leave and Pay for employed parents who lose a child on or after 6 April 2020. The legislation gives bereaved parents who are employees at least a right to time off work to grieve.

Specifically:

- The Parental Bereavement Leave Regulations 2020 implemented a new entitlement for bereaved parents who are employees to two weeks' leave from their job; and

- The Statutory Parental Bereavement Pay (General) Regulations 2020 implemented an entitlement for bereaved parents who meet certain eligibility criteria to receive a statutory payment whilst absent from work. This is paid at either the statutory flat rate of £172.48 per week for 2023/24, or 90% of average earnings calculated over a set reference period, whichever is the lower.

An employee is entitled under section 47C(1) of the ERA 1996 Act not to be subjected to any detriment by any act, or any deliberate failure to act, by an employer because they took or sought to take parental bereavement leave.

Parental leave

(see also *Detriment; Parental bereavement leave*)

Parents with at least one year's service are permitted to take up to 18 weeks' unpaid leave before a child's 18th birthday.

A system of Shared Parental Leave applies to births and adoptions from 5 April 2015 onwards.

An employee may present a complaint to an employment tribunal that his employer:

a)   has unreasonably postponed a period of parental leave requested by the employee; or

b)   has prevented or attempted to prevent the employee from taking parental leave (s80 ERA 1996).

Remedy: By s80(4) ERA 1996 the amount of compensation shall be such as the tribunal considers just and equitable in all the circumstances having regard to:

a)   the employer's behaviour; and

b)   any loss sustained by the employee which is attributable to the matters complained of.

Gross or net: Whether this is paid gross or net will depend on whether payment amounts to earnings or some other loss.

Limit on a week's pay: None

Limit on number of weeks: No, except in relation to the amount of leave the employee is entitled to by statute.

Any maximum or minimum: None

Adjustments: None

Tax: The tax treatment of any award is unclear. To the extent that the sum awarded is compensation for lost earnings, it is likely to be taxed under s62 ITEPA 2003 (see *Tax and termination payments*).

Recoupment: N/A

Statutory authorities: ERA 1996 *s80*

Part-time worker protection

A worker working part time has the right not to be treated by his employer less favourably than the employer treats a comparable permanent employee, on the ground that the worker is a part time worker, either as regards the terms of his contract; or by being subjected to any other detriment by any act, or deliberate failure to act, of his employer. Less favourable treatment will be permitted where it can be objectively justified. In assessing whether a part time worker has been less favourably treated, the tribunal will apply the pro rata principle unless that is inappropriate (Reg 5 PTW(PLFT) Regs 2000).

A worker has the right to request written reasons for any treatment which he or she considers might infringe the Reg 5 right, and is entitled to be provided with such a statement within 21 days of the request (Reg 6(1) PTW(PLFT)).

Reg 7 PTW(PLFT) establishes automatic unfair dismissal and detriment protections for the actions of individuals related to exercising and enforcing their Reg 5 and 6 rights (see *Unfair dismissal* and *Detriment*).

A worker may present a complaint to the tribunal that a right conferred on him or her by Reg 5 has been infringed (Reg 8(1) PTW(PLFT)).

Remedy: Where a tribunal upholds a complaint that a worker has been subject to less favourable treatment, the tribunal may take any of the following steps as it considers just and equitable (Reg 8(7) PTW(PLFT)):

• make a declaration as to the rights of the complainant and the employer in relation to the complaint;

• order the employer to pay compensation to the complainant;

• make a recommendation that the employer take certain steps to obviate or reduce any relevant adverse effect.

Where compensation is awarded the amount will be that which the tribunal considers just and equitable in all the circumstances (this phrase is used in the assessment of the compensatory award for unfair dismissal and similar principles will apply). The tribunal will have regard to the infringement and any loss which is attributable to it. Losses suffered by the complainant will be taken to include any expenses reasonably incurred as a consequence of the infringement and the loss of any benefit he would have had but for the infringement (see Regs 8(9) and (10) PTW(PLFT)). The common law principles of mitigation apply and the tribunal may reduce any award for contributory fault (Reg 8(13) PTW(PLFT)).

There is no right to compensation for injury to feelings where there has been infringement of the right not to be less favourably treated under Reg 5 PTW(PLFT) (however, an award for detriment under Reg 7 PTW(PLFT) may include such an award (see *Detriment* and *Injury to feelings*).

If an employer fails, without reasonable justification, to comply with a recommendation (see above), the tribunal may make an award of compensation if it has not already done so, or increase an award of compensation it has already made (Reg 8(14) PTW(PLFT)).

Gross or net: This will depend on whether the sums paid are treated as suppressed wages, an award for discrimination or injury to feelings (see *Tax* below within this entry). Where a sum is paid to represent a net loss it will be calculated on the net figure and grossed up where appropriate to make the final award. Where the sum is viewed as suppressed wages the award will be calculated on gross earnings, with the employer deducting tax and NI.

Any maximum or minimum: No, there is no statutory cap.

Adjustments: A percentage deduction for contributory conduct can be applied (Reg 8(13) PTW(PLFT)). Also, if the employer fails to comply with a tribunal's recommendation, any award may be increased (Reg 8(14) PTW(PLFT)).

Mitigation: The usual principles of mitigation apply.

Tax: Any payment to compensate for an employee's reduced wages or benefits would probably be classed as arrears of pay and taxed under s62 ITEPA 2003 in the normal way (see *EIM02550* and *EIM02530*, HMRC). The tax to be paid should be calculated according to the tax year in which the pay was withheld, not the tax year in which the repayment is made.

However, *EIM12965* of the Employment Income Manual states that payments of compensation for discrimination which occurs before termination is not employment income for the purposes of s401 and that they are therefore not taxable. It is arguable that the award for infringement of Reg 5 would not be subject to tax as it would be compensation for discrimination (in its broadest sense).

Statutory authorities: PTW(PLFT) Regs 2000 Regs 5 to 8

Paternity leave: see *Detriment*; *Table 16*; *Unfair dismissal*

Payment in lieu of notice (PILON)

(See also *Effective date of termination*; *Tax and termination payments*)

Where an employee's employment contract is terminated and the employee does not work a notice period, but instead receives a payment equivalent to what would have been earned during that period, this is often described as a payment in lieu of notice or a 'PILON'. It is not the same as payment during 'gardening leave', where the employee is still in employment during the notice period, even though he or she is not present at work.

There are four types of PILON:

- Contractual PILON, where the payment is made under an express contractual term (or occasionally an implied term);

- Automatic PILON, where payment is made as an automatic response by the employer to termination;

- Discretionary PILON, where payment is made under a discretionary power provided by a contractual term; and

- PILONs paid as compensation for breach of contractual entitlement to notice.

If the contract provides that termination can be achieved by making a payment in lieu of notice, the amount to be paid is a matter of the interpretation of the contract.

The employment contract is terminated when the terms of the PILON clause have been satisfied (such as payment being received by the employee), with the EDT being the date of termination of the contract (see *Société Générale, London Branch v Geys* [2013] IRLR 122).

If there is no contractual provision for PILON, a termination of employment with PILON is likely to be a breach of the employment contract. The value of the PILON sufficient to cover an employee's right to damages will be determined by what the terms of the contract establish the employee would have been entitled to receive had they been given their proper notice.

All payments in lieu of notice, not just contractual payments in lieu of notice, are taxable earnings. All employees will pay tax and Class 1 NICs on the amount of basic pay that they would have received if they had worked their notice in full, even if they are not paid a contractual payment in lieu of notice. This means the tax and NICs consequences will no longer depend on how the employment contract is drafted or whether payments are structured in some other form, such as damages.

Penalty for leaving pension scheme early: see *Pension loss*

Pension loss

(see also *State pension: Tables 25 to 39*)

Following the withdrawal of the 2003 edition of 'Compensation for Loss of Pension Rights: Employment Tribunals', a working party of Employment Judges developed the "Principles for compensating pension loss" which were published in August 2017. The *Principles* were revised in December 2019 and again in March 2021 to take account of the 8th edition of the Ogden Tables which were published in 2020. This entry explains how the loss of state pension, pension under a defined contribution scheme and under a defined benefit scheme is calculated.

Some definitions

Deferred pension

This is the pension entitlement built up by an employee who left employment before normal retirement date.

Final salary (defined benefit) pension scheme

This is a pension scheme where the value of a person's pension on retirement is calculated by reference to their final salary. Sometimes, the pension may be calculated according to the average of the last few years' salary. The value of the pension will also be calculated according to the number of years' service - typically entitlement will increase by a particular fraction of final salary for each year of employment. Some pension fractions are more generous than others - a pension fraction of 1/60 is more generous than a pension of 1/80 for example. A person who works for 30 years with a pension fraction of 1/60 will retire on half their final salary, whereas a person with a pension fraction of 1/80 will have to work for 40 years to retire on half their salary.

Gross weekly pensionable pay

The pensionable pay is that part of the employee's salary which will be used to calculate employer and employee pension contributions and may not be the same as their gross weekly pay. If pension loss is to be calculated on the basis of loss of employer contributions according to the Principles, the employee's gross weekly pensionable pay will first have to be ascertained, usually from the pension provider or the employer.

Money purchase (defined contribution) pension scheme

In such a scheme, a private provider, usually chosen by the employer, invests the pot or fund with a view to increasing it. The usual situation is that both the employer and the employee have contributed defined amounts to the pot or fund, expressed as percentages of salary. The amount of the resulting pension will depend on the performance of that pot or fund and the size of the annuity it can purchase.

Normal retirement date

There is no longer a normal retirement age as between employers and their employees (see *Employment Equality (Repeal of Retirement Age Provisions) Regulations 2011/1069*). Any dismissal on grounds of age will be discriminatory, subject to any justification defence, and so far as unfair dismissal is concerned the usual protections, regardless of age, will apply. However, pension scheme rules may specify a normal age at which employees are able to begin to receive a pension, and some schemes may make provision for earlier receipt of benefits.

Ogden Tables

The Ogden Tables are primarily used to assess lump sum damages for personal injury awards but they can also be used to calculate pension loss in certain cases for state pension and defined benefit pension schemes. They provide **multipliers** for different **discount rates** which are then multiplied by the **multiplicand** to arrive at a lump sum figure. The latest tables, the 8th edition, were published in July 2020 where the multipliers have been calculated using the projected mortality rates underlying the 2018-based principal population projection for the United Kingdom and assuming a date of trial in 2022. Additional Tables to the 8th edition of the Ogden Tables have also been produced which provide multipliers at selected rates of discount that can be used to capitalise multiplicands payable from any age at the date of trial to any future age (up to age 125).

Essentially, the **multiplier** is the number of years for which the loss will be incurred and will depend on the sex, age at EDT, retirement age of the claimant, and the current rate of return. The multipliers have been calculated with reference to 2018 mortality rates for the population at large - these rates are not the same as for the population in DB schemes. A **2 year mortality adjustment** to both age and date of retirement will therefore need to be applied for loss of pension (but not earnings).

The **discount rate** is an adjustment to reflect the interest a claimant can expect to earn by investing a lump sum representing pension loss, as well as the effects of tax, expenses and inflation on these returns. The discount rate should ensure that people receive the full compensation that they were awarded - no more or less - by taking into account what they are likely to earn on that money before they are expected to have spent it. It is currently a negative figure, -0.25%, although in Scotland, the ET has decided to keep the previous discount rate of -0.75%. This negative discount rate effectively means that it is assumed a lump sum invested will actually lose money rather than increase in value - the rate has therefore been calculated to mitigate the claimant against this potential loss.

The *multiplicand* is the present-day value of the future loss of annual pension.

All of the Ogden Tables have been summarised at the back of this book (Tables 25 to 39) to include the multipliers for discount rates of -0.25% and -0.75%, and for all the retirement ages between 50 and 75. Tables 26 to 33 list the multipliers with and without the 2 year adjustment.

All references to the tables in the examples below refer to the number of the table at the back of this book, not to the Ogden Table number. In each example the discount rate for England and Wales has been used and the 2 year adjustment applied to loss of pension (but not earnings).

Loss of State Pension

Since 6 April 2016, the state pension has been called the new State Pension or nSP. An individual needs to accrue 10 qualifying years on their NI record to get some nSP and will be entitled to the full nSP (currently £203.85 a week, or £10,600.20 a year, (2023/24)) if they accrue 35 qualifying years.

Dismissal interrupts an individual's NI record. In most cases it will not interrupt it for long enough to result in a loss of nSP benefits. This is because it will rarely stop a person from going on to accrue the 35 qualifying years needed to receive the full amount of nSP. Nonetheless, in exceptional cases, dismissal might be said to reduce nSP benefits if NI credits were not available and dismissal means that the claimant will fail to reach 35 qualifying years (or will accrue fewer years) than if not dismissed.

If a tribunal decides it is appropriate to award a sum for loss of state pension rights, the Ogden Tables for loss of pension will be needed.

Example

- Male
- Aged 63 at date of dismissal
- State pension age of 66 and no prospect of finding alternative work
- Number of qualifying years already accrued: 32
- nSP at date of dismissal: £10,600.20 a year (using current figures).

The individual will lose 3 qualifying years resulting in a reduction by 3/35ths of his full state pension from retirement until death.

It is necessary first of all to calculate the annual loss which is 3/35 x 10,600.20 = 908.59 (this is called the multiplicand – see above for more detail).

Next, the Ogden tables should be used to obtain the number of years for which this loss is likely to be incurred (this is called the multiplier). Using Table 26, the multiplier for a man aged 63 who will retire at age 66 is 21.75.

Therefore the capital sum which represents loss of nSP = 908.59 x 21.75 = £19,761.80.

As the example above demonstrates, the loss of nSP may not be an insignificant sum especially if the claimant is close to retirement and is unlikely to secure alternative employment.

Defined Contribution (DC or money purchase) schemes

Method of calculation in simple cases

Where the claimant has lost benefits from a DC scheme, pension loss will be calculated on the basis of lost employer contributions as follows:

- obtain details of the claimant's pay and employer contributions (the tribunal may assume auto-enrolment levels if there is no evidence);
- identify the date at which the period of loss ends;
- calculate the employer contributions to the remedy hearing (no recoupment);
- calculate the future loss of employer contributions (taking account of future pay rises);
- credit any employer contributions made by a new employer against the award (again the tribunal may assume auto-enrolment with new employer, rebuttable by evidence).

There is no loss by reason of lost facility to make Additional Voluntary Contributions.

Career long loss

The tribunal may consider that the contributions method is not appropriate if there is significant disparity between the level of employer contributions in the new job compared to the old job which will remain through to the claimant's retirement. Instead, the tribunal may add the employer contributions to net salary and use the Ogden Tables to calculate net loss of earnings. The relevant Ogden tables in these cases are Multiples for loss of Earnings (Ogden Tables 3 to 18) (Tables 34 to 37 listed at the back of this book).

Example

- Female

- Aged 54 at date of dismissal

- Pension age 70

- Pension contributions in old job = £9,750 per year

- Pension contributions in new job = £2,250 per year

- Loss each year = 9,750 – 2,250 = 7,500

- Table 35 without 2 year adjustment 15.78

- Loss of pension, before grossing up = 7,500 x 15.78 = £118,350.

Defined Benefit (DB or final salary) schemes

There are two methods of calculation depending on the complexity of the case.

Simple cases

These could include cases where it is disproportionate to engage in complex analysis (e.g. because of the compensation cap or a relatively short period of loss).

Method of calculation

There will usually be no award for loss of enhancement of accrued pension rights. The pension loss in simple cases should be calculated according to loss of contributions as for DC schemes as follows:

- obtain details of the employer's contribution rate (which could be an average for scheme members);

- identify the date at which the period of loss ends;

- calculate the employer contributions to the remedy hearing (no recoupment) by applying the average employer contribution rate to the claimant's gross salary at EDT;

- calculate the future loss of employer contributions in the same way (taking account of future pay rises);

- credit any employer contributions made by a new employer against the award (again the tribunal may assume auto-enrolment with the new employer, rebuttable by evidence).

Complex cases

These cases are typically cases with longer periods of loss (e.g. career-long loss cases) and no compensation cap, warranting more complex analysis.

Case management

Cases which could be described as complex should be identified at an early stage and parties should include a pension loss element on the schedule of loss at the start of the process i.e. before any liability is found. The Employment Tribunal's *Agenda for Case Management for Preliminary Hearing* contains a section to identify

this at a Case Management Preliminary Hearing. Use of expressions such as "to be confirmed" are discouraged.

For complex cases, there will be a split liability and remedy hearing, the remedy hearing being in two stages:

1) The first stage will identify the non-pension losses and make findings of fact relevant to pension losses. There will then be a period for the parties to try and agree the pensions figure between themselves.

2) The second stage will identify the pension loss, either by using Ogden tables or expert actuarial evidence.

Calculation

There could be two types of loss to be considered: loss of annual pension and loss of a lump sum.

Method of calculation of loss of annual pension using Ogden tables

The Principles identity seven steps that the tribunal and the parties should follow when calculating loss of DB pension rights using the Ogden Tables.

Step 1: Identify what the claimant's net pension income would have been at their retirement age if the dismissal had not occurred.

Step 2: Identify what the claimant's net pension income will be at their retirement age in the light of their dismissal.

Step 3: Deduct the result of Step 2 from the result of Step 1, which produces a figure for net annual loss of pension benefits. This is the ***multiplicand***.

Step 4: Identify the period over which that net annual loss is to be awarded, using Tables 26 to 33 at the back of this book to identify the ***multiplier*** as follows:

- Choose the correct table depending on the sex of the individual, the discount rate (-0.25% for claims in England and Wales; -0.75% for claims in Scotland) and whether the 2 year adjustment applies;

- Identify the age of the claimant at the date of the remedy hearing (the numbers down the side) and the claimant's retirement age (the numbers across the top).

Step 5: Multiply the multiplicand by the multiplier to obtain the capitalised value of the lost pension, subject to any further adjustment the tribunal considers appropriate.

Step 6: Check the lump sum position and perform a separate calculation if required (see below).

Step 7: Taking account of the other sums awarded by the tribunal, gross up the compensation awarded.

Example

- Male
- Aged 59 at dismissal
- Normal retirement age: 75
- Annual pension if not been dismissed: £15,000
- Annual pension having been dismissed: £7,000
- Annual pension loss: £8,000
- Multiplier from Table 26: 13.50
- Capital sum representing pension loss = 8,000 x 13.50 = £108,000

Lump sums

At retirement, claimants could receive either (i) a commuted lump sum (i.e. a lump sum in return for giving up some of their annual pension) or (ii) a non-commuted lump sum (i.e. one where the annual pension is not reduced). It may be appropriate to apply a discount factor, using Table 38, to any lost non-commuted lump sum to reflect the fact that it is being received early (any lost commuted lump sum will be ignored as this will already have been factored in when calculating annual pension loss).

Calculation method

The calculation of loss of lump sum is as follows:

- Identify the multiplicand. This is:

  the lump sum that would have been paid at retirement if the claimant had not been dismissed

  minus

  the lump sum they will now receive, taking account of withdrawal factors.

- Identify the number of years between dismissal and retirement date. This is the number down the side of Table 38.

- Identify the discount rate (along the top, which is currently -0.25% in England and Wales and -0.75% in Scotland).

- Find the appropriate multiplier.

- Multiply the multiplicand by the multiplier to find the present capital value of that loss.

Example

- Number of years to retirement: 25
- Lump sum payable but for dismissal: £25,000
- Lump sum payable having been dismissed: £20,000
- Lump sum loss = £5,000
- Table 38 multiplier: 1.0646

- Capital value of loss = £5,000 x 1.0646 = £5,323

Perks: see *Financial losses*

Permanent employment: see *Damages for wrongful dismissal*

Physical and psychiatric injury

(see also *Discrimination*; *Interest*)

Claimants can claim damages for personal injury caused by unlawful discriminatory acts including detriment for whistleblowing (see *Sheriff v Klyne Tugs (Lowestoft) Ltd* [1999] IRLR 481 and *Virgo Fidelis Senior School v Boyle* [2004] IRLR 268). However, it is not always easy to identify where injury to feelings ends and physical and psychiatric injury starts and there is a risk of double counting.

Although there is no absolute requirement for medical evidence to establish a claim for personal injury in employment tribunals, obtaining such evidence is advisable where possible, especially where claims are complex and there are issues over causation or divisibility (*Hampshire County Council v Wyatt* UKEAT/0013/16).

Divisible and Indivisible Harm

In some cases, issues may arise where a claimant has suffered an injury through multiple causes. In such cases, the tribunal will need to consider whether the harm is 'divisible' or 'indivisible'.

Divisible Harm is where different acts cause *different* damage, or *quantifiable parts* of the damage. In these cases, the tribunal must establish and award compensation only for that part of the harm for which the respondent is truly responsible.

Indivisible Harm is where multiple acts result in the *same* damage, usually either:

Monocausally: where all of the acts operate in the same way to cause the damage, only one act could have actually caused the damage, but it is impossible to tell which of them was the actual cause; or

Multicausally: where a single condition or harm is caused by a combination of separate acts or factors. For example, where the cumulative effect of their separate acts crosses a threshold that gives rise to that damage, or distinct acts combine to produce a single form of damage.

If the harm is indivisible, any respondent whose act has been the proximate cause of the injury must compensate for the *whole* of it. That others had a part to play in the injury is a matter for *contribution*, not apportionment.

Whether an injury is divisible or indivisible will depend on evidence, but it is *'more likely that an injury will be held to be indivisible if the competing causes are closely related to the injury and it is difficult to separate out the consequences'* (*Olayemi v Athena Medical Centre & Anor* UKEAT/0140/15, paragraph 25).

The issue of divisibility of harm was considered by the Court of Appeal in *BAE Systems (Operations) Ltd v Konczak* [2017] EWCA Civ 1188. The case confirmed the following propositions:

1) Where the harm has more than one cause, a respondent should only pay for the proportion attributable to their wrongdoing unless the harm is truly indivisible.

2) The burden is on the employer to raise the issue of apportionment.

3) Tribunals should try to *'identify a rational basis on which the harm suffered can be apportioned between a part caused by the employer's wrong, and a part which is not so caused.'* The tribunal should see if it *'can identify, however broadly, a particular part of the suffering which is due to the wrong'*.

4) Where such a *'rational basis'* can be found, the tribunal should apportion accordingly, even if the basis for doing so is *'rough and ready'*.

5) Any such assessment must consider any pre-existing disorder or vulnerability, and account for the chance that the claimant would have succumbed to the harm in any event, either at that point or in the future.

6) In cases of psychiatric injury, careful evidence should be obtained from experts, particularly in relation to the likelihood of suffering the harm in any event. Paragraph 93 of Irwin LJ's judgment identifies some of the matters that may be useful to put to such an expert.

Remedy: When it comes to the assessment of damages in relation to a proven psychiatric injury, tribunals are *'obliged to approach the assessment of damages for psychiatric injury on the same basis as a common law court in an ordinary action for personal injuries'* (*HM Prison Service v Salmon* [2001] IRLR 425).

The Judicial College has published guidelines for the assessment of general damages in personal injury cases. The latest 16th edition was published in April 2022. According to the College, the following factors need to be taken into account when valuing claims of psychiatric injury:

a) the injured person's ability to cope with life and work;

b) the effect on the injured person's relationships with family, friends and those with whom he comes into contact;

c) the extent to which treatment would be successful;

d) future vulnerability;

e) prognosis;

f) whether medical help has been sought;

g) whether the injury results from sexual and/or physical abuse and/or breach of trust; and if so, the nature of the relationship between victim and abuser, the nature of the abuse, its duration and the symptoms caused by it.

There are 4 categories of award (including the *Simmons v Castle* uplift):

1) Less Severe: between £1,540 and £5,860. Where the claimant has suffered temporary symptoms that have adversely affected daily activities;

2) Moderate: between £5,860 and £19,070. Where, while the claimant has suffered problems as a result of the discrimination, marked improvement has been made by the date of the hearing and the prognosis is good;

3) Moderately Severe: between £19,070 and £54,830. Moderately severe cases include those where there is work-related stress resulting in a permanent or long-standing disability preventing a return to comparable employment. These are cases where there are problems with factors a) to d) above, but there is a much more optimistic prognosis than Severe;

4) Severe: between £54,830 and £115,730. Where the claimant has serious problems in relation to the factors at a) to d) above, and the prognosis is poor.

Separate criteria apply for cases of Post-Traumatic Stress Disorder, and the Guidelines should be consulted accordingly in an appropriate case.

Any maximum or minimum: Only so far as the guidelines have suggested.

Adjustments:

Causation: The award can be adjusted to allow for the extent to which the act of discrimination caused the illness. So, if it is found that the discriminatory act caused the illness to the extent of 30%, the award will be reduced by 70%.

Double counting: Injury to feelings and physical and psychiatric injury are distinct heads of loss, but care should be taken that no double counting has taken place. Either one could be reduced if this is the case.

Discount rate: Where an employee suffers a life-changing personal injury resulting in long-term loss of earnings, the discount rate is applied to reflect early receipt. As of July 2019, that rate is now -0.25% in England and Wales and -0.75% in Scotland (see also *Accelerated/decelerated receipt*).

Interest: Interest could also be awarded (see *Interest*).

Simmons v Castle uplift: The figures quoted above include the *Simmons v Castle* 10% uplift (see *De Souza v Vinci Construction (UK) Ltd* [2017] EWCA Civ 879 paragraph 26).

Scotland:

- The discount rate remains at -0.75%;

- The tribunal can choose not to apply the *Simmons v Castle* uplift, but must set out reasons for doing so.

Mitigation: N/A

Tax: Awards for injury are exempted from tax under s406 ITEPA 2003 (see *Tax and termination payments*).

Recoupment: N/A

Relevant case law: *De Souza v Vinci Construction (UK) Ltd* [2017] EWCA Civ 879; *HM Prison Service v Salmon* [2001] IRLR 425; *Sheriff v Klyne Tugs (Lowestoft) Ltd* [1999] IRLR 481; *Virgo Fidelis Senior School v Boyle* [2004] IRLR 268

Polkey

(see also *Adjustments and order of adjustments*)

A '*Polkey*' deduction is the phrase used in unfair dismissal cases to describe the reduction in any award for future loss to reflect the chance that the individual would have been dismissed fairly in any event (*Polkey v AE Dayton Services Ltd* [1987] IRLR 50 (HL)).

This may take the form of a percentage reduction, or it may take the form of a tribunal making a finding that the individual would have been dismissed fairly after a further period of employment (for example a period in which a fair procedure would have been completed). Alternatively, a combination of the two approaches could be used, but not in the same period of loss (as confirmed in *Zebrowski v Concentric Birmingham Ltd* UKEAT/0245/16/DA)). The question for the tribunal is whether the *particular employer* (as opposed to a hypothetical reasonable employer) would have dismissed the claimant in any event had the unfairness not occurred.

There are useful reviews of the case law (which is not without its difficulties) in *Software 2000 Ltd v Andrews* [2007] IRLR 568, *V v Hertfordshire County Council and another* UKEAT/0427/14/LA and *Contract Bottling Ltd v Cave & Anor* UKEAT/0100/14/DM).

The *Polkey* adjustment is only applicable to the compensatory award, not the basic award (apart from in very limited circumstances where such a (fair) dismissal might have taken place virtually contemporaneously with the unfair dismissal which actually occurred, presumably applying s122(2) ERA 1996 - see *Granchester Construction (Eastern) Ltd v Attrill* UKEAT/0327/12/LA, paragraph 19). A similar approach to a *Polkey* deduction is taken in discrimination cases where the tribunal will assess the chance that a particular future loss has been suffered (see *Loss of chance*).

The tribunal must assess any *Polkey* deduction in two respects:

1) If a fair process had occurred, would it have affected when the claimant would have been dismissed? and

2) What is the percentage chance that a fair process would still have resulted in the claimant's dismissal?

Where there is a significant overlap between the factors taken into account in making a *Polkey* deduction and when making a deduction for contributory conduct, the ET should consider expressly, whether in the light of that overlap, it is just and equitable to make a finding of contributory conduct, and, if so, what its amount should be. This is to avoid the risk of penalizing the claimant twice for the same conduct (see *Lenlyn UK Ltd v Kular* UKEAT/0108/16/DM).

Relevant case law: *Contract Bottling Ltd v Cave & Anor* UKEAT/0100/14/DM; *Granchester Construction (Eastern) Ltd v Attrill* UKEAT/0327/12/LA; *Lenlyn UK Ltd v Kular* UKEAT/0108/16/DM; *Polkey v AE Dayton Services Ltd* [1987] IRLR 50 (HL);*Software 2000 Ltd v Andrews* [2007] IRLR 568; *V v Hertfordshire County Council and another* UKEAT/0427/14/LA; *Zebrowski v Concentric Birmingham Ltd* UKEAT/0245/16/DA

Pregnancy: see *Discrimination*; *Time off for ante-natal care*

Prescribed element: see *Recoupment*

Prescribed period: see *Recoupment*

Presidential guidance on remedy

APPENDIX 1 reproduces Guidance Note 6 from the Presidential Guidance - General Case Management which was amended and re-issued in 2018. This sets out in easily readable form the tribunal's procedure and expectations for dealing with remedy. The tribunal will expect parties to comply with the guidance.

Profit related bonus: see *Financial losses*; *Bonuses*

Protected act: see *Discrimination*

Protected disclosure

(see also *Detriment*; *Unfair dismissal*)

Where an employee has suffered a detriment, or has been dismissed, for making a protected disclosure, the tribunal may award financial compensation.

The right to bring a claim for detriment is established by s47B ERA 1996, and the right to not be unfairly dismissed for the sole or principal reason of making a protected disclosure is established by s103A ERA 1996.

For detriment (not dismissal) the tribunal must award such an amount as it considers is just and equitable having regard to:

1)   the infringement to which the complaint relates;

2)   any loss which is attributable to the act, or failure to act, which infringed the claimant's right (s49(2) ERA 1996).

If the employee has been dismissed, awards can be made for unfair dismissal (see *Additional award; Basic award; Compensatory award; Unfair dismissal*).

Remedy: For detriment (not dismissal) the loss to be compensated shall be taken to include: any expenses reasonably incurred by the claimant in consequence of the act, or failure to act, to which the complaint relates; and loss of any benefit which the claimant might reasonably be expected to have had but for the act or failure to act (s49(3) ERA 1996).

Such a detriment award may also include compensation for injury to feelings. Where a worker has brought the claim under s47B and the detriment is termination of the contract, which is akin to a claim for unfair dismissal of an employee, it is arguable that injury to feelings may be awarded, but only up to the amount of a basic award (see *Injury to feelings*). Compensation for injury to feelings is not available in an award for unfair dismissal.

Gross or net: If the claimant has been dismissed, see the individual awards for unfair dismissal. Otherwise, it will be a figure that the tribunal considers just and equitable (see *Detriment*).

Any maximum or minimum: The award is unlimited unless the detriment is termination of the contract of a worker when any compensation must not exceed the compensation that would be payable if the worker had been an employee and had been dismissed for making a protected disclosure (there is currently no limit to such financial losses) (s49(6) ERA 1996).

Adjustments: If the tribunal considers that the act or failure to act was caused or contributed to by action of the claimant, it may reduce the award if it thinks that it would be just and equitable to do so (ss49(4) and (5) ERA 1996).

The tribunal can also reduce the award of compensation by up to 25% if they find that any disclosure was not made in good faith.

ACAS uplift: The ACAS Code of Practice on Disciplinary and Grievance Procedures defines a grievance as *'concerns, problems or complaints that employees raise with their employers'*. A protected disclosure is likely to satisfy this definition, and thus may justify an uplift in compensation if there is any unreasonable failure to comply with the Code's requirements for handling grievances (*Ikejiaku v British Institute of Technology Ltd* UKEAT/0243/19).

Cap: The statutory cap on unfair dismissal does not apply if the employee has been dismissed as a result of making the protected disclosure, and there is no statutory cap if the claim is for detriment.

Mitigation: The tribunal may reduce the amount if it considers that the claimant has failed to mitigate his/her loss.

Tax: The award will be taxable under s401 ITEPA 2003 if the employee has been dismissed, although the tax treatment is unclear in the case of an employee who receives a payment because of suffering detriment but is still employed (see *Detriment; Tax and termination payments*).

Recoupment: Recoupment will only apply to unfair dismissal awards.

Statutory authorities: ERA 1996 *ss49* and *103A*

Protective award

Where an employer is proposing to dismiss as redundant 20 or more employees at one establishment within a period of 90 days or less, the employer shall consult about the dismissals all the persons who are appropriate representatives of any of the employees who may be affected by the proposed dismissals or may be affected by measures taken in connection with those dismissals (s188 and s188A TULR(C)A 1992).

The consultation shall begin in good time and in any event:

a)   where the employer is proposing to dismiss 100 or more employees, at least 45 days; and

b)   otherwise, at least 30 days,

before the first of the dismissals takes effect.

Where it is alleged that an employer has failed to comply with the consultation requirements the appropriate representatives, or in some limited situations an affected employee, may bring a complaint to a tribunal who, if the complaint is well founded, shall make a declaration to that effect and may make a 'protective award' covering the employees affected by the failure.

The protective award is remuneration for the 'protected period', of up to 90 days.

If the employer is insolvent, the employees may make a claim to the National Insurance Fund for payment of some (or in some cases all) of this award (see *Insolvency*).

Remedy (1): Under TULR(C)A 1992 s189(3), (4) and s190 the tribunal may make an award of up to 90 days' pay, with the length of the period determined by what is just and equitable in all the circumstances having regard to the seriousness of the employer's failure to comply with TULR(C)A 1992 s188. The award is calculated as starting on the day the first dismissals took effect. The award will identify the description of employees to whom it applies, who will be those employees whose representative has not been consulted properly.

The rate of remuneration payable is a week's pay for each week of the protected period; and remuneration in respect of a period less than one week shall be calculated by reducing proportionally the amount of a week's pay (s190(2)).

A day's pay is found by dividing the employee's actual gross weekly pay by 7.

The principles for determining the size of a protective award are set out in *Susie Radin Ltd v GMB & Ors* [2004] ICR 893. The award is designed to be punitive, not to compensate the employee for losses suffered, with the calculation starting at 90 days where there has been no consultation and being reduced to reflect the seriousness of the breach and any mitigating factors. It is important to remember that, even if the consultation period is only 30 days, the starting point and maximum protected period is still 90 days.

Remedy (2): If the employer fails to comply with s190 by not paying an employee within the description the amount due under the award, the employee may bring a complaint to the tribunal who may order the employer to pay the amount of remuneration due (s192(1) and (3)).

Gross or net: Gross. A week's pay is as defined in ss220 to 229 ERA 1996 (see *Week's pay*). Part weeks are to be calculated pro rata. Only the basic pay should be taken into account and not any discretionary bonus (see *Canadian Imperial Bank of Commerce v Beck* UKEAT/0141/10/RN).

Limit on a week's pay: None. The limit on a week's pay does not apply.

Limit on number of days: 90.

An employee will be entitled to payment of the protective award from the date the protected period begins but will cease being entitled at the date he is fairly dismissed, unreasonably terminates his contract of employment or unreasonably refuses an offer of employment during the protected period (see s191 TULR(C)A 1992).

Any maximum or minimum: None

Adjustments: None

Cap: There is no cap on the award.

Mitigation: N/A, as the award is a sanction for breach, not compensation for losses suffered.

Tax: The award will be taxable under s401 ITEPA 2003 if the employee is no longer in employment (EIM02550, HMRC). Also, see *Mimtec Ltd v Inland Revenue* [2001] UKSC SPC00277 (see *Tax and termination payments*).

Recoupment: Yes, the prescribed element being any amount ordered to be paid to the employee in respect of so much of the relevant protected period as falls before the date of the conclusion of the tribunal proceedings (see *Table 19*).

Statutory authorities: ITEPA 2003 s401; *The Employment Protection (Recoupment of Jobseeker's Allowance and Income Support) Regulations 1996*; TULR(C)A 1992 *ss189 and 190*

Relevant case law: *Canadian Imperial Bank of Commerce v Beck* UKEAT/0141/10/RN; *Mimtec Ltd v Inland Revenue* [2001] UKSC SPC00277; *Susie Radin Ltd v GMB & Ors* [2004] ICR 893

Example

The claimant's gross weekly pay is £500 (which has been calculated in accordance with ss220 to 229 ERA as above) and is awarded 80 days' protective award.

A day's pay = 500/7 = £71.43 (note: the weekly pay must be divided by 7, not the number of days per week actually worked)

Thus, the protective award = £71.43 x 80 = £5,714.40

Qualifying period

(see also *Effective date of termination*)

This is the length of continuous employment (see *s211 ERA 1996*) that must have been worked by the claimant before a tribunal will consider any particular complaint. Different qualifying periods apply for different types of claim (see *Table 18*).

The employee's continuous employment begins with the day on which the employee starts work, and ends with the day by reference to which the length of the employee's period of continuous employment is to be ascertained for the purposes of the provision.

But, if an employee's period of continuous employment includes one or more periods which (by virtue of ss*215*, *216* or *217* ERA 1996) while not counting in computing the length of the period do not break continuity of employment, the beginning of the period shall be treated as postponed by the number of days falling within that intervening period, or the aggregate number of days falling within those periods, calculated in accordance with the section in question.

Rate of pay: see *Week's pay*

Recoupment

(see also *Non-recoupable state benefits*)

A number of awards made by tribunals are subject to recoupment, whereby the state recovers from the respondent the value of certain state benefits paid to the claimant. This involves the tribunal identifying a part of the award that corresponds to a period of loss during which the claimant was in receipt of job seeker's allowance, income-related employment support allowance, income support or universal credit. The respondent is required to not pay the claimant the sum the tribunal identifies, but to wait until the DWP recoups from them any benefits paid, with the remainder then being paid to the claimant by the respondent. The principles to be applied are contained in the *Employment Protection (Recoupment of Jobseeker's Allowance and Income Support) Regulations 1996* (SI 1996/2349).

The types of award which may be covered by the prescribed element (see below) are listed in *Table 19*, the most common awards being for unfair dismissal, failure to make a guarantee payment, failure to pay during a period of maternity or medical suspension and protective awards (see Column 1 of the Schedule to the regulations, and Reg 3(1)(a)).

The recoupment regulations do not apply if the claimant has not claimed the relevant benefits, or if the award is compensation for discrimination statutes or for dismissal by reason of redundancy.

The recoupment regulations do not apply to settlements - this may create an incentive to settle where, because the Secretary of State will not recoup the benefits paid, a smaller sum paid by the respondent than that which would be awarded by the tribunal may well result in a higher sum being received by the claimant.

Required information

The tribunal must in its judgment identify four items of information that will then be provided to the DWP:

the amount of any 'prescribed element', the prescribed period, the total amount of the award and the balance. In essence, this will define the sum within any award from which the state may seek recoupment. No greater sum will be recouped, and the respondent will be ordered by the tribunal to pay the remainder to the claimant.

Prescribed element

The prescribed element is that part of the award which is held back from the claimant until the value of any state benefits subject to the recoupment procedures is known. It is defined in Reg 3(1)(a) and Column 3 of the Schedule, and is that part of the monetary award attributable to loss of wages or arrears of pay or losses due to the claimant (including a protective award) for the period before the conclusion of the tribunal proceedings, or if it covers a protective award or award for failure to inform or consult under TUPE, up to the final day of the period covered by that protective award. The prescribed element does not include the figure that may have been awarded for loss of statutory rights, right to written particulars or the loss of benefits or pension.

The prescribed element will be reduced in line with any deduction for contributory fault that may have been made to the compensatory award. Further, the prescribed element will be reduced by the same proportion as the compensatory award when applying the statutory cap. For example, if the compensatory award has been reduced from £117,452 to the cap of £105,707 (that is, by 10%), the prescribed element will also be reduced by 10% (see Reg 4(2)).

Prescribed period

The prescribed period is identified in column 3 of the Schedule to the regulations. For straightforward unfair dismissal claims the prescribed period is the period between the EDT and the date of the remedy hearing (or the date at which the tribunal sent the remedy judgment to the parties). For concurrent wrongful and unfair dismissal claims, since recoupment does not apply to the award for breach of contract, the prescribed period is the period between the end of the period over which damages have been awarded and the date of the hearing (or the date at which the parties were sent the remedy judgment).

Total award

This is the total of all the awards that have been made by the tribunal.

Balance

This is the difference between the total and the prescribed element and must be paid to the claimant.

Once the actual state benefits that are subject to recoupment are known, the DWP will claim this figure from the prescribed element retained by the respondent and any remaining monies must be paid by the employer to the employee.

Statutory authorities: *Employment Protection (Recoupment of Jobseeker's Allowance and Income Support) Regulations 1996*

Example 1 (where the statutory cap is not applicable)

Basic award = £500

Immediate loss of earnings = £2,000

Future loss of earnings = £700

Loss of statutory rights = £200

Contributory conduct of 20% applies to compensatory award only

Calculation

Prescribed element applies only to the immediate loss of earnings, i.e. £2,000

But this amount has been reduced by 20% and is now 2,000 x 0.8 = £1,600

Total award = 500 + 1,600 + 700 + 200 = £3,000

Prescribed element is therefore £1,600 which should be held back from the claimant. Balance payable immediately to claimant = 500 + 700 + 200 = £1,400, the other £1,600 being payable if the DWP does not serve a recoupment notice on the employer. If the DWP does serve a recoupment notice, and the value of the state benefits received by the claimant is, say, £500, the employer must pay £500 to the DWP and the remaining £1,100 to the claimant.

Example 2 (where adjustments have to be made for the statutory cap)

Basic award = £11,000

Compensatory award = £120,000, of which immediate loss = £30,000 and future loss is £90,000

Loss of statutory rights = £200

Contributory conduct of 20% applies to compensatory award only

Calculation

First, the basic award remains intact.

Secondly, the compensatory award AND the loss of statutory rights should be reduced for contributory conduct = (£120,000 + £200) x 0.8 = £96,160

Thirdly, a grossing up calculation needs to be performed:

Gross up £11,000 + £96,160 - £30,000 = £77,160

Grossing up £77,160 at, say, 20% = 77,160 ÷ 0.8 = £96,450

The compensatory award is now the remainder of £30,000 - £11,000 = £19,000 plus the grossed up figure of £96,450 which comes to £115,450. This will be capped at £105,707.

Before the contributory conduct and the cap, the compensatory award was £120,200, and after these adjustments the award was £105,707 so we need to calculate the proportion by which the compensatory award has been reduced as a result. The calculation is (120,200 − 105,707) x 100/120,200 = 12.05% approximately.

So, the prescribed element of £30,000 (i.e. the immediate loss) should be reduced by 12.05%. Therefore, the prescribed element = 30,000 (immediate loss) x 0.8795 = £26,385.

Redundancy

An employee with 2 years' service is entitled to be paid a redundancy payment if he or she is dismissed by reason of redundancy, or eligible by reason of being laid off or kept on short-time (see s135 ERA 1996). An employee may also be entitled to an enhanced redundancy payment by virtue of an express, incorporated or implied term of their contract of employment.

Statutory redundancy pay (see also *Basic award*)

If an employee has been dismissed by reason of redundancy and has not been paid the statutory redundancy pay to which they are entitled, s163 ERA 1996 permits the employee to bring a claim to the tribunal, which may order the employer to pay such amount as it thinks appropriate to compensate the worker for any financial loss arising from this non-payment (s163(5)). However, the claimant is not entitled to receive both a redundancy payment and a basic award, and any redundancy pay already paid will reduce the basic award accordingly. If redundancy was not the real reason for dismissal, the redundancy payment will not be set off against any basic award (*Boorman v Allmakes Ltd* [1995] IRLR 553).

Calculation: The redundancy payment is calculated according to the employee's length of service, age and gross weekly pay (up to the specified limit) (s162 ERA 1996). The calculation is identical to that for working out the basic award.

The employee will receive 1 ½ weeks' gross pay for each year of employment in which they were not below the age of 41, 1 week's gross pay for each year of employment in which they were at some point below the age of 41 but not below the age of 22 and ½ a week's gross pay for each year of employment in which they were at any point below the age of 22. The maximum number of reckonable years is 20.

Limit on a week's pay: £643. A week's pay as defined in ss220 to 229 ERA 1996 applies (see *Week's pay* and *Table 1* for historical rates).

Limit on the number of weeks: 30

Adjustments: The ACAS uplift does not apply. The 2015 ACAS Code of Practice states that the Code does not apply to redundancy dismissals, and therefore nor does the ACAS adjustment. *Holmes v Qinetiq Ltd* UKEAT/0206/15 confirms that the Code only applies to dismissals involving some form of *'culpable conduct'*.

The redundancy payment can be reduced or in certain circumstances withheld completely, for example if the employee commits an act of misconduct, leaves before the redundancy notice period has expired or the employee had taken part in a strike and refused to comply with a notice of extension served by the employer (see ss140 to 143 ERA 1996).

Mitigation: N/A

Tax: Any redundancy pay will be taxed under s401 ITEPA 2003 and therefore be counted towards the £30,000 tax free allowance.

Recoupment: N/A

Enhanced redundancy payment (awarded at tribunal)

An employee entitled to an enhanced redundancy payment may claim this from the tribunal.

Remedy: Any amount that the employee would have been entitled to over and above the statutory redundancy payment can be claimed.

Adjustments: Any enhanced redundancy payment will be part of the compensatory award and adjusted accordingly.

Cap: The statutory cap will apply to the whole of the compensatory award which includes any enhanced redundancy payment.

Tax: The enhanced redundancy payment, if awarded, will form part of the compensatory award and will be taxed under s401 ITEPA 2003 and therefore be counted towards the £30,000, tax free allowance.

Recoupment: Recoupment does not apply to any enhanced redundancy pay awarded.

Statutory authorities: ERA 1996 *ss155, 162* and *163*

Enhanced redundancy payment (paid on termination of employment)

The employee is not permitted to receive both a statutory redundancy payment and a basic award. The basic award will be reduced by the equivalent of the statutory redundancy payment made (s122(4) ERA 1996), and any enhanced redundancy payment that has been paid in excess of the statutory redundancy figure will go towards reducing the compensatory award

(s123(7) ERA 1996). Note that the employer will enjoy the full benefit of any enhanced redundancy paid. In other words, any adjustments, such as contributory conduct, are made before the enhanced redundancy payment is taken off the compensatory award but interest will apply after the enhanced redundancy payment. The statutory cap is applied after the enhanced redundancy payment has been taken into account. It is important that the order is complied with, as in the following example:

Example

Compensatory award before adjustments = £50,000

After contributory conduct of 10% has been applied, compensatory award = £45,000

Enhanced redundancy payment of £25,000 reduces the compensatory award to £20,000

Example (where the redundancy pay received reduces the tax free sum available for other awards)

Redundancy payment received (tax free) = £5,000

The tax free sum available after the redundancy payment has been made is £30,000 - £5,000 = £25,000

Basic award = £11,000

Compensatory award = £40,000

The amount that should be grossed up = £11,000 + £40,000 - £25,000 = £26,000.

Statutory and contractual redundancy payments (awarded at tribunal)

If a contractual claim is brought under the Employment Tribunal's Extension of Jurisdiction (England and Wales) Order 1994, the jurisdiction of the ET under that Order is subject to a cap of £25,000 on contractual claims: see Article 10 of the Order. But if a claim for a statutory redundancy payment is made in addition to the contractual redundancy payment, the EAT has ruled that there are two causes of action; a contractual cause of action and a statutory cause of action, and the claimant would be entitled to both payments. The respondent is entitled to set off the statutory redundancy payment against the contractual redundancy payment but the set off should be against the uncapped amount, not against the capped amount (see *Ugradar v Lancashire Care NHS Foundation Trust* UKEAT/0301/18/BA).

Example

Statutory redundancy entitlement = £10,000

Contractual redundancy entitlement = £60,000 of which £10,000 can be set off because of the statutory redundancy payment, leaving £50,000

Payment to claimant = £35,000, consisting of:

- £10,000 Statutory redundancy pay; and
- £25,000 Contractual redundancy pay (the remaining £50,000 capped)

Statutory authorities: ERA 1996 *ss122(4)* and *123(7)*

Re-engagement and reinstatement

(see also *Additional award*; *Unfair dismissal*)

When a claimant succeeds in an unfair dismissal claim the three remedies available are reinstatement, re-engagement and compensation (ss112 to 126 ERA 1996).

The tribunal is obliged to explain to a successful claimant the availability of these three orders (s112(2) ERA 1996) and ask them whether they wish the tribunal to make such an order. Although reinstatement and re-engagement are sometimes stated as the primary remedies for unfair dismissal, this is only true in the sense that they must be considered before any claim for compensation (*Park Chinois Ltd v Ozkara* [2019] UKEAT/0017/19). In practice such orders are rarely granted, with most cases resulting in an award of compensation only.

If the claimant has expressed a wish to be reinstated or re-engaged, and communicated that to the respondent not fewer than 7 days before the final hearing, the respondent is obliged to adduce reasonable evidence about the availability of the job from which the claimant was dismissed, or of comparable or suitable employment. If the respondent fails to do so without special reason, and this results in the postponement or adjournment of the final hearing, the tribunal is obliged to order that the respondent pay the costs incurred as a result of that postponement or adjournment (Employment Tribunals (Constitution and Rules of Procedure) Regulations 2013, r76(3)).

Reinstatement

This is an order that the employer shall treat the claimant in all respects as if they had not been dismissed (s114(1) ERA 1996)).

The claimant is to be reinstated to the same contractual rights, terms and conditions as they had before they were dismissed, and the tribunal has no right to order reinstatement that alters the terms of the claimant's employment (although there is a limited right to change job duties insofar as this is not a change to the contract of employment) (*McBride v Scottish Police Authority* [2016] UKSC 27).

In making such an order the tribunal shall:

- Specify an amount payable in respect of any

benefit the claimant might reasonably have expected to have had between the Effective Date of Termination and his reinstatement, including back pay.

In calculating this figure, the tribunal must reduce the respondent's liability by the amount of any payment in lieu of notice or *ex gratia* payments by the employer, and any remuneration by another employer in the period between the EDT and the date of reinstatement, as well as any such other benefits as the tribunal thinks appropriate in the circumstances;

- State any rights and privileges to be restored to the employee;
- Specify the date by which the order must be complied with; and
- Require that the claimant be treated as if they had benefited from any improvement to their terms and conditions of employment that they would have obtained had they not been dismissed.

Re-engagement

This is an order that the claimant be engaged by the employer, a successor or associated employer, 'in employment comparable to that from which he was dismissed or other suitable employment' (s115(1) ERA 1996)). There is an exception where the employee caused or contributed to their dismissal, in which case the tribunal can order re-engagement on less favourable terms.

Any such order must specify: the identity of the employer; the nature of the employment; remuneration; back pay (as with reinstatement above); any rights and privileges to be restored to the employee; and the date to comply with the order. There are identical provisions for reducing back pay liability for re-engaged employees as there are for reinstatement.

The terms of an order for re-engagement 'must be specified with a degree of precision'. It is not sufficient to simply order that the employer employ the claimant in a comparable role (*Lincolnshire County Council v Lupton* UKEAT/0328/15/DM).

Procedure

The tribunal must first consider reinstatement and, if it decides against it, then move on to consider re-engagement.

In assessing the suitability of each order, the tribunal must consider:

- the claimant's wishes;
- the practicability of compliance by the employer;
- if the claimant caused or contributed to his

dismissal, whether it is just to order reinstatement or re-engagement.

Practicability

This is considered in two stages: first on a provisional basis at the time of making the order; second on a conclusive basis if the employer fails to comply with the order. At this second stage the burden is on the employer to prove impracticability.

Practicability is a question of fact for the tribunal, not a matter of whether the employer's views fall within a band of reasonable responses. However, where the barrier to practicability is said to be a lack of trust and confidence in an employee (for example because of the employee's dishonesty), the tribunal need only consider whether that belief is genuinely held and based on rational grounds (*Kelly v PGA European Tour* [2021] EWCA Civ 559). The cause of the loss of trust and confidence need not be conduct that resulted in dismissal, and extend to matters of which the employer was unaware during the individual's employment.

However, just because the person who took the decision to dismiss genuinely believed the claimant committed misconduct, it does not automatically follow that the employer as a whole (particularly if it is a large organisation) has lost trust and confidence in the claimant (*Keable v LB Hammersmith and Fulham* [2021] EA-2019-00733).

The matter is to be judged in a broad common-sense fashion and is to be assessed at the time an order would take effect. It is a question of possibility bearing in mind the circumstances of the employer's business and industrial relations realities. It means more than merely possible, but *'capable of being carried into effect with success'* (*Coleman v Magnet Joinery Ltd* [1985] ICR 46). It is also based on the specific employer rather than a hypothetical reasonable employer (*Kelly*, above). Relevant factors include matters such as:

- whether the parties are able to trust each other;

- whether the nature of the allegations makes it impossible for the employee and the subjects of those allegations to work together;

- whether the industrial atmosphere has been poisoned against the employee or their reinstatement or re-engagement is otherwise likely to lead to strife; or

- (Re-engagement only) whether the employee meets the essential requirements of a particular post (*Kelly*, above).

In reaching such a decision, however, the tribunal is not to take into account the fact that the employer has engaged a permanent replacement for the claimant unless the employer shows that it is not practicable to arrange for the work to be done without engaging a permanent replacement. This principle does not extend to *'comparable or suitable alternative posts [that] had become vacant, but had been filled before the remedies hearing'* (*Kelly*, above).

A tribunal is also not bound to conclude reinstatement is impracticable *'just because reinstatement may require the employer to make some adjustments to the business to accommodate the returning employee'* (*Ozkara*, above).

Non-Compliance

If an employer fails to comply with an order for reinstatement or re-engagement the tribunal will, as noted above, consider practicability on a conclusive basis with the burden of proof on the employer. If the employer fails to establish impracticability, the tribunal will make an Additional Award (see *Additional award*). Where an employer declines to re-engage (or, probably, reinstate) an employee, no interest accrues on any sum awarded under it (*Fotheringhame v Barclays Services Ltd* UKEAT/0208/19/BA).

Statutory authorities: ERA 1996 ss112 to 126

Retirement: see *Pension loss*; *Table 20*; *Table 21*

Schedule of loss

The schedule of loss is an integral part of the claim and needs to be devised with care. The sum being claimed must reflect the claimant's reasonable losses, and several versions of the schedule of loss might need to be designed to illustrate the effect of any adjustments that could be made for contributory fault for example.

In particular, future loss is notoriously difficult to calculate due the high degree of speculation involved, but the period needs to be justified, for example by taking into account the health and age of the claimant, their particular expertise and the state of the job market. Any representative should ask very direct questions of their client and check carefully all the information that has been given to them before serving a schedule of loss on the other parties and the tribunal.

See *APPENDIX 2* for an example schedule of loss.

Settlement agreements

(see also *Tax and termination payments*)

Employment may be terminated by mutual agreement, as may tribunal proceedings. Tribunal claims may be settled through early conciliation through ACAS, after the proceedings have begun through a COT3 by ACAS, by agreement between the parties or in the form of a tribunal order dismissing the proceedings upon agreement having been reached between the parties. Agreement between the parties may be reached by a number of routes both informal and formal including mediation, with some cases being mediated by tribunal judges under the official judicial mediation schemes.

Formalities

Where the agreement between the parties is reached other than by use of the COT3 procedure, any agreement by an individual that they will not bring any of a number of employment rights will be ineffective unless certain formalities have been undertaken (see for example s203 ERA 1996 and ss144 and 147 EA 2010). For the compromise of a claim to be valid:

- The contract must be in writing;

- The contract must relate to a particular complaint;

- The individual must, before entering into the contract, have received advice from a relevant independent legal advisor about its terms and effect;

- On the date of giving the advice there must have been in force insurance or an indemnity against losses arising from giving the advice;

- The contract must identify the advisor;

- The contract must state that bullet points 3 and 4 above have been complied with.

A settlement agreement or COT3 can be set aside by an Employment Tribunal on the same common law grounds as any other agreement (e.g. misrepresentation, duress, undue influence): *Cole v Elders' Voice* UKEAT/0251/19.

Non-Disclosure Agreements (NDAs)

It is common for settlement agreements to contain clauses requiring parties to keep the nature and terms of the agreement, and/or the circumstances giving rise to it, confidential. These clauses are the subject of ongoing public, political and regulatory scrutiny and controversy.

It is beyond the scope of this work to address the matter in detail, but representatives are advised to keep an eye on the potential for ongoing regulatory and legal developments in this area, and to have particular regard to the Law Society's practice note: *Non-disclosure agreements and confidentiality clauses in an employment law context*.

Contractual entitlements

Where a settlement agreement makes payment for contractual payments that have already crystallised, it may well be that such sums would be taxable as earnings rather than under s401 ITEPA 2003 (see *EIM12856*).

Legal expenses

The employer may agree to pay legal costs incurred by the employee. Such a payment may be within s401 ITEPA 2003 since it is made in connection with the termination (see *EIM13010*), but there is a potential tax exemption where the fees are paid directly to the employee's lawyers (see *Tax and termination payments*).

What tax rate should be used when deducting tax?

PAYE74015 explains the different rules when deducting tax.

Termination payment made on or before date of P45

If the termination payment is paid on or before the P45 is issued, tax and NI will be deducted from any taxable termination payment through the normal payroll using the employee's tax code at that date.

Termination payment made after the date of P45

Any taxable termination payments made after the P45 is issued should have tax deducted using the tax code 0T (effectively ignoring any personal tax allowance) and on a non-cumulative basis (which treats each pay period as a separate tax period). This can mean that the employee pays too much tax initially and would have to claim it back from HMRC on their self-assessment.

Sometimes payments paid in instalments may benefit the cash flow for both parties. Each tranche of the termination payment will be taxable independently on the above 0T basis, on the date of entitlement.

For monthly paid employees (using 2023/2024 tax bands)

Only the first £3,142 (i.e. 1/12 x £37,700) of the settlement payment will be charged at the basic rate of 20%;

The next £9,358 (i.e. 1/12 x (£150,000 - £37,700) = 1/12 x £112,300) will be charged to tax at the higher rate of 40%; and

Any remaining balance of the termination payment will be taxed at the additional rate of 45%.

Example

A termination payment of £75,000 is paid to an employee on 01/05/2023 after his P45 has been issued. £55,000 of this payment is taxable. He will pay:

20% of £3,142 = £628.40, plus

40% of £9,358 = £3,743.20, plus

45% of (£55,000 − £3,142 − £9,358) = 45% of £42,500 = £19,125

So his total tax liability, which is payable immediately by the employer, is £23,496.60.

Sex discrimination: see *Discrimination*

Sex Equality Clause

A 'sex equality clause' is implied into every contract of employment, if one is not already present (s66 EA 2010). The effect of a sex equality clause is that any term of an individual's contract of employment, if it is less favourable to him or her than the same term is to a comparable employee of the opposite sex, will be modified so as to not be less favourable. A comparable employee will be of the opposite sex, and the work they are employed to do will be equal (s64 and 65 EA 2010).

This applies to all the parts of the contract including:

- wages and salaries;
- non-discretionary bonuses;
- holiday pay;
- sick pay;
- overtime;
- shift payments;
- occupational pension benefits; and
- non-monetary terms such as holiday or other leave entitlements or access to sports and social benefits.

An employee may bring a claim to the tribunal for breach of his/her sex equality clause under s132 EA 2010.

Remedy: If a tribunal finds that there has been a breach of the sex equality clause it may make a declaration as to the rights of the parties (for example, stating what pay or rate of pay the individual is entitled to). The tribunal may also order an award of arrears of pay or damages (s132 EA 2010).

A limit is imposed on the period over which arrears of pay may be claimed (see s132(4)). In the standard case arrears over the preceding 6 years may be awarded, but where the breach of the clause has been concealed or the individual had an incapacity at the date of the breach, and the claim was presented within 6 years of the date the claimant knew of the claim or was capable of bringing the claim, arrears may be claimed from the date the arrears first occurred (s132(3) EA 2010).

Gross or net: Gross (but then taxed by the employer in the normal way through the payroll).

Limit on a week's pay: None

Limit on number of years: Normally 6

Adjustments: Interest can be awarded for arrears of pay and will be calculated according to the mid-point rule (see *Interest*).

Any maximum or minimum: None

Tax: Awards (or settlements) in respect of claims under the Equal Pay Act 1970 (now EA 2010 Part V, Ch 3) are arrears of pay and therefore should be taxed under s62 ITEPA 2003 (see *EIM02530* HMRC). The tax liability arises in the year of entitlement not in the year of eventual payment. It is unclear whether any interest would also be taxed.

Statutory authorities: EA 2010 *ss66* and *132*; *Employment Tribunals (Interest on Awards in Discrimination Cases) Regulations 1996*

Share options: see *Financial losses*

Shared parental leave (SPL): see *Parental leave*

Short time working: see *Guarantee payment*; *Week's pay*

Sickness: see *Holiday pay*

Social security benefits: see *Income support*; *Job seekers allowance*; *Non-recoupable state benefits*; *Recoupment*

State pension

This is the pension based on previous NI contributions paid. Women born after 5 April 1953 and men born after 5 April 1951 will claim the new State Pension (nSP) and will need a certain number of NI qualifying years to receive any nSP. See *Table 20* and *Table 21* for state pension ages for men and women and *Table 22* for the current weekly state pension and the number of qualifying years required.

Claimants are not expected to give credit for any state pension benefits received when a tribunal assesses losses suffered by a claimant.

Loss of state pension on termination of employment can be claimed in some circumstances - see *Pension loss* for more information.

Statutory cap

(see also *Additional award*; *Arrears of pay (reinstatement/re-engagement)*; *Compensatory award*; *Discrimination*; *Recoupment*; *Table 1***)**

A statutory cap applies to a compensatory award under s117(1) and (2) ERA and s123. The applicable statutory cap is the lower of the current figure of £105,707 or 52 weeks' gross pay (as defined in ss220 to 229 ERA

1996) (see s124 ERA 1996). *Table 1* lists the historical statutory caps.

Because the definition of a week's pay does not cover all pay or valuable benefits received, an employee may not be compensated for an entire year's losses. However, the cap applies to 52 weeks' gross pay, which effectively means that a claimant could be awarded up to 15 to 16 months' net pay, assuming a combined tax/NI rate of 30%.

There are three situations in which the cap does not apply:

- If the reason for dismissal was discriminatory, the financial losses will be awarded under the discrimination legislation where there is no cap;

- If the employee is regarded as unfairly dismissed by virtue of s100 or 105(3) (Health and Safety cases), 103A or 105(6A) (Whistleblowing);

- If an award under s117 would otherwise not fully reflect the amount of arrears payable to the employee (see also *Arrears of pay (reinstatement/re-engagement)*).

The cap is applied after all the adjustments such as contributory conduct and *Polkey* have been applied. It is imposed after any deduction is made for sums paid on account e.g. due to an order for reinstatement (*Dafiaghor-Olomu v Community Integrated Care* [2022] EAT 84). It is also applied **after** any grossing up calculation has been done.

Example

Basic award = £11,000

Compensatory award after all adjustments (see *Adjustments and order of adjustments*) = £90,000

Grossing up calculation (assuming marginal tax rate of 25%)

Gross up £11,000 + £90,000 - £30,000 = £71,000

Grossed up compensatory award of £71,000 = 71,000 ÷ 0.75 = £94,666.67

Compensatory award now = £19,000 + £94,666.67 = £113,666.67

Statutory cap = £105,707

Total award = £11,000 + £105,707 = £116,707

Note: the grossing up should be done **before** the cap is applied.

Statutory authorities: ERA 1996 *ss117(1) & (2), 100, 103A, 105(3), 105(6A), 123* and *124*

Statutory notice period

(see also *Contractual notice period*; *Effective date of termination*; *Table 14***)**

Section 86 ERA 1996) provides for minimum notice of termination to be given by the parties to the contract of employment. Under normal circumstances, an employee with more than 1 month's continuous service is entitled to 1 week's notice, and having completed 2 years' service is entitled to 2 weeks, with the number of weeks increasing by one each year until a maximum of 12 weeks' notice. The notice an employee must give an employer, having completed 1 month's service, is 1 week (see *Table 14*).

By s86(6) no notice need be given by either party where the other has so seriously breached the contract as to be regarded as having repudiated the contract, in which case the other party may accept the breach and terminate the contract without notice, for example where an employee has committed gross misconduct.

The parties to an employment contract may agree to a longer, contractual notice period. The parties may also waive their right to notice on any occasion or accept payment in lieu of notice (see s86(3)).

Statutory redundancy: see *Redundancy*; *Table 13*; *Table 14*

Statutory rights

One of the heads of loss for which a tribunal may award compensation is the value of accrued statutory rights that have been lost: where an employee begins a new job following the termination of their employment, they will need to accrue 2 years' continuous service before they will have acquired the right to claim unfair dismissal or a statutory redundancy payment, and may have lost the right to a lengthy statutory notice period if they have been employed for several years. The sum awarded is usually between £250 and £500, and is not generally governed by the personal circumstances of the employee such as would increase or decrease the actual value of the loss.

Remedy: There is no particular figure that should be awarded, but it is usually around £250 to £500. In *Countrywide Estate Agents & Ors v Turner* UKEAT/0208/13/LA, the EAT held that the ET was entitled to award 2 weeks' gross pay (limited to the weekly pay in force) for loss of statutory rights, as the claimant would take another 2 years to accrue those rights.

No award should be made where there is a finding that the claimant would have been fairly dismissed in any event (*Puglia v C James and Sons* [1996] IRLR 70).

Any maximum or minimum: None

Adjustments: The award is part of the compensatory award and will be adjusted accordingly (see *Hope v Jordan Engineering Ltd* [2008] UKEAT/0545/07). This includes *Polkey* deductions (*Gardner v The Coopers Company & Coborn School* UKEAT/0235/19/BA).

Cap: The award is part of the compensatory award (see *Statutory cap*).

Tax: The award is part of the compensatory award and will be subject to the grossing up calculation, if appropriate, in the normal way.

Recoupment: Recoupment will not apply to this head of loss.

Relevant case law: *Countrywide Estate Agents & Ors v Turner* UKEAT/0208/13/LA; *Gardner v The Coopers Company & Coborn School* UKEAT/0235/19/BA; *Hope v Jordan Engineering Ltd* [2008] UKEAT/0545/07; *Puglia v C James and Sons* [1996] IRLR 70

Summary dismissal: see *Effective date of termination*; *Notice pay*

Suspension

Part VII ERA 1996 provides the express right for an employee to be paid whilst suspended for particular reasons:

1) An employee who is suspended from work by his employer on medical grounds is entitled to be paid by his employer remuneration while he is so suspended for a period not exceeding 26 weeks (s64(1) ERA 1996);

2) An employee who is suspended from work on maternity grounds is entitled to be paid remuneration by her employer while she is so suspended (s68(1) ERA 1996). Suspension on maternity grounds in effect means suspension on grounds that a woman is pregnant, has recently given birth or is breastfeeding;

3) However, the employee has a right to be offered suitable alternative work, where it exists, before being suspended from work on maternity grounds (s67(1) ERA 1996);

4) Related rights to remuneration or alternative work apply to agency workers, see ss68A to 68D ERA 1996.

A common thread between these rights is that the suspension must be required by other legislative provisions, generally regarding the health and safety of workers (see ss64(2) to (4) and s66 ERA 1996).

An employee may bring a claim that his or her employer has not paid them the remuneration to which they are entitled (see s70 ERA 1996). A similar right exists for agency workers, regarding their maternity suspension rights (see s70A ERA 1996).

Remedy: Where the tribunal finds that the employee or agency worker has not been paid the remuneration to which he or she was entitled, the tribunal will order the employer (or agency) to pay the individual the amount of remuneration which it finds is due to him or her (ss70(3) and 70A(3) ERA 1996). Remuneration is calculated according to the definition of a week's pay (see *Week's pay*) in s220 to s229 (see s69), save that the limit on a week's pay does not apply.

Where a tribunal finds that suitable alternative work has not been provided to an employee or agency worker, the tribunal may make an award of compensation (see s70(6) and (7) and s70A(6) and (7) ERA 1996). The amount of the compensation is that which the tribunal considers just and equitable in all the circumstances having regard to:

a) the infringement of the employee's right under s67 by the failure on the part of the employer to which the complaint relates; and

b) any loss sustained by the employee which is attributable to that failure.

It is likely that an award for injury to feelings can be made where there has been a failure to provide suitable alternative work, since the statutory wording for calculating the loss is that used in the detriment provisions (s49 ERA 1996) and the protection of a woman who may be suspended on maternity grounds may be seen to be akin to the protection provided by discrimination legislation.

Gross or net: The award for lost remuneration will be calculated gross, as the definition of a week's pay in ss220 to 229 ERA 1996 applies (see *Week's pay*).

The award for a failure to provide suitable alternative work will be based on net losses, and also any injury to feelings award.

Limit on a week's pay: None

Limit on number of weeks: 26 weeks' remuneration for suspension on medical grounds (see s64(1)); otherwise unlimited

Any maximum or minimum: None, other than the maximum award will be 26 weeks' actual gross pay where the award is for remuneration for suspension on medical grounds (see s64(1)).

Adjustments: None

Tax: To the extent that the sum awarded is compensation for lost earnings, it is likely to be taxed under s62 ITEPA 2003 (see *Tax and termination payments* and EIM02550).

Recoupment: Recoupment applies to awards made in

respect of a failure to pay remuneration (see Schedule to *The Employment Protection (Recoupment of Jobseeker's Allowance and Income Support) Regulations 1996)*.

Statutory authorities: ERA 1996 *ss64(1), 67(1)* and *s68(1)*; Schedule to *The Employment Protection (Recoupment of Jobseeker's Allowance and Income Support) Regulations 1996*

Tax and termination payments

(see also *Gourley principle*; *Grossing up*; *Injury to feelings***)**

Specific tax regimes apply to income and benefits derived from employment (*s62* ITEPA 2003), and to payments made in connection with employment (*ss401 to 416* ITEPA 2003). Where a tribunal makes a monetary award it will take into account how that sum will be treated for tax: the award may amount to an order that the employer pay salary; the award may be for a sum due in connection with employment; an award may fall outside the tax regimes or fall within an exception or allowance. Where tax will be paid by the claimant on the sum he receives, the tribunal will gross up the award to ensure that the sum received after tax is appropriate.

The tax regimes apply to a variety of sums including earnings, *ex gratia* payments, sums paid under settlement agreements and tribunal awards. The tax treatment of any sum will depend on the nature of the underlying sum, and the circumstances of its payment. Essentially, any sum will be taxed under the applicable employment provisions (see further below) - if none of them apply then the sum may be taxed as being paid in connection with termination. If none of the foregoing regimes apply, the payment will not be subject to tax.

By way of example:

- Earnings and benefits will be taxed (and have NIC deducted) by the employer under the applicable tax code;

- An award by a tribunal that an employer pay unlawfully deducted wages will be calculated gross, and the employer will pay the sum (and deduct tax on it) as he does wages;

- Sums paid under a termination agreement between employer and employee, providing for sums owing under the contract that are earnings, will be taxed by the employer under the applicable tax code;

- Sums paid under a termination agreement between employer and employee, which do not amount to sums owing under the contract that

are earnings, such as an enhanced redundancy payment, may fall within the regime for payments made in connection with termination. A £30,000 allowance applies to such sums;

- An award by a tribunal for losses arising from unfair dismissal, including the failure to pay an enhanced redundancy payment, will be treated as a payment made in connection with termination, where the £30,000 allowance applies.

Some sums do not fall within easily identifiable categories, for example, punitive awards such as a protective award, injury to feelings and an award for discrimination occurring independently of termination.

The applicable principles are dealt with below.

Identifying the applicable tax regime

The starting point is to ascertain whether the payment could be classed as earnings, in which case tax and employee and employer NI will be payable under *s62* ITEPA 2003, or as a taxable benefit under Part 3 Chapters 2 to 11 ITEPA 2003.

If the payment does not fall under the category of earnings, the next consideration is whether it is a payment in consideration of a restrictive covenant, in which case it is fully taxable (*s225* ITEPA 2003).

If neither of the first two conditions apply, the next question is whether the payment is in respect of an employer-financed retirement benefit, taxable under Part 6 Chapter 2 of ITEPA 2003.

If the answer to all the previous questions is in the negative, and the payment is '*received directly or indirectly in consideration of or in consequence of or otherwise in connection with the termination of employment, a change in the duties of a person's employment, or a change in the earnings from a person's employment*', it will be taxed under Part 6 Chapter 3 of ITEPA. A tax free allowance of £30,000 applies to such payments.

From 6 April 2020, in respect of any payments which fall under s401 ITEPA 2003, employer (but not employee) National Insurance is payable on any amount exceeding £30,000.

If none of the above apply, the compensation is unconnected with the employment or its termination and is therefore outside the scope of income tax and NIC. For example, payments or awards for damages for breach of contract prior to termination do not fall within the above provisions, neither do awards for injury to feelings from discrimination unconnected with termination.

Fully taxable and subject to NI deductions

- Earnings from employment;

- Arrears of pay (but see 'Reinstatement or re-engagement' later in this entry);

- Accrued holiday pay;

- Payments made in consideration of restrictive covenants (s225 ITEPA 2003), unless the specific consideration is attached to the restatement of existing covenants or an agreement to discontinue proceedings (see *Appellant v Inspector of Taxes* [2001] STC (SCD) 21);

- Payment in respect of a non-approved retirement benefit;

- Contractual and non-contractual PILONs;

- Implied contractual right to a PILON;

- Termination payments/'post employment notice pay';

- Contractual benefits in kind;

- Payments during garden leave;

- Payments to an employee suspended from work on medical grounds under Sections *64* and *70(3)* ERA 1996 (EIM02550, HMRC);

- Maternity suspension payments under Sections 68 and 70(3) ERA 1996 (EIM02550, HMRC);

- Payments under Sections 51(3)(b) or 63(4) ERA 1996 for infringing the employee's rights to time off for public duties under s50 or Trade Union duties or activities under ss61 and 62 respectively (EIM02550, HMRC);

- Payments under the Sex Discrimination Acts, the Equal Pay Act 1970 (see *EIM02530*), the Wages Act 1986, the Trade Union and Labour Relations (Consolidation) Act 1992 and the National Minimum Wage Act 1998 for wrongfully depressing the employee's remuneration in the employment (*EIM02550*, HMRC).

Payments which are fully taxable by the employer before payment to the individual should not be grossed up by the tribunal.

Payments in lieu of notice (PILONS)

From 6 April 2018, payments in lieu of notice, whether contractual or otherwise, are taxable as earnings and are not taxed under, or qualify for, any exemptions in ss401 to 416 ITEPA 2003. The taxable component is defined as "post employment notice pay" and calculated In line with the formula in s402D ITEPA 2003. This is fully subject to income tax and Class 1 NICs. Any element that exceeds this, however, is subject to the £30,000 threshold under ITEPA 2003. Previously, only payments where there was an express or implied contractual right to a PILON, or where there was a discretion to make a PILON, were fully taxable (see *EMI Group Electronics Ltd v Coldicott* [1999] IRLR 630).

Subject to the above, where a payment made on termination, in a settlement agreement or in the form of a tribunal award, falls within Part 6 Chapter 3 of ITEPA, that particular regime will apply. This includes a £30,000 allowance, so for example in a straightforward unfair dismissal award made by a tribunal the first £30,000 will be exempt from tax, and any award above this will be grossed up by the tribunal to ensure the individual retains the value of his net loss. However, note *Hill v Revenue & Customs* [2015] UKFTT 295 (TC) where the claimant was transferred under TUPE and the tribunal did not accept his argument that a payment of £30,000 in settlement of his grievance was not taxable because his employment was ongoing.

Payments and other benefits that fall within this regime include:

- Non-contractual benefits in kind;

- Statutory, non-contractual and contractual redundancy payments, provided that they are genuinely on account of redundancy (see *Mairs v Haughey* [1994] 1 AC 303);

- Basic award;

- Awards for financial loss whether for unfair dismissal or as a result of discrimination;

- Damages for wrongful dismissal;

- An additional award;

- An award for employer failing to provide a statement of written particulars (see *EIM12960*);

- Protective awards;

- Payment by the employer of the employee's legal expenses (but see 'Specific categories of award' below).

Any part of the total award in excess of the £30,000 tax free allowance and which has been calculated on a net basis should be grossed up to ensure the employee receives the sum that has been awarded. This means that any of the compensatory award or award of damages which forms part or all of the excess figure should be grossed up.

Exempt from taxation

Certain payments are exempted from taxation under s401 ITEPA 2003 and will therefore not be taxed at all. Payments include:

- Payment made by reason of the death of an employee or on account of an injury to, or disability of, the employee (but **not** for injured feelings – see *Injury to feelings*);

- Payment of legal expenses where the sum is either awarded by the tribunal or paid under a settlement agreement directly to the individual's lawyer (*Enactment of Extra-Statutory Concessions Order 2011 SI 2011/1037*, Article 10);

- Certain costs in connection with counselling, outplacement and retraining courses (ss310 and 311 ITEPA 2003).

Payments which are exempt from tax should not be grossed up.

Foreign service exemption

Prior to 6 April 2018, full and partial exemptions applied to payments made in respect of foreign service, where an employee was both non-resident and non-ordinarily resident in the UK (s413 ITEPA 2003). From 6 April 2018, employees who are UK resident in the tax year their employment is terminated will not be eligible for foreign service relief on their termination payment.

Specific categories of award

Unlawful deduction from wages

A tribunal ought to award payment for unlawful deduction from wages under s13 ERA 1996 gross, with the employer deducting tax and NIC at source, as such payments fall within s62 ITEPA 2003.

Reinstatement or re-engagement

Where a tribunal has made an award for lost salary between the date of dismissal and the reinstatement or re-engagement, that sum is not taxed as earnings under s62 ITEPA 2003 but will fall within s401 (*Wilson v Clayton* [2005] IRLR 108). Such sums will be calculated on a net basis and grossed up where appropriate (see *EIM12960*).

Discrimination not involving termination

According to HMRC in EIM12965 and *Yorkshire Housing Ltd v Cuerden* UKEAT/0397/09, compensation payments made for discrimination that does not cause termination will not be subject to tax. See also *Mr A v Revenue & Customs (Income tax/Corporation tax: Employment income)* [2015] UKFTT 189 where the claimant accepted £600,000 in settlement of his threatened claim for discrimination. The first tier tribunal ruled that the reason the payment was made by the employer was (rightly or wrongly on their part) to settle a discrimination claim and not to pay back money which they thought the appellant was entitled to in respect of underpaid salary and bonus.

Compensation payments would include any financial and non-financial losses such as an award for injury to feelings. Such an award should be calculated on a net basis, and there will not be a need to gross up.

Discrimination involving termination

Awards made in connection with termination arising from discrimination will be taxable under s401 ITEPA 2003 (*Walker v Adams* [2001] STC 101, *Orthet v Vince*

Cain [2004] IRLR 857 and *Oti-Obihara v Commissioners for HM Revenue & Customs* [2011] IRLR 386 and *Moorthy v The Commissioners for Her Majesty's Revenue & Customs* [2014] UKFTT 834 (TC), and *Moorthy v Revenue & Customs* [2016] UKUT 13 (TC).

Equality clauses

Where an award is made for breach of an equality clause, the award will be subject to tax on the basis of the tax due in the year the sum ought to have been paid (EIM02530). The award should be calculated on a gross basis, with the employer operating an appropriate special PAYE procedure.

Injury to feelings

Awards for injury to feelings unrelated to termination of employment are tax-free, as are such awards related to the termination of employment prior to 6 April 2018 (*Moorthy v HMRC* [2018] EWCA Civ 847). However, from 6 April 2018, any compensation for injury to feelings in a termination payment is taxable to the extent that the £30,000 'allowance' has been exceeded, following an amendment to s406 ITEPA 2003, except where the compensation is for a psychiatric injury.

The breadth of the wording of s401 means that it does not apply solely to awards for injury to feelings in consequence of a claimant's dismissal, but also those *"in connection with"* them (*Slade v Biggs* [2021] EA-2019-000687).

Protective awards and TUPE consultation

Though protective awards are calculated by reference to pay over a protected period, such sums are not paid by reference to the individual acting as an employee, but under statute (and as punishment for breach of a statutory obligation) (see *Mimtec Ltd v Inland Revenue* [2001] UKSC SPC00277). They therefore fall under s401 rather than s62 ITEPA 2003.

The logic applied in *Mimtec* might suggest that where an award has been made for failure to inform and consult under TUPE, which is unconnected to any termination, the award would not be subject to tax at all. Where an individual in receipt of such an award has been subject to a transfer, it might be argued that the transfer, for the purposes of the tax regime, did amount to a termination (see *Kuehne & Nagel Drinks Logistics Ltd, Scott & Joyce v HMRC* [2009] UKFTT 379 (TC)). That argument would not however apply to an individual affected by the transfer, whose representatives were not appropriately consulted, but who did not themselves transfer.

Payments unrelated to termination

Where an award is made for breach of a statutory right, for example if the employer has not complied with the right of an employee to be accompanied at a disciplinary hearing, this is unrelated to the individual's termination and may well not be earnings. There is no official guidance on how such sums should be treated. However, the logic in *Mimtec Ltd v Inland Revenue* [2001] UKSC SPC00277, that such sums are not paid by reference to the individual acting as an employee but under statute (and as punishment for breach of a statutory obligation), could apply. Such payments may well not be subject to tax and should not be grossed up.

Payment of employee's legal expenses by the employer

An employer may agree to pay legal costs incurred by an employee in relation to a claim against the employer after the contract of employment has been terminated. Such a payment falls within s401 ITEPA 2003 since it is made in connection with the termination (see EIM13010), but as a concession the sum will not be charged where:

1) the dispute is settled without recourse to the courts and three conditions are met:

   a) the payment is made direct to the employee's solicitor rather than to the employee himself or herself; and

   b) the payment is applied to discharge the bill for solicitor's costs that the employee has incurred only in connection with the termination of the employment; and

   c) the payment is made under a specific term in the agreement that settles the dispute;

or

2) the payment of costs by the employer is made in accordance with a court order. This applies even if the payment is made directly to the employee.

Note that the concession:

- applies only to legal costs, not to any other professional costs (such as accountancy fees). However, it does include the expenses of expert professional witnesses incurred by the employee's legal advisor;

- does not allow an employee to claim a deduction for his or her own legal costs in any way.

Interim relief

Payments made under a continuation order are taxable as payments in connection with termination under s401, not in full as earnings under s62 ITEPA (see also *Interim relief*). See *Turullols v HMRC* [2014] UKFTT 672 (TC) where the First Tier Tribunal held that the claimant, who was found to have been unfairly dismissed, could claim back the tax that had been paid on the salary payments made under the interim relief order because they were payments in connection with the termination of her employment and therefore should have been tax-free up to £30,000. This would also have been the case even if the ET had not upheld the unfair dismissal claim.

National Insurance

From 6 April 2020, Employer National Insurance, but not employee NI, is payable at 13.8% on any amount above £30,000.

Time off to accompany to ante-natal appointment

(see also *Time off for ante-natal care*)

An expectant father, or the partner of a pregnant woman, and other employees who have a qualifying relationship with a pregnant woman or her expected child are entitled to be permitted by his or her employer to take time off during the employee's working hours in order that he or she may accompany the woman when she attends by appointment at any place for the purpose of receiving ante-natal care (s57ZE ERA 1996).

An employee may present a complaint to an employment tribunal that his or her employer has unreasonably refused to let him or her take time off as required by s57ZE.

Equivalent rights to time off and remuneration for the period of absence are given to agency workers, with the remuneration to be paid by the agency (see s57ZH).

Remedy: Where a tribunal finds a complaint well founded, it will make a declaration to that effect (s57ZF(4a)).

Further, if the tribunal has found that the employer has unreasonably refused to permit the employee to take time off, the tribunal will also order the employer to pay compensation to the employee according to the following formula (s57ZF(5)):

> Amount to be paid = Appropriate hourly rate for the employee x Number of working hours for which the employee would have been entitled under s57ZE to be absent if the time off had not been refused x 2

Unless the employee works a varying number of working hours, the appropriate hourly rate is one week's pay divided by the normal working hours in a week when the time off would have been taken. For employees whose hours of work vary over a week or longer period, the appropriate hourly rate is obtained by dividing one week's pay by the average number of hours worked over the previous 12 weeks, or where the employee has not been employed for 12 weeks, a number which fairly represents the number of normal working hours in a week (see s57ZF(7)).

A week's pay will be calculated in accordance with s220 to s229 ERA 1996 (see *Week's pay*).

Gross or net: The sum for unpaid earnings will be calculated gross and paid through payroll as with ordinary remuneration.

Any maximum or minimum: None

Adjustments: The claimant will have to give credit for any amount paid towards the entitlement under the contract.

Mitigation: N/A

Tax: The tax treatment is not clear. To the extent that the sum awarded is compensation for lost earnings for work done, it is likely to be taxed under s62 ITEPA 2003 (see *Tax and termination payments*).

Recoupment: N/A

Statutory authorities: ERA 1996 ss57ZE and 57ZF

Time off to attend adoption appointments

Employees proposing to adopt a child may take time off to attend up to 5 adoption appointments. The time off must be paid where the employee is adopting the child on their own (ss57ZJ to ZL ERA 1996).

If the employee is adopting jointly, then one of the parents may elect to receive the time off as paid and the other will be entitled to take unpaid leave for up to 2 appointments.

A maximum of 6 ½ hours is allowed for each appointment in all cases.

An employee may present a complaint to an employment tribunal that his or her employer has unreasonably refused to let him or her take time off as required by s57ZJ to L. Equivalent rights to time off and remuneration for the period of absence are given to agency workers, with the remuneration to be paid by the agency (see s57ZN).

Remedy: Where a tribunal finds a complaint well founded, it will make a declaration to that effect (s57ZM(4)).

If the complaint is that the employer has failed to pay the employee the whole or part of any amount to which the employee is entitled under s57ZK (paid time off), the tribunal must order the employer to pay compensation to the employee the amount which it finds due to the employee.

Further, if the tribunal has found that the employer has unreasonably refused to permit the employee to take time off, the tribunal will also order the employer to pay to the employee according to the following formula (s57ZM(7)):

Amount to be paid = Appropriate hourly rate for the

employee x Number of working hours for which the employee would have been entitled under s57Z to be absent if the time off had not been refused x 2

Unless the employee works a varying number of working hours, the appropriate hourly rate is one week's pay divided by the normal working hours in a week when the time off would have been taken. For employees whose hours of work vary over a week or longer period, the appropriate hourly rate is obtained by dividing one week's pay by the average number of hours worked over the previous 12 weeks, or where the employee has not been employed for 12 weeks, a number which fairly represents the number of normal working hours in a week (see s57ZK).

A week's pay will be calculated in accordance with s220 to s229 ERA 1996 (see *Week's pay*).

Gross or net: The sum for unpaid earnings will be calculated gross and paid through payroll as with ordinary remuneration.

Any maximum or minimum: None

Adjustments: The claimant will have to give credit for any amount paid towards the entitlement under the contract.

Mitigation: N/A

Tax: The tax treatment is not clear. To the extent that the sum awarded is compensation for lost earnings for work done, it is likely to be taxed under s62 ITEPA 2003 (see *Tax and termination payments*).

Recoupment: N/A

Statutory authorities: ERA 1996 ss57ZJ to 57ZN

Time off for ante-natal care

(see also *Time off to accompany to ante-natal appointment*)

An employee who has an appointment for the purpose of receiving ante-natal care is entitled to be permitted by her employer to take time off during the employee's working hours in order to enable her to keep the appointment (s55 ERA 1996).

The employee is entitled to be paid at their 'appropriate hourly rate' for their period of absence. Unless the employee works a varying number of working hours, the appropriate hourly rate is one week's pay divided by the normal working hours in a week when the time off was taken. For employees whose hours of work vary over a week or longer period, the appropriate hourly rate is obtained by dividing one week's pay by the average number of hours worked over the previous 12 weeks, or where the employee has not been employed for 12 weeks, a number which fairly represents the number of normal working hours in a week (see s56(2), (3) and (4) ERA 1996).

A week's pay will be calculated in accordance with ss220 to 229 ERA 1996 (see *Week's pay*).

Any contractual remuneration paid to an employee in respect of such a period of time off goes towards discharging the liability under s56 (see s56(5) and (6) ERA 1996).

An employee may bring a complaint to a tribunal that her employer has unreasonably refused to permit her to take the time off under s55, or has failed to pay the sums due under s56 (see s57(1) ERA 1996).

Equivalent rights to time off and remuneration for the period of absence are given to agency workers, with the remuneration to be paid by the agency (see ss57ZA to 57ZD).

Remedy: Where a tribunal finds a complaint well founded, it will make a declaration to that effect (s57(3)).

Further, if the tribunal has found that the employer has unreasonably refused to permit the employee to take time off, the tribunal will also order the employer to pay to the employee an amount equal to the remuneration to which she would have been entitled under s56 if the employer had not refused (s57(4)). Also, if the tribunal finds that the employer has failed to pay the employee the whole or part of any amount to which she is entitled under s56, the tribunal will also order the employer to pay to the employee the amount she is owed (s57(5)).

For employees working fixed number of hours per week

Sum to which the employee is entitled = (gross weekly pay) x 1/(number of normal working hours in a week) x (number of hours absent) (s56(2) ERA 1996)

For employees with varying number of hours worked per week

Sum to which the employee is entitled = gross weekly pay x 12/(number of normal hours worked in the last 12 weeks ending with the last complete week before the day on which the time off is taken) x (number of hours absent) (s56(3) ERA 1996)

For employees with varying number of hours worked per week and who have worked for less than 12 weeks

Sum to which the employee is entitled = (gross weekly pay) x 1/(number of normal hours which fairly represents the number of normal working hours in a week) x (number of hours absent) (s56(3) and (4) ERA 1996)

Gross or net: The sum for unpaid earnings will be calculated gross and paid through payroll as with ordinary remuneration.

Any maximum or minimum: None

Adjustments: The claimant will have to give credit for any amount paid towards the entitlement under the contract.

Mitigation: N/A

Tax: The tax treatment is not clear. To the extent that the sum awarded is compensation for lost earnings for work done, it is likely to be taxed under s62 ITEPA 2003 (see *Tax and termination payments*).

Recoupment: N/A

Statutory authorities: ERA 1996 *ss55, 56* and *ss57ZA to 57ZD*

Time off for dependants

An employee is entitled to be permitted by his employer to take a reasonable amount of time off during the employee's working hours in order to care for or sort out issues in relation to a dependant (s57A ERA 1996). The definition of a dependant includes amongst others a spouse, a civil partner, a child and a parent.

An employee may bring a complaint to a tribunal that his employer has unreasonably refused to permit him to take this time off (s57B ERA 1996).

Remedy: Where the tribunal finds such a complaint well founded it will make a declaration to that effect (s57B(3)(a)).

It may also make an award of compensation to be paid by the employer (s57B(3)(b) and (4)).

The amount of compensation will be that which it considers just and equitable in all the circumstances having regard to:

a)   the employer's default in refusing to permit time off to be taken by the employee; and

b)   any loss sustained by the employee as a result.

Any maximum or minimum: There is no statutory limit to the compensation.

Adjustments: N/A

Mitigation: It is likely that the principle of mitigation would be applied in an appropriate case. However, this would most likely operate to restrict the losses that would be compensated for where it would have been reasonable for the employee to have incurred a lower level of losses than were in fact incurred, for example where the alternative care was unreasonably expensive and reasonably avoidable.

Tax: The tax treatment is not clear. To the extent that the sum awarded is compensation for lost earnings for work done, it is likely to be taxed under s62 ITEPA 2003 (see *Tax and termination payments* and EIM02550).

Recoupment: N/A

Statutory authorities: ERA 1996 *s57A and 57B*

Time off for employee representatives

An employee representative for the purposes of collective consultation or TUPE consultation is entitled to take reasonable time off during the employee's working hours to perform his functions as such an employee representative, or candidate in an election for such a role, or in order to undergo training to perform such functions (s61 ERA 1996).

The employee is entitled to be paid at their 'appropriate hourly rate' for their period of absence. Unless the employee works a varying number of working hours, the appropriate hourly rate is one week's pay divided by the normal working hours in a week when the time off was taken.

For employees whose hours of work vary over a week or longer period, the appropriate hourly rate is obtained by dividing one week's pay by the average number of hours worked over the previous 12 weeks, or where the employee has not been employed for 12 weeks, a number which fairly represents the number of normal working hours in a week (s62 ERA 1996).

A week's pay will be calculated in accordance with ss220 to 229 ERA 1996 (see *Week's pay*).

Any contractual remuneration paid to an employee in respect of such a period of time off goes towards discharging the liability under s62 (see s62(5) and (6)).

An employee may bring a complaint to a tribunal that his or her employer has unreasonably refused to permit him or her to take the time off under s61, or has failed to pay the sums due under s62 (see s63(1) ERA 1996).

Remedy: Where a tribunal finds a complaint well founded, it will make a declaration to that effect (s63(3) ERA 1996).

Further, if the tribunal has found that the employer has unreasonably refused to permit the employee to take time off, the tribunal will also order the employer to pay to the employee an amount equal to the remuneration to which he or she would have been entitled under s62 if the employer had not refused (s63(4) ERA 1996).

Also, if the tribunal finds that the employer has failed to pay the employee the whole or part of any amount to which he or she is entitled under s62, the tribunal will also order the employer to pay to the employee the amount he or she is owed (s63(5) ERA 1996).

For employees working fixed number of hours per week

Sum to which the employee is entitled = (gross weekly pay) x 1/(number of normal working hours in a week) x (number of hours absent) (s62(2) ERA 1996)

For employees with varying number of hours worked per week

Sum to which the employee is entitled = gross weekly pay x 12/(number of normal hours worked in the last 12 weeks ending with the last complete week before the day on which the time off is taken) x (number of hours absent) (s62(3)(a) ERA 1996)

For employees with varying number of hours worked per week and who have worked for less than 12 weeks

Sum to which the employee is entitled = (gross weekly pay) x 1/(number of normal hours which fairly represents the number of normal working hours in a week) x (number of hours absent) (s62(3) and (4) ERA 1996)

Gross or net: The sum will be calculated gross and paid through payroll as with ordinary remuneration.

Any maximum or minimum: None

Adjustments: The claimant will have to give credit for any amount paid towards the entitlement under the contract.

Mitigation: N/A

Tax: Taxable under s62 ITEPA 2003 (see *EIM02550*).

Recoupment: N/A

Statutory authorities: ERA 1996 *ss61 to 63*

Time off for employee representatives (ICE)

An employee representative who is a negotiating representative or an information and consultation representative within the Information and Consultation of Employees Regulations 2004 is entitled to take reasonable time off during the employee's working hours to perform his functions as such a representative (Reg 27 ICE Regs 2004).

The employee is entitled to be paid at their 'appropriate hourly rate' for their period of absence. Unless the employee works a varying number of working hours, the appropriate hourly rate is one week's pay divided by the normal working hours in a week when the time off was taken. For employees whose hours of work vary over a week or longer period, the appropriate hourly rate is obtained by dividing one week's pay by the average number of hours worked over the previous 12 weeks, or where the employee has not been employed for 12 weeks, a number which fairly represents the number of normal working hours in a week (see Reg 28(3), (4) and (5)).

A week's pay will be calculated in accordance with ss220 to 229 ERA 1996 (see *Week's pay*) (Reg 28(2)).

Any contractual remuneration paid to an employee in respect of such a period of time off goes towards discharging the liability under Reg 28 (see Reg 28(6) and (7)).

An employee may bring a complaint to a tribunal that his or her employer has unreasonably refused to permit him or her to take the time off under Reg 27, or has failed to pay the sums due under Reg 28 (see Reg 29).

Remedy: Where a tribunal finds a complaint well founded, it will make a declaration to that effect (Reg 29(3)).

Further, if the tribunal has found that the employer has unreasonably refused to permit the employee to take time off, the tribunal will also order the employer to pay to the employee an amount equal to the remuneration to which he or she would have been entitled under Reg 28 if the employer had not refused (Reg 29(4)).

Also, if the tribunal finds that the employer has failed to pay the employee the whole or part of any amount to which he or she is entitled under Reg 28, the tribunal will also order the employer to pay to the employee the amount he or she is owed (Reg 29(5)).

For employees working fixed number of hours per week

Sum to which the employee is entitled = (gross weekly pay) x 1/(number of normal working hours in a week) x (number of hours absent) (Reg 28(3))

For employees with varying number of hours worked per week

Sum to which the employee is entitled = gross weekly pay x 12/(number of normal hours worked in the last 12 weeks ending with the last complete week before the day on which the time off is taken) x (number of hours absent)

For employees with varying number of hours worked per week and who have worked for less than 12 weeks

Sum to which the employee is entitled = (gross weekly pay) x 1/(number of normal hours which fairly represents the number of normal working hours in a week) x (number of hours absent) (Reg 28(4) and (5) ICE 2004)

Gross or net: Gross. A week's pay as defined in ss220 to 229 ERA 1996 applies (see *Week's pay*) (Reg 28(2)).

Limit on a week's pay: None. The calculation is based on actual gross weekly pay.

Limit on number of weeks: None

Any maximum or minimum: None

Adjustments: None

Mitigation: N/A

Tax: The tax treatment is not clear. To the extent that the sum awarded is compensation for lost earnings for work done, it is likely to be taxed under s62 ITEPA 2003 (see *Tax and termination payments* and EIM02550).

Recoupment: N/A

Statutory authorities: ICE 2004 (SI 2004/3426) Regs *27* and *29*

Time off for employee representatives (OPPS)

A 'consulted representative' within the Occupational and Personal Pension Schemes (Consultation by Employers and Miscellaneous Amendment) Regulations 2006 (OPPS Regs 2006) is entitled to take reasonable time off during the employee's working hours to perform his functions as such a representative (Sch para 2 OPPS 2006). A 'consulted representative' is an employee who is a trade union representative, appointed representative, elected representative or one identified in an appropriate agreement (Reg 12(2)(a) and (3) and Reg 13(2) of OPPS Regs 2006).

The employee is entitled to be paid at their 'appropriate hourly rate' for their period of absence. Unless the employee works a varying number of working hours, the appropriate hourly rate is one week's pay divided by the normal working hours in a week when the time off was taken. For employees whose hours of work vary over a week or longer period, the appropriate hourly rate is obtained by dividing one week's pay by the average number of hours worked over the previous 12 weeks, or where the employee has not been employed for 12 weeks, a number which fairly represents the number of normal working hours in a week (see Sch para 3(3), (4) and (5)).

A week's pay will be calculated in accordance with ss220 to 229 ERA 1996 (see *Week's pay*) (Sch para 3(2)).

Any contractual remuneration paid to an employee in respect of such a period of time off goes towards discharging the liability under Sch para 3 (see Sch para 3(6) and (7)).

An employee may bring a complaint to a tribunal that his or her employer has unreasonably refused to permit him or her to take the time off under Sch para 2, or has failed to pay the sums due under Sch para 3 (see Sch para 4 OPPS 2006).

Remedy: Where a tribunal finds a complaint well

founded, it will make a declaration to that effect (Sch para 4(3) OPPS 2006).

Further, if the tribunal has found that the employer has unreasonably refused to permit the employee to take time off, the tribunal will also order the employer to pay to the employee an amount equal to the remuneration to which he or she would have been entitled under Sch para 3 if the employer had not refused (Sch para 4(4)).

Also, if the tribunal finds that the employer has failed to pay the employee the whole or part of any amount to which he or she is entitled under Reg 28, the tribunal will also order the employer to pay to the employee the amount he or she is owed (Sch para 4(5)).

For employees working fixed number of hours per week

Sum to which the employee is entitled = (gross weekly pay) x 1/(number of normal working hours in a week) x (number of hours absent) (Sch para 3(3) OPPS Regs 2006)

For employees with varying number of hours worked per week

Sum to which the employee is entitled = gross weekly pay x 12/(number of normal hours worked in the last 12 weeks ending with the last complete week before the day on which the time off is taken) x (number of hours absent) (Sch para 3(4) OPPS Regs 2006)

For employees with varying number of hours worked per week and who have worked for less than 12 weeks

Sum to which the employee is entitled = (gross weekly pay) x 1/(number of normal hours which fairly represents the number of normal working hours in a week) x (number of hours absent) (Sch para 3(4) and (5) OPPS Regs 2006)

Gross or net: Gross. A week's pay as defined in ss220 to 229 ERA 1996 applies (see *Week's pay*).

Limit on a week's pay: None. The calculation is based on actual gross weekly pay.

Limit on number of weeks: None

Any maximum or minimum: None

Adjustments: None

Mitigation: N/A

Tax: The tax treatment is not clear. To the extent that the sum awarded is compensation for lost earnings for work done, it is likely to be taxed under s62 ITEPA 2003 (see *Tax and termination payments* and EIM02550).

Recoupment: N/A

Statutory authorities: OPPS Regs 2006 (SI 2006/349) Regs *12, 13* and *Schedule paragraphs 2 to 4*

Time off for members of a European Works Council

An employee who is:

a) a member of a special negotiating body;

b) a member of a European Works Council;

c) an information and consultation representative; or

d) a candidate in an election in which any person elected will, on being elected, be such a member or representative,

is entitled to take reasonable time off during the employee's working hours to perform his functions as such a representative (Reg 25 Transnational Information and Consultation of Employees Regulations 1999 (SI 1999/3323) (TICE 1999)).

An employee who is:

a) a member of a special negotiating body;

b) a member of a European Works Council,

is entitled to take reasonable time off during the employee's working hours to undertake the training permitted by Reg 19B (Reg 25(1A) TICE Regs 1999).

The employee is entitled to be paid at their 'appropriate hourly rate' for their period of absence. Unless the employee works a varying number of working hours, the appropriate hourly rate is one week's pay divided by the normal working hours in a week when the time off was taken. For employees whose hours of work vary over a week or longer period, the appropriate hourly rate is obtained by dividing one week's pay by the average number of hours worked over the previous 12 weeks, or where the employee has not been employed for 12 weeks, a number which fairly represents the number of normal working hours in a week (see Reg 26(3), (4) and (5)).

A week's pay will be calculated in accordance with ss220 to 229 ERA 1996 (see *Week's pay*) (Reg 26(2)).

Any contractual remuneration paid to an employee in respect of such a period of time off goes towards discharging the liability under Reg 26 (see Reg 26(6) and (7)).

An employee may bring a complaint to a tribunal that his or her employer has unreasonably refused to permit him or her to take the time off under Reg 25, or has failed to pay the sums due under Reg 26 (see Reg 27 TICE 1999).

Remedy: Where a tribunal finds a complaint well founded, it will make a declaration to that effect (Reg 27(3)).

Further, if the tribunal has found that the employer has unreasonably refused to permit the employee to take time off, the tribunal will also order the employer to pay to the employee an amount equal to the remuneration to which he or she would have been entitled under Reg 26 if the employer had not refused (Reg 27(4)).

Also, if the tribunal finds that the employer has failed to pay the employee the whole or part of any amount to which he or she is entitled under Reg 26, the tribunal will also order the employer to pay to the employee the amount he or she is owed (Reg 27(5)).

For employees working a fixed number of hours per week

Sum to which the employee is entitled = (gross weekly pay) x 1/(number of normal working hours in a week) x (number of hours absent) (Reg 26(3) TICE 1999)

For employees with varying number of hours worked per week

Sum to which the employee is entitled = gross weekly pay x 12/(number of normal hours worked in the last 12 weeks ending with the last complete week before the day on which the time off is taken) x (number of hours absent) (Reg 26(4) TICE 1999)

For employees with varying number of hours worked per week and who have worked for less than 12 weeks

Sum to which the employee is entitled = (gross weekly pay) x 1/(number of normal hours which fairly represents the number of normal working hours in a week) x (number of hours absent) (Reg 26(4) and (5) TICE 1999)

Gross or net: Gross. A week's pay as defined in ss220 to 229 ERA 1996 applies (see *Week's pay*).

Limit on a week's pay: None. The calculation is based on actual gross weekly pay.

Limit on number of weeks: None

Any maximum or minimum: None

Adjustments: None

Mitigation: N/A

Tax: The tax treatment is not clear. To the extent that the sum awarded is compensation for lost earnings for work done, it is likely to be taxed under s62 ITEPA 2003 (see *Tax and termination payments* and *EIM02550*).

Recoupment: N/A

Statutory authorities: TICE 1999 (SI 1999/3323) Regs 19B, 25 to 27

Time off for pension scheme trustees

An employee who is the trustee of his employer's pension scheme is permitted to take time off to perform the duties of a trustee and undergo relevant training. The amount of time off is that which is reasonable in all the circumstances having regard to how much time is required to be taken off and the effect of the employee's absence on the running of the employer's business (s58 ERA 1996).

The employee must be paid by his or her employer for the time taken off under s58 (s59). Where the employee's remuneration would not have varied with the amount of work done during the period of absence, the employee should be paid as if he or she had worked for the whole of that time (s59(2)). However, where the employee's remuneration would have varied with the amount of work done, he or she should be paid their average hourly earnings for the period (s59(3) and (4)).

Any contractual remuneration paid to an employee in respect of such a period of time off goes towards discharging the liability under s59 (see s59(5) and (6)).

An employee may bring a complaint to a tribunal that his or her employer has unreasonably refused to permit him or her to take the time off under s58, or has failed to pay the sums due under s59 (see s60 ERA 1996).

Remedy: Where the tribunal finds such a complaint well founded it will make a declaration to that effect (s60(3)(a)). It may also make an award of compensation to be paid by the employer (s60(3)(b) and (4) ERA 1996).

The amount of compensation will be that which it considers just and equitable in all the circumstances having regard to:

a)   the employer's default in refusing to permit the employee to take time off; and

b)   any loss sustained by the employee as a result.

Gross or net: Payment under s60(5): gross but taxable as normal under PAYE; Payment under s60(4): N/A

Limit on a week's pay: None. For payment under s60(5) the calculation is based on actual weekly pay.

Any maximum or minimum: There is no statutory limit to the award.

Mitigation: It is likely that the principle of mitigation would be applied in an appropriate case. However, this would most likely operate to restrict the losses that would be compensated for where it would have been reasonable for the employee to have incurred a lower level of losses than were in fact incurred, for example where the expenses incurred in making alternative arrangements were unreasonably expensive and reasonably avoidable.

Tax: The tax treatment is not clear. To the extent that the sum awarded is compensation for lost earnings for work done, it is likely to be taxed under s62 ITEPA 2003 (see *Tax and termination payments* and EIM02550).

Statutory authorities: ERA 1996 *ss58 to 60*

Time off for public duties

An employee who holds any of a number of specified public offices is entitled to take time off during his or her working hours for the purpose of performing specified duties. The duties that fall within the right depend on the office held. Offices include Justices of the Peace, and members of statutory tribunals, independent monitoring boards and visiting committees of a prison, volunteers in the criminal justice system, a relevant health or education body, the Environment Agency, the Scottish Environment Protection Agency and Scottish Water. Duties for which an individual is entitled to time off include meetings and discharging the functions of the body (see ss50(1) to (3) and (5) to 9B ERA 1996).

The amount of time off permitted is that which is reasonable in all the circumstances having regard to how much time is required to be taken off, how much time off the individual has taken off for trade union duties and activities and the effect of the employee's absence on the running of the employer's business (s50(4) ERA 1996).

An employee may bring a complaint to a tribunal that his or her employer has unreasonably refused to permit him or her to take the time off under s50 (s51 ERA 1996).

Remedy: Where the tribunal finds such a complaint well founded it will make a declaration to that effect (s51(3)(a)). It may also make an award of compensation to be paid by the employer (s51(3)(b) and (4)).

The amount of the compensation shall be such as the tribunal considers just and equitable in all the circumstances having regard to:

a)   the employer's default in refusing to permit the employee to take time off; and

b)   any loss sustained by the employee as a result.

Any maximum or minimum: There is no statutory limit to the compensation.

Mitigation: It is likely that the principle of mitigation would be applied in an appropriate case. However, this would most likely operate to restrict the losses that would be compensated for where it would have been reasonable for the employee to have incurred a lower level of losses than were in fact incurred, for example

where the expenses incurred in making alternative arrangements were unreasonably expensive and reasonably avoidable.

Tax: See EIM02550. To the extent that the sum awarded is compensation for lost earnings for work done, it is likely to be taxed under s62 ITEPA 2003 (see *Tax and termination payments* and EIM02550).

Statutory authorities: ERA 1996 *ss50 and 51*

Time off for study or training

Section 63D ERA 1996 creates the right to make a request for time off in relation to study or training where the purpose of the study or training is to improve the employee's effectiveness or performance in the employer's business. The procedure for making the application and for the employer's consideration of it are set out at s63D to 63H ERA 1996.

An employee may bring a complaint to an employment tribunal that his or her employer has failed to follow the required procedure, reached its decision on impermissible basis or based its decision on incorrect facts (s63I(1) ERA 1996). There are various procedural hurdles to bringing such a claim (s63I(2) to (6) ERA 1996).

Remedy: If an employment tribunal finds the complaint well founded it must make a declaration to that effect and may make an order for:

a)   reconsideration of the application; and/or

b)   an award of compensation.

The amount of any compensation will be that which the tribunal considers just and equitable in all the circumstances, limited to 8 weeks' pay (see s63J ERA 1996 and EST(ECR) Regs 2010).

Gross or net: Gross. The definition of a week's pay as defined in ss220 to 229 ERA 1996 will apply (see *Week's pay*).

Limit on a week's pay: Currently £643 (see *Table 1* for historical rates).

Limit on number of weeks: 8 (see the Employee Study and Training (Eligibility, Complaints and Remedies) Regulations 2010 SI No. 156)

Any maximum or minimum: Currently the maximum is £5,144

Adjustments: None

Mitigation: N/A

Tax: The tax treatment is not clear. To the extent that the sum awarded is compensation for lost earnings for work done, it is likely to be taxed under s62 ITEPA 2003 (see *Tax and termination payments* and *EIM02550*).

Statutory authorities: ERA 1996 *ss63D to K, The Employee Study and Training (Eligibility, Complaints and Remedies) Regulations 2010* (SI 2010/156)

Time off for union duties, activities and union learning reps

An employee who is an official of an independent trade union recognised by his or her employer is entitled to take time off during working hours to carry out various official union duties (s168 TULR(C)A 1992)

An employee who is a member of a recognised trade union and a learning representative of that trade union is entitled to take time off during his working hours for a number of training related activities (s168A).

An employee who is a member of a recognised trade union is entitled to take time off during his working hours to take part in activities of the union, and activities in relation to which the employee is acting as a representative of the union (s170).

The amount of time off which must be permitted is that which is reasonable in all the circumstances having regard to any relevant provisions of a code of practice issued by ACAS (s168(3), s168A(8) and s170(3)).

The employee must be paid by his or her employer for the time taken off under s168 or s168A, but not s170 (s169). Where the employee's remuneration would not have varied with the amount of work done during the period of absence, the employee should be paid as if he or she had worked for the whole of that time (s169(2)). However, where the employee's remuneration would have varied with the amount of work done, he or she should be paid their average hourly earnings for the period (s169(3) and (4)).

Any contractual remuneration paid to an employee in respect of such a period of time off goes towards discharging the liability under s169 (see s169(4)).

An employee may bring a complaint to a tribunal that his employer has unreasonably refused to permit him to take time off (s168(4), s168A(9) and s170(4)). An employee may bring a complaint to a tribunal that his or her employer has failed to pay them during their time off under s169 (s169(5)).

Remedy: Where the tribunal upholds a complaint for failure to permit time off it will make a declaration to that effect and may also make an award of compensation to be paid by the employer (s172(1) and (2) TULR(C)A 1992).

The amount of compensation will be that which it considers just and equitable in all the circumstances having regard to:

a) the employer's default in refusing to permit the employee to take time off; and

b) any loss sustained by the employee as a result.

Where a tribunal finds that an employer has failed to pay the employee during their time off, the tribunal will order that the employer pay the amount found to be due (s172(3)).

Gross or net: Net loss, or gross where taxable under s62 ITEPA 2003.

Adjustments: None

Mitigation: It is likely that the principle of mitigation would be applied in an appropriate case. However, this would most likely operate to restrict the losses that would be compensated for where it would have been reasonable for the employee to have incurred a lower level of losses than were in fact incurred, for example where the expenses incurred in making alternative arrangements were unreasonably expensive and reasonably avoidable.

Tax: The tax treatment is not clear. To the extent that the sum awarded is compensation for lost earnings for work done, it is likely to be taxed under s62 ITEPA 2003 (see *Tax and termination payments* and EIM02550).

Recoupment: N/A

Statutory authorities: TULR(C)A 1992 *ss168 to 173*

Time off for young person for study or training

An employee who is aged 16 or 17, is not receiving full-time secondary or further education, and has not attained such standard of achievement as is prescribed by regulations made by the Secretary of State, is entitled to take time off during his or her working hours to undertake study or training leading to a relevant qualification (s63A(1) and (2) ERA 1996). The right extends to such employees who are supplied by their employer to another 'principal' (s63A(3) ERA 1996). The right also extends to employees who have begun their study or training but have turned 18 (s63A(4) ERA 1996).

The amount of time off permitted is that which is reasonable in all the circumstances having regard to the requirements of the employee's study or training and the effect of the employee's absence on the running of the employer's business (s63A(5) ERA 1996).

The employee is entitled to be paid at their 'appropriate hourly rate' for their period of absence. Unless the employee works a varying number of working hours, the appropriate hourly rate is one week's pay divided by the normal working hours in a week when the time off was taken. For employees whose hours of work vary over a week or longer period, the appropriate hourly rate is obtained by dividing one week's pay by the average number of hours worked over the previous 12 weeks, or where the employee has not been employed for 12 weeks, a number which fairly represents the number of normal working hours in a week (see s63B(1) to (4) ERA 1996).

A week's pay will be calculated in accordance with ss220 to 229 ERA 1996 (see *Week's pay*). Any contractual remuneration paid to an employee in respect of such a period of time off goes towards discharging the liability under s63B (see s63B(5) and (6) ERA 1996).

An employee may bring a complaint to a tribunal that his or her employer has unreasonably refused to permit him or her to take the time off under s63A, or has failed to pay the sums due under s63B (see s63C ERA 1996).

Remedy: Where a tribunal finds a complaint well founded, it will make a declaration to that effect (s65C(3) ERA 1996).

Further, if the tribunal has found that the employer has unreasonably refused to permit the employee to take time off, the tribunal will also order the employer to pay to the employee an amount equal to the remuneration to which he or she would have been entitled under s63B if the employer had not refused (s63C(4) ERA 1996).

Also, if the tribunal finds that the employer has failed to pay the employee the whole or part of any amount to which he or she is entitled under s63B, the tribunal will also order the employer to pay to the employee the amount he or she is owed (s63C(5) ERA 1996).

For employees working fixed number of hours per week

Sum to which the employee is entitled = (gross weekly pay) x 1/(number of normal working hours in a week) x (number of hours absent) (s63B(2) ERA 1996)

For employees with varying number of hours worked per week

Sum to which the employee is entitled = gross weekly pay x 12/(number of normal hours worked in the last 12 weeks ending with the last complete week before the day on which the time off is taken) x (number of hours absent) (s63B(3) ERA 1996)

For employees with varying number of hours worked per week and who have worked for less than 12 weeks

Sum to which the employee is entitled = (gross weekly pay) x 1/(number of normal hours which fairly represents the number of normal working hours in a

week) x (number of hours absent) (s63B(3) and (4) ERA 1996)

Gross or net: Gross. The definition of a week's pay as defined in ss220 to 229 ERA 1996 will apply (see *Week's pay*).

Limit on a week's pay: None. The calculation is based on actual gross weekly pay.

Limit on number of weeks: None

Any maximum or minimum: None

Adjustments: None

Mitigation: N/A

Tax: The tax treatment is not clear. To the extent that the sum awarded is compensation for lost earnings for work done, it is likely to be taxed under s62 ITEPA 2003 (see *Tax and termination payments* and EIM02550).

Recoupment: N/A

Statutory authorities: ERA 1996 *ss63A to 63C*

Time off to look for work or arrange training after being made redundant

An employee who is given notice of dismissal by reason of redundancy and who has sufficient continuity of service to receive a statutory redundancy payment, is entitled to take reasonable time off during his or her working hours before the end of his notice in order to look for new employment, or make arrangements for training for future employment (s52 ERA 1996).

The employee is entitled to be paid at their 'appropriate hourly rate' for their period of absence. Unless the employee works a varying number of working hours, the appropriate hourly rate is one week's pay divided by the normal working hours in a week when the time off was taken. For employees whose hours of work vary over a week or longer period, the appropriate hourly rate is obtained by dividing one week's pay by the average number of hours per week worked over the previous 12 weeks (s53(1) to (3) ERA 1996).

If an employer unreasonably refuses to permit an employee to take the time permitted by s52, the employee is entitled to be paid the amount of remuneration he would have been entitled to if he had been given the time off (s53(4) ERA 1996). A week's pay will be calculated in accordance with ss220 to 229 ERA 1996 (see *Week's pay*). Any contractual remuneration paid to an employee in respect of such a period of time off goes towards discharging the liability under s53 (see s53(6) and (7) ERA 1996).

The total liability to pay remuneration for an

employee's time off is limited to 40% of a week's pay for that employee (s53(5) ERA 1996).

An employee may bring a complaint to a tribunal that his or her employer has unreasonably refused to permit him or her to take the time off under s52, or has failed to pay the sums due under s53 (see s54 ERA 1996).

Remedy: Where a tribunal finds a complaint well founded, it will make a declaration to that effect (s54(3)(a) ERA 1996) and will order the employer to pay the employee the amount which it finds due to him (s54(3)(b) ERA 1996).

For employees working fixed number of hours per week

Sum to which the employee is entitled = (gross weekly pay) x 1/(number of normal working hours in a week) x (number of hours absent) (s53(2) ERA 1996)

For employees with varying number of hours worked per week

Sum to which the employee is entitled = gross weekly pay x 12/(number of normal hours worked in the last 12 weeks ending with the last complete week before the day on which the time off is taken) x (number of hours absent) (s53(3) ERA 1996)

Gross or net: Gross. The definition of a week's pay as defined in ss220 to 229 ERA 1996 will apply (see *Week's pay*).

Limit on a week's pay: None. The calculation is based on actual gross weekly pay.

Limit on number of weeks: None

Any maximum or minimum: The maximum payable is 40% of an actual week's gross pay (s53(5) ERA 1996).

Tax: The tax treatment is not clear. To the extent that the sum awarded is compensation for lost earnings for work done, it is likely to be taxed under s62 ITEPA 2003 (see EIM02550). The sum may also be paid in connection with termination and be taxable under s401 (see *Tax and termination payments*).

Statutory authorities: ERA 1996 *ss52 to 54*

Trade unions: see *Union activities or collective bargaining (inducements)*; *Union member (deduction of contributions to political fund)*; *Union member (deduction of unauthorised or excessive subscriptions)*; *Union member (expelled or excluded)*; *Union member (refusal of employment)*; *Union member (unjustifiably disciplined)*

TUPE (information and consultation)

The employer of any employees affected by a TUPE transfer must inform and consult their appropriate representatives before the transfer to enable consultation with any affected employees. The information must include: the fact that the transfer is to take place, the date or proposed date of the transfer and the reasons for it; the legal, economic and social implications of the transfer for any affected employees; the measures which he envisages he will take in relation to any affected employees; and if the employer is the transferor, the measures, in connection with the transfer, which he envisages the transferee will take in relation to any affected employees who will become employees of the transferee after the transfer by virtue of regulation 4. The employer is under a duty to consult where they envisage that they will be taking measures in relation to any affected employee. Consultation must be with a view to seeking the agreement of the representatives to the intended measures (Reg 13 TUPE 2006).

Appropriate employee representatives will be the representatives of a recognised trade union, or if none exist, representatives appointed or elected with the authority to be informed and consulted (Regs 13(3) and 14). There is an exception for employers with fewer than 10 employees who, if certain conditions are met, may inform and consult the affected employees directly (Reg 13A).

Generally speaking, it is the representatives who may bring a claim to a tribunal for failure to inform and/or consult (Reg 15(1)). Once a tribunal has made an award, any employee who falls within the description of employees covered by that award may bring a complaint to a tribunal that the particular award to which he is entitled has not been paid to him (Reg 15(10)). However, where the claim is brought by affected employees rather than their representatives, then the award is only payable to those employees who have actually brought claims (*Ferguson and ors v Astrea Asset Management Ltd* [2020] UKEAT/0139/19).

Remedy: Where the tribunal finds a complaint under Reg 15(1) well founded it will make a declaration to that effect and can award such compensation as the tribunal considers just and equitable having regard to the seriousness of the failure of the employer to comply with the duty, of up to 13 weeks' pay. The compensation will be ordered to be paid to '*such descriptions of affected employees as may be specified*', which will reflect the employees in respect of whom there has been a failure (Reg 15(7) and (8)).

The award is punitive, not compensatory. Its purpose is to provide a sanction for breach of the obligation to inform and consult. The tribunal has a wide discretion but it will focus on the seriousness of the default, which may vary from the merely technical to a complete failure to comply with the duties, and it may consider the deliberateness of the failure.

The proper approach where there has been no consultation is to start at the maximum and reduce it if there are mitigating circumstances justifying a reduction (see *Susie Radin Ltd v GMB & Ors* [2004] ICR 893). This approach has recently been doubted by the EAT in *Ferguson and others v Astrea Asset Management Limited* [2020] UKEAT/0139/19. However, the reasoning for this is brief and it is unclear to what extent it truly changes the approach taken by tribunals given that it goes on to accept that there exists a *'paradigm "really serious" case where, for example, a transferor employer had wholly failed to inform or consult its employees and the first they had heard about a transfer was on the very day it was to take effect, causing serious alarm and distress'* (paragraph 54).

However, the tribunal should not take this approach where there has been some information given and/or some consultation (see *Todd v Strain & Ors* [2011] IRLR 11 and *London Borough of Barnet v Unison & Ors* UKEAT/0191/13).

It is wrong to make an award of zero where the only breach is a failure to inform the employee of the identity of the transferor. This is an essential obligation under TUPE and not a mere technicality (*Clark v Middleton* [2022] EAT 31).

Gross or net: Gross. A week's pay as defined in ss220 to 229 ERA 1996 applies (see *Week's pay*).

Limit on a week's pay: None. The calculation is based on actual gross weekly pay (see *Zaman & Ors v Kozee Sleep Products Ltd t/a Dorlux Beds UK* UKEAT/0312/10/CEA).

Limit on number of weeks: 13

Adjustments: None

Mitigation: N/A

Tax: The tax treatment is unclear but it is likely that HMRC would regard any payment made under TUPE to fall under s401 ITEPA 2003 (see *Tax and termination payments*).

Recoupment: N/A

Statutory authorities: TUPE 2006 *Regs 13 to 16*

Relevant case law: *Cable Realisations Ltd v GMB Northern* [2010] IRLR 42; *Clark v Middleton* [2022] EAT 31; *Ferguson and ors v Astrea Asset Management Ltd* [2020] UKEAT/0139/19; *London Borough of Barnet v Unison & Ors* UKEAT/0191/13; *Susie Radin Ltd v GMB & Ors* [2004] ICR 893; *Sweeting v Coral Racing* [2006] IRLR 252; *Todd v Strain & Ors* [2011] IRLR 11; *Zaman & Ors v Kozee Sleep Products Ltd t/a Dorlux Beds UK* UKEAT/0312/10/CEA

TUPE (failure to notify employee liability information)

The transferor is obliged to provide specified employee liability information to the transferee for any employees who will be transferred, at least 14 days before the relevant transfer (Reg 11 TUPE 2006). For any transfer occurring on or after 1 May 2014, the information must be provided at least 28 days before the relevant transfer (Reg 10 CRATU(PE) Regs 2014).

A transferee may present a complaint to a tribunal that the transferor has failed to comply with any provisions of Reg 11 (Reg 12(1)).

Remedy: Where a tribunal finds a complaint well founded it must make a declaration to that effect and may make an award of compensation to be paid by the transferor to the transferee (Reg 12(3)). The amount of compensation will be that which the tribunal considers just and equitable in all the circumstances having particular regard to the losses sustained by the transferee as a result of the failure to provide information, and any relevant terms of any contract between the transferor and transferee dealing with payment for such a failure (Reg 12(4)).

There are two further provisions that may influence the amount of any award:

- By Reg 12(5) the amount of compensation must be a minimum of £500 per employee whose liability information has not been provided, subject to the discretion of the tribunal to award a lesser sum if in all the circumstances it considers it just and equitable.

- By Reg 12(6) the tribunal must apply the common law rules as to mitigation in assessing the loss suffered by the transferee.

Gross or net: Loss will likely be calculated net of any tax that may be payable.

Any maximum or minimum: Minimum is £500 per employee whose liability information has not been provided, unless the tribunal considers it is just and equitable to award a lesser sum.

Adjustments: N/A

Mitigation: The transferee is under a duty to mitigate their loss.

Tax: The tax treatment is unclear.

Statutory authorities: TUPE 2006 *Regs 11 and 12*; *CRATU(PE) Regs 2014 Reg 10*

Unauthorised deductions: see
Unlawful deductions from wages

Unfair dismissal

(see also *Additional award; Adjustments and order of adjustments; Basic award; Compensatory award; Damages for wrongful dismissal; Mitigation***)**

The right not to be unfairly dismissed is established by *s94* ERA 1996. An individual may bring a complaint to a tribunal that he or she has been unfairly dismissed (*s111* ERA 1996).

The definition of a dismissal is set out at *s95*, and includes dismissal with or without notice, the termination of a fixed term contract and dismissal where the employer or employee has committed a repudiatory breach of contract entitling the other to terminate the contract immediately (constructive dismissal).

Whether a dismissal is fair or unfair will be determined by a tribunal applying the tests set out in *s98*, which include that the employer's reason for the dismissal must be one of a number of specified reasons (including misconduct and redundancy), and require the tribunal to assess whether the employer acted reasonably or unreasonably in treating its reason as a sufficient reason for dismissing the employee. This second stage is itself the subject of extensive further guideline cases, which are outside the scope of this work.

Automatic unfair dismissal

Where the reason, or if more than one reason the principal reason for the dismissal is one of a number of protected reasons, the dismissal will be automatically unfair. The protected reasons are:

- Being summoned to attend for jury service or being absent for attending jury service (*s98B* ERA 1996);

- Exercising rights to family leave (*s99* ERA 1996);

- Exercising various health and safety functions (*s100* ERA 1996);

- Refusing to work on a Sunday (if a specified shop or betting worker) (*s101* ERA 1996) or refusing to work additional hours on a Sunday (s101ZA ERA 1996);

- Taking various actions under the Working Time Regulations 1998 (*s101A* ERA 1996);

- Exercising various rights to participate in education or training (*s101B* ERA 1996);

- Performing various functions of the trustee of an occupational pension scheme (*s102* ERA 1996);

- Performing various functions related to being an employee representative (*s103* ERA 1996);

- Making a protected disclosure (whistleblowing) (*s103A* ERA 1996);

- Asserting one of a number of statutory rights (*s104* ERA 1996);

- Reasons related to action taken under the National Minimum Wage Act 1998 (*s104A* ERA 1996);

- Reasons related to actions taken under the Tax Credits Act 2002 (*s104B* ERA 1996);

- Exercising various rights to flexible working (*s104C* ERA 1996);

- Reasons related to actions taken relating to pension enrolment (*s104D* ERA 1996);

- Exercising various rights to study and training (*s104E* ERA 1996);

- Reasons related to the existence of trade union blacklist (*s104F* ERA 1996);

- Refusing to accept an offer of employee shareholder status (*s104G* ERA 1996);

- Reasons relating to actions taken related to trade union recognition (*para 161 Sch A1* TULR(C)A 1992);

- Reasons related to trade union membership or activities (*s152* TULR(C)A 1992); and

- Redundancy, but the reason or principal reason for selection for redundancy was one of a long list of protected reasons (*ss105(3) to (7N)*, *s153* TULR(C)A 1992 and *paragraph 162* Sch 1A TULR(C)A 1992).

The right to not be dismissed unfairly generally accrues to an employee after the completion of 2 years' service (see *s108(1)* ERA 1996). However, where the dismissal relates to a number of protected reasons, the period of continuous service required is either reduced or removed entirely (s108(2) to (4)). Most of the automatically unfair dismissal provisions can be relied upon by a dismissed employee who has not completed 2 years' continuous service.

Industrial action

Where the reason for a dismissal is related to industrial action, specific provisions apply (see *ss237 to 239* TULR(C)A 1992).

Interim relief

An individual may also bring a complaint to a tribunal that he or she has been unfairly dismissed and seek an order for continuation of the contract of employment under the interim relief provisions (ss128 to 132 ERA

1996 and ss161 to 167 TULR(C)A 1992). This remedy is limited to allegations of unfair dismissal where the alleged reason or principal reason for the dismissal falls within the automatically unfair dismissal provisions relating to representative roles, the existence of a blacklist, trade union membership and activities and making a protected disclosure.

Remedy: Where a tribunal has found a dismissal to be unfair the remedies available are reinstatement, re-engagement and compensation (ss112 to 126 ERA 1996). See *Re-engagement and reinstatement.*

The tribunal must explain to a successful claimant the three orders available to it (s112(2) ERA 1996). Though the primary remedies are reinstatement or re-engagement, this is rarely granted in practice and it is most often the case that claimants seek only an award of compensation.

Where an order for reinstatement or re-engagement is not fully complied with (and the respondent fails to establish that such reinstatement or re-engagement was not practicable), the tribunal will award compensation under s117(2) (s117(1) ERA 1996).

Where the tribunal is not asked to order reinstatement or re-engagement, or where a claimant has not been reinstated or re-engaged, the tribunal will make an award of compensation under ss118 to 126 ERA 1996 (s117(3) and (4) and s112(4) ERA 1996) (see also *Additional award*).

The award of compensation under ss118 to 126 ERA 1996 consists of a basic award and compensatory award (see *Basic award, Compensatory award*).

The basic award is calculated on the basis of (capped) gross weekly pay and the number of years' continuous service (the longer the service the higher the award).

The compensatory award compensates the individual for the financial losses suffered as a result of the dismissal and is based on actual net weekly pay. Except where the dismissal is for one of a limited number of protected reasons, the compensatory award is capped at the lesser of one year's gross pay and currently £105,707 (see *Statutory cap* and *Table 1*). Compensation for non-pecuniary losses, such as injury to feelings, is not available within a compensatory award (see *Dunnachie v Kingston upon Hull City Council* [2004] UKHL 36).

Awards of compensation for unfair dismissal may be adjusted for failure to comply with a relevant code of practice (see *Adjustments and order of adjustments*).

The specific interim remedy of a continuation order is available in limited circumstances where a claimant has sought interim relief under ss128 to 132 ERA 1996 and ss161 to 167 TULR(C)A 1992 (see *Interim relief*).

Statutory authorities: ERA 1996 s94, s95, ss98 to 104,

s108, s111, ss112 to 126, s117, ss128 to 132; TULR(C)A 1992 Schedule 1A, Schedule A1, s105, s152, s153, ss161 to 167, ss237 to 239

Union activities or collective bargaining (inducements)

A worker has the right not to have an offer made to him by his employer to induce the worker: not to be or seek to become a member of a trade union; not to take part in the activities of a trade union; not to make use of trade union services; or to be or become a member of any trade union (s145A of TULR(C)A 1992).

A worker who is a member of a trade union which is recognised, or seeking to be recognised, by his employer has the right not to have an offer made to him by his employer if: acceptance of the offer, together with other workers' acceptance of offers which the employer also makes to them, would have 'the prohibited result', and the employer's sole or main purpose in making the offers is to achieve that result. The 'prohibited result' is that the workers' terms will not or will not continue to be determined by collective bargaining (s145B of TULR(C)A 1992).

A worker or former worker may bring a complaint to a tribunal that the employer has made an offer in contravention of s145A or 145B (s145A(5) and s145B(5)).

Remedy: Where a tribunal finds such a complaint well founded, it will make a declaration to that effect and will make an award of £5,128 (s145E(1) to (3) TULR(C)A 1992).

Section 145E prescribes certain other consequences where an unlawful offer has been made, which exist without a claim having been brought to a tribunal. By s145E(4) any agreement to vary the terms of employment between the worker and employer will not be enforceable by the employer, however if merely as a result of the acceptance (e.g. because collectively agreed terms would have been different in those circumstances) nothing in s145A or s145B makes the variation unenforceable by either party.

Adjustments: s38 EA 2002 adjustment for failure to give statement of employment particulars applies. ACAS uplift applies (Schedule A2 TULR(C)A).

Mitigation: N/A

Tax: The tax treatment of this award is unclear.

Recoupment: N/A

Statutory authorities: TULR(C)A 1992 *ss145A, B & E*

Union member (deduction of contributions to political fund)

Trade unions may maintain political funds, and seek contributions to that fund from members. A member may object to contributing to the political fund. If a member of a trade union which has a political fund informs his employer in writing that he is exempt from the obligation to contribute to the fund, or he has notified the union in writing of his objection to contributing to the fund, the employer is obliged to ensure that no amount representing a contribution to the political fund is deducted by him from emoluments payable to that individual (see s84 and s86 TULR(C)A 1992).

A member may bring a claim to the tribunal alleging that his employer has made a deduction contrary to s86 (s87(1) TULR(C)A 1992).

A member may bring a further complaint in circumstances where an order granted under the first complaint to prevent a repetition of the failure has not been complied with (s87(5) TULR(C)A 1992).

Remedy: Where a tribunal finds a complaint under s87(1) well founded, it will make a declaration to that effect and may order the employer to pay to the complainant the amount deducted less any part of that amount already paid to him by the employer (s87(4)(a) TULR(C)A) The tribunal may also order the employer to take steps to prevent a repetition of the failure (s87(4)(b)).

A complainant may bring a complaint alleging that his or her employer has not complied with the order under s87(4)(b) (s87(5)). If the tribunal finds that the employer has without reasonable excuse failed to comply with the order, it will order the employer to pay the complainant 2 weeks' pay (s87(7)).

Gross or net:

Deductions under s87(4)(a): the actual amount of the deducted owing must be paid.

Non-compliance with s87(4)(b): gross weekly pay according to ss220 to 229 ERA 1996 (s87(8) TULR(C)A 1992).

Limit on a week's pay: None

Limit on number of weeks: For a complaint under s87(7) ERA 1996 the limit is 2 weeks' pay.

Any maximum or minimum: None

Adjustments: None

Mitigation: N/A

Tax: The actual deductions should be repaid, and there should be no impact on tax calculations. It is unclear whether the 2 weeks' pay will be subject to tax.

Recoupment: N/A

Statutory authorities: TULR(C)A 1992 *ss84 to 87*

Union member (deduction of unauthorised or excessive subscriptions)

Where arrangements exist between an employer and a trade union for the deduction of membership subscriptions from an employee, the employer must ensure that no subscription deductions are made for any worker if he or she has not authorised the deduction or has withdrawn authorisation (see s68 TULR(C)A 1992).

A worker may bring a complaint to a tribunal that that his employer has made such a deduction (s68A(1) TULR(C)A 1992).

Remedy: Where a tribunal finds that the complaint is well founded, it will make a declaration to that effect and will order the employer to pay to the worker the amount of the deduction owing to the employee (s68A(3)). s68A(4) makes provision to ensure there is no double recovery where the sum deducted might also be claimed under another jurisdiction, such as s13 ERA 1996 (unlawful deductions from wages).

Gross or net: The actual amount of any deductions owing should be paid.

Any maximum or minimum: None

Statutory authorities: TULR(C)A 1992 *ss68 and 68A*

Union member (expelled or excluded)

An individual is protected from being excluded or expelled from a trade union unless the exclusion or expulsion is permitted by s174(2) TULR(C)A. The legitimate reasons for exclusion or expulsion include that the individual no longer satisfies enforceable membership criteria or has committed misconduct.

This right gives rise to two circumstances in which a claim may be brought to a tribunal. First, a member may bring a claim alleging that he or she has been excluded or expelled from a trade union (s174(5)). Second, where such a claim has been declared well founded it is envisaged the parties may reach agreement to deal with the issue between them, but the individual is may bring a claim under s176(2) to enforce such an agreement or seek compensation.

Remedy: The primary remedy, following a complaint under s174(5), is a declaration from the tribunal that the claim is well founded (s176(1)). The tribunal must also make a declaration, stating that effect, where the exclusion or expulsion was mainly attributable to a reason relating to the individual being a member of a political party (s176(1A)) and (if it applies) that the exclusion or expulsion was otherwise wholly or mainly attributable to conduct of the individual contrary to a rule of the union or an objective of the union (s176(1B)).

Where the individual has succeeded under a s176(1) claim, the individual may bring a claim under s176(2) to seek compensation. The amount of compensation awarded will be that which the employment tribunal considers just and equitable in all the circumstances (s176(4)). The tribunal may reduce any award for contributory fault (s176(5)).

Gross or net: It is likely that this will be paid gross.

Any maximum or minimum:

Minimum: The amount of compensation will not be less than £11,967 where on the date the s176(1) application was made the union has not admitted or readmitted the member (TULR(C)A 1992 s67(8A) and s176(6A)), unless the tribunal also made declarations under s176(1A) and (1B) (see s176(6B)).

Maximum: The total award will not exceed the aggregate of 30 times the limit on a week's pay under s227(1)(a) ERA 1996 (£19,290) and the maximum compensatory award (£105,707) i.e. £124,997 (TULR(C)A 1992 s176(7) and ERA 1996 s227(1)(a) and s124(1)).

Adjustments: Yes, for contributory conduct.

Cap: A cap applies (see above).

Mitigation: The member is likely to be under a duty to mitigate any losses for which he or she seeks compensation

Tax: It is likely that this will be treated as a punishment or fine, and not taxed.

Recoupment: N/A

Statutory authorities: ERA 1996 *ss113, 124(1)* and *227(1)*; TULR(C)A 1992 *ss174 to 176*

Union member (refusal of employment)

It is unlawful to refuse a person employment because he is or is not a member of a trade union, or because he is unwilling to accept a requirement that he take steps to cease to be or to remain or to become a member of a trade union, or a requirement to make payments or suffer deductions in the event of him not being a member of a trade union (s137 TULR(C)A 1992).

An equivalent right applies where an employment agency refuses such a person any of its services (s138 TULR(C)A 1992).

An individual may bring a complaint to a tribunal that this right has been infringed (s137(2) and s138(2) TULR(C)A 1992).

Remedy: Where a tribunal finds such a complaint well founded, it will make a declaration to that effect and may make an order of compensation (s140(1)(a)) and/ or a recommendation (s140(1)(b)).

Compensation will be assessed on the same basis as damages for breach of statutory duty (as are discrimination claims) and may include compensation for injury to feelings (s140(1)(a) and s140(2) TULR(C)A). The total compensation is limited to the maximum sum available under a compensatory award (s140(4)).

Any recommendation will require the respondent to take action to obviate or reduce the adverse effect on the complainant of the conduct that forms the basis of the complaint (s140(1)(b)).

Where the respondent fails without reasonable justification to comply with a recommendation, the tribunal may make an award of compensation, or increase it if it has already made an award (s140(3)).

Gross or net: The award of compensation will be made on the basis of net loss.

Limit on a week's pay: None

Limit on number of weeks: None

Any maximum or minimum: The maximum award is that of the statutory cap on unfair dismissal in force at the date of the breach under s124(1) ERA 1996, currently the lesser of £105,707 and 52 weeks' gross pay. There is no minimum.

Adjustments: None

Compensation cap: See maximum above.

Mitigation: The usual rules as to mitigation in discrimination claims will apply.

Tax: The tax treatment of this award is unclear.

Recoupment: N/A

Statutory authorities: ERA 1996 *s124(1)*; TULR(C)A 1992 *ss137 to 143*

Union member (unjustifiably disciplined)

An individual who is or has been a member of a trade union has the right not to be unjustifiably disciplined by the union (s64(1) TULR(C)A 1992). Section 64(2) identifies what actions of the union amount to 'discipline', whilst s65 identifies those reasons for the discipline which render the discipline 'unjustified'.

This right gives rise to two circumstances in which a claim may be brought to a tribunal. First, a member may bring a claim alleging that he or she has been unjustifiably disciplined (s66(1)). Second, where such a claim has been declared well founded it is envisaged the parties may reach agreement to deal with the issue between them, but the individual may bring a claim under s67(1) to enforce such an agreement or seek compensation.

Remedy: The primary remedy, following a complaint under s66(1), is a declaration from the tribunal that the individual has been unjustifiably disciplined (s66(3)).

Where the individual has succeeded under a s66(1) claim, it is envisaged the parties may reach agreement to deal with the issue between them, but the individual may bring a claim under s67(1) to enforce such an agreement or seek compensation.

The amount of compensation awarded will be that which the employment tribunal considers just and equitable in all the circumstances (s67(3)). The tribunal will apply the common law principles of mitigation (s67(4)) and may reduce any award for contributory fault (s67(5)).

Gross or net: It is likely that this will be paid gross.

Any maximum or minimum:

Minimum: The amount of compensation will not be less than £11,967 where on the date the s67(1) application was made the union has not revoked the decision to discipline the member or taken all necessary steps to secure the reversal of anything done to give effect to the disciplinary sanction (TULR(C)A 1992 s67(8A) and s176(6A)).

Maximum: The total award will not exceed the aggregate of the maximum basic award (£19,290) and the maximum compensatory award (£105,707) i.e. £124,997 (TULR(C)A 1992 s67(7) and ERA 1996 s227(1)(a) and s124(1)).

Adjustments: Yes, for contributory conduct.

Cap: A cap applies (see above).

Mitigation: Yes, the member is under a duty to mitigate any losses.

Tax: It is likely that this will be treated as a punishment or fine, and not taxed.

Recoupment: N/A

Statutory authorities: ERA 1996 *s227(1)(a)* and *s124(1)*; TULR(C)A 1992 *ss64 to 67*

Union membership (blacklists, unfair dismissal/redundancy): see *Basic award, minimum*; *Unfair dismissal*

Union membership or activities (detriment): see *Detriment*

Unlawful deductions from wages

(see also *Holiday pay*; *National Minimum Wage*)

A worker has the right not to suffer deductions from wages except under prescribed circumstances, which are as follows:

- Deductions required or authorised by statute (such as PAYE) or by a provision in the worker's contract (s13(1)(a) ERA 1996);

- Deductions previously agreed to and signified in writing by the worker (s13(1)(b) ERA 1996);

- Deductions for reimbursement of an overpayment of wages or expenses (s14(1) ERA 1996);

- Payment to third parties for which the individual has given written consent (s14(4) ERA 1996);

- Deductions on account of the worker's participation in industrial action (s14(5) ERA 1996);

- Deductions made in respect of an attachment of earnings order made by a court, where the individual has given written consent (s14(6) ERA 1996);

- Deductions made to a public authority as required under statute (s14(3) ERA 1996).

Wages is broadly interpreted, including salaries, fees, bonuses, commissions and holiday pay (both contractual and under the WTR 1998 (see *HMRC v Stringer* [2009] IRLR 677). The definition of wages does not usually include pay in lieu of notice (see *Delaney v Staples* [1992] ICR 483). Also, where the sum claimed is dependent on the exercise of a discretion by the employer that has yet to be determined, such as a discretionary bonus, no identifiable sum exists and the claim must be brought as a breach of contract claim in the tribunal or the civil courts, rather than as an unlawful deduction claim (see *Adcock v Coors Brewers Ltd* [2007] IRLR 440).

Workers in the retail industry have special protection, whereby deductions to compensate for cash or stock shortages within a period may not exceed 10% of the worker's gross wages in that period (see ss17 to 22 ERA 1996).

A worker may bring a claim to a tribunal that his employer has made unlawful deductions from his wages (s23(1) ERA 1996).

The Court of Appeal in *Agarwal v Cardiff University & Anor* [2018] EWCA Civ 1434 has confirmed that employment tribunals have the power to interpret the relevant provisions of a contract of employment to determine the amount properly payable to an employee.

Remedy: Where a tribunal finds a complaint under s23 well founded, it will make a declaration to that effect and will order the employer to pay the worker the sum found to have been deducted unlawfully (s24(1)). The tribunal may also make such award as it considers appropriate in all the circumstances to compensate the worker for any financial loss sustained by him which is attributable to the unlawful deduction (s24(2)).

Gross or net: The sums awarded ought to be calculated on a gross basis, since they will be taxable under s62 ITEPA 2003.

Adjustments: The ACAS uplift applies (Schedule A2 TULR(C)A).

Cap: There is no statutory cap on the sums that may be awarded by the tribunal but sums can only be claimed for the previous 2 years before the claim was made (*Deductions from Wages (Limitation) Regulations* 2014 SI 2014/3322, effective 1 July 2015). This includes holiday pay as well as any other deduction. For claims before this period there is no such limit, and the Limitation Act 1980 does not apply (*Bath Hill Court (Bournemouth) Management Co Ltd v Coletta* [2019] EWCA Civ 1707).

Mitigation: The usual principles of mitigation will likely apply to any award under s24(2), but the award for repayment of deductions does not need to be mitigated.

Tax: Taxable under s62 ITEPA 2003

Recoupment: N/A

Statutory authorities: ERA 1996 *ss13 to 26*; *Deductions from Wages (Limitation) Regulations* 2014 SI 2014/3322

Relevant case law: Adcock v Coors Brewers Ltd [2007] IRLR 440; *Agarwal v Cardiff University & Anor* [2018] EWCA Civ 1434; *Bath Hill Court (Bournemouth) Management Co Ltd v Coletta* [2019] EWCA Civ 1707; *HMRC v Stringer* [2009] IRLR 677

Unreasonable refusal to be reinstated: see *Additional award*

Variable hours: see *Holiday pay*; *Week's pay*

Varying pay with output: see *Holiday pay*; *Week's pay*

Victimisation: see *Discrimination*

Week's pay

The concept of a week's pay is defined by ss220 to 229 and s234 ERA 1996. It is used for calculating a remedy in each of the following employment rights (see *Table 5* for a list of claims, the relevant calculation date and whether a limit on a week's pay applies):

- Additional award (s117(1) ERA 1996);
- Basic award/Redundancy pay (s119(2), s121 and s162(2) ERA 1996);
- Guarantee pay (s30(2) ERA 1996);
- Payments on the insolvency of an employer (s182 ERA 1996);
- Protective award (s190(2) TULR(C)A 1992);
- Remuneration whilst suspended on medical or maternity grounds (s69(1) ERA 1996);
- Right for union member not to be unjustifiably disciplined/expelled and blacklisting claims (ss67(8)(a) and 176(6)(a) TULR(C)A 1992);
- Failure to inform and consult union on training for workers (s70C(4) TULR(C)A 1992);
- Time off to look for work or arrange training after being made redundant (s54(4) ERA 1996);
- Time off for antenatal care (s56(2) ERA 1996);
- Absence during statutory notice period (ss88(1) to 89(1) ERA 1996);
- Time off for employee representatives (including ICE and OPPS) (s62(2) ERA 1996, Reg 28(2) ICE Regs 2004, Sch para 3(2) OPPS Regs 2006);
- Time off for study or training (s63J(3) ERA 1996);
- Time off for young person for study or training (s63B(2) ERA 1996);
- Time off for members of a European Works Council (Reg 26(2) TICE 1999);
- Failure to inform and consult under TUPE (Reg 16(3) TUPE Regs 2006);
- Right to be accompanied at a disciplinary or grievance meeting (s11(3) ERelA 1999);
- Infringement of right to be accompanied at flexible working meeting (Reg 15(3) FW(PR) Regs 2002);

- Rejection of flexible working application (Reg 7 FW(ECR) Regs 2002);

- Written reasons for dismissal (s93(2) ERA 1996);

- Written statement of particulars (s38 EA 2002); and

- Paid annual leave under the Working Time Regulations (Reg 16(1) WTR 1998).

What is a week's pay?

In essence, a week's pay is the gross contractual remuneration an employee is entitled to be paid when working their normal hours each week. Difficulties emerge in the calculation where an individual typically receives pay in addition to their contractual salary (such as voluntary overtime), or where they do not have normal working hours each week, such as when working irregular shift patterns.

For the purpose of calculating maximum compensation, a week's pay can include employer pension contributions (see *University of Sunderland v Drossou* UKEAT/0341/16/RN).

Since pay will vary over the period of employment of an individual, for each remedy that uses the definition of a week's pay, a calculation date is specified (see *Table 5*). For a number of remedies, a week's pay is capped, currently at £643 (again, see *Table 5* for a full list).

Working hours

An employee's normal working hours will often be identified in their written particulars (s221(1)) or other contractual documentation. Failing this, it may be clear from the hours actually worked.

Matters are complicated where a contract specifies a minimum number of hours to be worked each week and also provides for an increased overtime wage to be paid beyond a certain number of hours. By s234, in that situation the normal working hours will be the minimum number of hours specified, even if overtime is paid for a smaller number of hours, and even if the minimum number of hours can be reduced in certain circumstances.

- Where overtime is obligatory for the employee, but is not guaranteed by the employer, the normal working hours will not include those additional hours - they will only amount to normal working hours if the obligation to work and provide work for that period is mutual (see *Tarmac Roadstone Holdings Ltd v Peacock* [1973] ICR 273). Further, where employees are paid on the basis of a pre-estimate of the number of hours a task will take, though the time taken may vary, the pre-estimate will not amount to normal working hours (see *Sanderson v Exel Management Services Ltd* [2006] ICR 1337).

- Remuneration where an employee has normal working hours is calculated as the contractual payments made to the employee for the work they have done.

- Contractual bonuses are usually included, such as a regular shift bonus (see *Mole Mining Ltd v Jenkins* [1972] ICR 282). It may be possible to infer a contractual term that a regular bonus, such as a site bonus in the construction industry, will be paid unless certain conditions are met, such that it falls within remuneration (see *Donelan v Kerrby Constructions* [1983] ICR 237).

- Discretionary bonuses will not form part of the remuneration, unless deemed a contractual payment (see *Canadian Imperial Bank of Commerce v Beck* EAT/0141/10/RN and *Hoyland v Asda Stores Ltd* [2006] IRLR 468).

- Tips paid by the employer (but not by customers to the employee in cash) will count as remuneration (see *Palmanor Ltd v Cedron* [1978] ICR 1008 and *Nerva v RL&G Ltd* [1997] ICR 11). However, it may be that non-cash tips distributed through a tronc system set up by the employer do not count as remuneration, as they do not count towards the minimum wage (see *Revenue and Customs Commissioners v Annabel's (Berkeley Square) Ltd* [2009] ICR 1123).

- Commission which is a regular part of an employee's earnings will amount to remuneration, and can be apportioned as the tribunal deems appropriate (see *Weevsmay Ltd v Kings* [1977] ICR 244 and *J and S Bickley Ltd v Washer* [1977] ICR 425).

- Benefits in kind, such as free lodging, will not count as remuneration.

- Where an individual has been paid less than the minimum wage, the calculation of a week's pay should be based on the pay the individual ought to have received, but at the rate applicable at the date of the hearing (see *Paggetti v Cobb* [2002] IRLR 861).

- A profitability bonus, where completion of normal working hours is a necessary but not sufficient condition for payment, does not fall to be included in the calculation of a week's pay under section 221(2) ERA 1996 (*Econ Engineering Ltd v Dixon* UKEAT/0285/19).

Where an employee has normal working hours

There are three alternative routes to calculating a week's pay:

- **'time workers'**, where the remuneration does not vary with the amount of work done, which includes work where commission is awarded for success achieved, as opposed to being awarded for the work actually done (see *Evans v Malley Organisation Ltd t/a First Business Support* [2003] ICR 432). A week's pay is the amount payable by the employer to the employee under the contract in force at the calculation date if the individual works the normal working hours in a week (s221(2));

- **'piece workers'**, where the remuneration varies according to the amount of work done during normal working hours but does not vary according to the times or days when the work is done. A week's pay is the average hourly rate for the normal working hours calculated over the previous 12 weeks (s221(3)). For these purposes remuneration will include commission which is awarded for success achieved, as opposed to being awarded for the work actually done (see *Evans v Malley Organisation Ltd t/a First Business Support* [2003] ICR 432);

- **'shift workers'**, where normal working hours are worked at times of the day or days of the week that vary from week to week and where remuneration also varies from week to week. A week's pay is calculated over a period of 12 weeks by reference to the average hourly rate multiplied by the average number of normal weekly hours (s222).

Where an employee has no normal working hours

A week's pay is calculated by reference to average weekly remuneration over a 12 week period (s224). In this situation, any overtime payments received will count towards remuneration, whether or not there is a mutual obligation to work and provide overtime (see above re normal working hours).

The 12 week period is based on complete weeks worked (s221(3) and (4) and s235(1)). Any week in which the individual was not working or was not paid remuneration will not count, and an earlier week will be brought in to make up the 12 weeks (s223(2) and s224(3)).

Is the calculation of a week's pay in compliance with EU law?

The concept of a week's pay is used in the working time regulations to calculate holiday pay entitlement. However, the particular means to calculate a week's pay frequently leads to individuals receiving less money than they would have received had they not taken the holiday, for example where regular overtime is required but there is no obligation on the employer to offer it. Please see the section on *Holiday pay* for a more detailed discussion of this issue.

The following examples demonstrate the calculation of a week's pay.

Normal working hours

Straightforward number of hours and constant pay per hour/week/month

1. Weekly pay for hourly paid employees
Weekly pay for hourly paid employees = Number of normal hours worked per week x (hourly rate + hourly commission/bonus if they are constant).

If the commission is not constant, this calculation does not apply (see below). If the period of commission does not coincide with the period of payment, the weekly pay should be calculated in a manner which is just, over the whole period (s229(2)).

2. Weekly pay for monthly, annual or other period paid employees
The tribunal must apportion the payment in the manner that is considers just (ERA 1996 s229(2)).

One way in which this could be done is as follows:

Weekly pay = Monthly salary ÷ 4.3 (or alternatively, monthly salary x 12 ÷ 365 x 7 which produces a slightly different answer because of rounding errors)

Weekly pay = Annual salary ÷ 52

Weekly pay = Other period salary ÷ number of days in which it was earned x 7

3. Weekly pay with differing commission
Weekly pay with differing commission = Number of hours worked in a week x hourly rate + (total commission earned ÷ number of weeks in which it was earned)

Straightforward but pay and/or commission/bonus varying with output (piece workers)

Weekly pay = Average hourly rate x hours in a normal working week = (Total remuneration, including overtime, in the previous 12 week period ÷ total hours worked in the 12 week period) x hours in a normal working week

However, note that overtime hours are rated as basic hours - overtime premiums are ignored.

Variable hours (shift workers)

Weekly pay = Average hourly rate x average hours in a normal working week = (Total remuneration in previous 12 weeks ÷ Total hours worked in previous 12 weeks, including overtime hours if they form part of the normal working hours) x (number of hours worked in the 12 week period ÷12)

Note: the 12 weeks needs to be taken prior to the pay date or the calculation date, whichever is the earlier.

Also, if in any week no remuneration or guaranteed pay was paid, those weeks are ignored and an earlier week is used in the calculation.

No normal working hours (casual workers)

Weekly pay = Total remuneration, including overtime and overtime rates, in 12 weeks immediately before calculation date (or the pay day immediately before the calculation date if calculation date is not the same as the pay date) ÷ 12

Statutory authorities: Chapter II ERA 1996

COVID-19: The coronavirus pandemic resulted in large numbers of employees being placed on furlough under the Coronavirus Job Retention Scheme. The Employment Rights Act 1996 (Coronavirus, Calculation of a Week's Pay) Regulations SI 2020/814 (as amended) provide, in effect, that the calculation of an employee's week's pay should be calculated as if their furloughed hours were normal working hours and disregarding any reduction in pay as a result of being furloughed.

Relevant case law: *BA v Williams* [2011] IRLR 948; *Bear Scotland & Ors v Fulton & Ors* UKEATS/0047/13/BI; *Canadian Imperial Bank of Commerce v Beck* EAT 0141/10; *Donelan v Kerrby Constructions* [1983] ICR 237; *Econ Engineering Ltd v Dixon* UKEAT/0285/19; *Evans v Malley Organisation Ltd t/a First Business Support* [2003] ICR 432; *Fox v C Wright (Farmers) Ltd* [1978] ICR 98; *Hoyland v Asda Stores Ltd* [2006] IRLR 468; *J and S Bickley Ltd v Washer* [1977] ICR 425; *Mole Mining Ltd v Jenkins* [1972] ICR 282; *Nerva v RL&G Ltd* [1997] ICR 11; *Paggetti v Cobb* [2002] IRLR 861; *Palmanor Ltd v Cedron* [1978] ICR 1008; *Revenue and Customs Commissioners v Annabel's (Berkeley Square) Ltd* [2009] ICR 1123; *Sanderson v Exel Management Services Ltd* [2006] ICR 1337; *Tarmac Roadstone Holdings Ltd v Peacock* [1973] ICR 273; *Toni & Guys (St Pauls) Ltd v Georgiou* UKEAT/0085/13/DM; *Weevsmay Ltd v Kings* [1977] ICR 244; *Z.J.R. Lock v British Gas Trading Ltd and Others* [2014] ICR 813 (CJEU)

Working Time Regulations

An adult worker is entitled to various periods of rest as detailed in the *WTR 1998.* A breach of these regulations could entitle the worker to bring a claim at the ET.

By Reg 30(1)(a) a worker may bring a claim to the tribunal that his employer has denied him the following rights:

- Sufficient daily rest under Reg 10(1) or (2);

- Sufficient weekly rest under Reg 11(1), (2) or (3);

- Sufficient rest breaks within a working day under Reg 12(1) or (4);

- Sufficient annual leave under Reg 13;

- Entitlement to additional annual leave under Reg 13A;

- Compensatory rest under Reg 24;

- Adequate rest (if a mobile worker) under Reg 24A;

- Compensatory rest (if a young worker in the armed forces) under Reg 25(3);

- Compensatory rest (during night work if a young worker) under Reg 27A(4)(b); or

- Compensatory rest (if a young worker and certain exceptional circumstances apply) under Reg 27(3).

By Reg 30(1)(b) a worker may bring a bring a claim to the tribunal that his employer has failed to pay him the whole or any part of his or her entitlement to paid leave or payment in lieu of leave untaken at termination (Reg 30(1)(b)). Such a claim may also be brought as a deduction from wages claim under s13 ERA 1996 (see *Stringer v HM Revenue and Customs* [2009] IRLR 677).

Remedy: Where a tribunal finds a complaint under Reg 30(1)(a) well founded, it will make a declaration to that effect and may make an award of compensation.

Compensation will be determined as that which the tribunal considers to be just and equitable in all the circumstances having regard to the employer's default in refusing to permit the worker to exercise his right and any loss sustained by the worker as a result. Such an award does not include injury to feelings, as these claims are akin to breach of contract rather than discrimination (*Gomes v Higher Level Care Ltd* [2018] EWCA Civ 418). They can, however, include a claim for injury to health (*Grange v Abellio London Limited* UKEAT/0304/17/JOJ).

Where a tribunal finds a complaint under Reg 30(1)(b) that certain pay for leave entitlement has not been paid, it will order the employer to pay the worker the sums owing (Reg 30(5)).

Gross or net: N/A for Regs 10, 11, 12, 13, 24 or 24A; Gross for Regs 14 and 16

Tax: The tax treatments is unclear for payments under Regs 10, 11, 12, 13, 24 or 24A. However, tax should be paid under s62 ITEPA 2003 for payments under Regs 14 and 16.

Statutory authorities: WTR 1998 Regs 10 to 13, Reg 24, Reg 24A, Reg 25, Reg 27, Reg 27A, Reg 30(1)(a)

Relevant case law: *Gomes v Higher Level Care Ltd* [2018] EWCA Civ 418; *Grange v Abellio London Limited* UKEAT/0304/17/JOJ; *Stringer v HM Revenue and Customs* [2009] IRLR 677

Written reasons for dismissal

An employee is entitled to a written statement of reasons for dismissal from his or her employer where the dismissal arises from either: a) the employer giving notice; b) the employer terminating without notice; or c) if a limited term contract terminates by virtue of its limiting event (s92(1) ERA 1996). Generally, the employee must have made a request for the written reasons and must have been continuously employed for 2 years (s92(2) and (3)). The exception is where someone is dismissed when she is pregnant or on maternity leave until dismissed (s92(4)), or he or she is on adoption leave until dismissed (s92(4A)).

An employee may make a complaint to a tribunal that his or her employer has unreasonably failed to provide the statement or that the particulars of the statement given are inadequate or untrue (s93(1)).

Remedy: Where a tribunal finds such a complaint well founded, it may make a declaration as to what it finds the employer's reasons were for dismissing the employee and will make an award of 2 weeks' pay.

Gross or net: Gross. A week's pay as defined in ss220 to 229 ERA 1996 applies (see *Week's pay*).

Limit on a week's pay: None

Limit on number of weeks: 2

Any maximum or minimum: The award is simply 2 weeks' pay.

Adjustments: None

Cap: The award will form part of the compensatory award and the cap will apply in non-discriminatory unfair dismissal cases.

Mitigation: N/A

Tax: Any payment made in connection with the termination of employment will be taxed under s401 ITEPA 2003, of which this award will form a part.

Recoupment: The award should not form part of the prescribed element.

Statutory authorities: ERA 1996 *ss92 and 93*

Written statement of particulars

The *Employment Rights (Employment Particulars and Paid Annual Leave) (Amendment) Regulations 2018* amended sections 1 to 7B of Part I of the Employment Rights Act 1996. The amendments, which came into force on 6 April 2020, have the effect of making the right to a written statement of employment particulars a 'day 1' right for all workers (not just employees) and adding additional contents to the written statement. This means:

1) They are entitled to receive the 'principal statement' of the written statement no later than the first day of their new job (before 6 April 2020 the employer had a period of two months in which to provide the statement).

2) There is no qualifying period of employment (prior to 6 April 2020 employees were entitled to a written statement only if their employment had continued for at least one month).

An employee may bring a claim to a tribunal alleging that his or her employer has not complied with these obligations (s11(1)), and either party may bring a reference to a tribunal to determine what particulars ought to have been supplied (s11(2)).

Remedy (1): The tribunal has the power to determine the particulars of employment between the parties (s12(1) and (2)). Where an itemised pay statement has not been provided, or where deductions have been made which were not itemised on such a statement, the tribunal will make a declaration to that effect and may order the employer to pay the employee the value of the deductions (s12(3) and (4)).

Remedy (2): There is an additional right to a remedy from a tribunal where a claim has been brought within the list of jurisdictions in Sch 5 to EA 2002 (the list is extensive and includes many of the common, and not so common, claims). Where under such a claim the tribunal finds for the employee, whether or not it makes an award in respect of that claim, and where when the proceedings were brought the employer was in breach of the duty to give written particulars, the tribunal will make an award of 2 weeks' pay unless it would be unjust and inequitable to do so, and may if it considers it just and equitable in all the circumstances make an award of 4 weeks' pay (see ss38(1) to (5) EA 2002). For such an award to be made, the employer must be in breach of the obligation at the time the proceedings have begun. Where the employer has complied with its obligations under section 1, even belatedly, before the proceedings have begun, the tribunal has no power to make such an award (*Govdata Ltd v Denton* UKEAT/0237/18/BA).

Gross or net: Gross. A week's pay as defined in ss220 to 229 ERA 1996 applies (see *Week's pay*).

Limit on a week's pay: The current weekly limit is £643 (see *Table 1* for historical rates).

Limit on number of weeks: Minimum is 2; Maximum is 4 (s38(4) EA 2002).

Any maximum or minimum: Minimum is 2 weeks' pay, capped; Maximum is 4 weeks' pay, capped.

Adjustments: Contributory conduct applies. See *Adjustments and order of adjustments* for information about the order in which they apply when this head of loss is being claimed.

Cap: The award or increase of any award will fall within any applicable statutory cap for that award.

Mitigation: The usual rules of mitigation apply to the compensatory award.

Tax: The tax rules applicable to the particular award that has been made or increased will apply.

Recoupment: The award should not be included in the prescribed element.

Statutory authorities: EA 2002 *s38*; ERA 1996 *ss1 to 12,* and *ss220 to 229; Employment Rights (Employment Particulars and Paid Annual Leave) (Amendment) Regulations 2018* (SI 2018/1378)

Relevant case law: Govdata Ltd v Denton UKEAT/0237/18/BA

Wrongful dismissal: see *Damages for wrongful dismissal*

Zero-hours contracts

A zero-hours contract is one in which the employer does not guarantee the individual any hours of work. The employer offers the individual work when it arises, and the individual can either accept or decline the work offered on that occasion. Individuals on a zero-hours contract may have the employment status of a 'worker' or an 'employee'. The term is a political rather than a legal concept, potentially covering a range of different contracts and working arrangements.

Regardless of how many hours are actually offered, the employer must pay at least the National Minimum Wage.

Section 27A(3) of the ERA 1996 (as inserted by the Small Business, Enterprise and Employment Act, s153(1) and (2)) provides that, from 26 May 2015, a provision in a zero hours contract which prohibits the worker from doing work under any other arrangement is unenforceable.

Regulation 2 of the Exclusivity Terms in Zero Hours Contracts (Redress) Regulations 2015) (ETZHC (R) Regs 2015) makes provision in relation to the right for individuals on a zero hours contract not to be unfairly dismissed or subjected to a detriment (see *Detriment*) for a reason relating to a breach of a provision of a zero hours contract to which s27A(3) of the 1996 Act applies.

There is no qualifying period for an employee bringing such an unfair dismissal or detriment claim to the ET.

Remedy

Where an employment tribunal finds that a complaint is well founded, it must take such of the following steps as it considers just and equitable:

a) making a declaration as to the rights of the complainant and the employer in relation to the matters to which the complaint relates; and

b) ordering the employer to pay compensation to the complainant (Reg 4(1) ETZHC (R) Regs 2015).

The amount of the compensation awarded must be such as the tribunal considers just and equitable in all the circumstances having regard to:

a) the infringement to which the complaint relates; and

b) any loss which is attributable to the act, or failure to act, which infringed the complainant's right (Reg 4(2) ETZHC (R) Regs 2015).

The loss must be taken to include:

a) any expenses reasonably incurred by the complainant in consequence of the act, or failure to act, to which the complaint relates; and

b) loss of any benefit which the complainant might reasonably be expected to have had but for that act or failure to act (Reg 4(3) ETZHC (R) Regs 2015).

Gross or net: The basic award will be calculated gross and the compensatory award will be calculated on the basis of net loss.

Limit on a week's pay: £643 for the basic award element.

Any maximum or minimum: If the detriment to which the worker is subjected is the termination of the worker's contract, but that contract is not a contract of employment, the total award will not exceed the aggregate of the maximum basic award (£19,290) and the maximum compensatory award (£105,707) i.e. £124,997 (Reg 4(6) ETZHC (R) Regs 2015).

Adjustments: The award can be reduced for contributory fault (Reg 4(7) ETZHC (R) Regs 2015).

Mitigation: The individual is expected to mitigate their loss (Reg 4(4) ETZHC (R) Regs 2015).

Tax: If the combined sum of any basic and compensatory award is greater than £30,000 then the excess figure will be subject to tax (see *Grossing up*).

Recoupment: It is assumed that recoupment will be apply to immediate loss of earnings.

Statutory authorities: Exclusivity Terms in Zero Hours Contracts (Redress) Regulations 2015 Regs 2,3 and 4; Small Business, Enterprise and Employment Act 2015 s153; ERA 1996 s27A

Caps and limits

Table 1: Statutory cap, maximum basic award and the limit on gross weekly pay

Date	Maximum Compensatory Award	Maximum Basic Award	Maximum Total	Gross Weekly Pay Limit
06/04/2017 to 05/04/2018	£80,541 or gross annual pay, whichever is the smaller	£14,670	£95,211	£489
06/04/2018 to 05/04/2019	£83,682 or gross annual pay, whichever is the smaller	£15,240	£98,922	£508
06/04/2019 to 05/04/2020	£86,444 or gross annual pay, whichever is the smaller	£15,750	£102,194	£525
06/04/2020 to 05/04/2021	£88,519 or gross annual pay, whichever is the smaller	£16,140	£104,659	£538
06/04/2021 to 05/04/2022	£89,493 or gross annual pay, whichever is the smaller	£16,320	£105,813	£544
06/04/2022 to 05/04/2023	£93,878 or gross annual pay, whichever is the smaller	£17,130	£111,008	£571
06/04/2023 to 05/04/2024	£105,707 or gross annual pay, whichever is the smaller	£19,290	£124,997	£643

Notes

1. The cap on gross weekly pay is only applicable to claims of Statutory redundancy pay, Basic award; Right to written particulars of employment; Right to be accompanied at a disciplinary hearing; Right to request flexible working; Insolvency provisions; Additional award

2. The Employment Rights (Increase of Limits) Order 2023 increased the limits to take effect from 06/04/2023. Limits are increased in line with inflation every 6th April.

Table 2: Limits on awards (other)

See Employment Rights (Increase of limits) Orders

	Award	06/04/2020 to 05/04/2021	06/04/2021 to 05/04/2022	06/04/2022 to 05/04/2023	06/04/2023 to 05/04/2024
s145E(3) TULR(C)A 1992	Amount of award for unlawful inducement relating to trade union membership or activities or for unlawful inducement relating to collective bargaining.	£4,294	£4,341	£4,554	£5,128
s156(1) TULR(C)A 1992	Minimum amount of basic award of compensation where dismissal is unfair by virtue of section 152(1) or 153 of the 1992 Act.	£6,562	£6,634	£6,959	£7,836
s176(6A) TULR(C)A 1992	Minimum amount of compensation where individual excluded or expelled from union in contravention of section 174 of the 1992 Act and not admitted or re-admitted by date of tribunal application.	£10,022	£10,132	£10,628	£11,967
s31(1) ERA 1996	Limit on amount of guarantee payment payable to an employee in respect of any day.	£30	£30	£31	£35
s120(1) ERA 1996	Minimum amount of basic award of compensation where dismissal is unfair by virtue of section 100(1)(a) and (b), 101A(d), 102(1) or 103 of the 1996 Act.	£6,562	£6,634	£6,959	£7,836

Table 3: Guarantee Payments

Date	Daily limit	Maximum amount in any 3 month period (5 days)
06/04/2019 to 05/04/2020	£29.00	£145.00
06/04/2020 to 05/04/2021	£30.00	£150.00
06/04/2021 to 05/04/2022	£30.00	£150.00
06/04/2022 to 05/04/2023	£31.00	£155.00
06/04/2023 to 05/04/2024	£35.00	£175.00

Table 4: Time limits for appeals

Review of ET decision	14 days
Appeal to EAT from ET	42 days
Review of EAT decision	14 days
Appeal to Court of Appeal from EAT	14 days

Table 5: Gross weekly pay: claims for which gross weekly pay is used in the calculation and the related calculation dates

Claim	Calculation date	Limit on a week's pay
Additional award	Date on which employee is given notice or the EDT.	£643
Basic award	If the employee is summarily dismissed or dismissed with less than the statutory notice, the calculation date is the date on which the employment ended. If the employee was dismissed with notice equal to or more than the statutory notice, the calculation date is found by subtracting the statutory notice period from the actual notice given. This means that if statutory notice is given, the calculation date is the date that notice was given. If statutory notice is 3 weeks and actual notice given is 4 weeks, the calculation date is the day after the end of the first week of notice.	£643
Guarantee pay	The day when the guarantee pay is due.	See separate limits
Insolvency	For arrears of pay and holiday, the date on which the employer became insolvent. For the Basic award the latest of (i) the date on which the employer became insolvent, (ii) the date of the termination of the employee's employment, and (iii) the date on which the award was made. In relation to any other debt whichever is the later of (i) the date on which the employer became insolvent, and (ii) the date of the termination of the employee's employment.	£643
Protective award	The date on which the protective award was made or, in the case of an employee who was dismissed before the date on which the protective award was made, the calculation date for the purpose of computing the amount of a redundancy payment.	Unlimited
Remuneration whilst suspended on medical grounds	The day before suspension began.	Unlimited
Right for union member not to be unjustifiably disciplined/expelled and blacklisting claims	N/A	£643 for the Basic award element
Time off to look for work or arrange training after being made redundant	The day on which the employer's notice was given.	Actual gross weekly pay is used but limited to 40% of a week's pay

Table 5: Gross weekly pay: claims for which gross weekly pay is used in the calculation and the related calculation dates

Claim	Calculation date	Limit on a week's pay
Time off for antenatal care	The day of ante-natal appointment.	Unlimited
Time off for employee representatives (including ICE and OPPS); pension trustees; union duties, activities and union learning reps; study or training; young person for study or training; members of a European Works Council	Date on which time off was taken or should have been permitted.	No limit apart from for Study or training (not Young person study or training) where the limit is £643
TUPE claims	In the case of an employee who is dismissed by reason of redundancy the date which is the calculation date for the purposes of any entitlement of his to a redundancy payment. In the case of an employee who is dismissed for any other reason, the effective date of termination. In any other case, the date of the relevant transfer.	Unlimited
Right to be accompanied at a disciplinary or grievance meeting	Date of dismissal/EDT or if no dismissal the date of the hearing.	£643
Right to request flexible working	Date on which the application was made.	£643
Written reasons for dismissal	Date notice was given or if no notice the EDT.	Unlimited
Written statement of particulars	If the employee was employed by the employer on the date the proceedings were begun, that date. If he was not, the effective date of termination.	£643
Paid annual leave under the Working Time Regulations	Payment based on a normal week's pay on the first day of the period of leave in question.	Unlimited
Redundancy payments	Depends on the circumstances.	£643

Holiday

Table 6: Holiday Pay crib sheet

Reproduced from Holidays and holiday pay leaflet – ACAS

Working Pattern	Before 1 April 2009	After 1 April 2009
Full-time (5 day week)	4.8 weeks (24 days)	5.6 weeks (28 days)
Part-time (4 day week)	4.8 weeks (19.2 days)	5.6 weeks (22.4 days)
Part-time (3 day week)	4.8 weeks (14.4 days)	5.6 weeks (16.8 days)
6 day week	4.8 weeks (28 days – the maximum statutory entitlement)	5.6 weeks (28 days – the maximum statutory entitlement)
Compressed hours e.g. 36 hours in 4 days	36 hours x 4.8 weeks = 172.8 hours per year	36 hours x 5.6 weeks = 201.6 hours per year
Annualised hours e.g. 1,600 hours at an average of 33.5 hours week	33.5 hours x 4.8 weeks = 160.8 hours per year	33.5 hours x 5.6 weeks = 187.6 hours per year
Bank Holidays	Can be included in the 4.8 weeks leave – check the contract	Can be included in the 5.6 weeks leave – check the contract

Income Tax and National Insurance

Table 7: Income Tax Rates and Taxable Bands (England & Wales)

Rate	2021-2022	2022-2023	2023-2024
Zero rate: 0% (Personal allowance) [1]	£0 - £12,570	£0 - £12,570	£0 - £12,570
Basic rate: 20%	The next £37,700	The next £37,700	The next £37,700
Higher rate: 40%	The next £99,730	The next £99,730	The next £74,870
Additional rate: 45%	Over £150,000	Over £150,000	Over £125,140
Starting rate for savings	£0 - £5,000	£0 - £5,000	£0 - £5,000
Savings allowance (basic rate tax payers)	£1,000	£1,000	£1,000
Savings allowance (higher rate tax payers)	£500	£500	£500
Savings allowance (additional rate tax payers)	NIL	NIL	NIL

[1] But remember that the personal allowance will decrease by £1 for every £2 of earnings over £100,000 so this will need to be taken into account.

Table 8: Income Tax Rates and Taxable Bands (Scotland)

Rate	2021-2022	2022-2023	2023-2024
Zero rate: 0% (Personal allowance) [1]	£0 - £12,570	£0 - £12,570	£0 - £12,570
Starter rate: 19%	The next £2,097	The next £2,162	The next £2,162
Basic rate: 20%	The next £10,629	The next £10,956	The next £10,956
Intermediate rate: 21%	The next £18,366	The next £17,974	The next £17,974
Higher rate: 42% (41% in 2021/22/23)	The next £106,338	The next £106,338	The next £81,478
Top/Additional rate: 47% (46% in 2021/22/23)	Over £150,000	Over £150,000	Over £125,140

[1] But remember that the personal allowance will decrease by £1 for every £2 of earnings over £100,000 so this will need to be taken into account.

Table 9: Income Tax Allowances (England, Wales & Scotland)

Income Tax allowances	2021-2022	2022-2023	2023-2024
Personal Allowance	£12,570	£12,570	£12,570
Income limit for Personal Allowance [1]	£100,000	£100,000	£100,000
Maximum amount of Married Couple's Allowance [2] [3]	£9,125	£9,415	£10,375
Minimum amount of Married Couple's Allowance [2] [4]	£3,530	£3,640	£4,010
Blind Person's Allowance	£2,520	£2,600	£2,870
Transferable Tax Allowance for married couples and civil partners [5]	£1,260	£1,260	£1,260
Dividend allowance	£2,000	£2,000	£1,000

[1] The personal allowance reduces where the individual's income is above this limit by £1 for every £2 above the limit. This applies regardless of the individual's date of birth.

[2] Available to people born before 6 April 1935. Tax relief for this allowance is restricted to 10%.

[3] This allowance is reduced when the individual's income is above the income limit. This is at a rate of £1 for every £2 above the income limit until it reaches the minimum amount. Any reduction in the married couple's allowance applies after any reduction to the individual's personal allowance.

[4] This is also the maximum relief for maintenance payments where at least one of the parties is born before 6 April 1935.

[5] Available to spouses/civil partners born after 5 April 1935. This allowance is 10% of the personal allowance for those born after 5 April 1938. It allows a spouse or civil partner who is not liable to income tax above the basic rate to transfer this amount of their personal allowance to their spouse/civil partner. The recipient must not be liable to tax above the basic rate. The recipient is eligible to a tax reduction of 20% of the transferred amount.

Table 10: National Insurance Contributions: Rates and Allowances (England, Wales & Scotland)

	2021-22	2022-2023	2023-2024
Lower earnings limit, primary Class 1	£120	£123	£123
Upper earnings limit, primary Class 1	£967	£967	£967
Primary threshold (employee contribution)	£184	£190[1]	£242
Secondary threshold (employer contribution)	£170	£175	£175
Employees' primary Class 1 rate between primary threshold and upper earnings limit (not contracted out)	12%	12%	12%
Employees' primary Class 1 rate above upper earnings limit	2%	2%	2%
Class 1A rate on employer provided benefits [2]	13.8%	13.8%	
Employers' secondary Class 1 rate above secondary threshold – no limit (not contracted out)	13.8%	13.8%	13.8%
Employment Allowance	£4,000 per year, per employer	£4,000 per year, per employer	£5,000 per year, per employer
Apprentice Upper Secondary Threshold (AUST) for under 25s	£967	£967	£967
Class 2 Rate	£3.05 per week	£3.15 per week	£3.45 per week
Class 2 small earnings exception/Small Profits Threshold	£6,515 per year	£6,725 per year	£6,725 per year
Special Class 2 rate for share fishermen	£3.70 per week	£3.80 per week	£4.10 per week
Special Class 2 rate for volunteer development workers	£6.00 per week	£6.15 per week	£6.15 per week
Class 3 rate	£15.40 per week	£15.85 per week	£17.45 per week
Class 4 lower profits limit	£9,568 per year	£9,880 per year	£12,570 per year
Class 4 upper profits limit	£50,270 per year	£50,270 per year	£50,270 per year
Class 4 rate between lower profits limit and upper profits limit	9%	10.25%	9.73%
Class 4 rate above upper profits limit	2%	3.25%	2.73%

[1] On 23 March 2022 the then Chancellor, Rishi Sunak, announced an increase in the threshold for payment of Employee's National Insurance from £190 per week to £242 per week, with effect from July 2022. This reduces the amount of NI that employees will pay from that date, but payments made between April and June will have the previous threshold applied.

[2] Class 1A NICs are payable in July and are calculated on the value of taxable benefits provided in the previous tax year, using the secondary Class 1 percentage rate appropriate to that tax year.

Table 11: Income Tax and National Insurance: Gross to Net Salaries 2023 - 2024

Gross Annual Salary	Tax (England & Wales)	Tax (Scotland)	Employee National Insurance (England, Wales and Scotland)	Net Annual Salary (England & Wales)	Net Annual Salary (Scotland)
13,000	86.00	81.70	51.60	12,862.40	12,866.70
14,000	286.00	271.70	171.60	13,542.40	13,556.70
15,000	464.38	464.38	291.60	14,222.40	14,244.02
16,000	686.00	664.38	411.60	14,902.40	14,924.02
17,000	886.00	864.38	531.60	15,582.40	15,604.02
18,000	1,086.00	1,064.38	651.60	16,262.40	16,284.02
19,000	1,286.00	1,264.38	771.60	16,942.40	16,964.02
20,000	1,486.00	1,464.38	891.60	17,622.40	17,644.02
21,000	1,686.00	1,664.38	1,011.60	18,302.40	18,324.02
22,000	1,886.00	1,864.38	1,131.60	18,982.40	19,004.02
23,000	2,086.00	2,064.38	1,251.60	19,662.40	19,684.02
24,000	2,286.00	2,264.38	1,371.60	20,342.40	20,364.03
25,000	2,486.00	2,464.38	1,491.60	21,022.40	21,044.02

Table 11: Income Tax and National Insurance: Gross to Net Salaries 2023 - 2024

Gross Annual Salary	Tax (England & Wales)	Tax (Scotland)	Employee National Insurance (England, Wales and Scotland)	Net Annual Salary (England & Wales)	Net Annual Salary (Scotland)
26,000	2,686.00	2,667.50	1,611.60	21,702.40	21,720.90
27,000	2,886.00	2,877.50	1,731.60	22,382.40	22,390.90
28,000	3,086.00	3,087.50	1,851.60	23,062.40	23,060.90
29,000	3,286.00	3,297.50	1,971.60	23,742.40	23,730.90
30,000	3,486.00	3,507.50	2,091.60	24,422.40	24,400.90
35,000	4,486.00	4,557.50	2,691.60	27,822.40	27,750.90
40,000	5,486.00	5,607.50	3,291.60	31,222.40	31,100.90
45,000	6,486.00	6,938.48	3,891.60	34,622.40	34,169.92
50,000	7,486.00	9,038.48	4,491.60	38,022.40	36,469.92
55,000	9,432.00	11,138.48	4,618.60	40,949.40	39,242.92
60,000	11,432.00	13,238.48	4,718.60	43,849.40	42,042.92
65,000	13,432.00	15,338.48	4,818.60	46,749.40	44,842.92
70,000	15,432.00	17,438.48	4,918.60	49,649.40	47,642.92
75,000	17,432.00	19,538.48	5,018.60	52,549.40	50,442.92
80,000	19,432.00	21,638.48	5,118.60	55,449.40	53,242.92
85,000	21,432.00	23,738.48	5,218.60	58,349.40	56,042.92
90,000	23,432.00	25,838.48	5,318.60	61,249.40	58,842.92
95,000	25,432.00	27,938.48	5,418.60	64,149.40	61,642.92
100,000	27,432.00	30,038.48	5,518.60	67,049.40	64,442.92
125,000	37,432.00	45,788.48	6,018.60	81,549.40	73,192.92
150,000	53,703.00	57,560.88	6,518.60	89,778.40	85,920.52
175,000	64,953.00	69,310.88	7,018.60	103,028.40	98,670.52
200,000	76,203.00	81,060.88	7,518.60	116,278.40	111,420.523

Assumption: the above figures are based on a tax code of 1257L (the personal allowance for 2023-24 is £12,570, unchanged from the previous year). For any net earnings above £100,000 the standard personal allowance has been reduced by £1 for every £2 above £100,000 and the tax calculated accordingly..

Interest

Table 12: Interest Rates

Date	Interest rate
From 01/08/1999	7%
From 01/02/2002	6%
From 01/02/2009	3%
From 01/06/2009	1.5%
From 01/07/2009	0.5%
From 29/07/2013	8%

Redundancy and Statutory Notice

Table 13: Statutory Redundancy - number of weeks redundancy pay

Age	Number of years' continuous service																		
	2	3	4	5	6	7	8	9	10	11	12	13	14	15	16	17	18	19	20
17	1	-	-	-	-	-	-	-	-	-	-	-	-	-	-	-	-	-	-
18	1	1½	-	-	-	-	-	-	-	-	-	-	-	-	-	-	-	-	-
19	1	1½	2	-	-	-	-	-	-	-	-	-	-	-	-	-	-	-	-
20	1	1½	2	2½	-	-	-	-	-	-	-	-	-	-	-	-	-	-	-
21	1	1½	2	2½	3	-	-	-	-	-	-	-	-	-	-	-	-	-	-
22	1	1½	2	2½	3	3½	-	-	-	-	-	-	-	-	-	-	-	-	-
23	1½	2	2½	3	3½	4	4½	-	-	-	-	-	-	-	-	-	-	-	-
24	2	2½	3	3½	4	4½	5	5½	-	-	-	-	-	-	-	-	-	-	-
25	2	3	3½	4	4½	5	5½	6	6½	-	-	-	-	-	-	-	-	-	-
26	2	3	4	4½	5	5½	6	6½	7	7½	-	-	-	-	-	-	-	-	-
27	2	3	4	5	5½	6	6½	7	7½	8	8½	-	-	-	-	-	-	-	-
28	2	3	4	5	6	6½	7	7½	8	8½	9	9½	-	-	-	-	-	-	-
29	2	3	4	5	6	7	7½	8	8½	9	9½	10	10½	-	-	-	-	-	-
30	2	3	4	5	6	7	8	8½	9	9½	10	10½	11	11½	-	-	-	-	-
31	2	3	4	5	6	7	8	9	9½	10	10½	11	11½	12	12½	-	-	-	-
32	2	3	4	5	6	7	8	9	10	10½	11	11½	12	12½	13	13½	-	-	-
33	2	3	4	5	6	7	8	9	10	11	11½	12	12½	13	13½	14	14½	-	-
34	2	3	4	5	6	7	8	9	10	11	12	12½	13	13½	14	14½	15	15½	-
35	2	3	4	5	6	7	8	9	10	11	12	13	13½	14	14½	15	15½	16	16½
36	2	3	4	5	6	7	8	9	10	11	12	13	14	14½	15	15½	16	16½	17
37	2	3	4	5	6	7	8	9	10	11	12	13	14	15	15½	16	16½	17	17½
38	2	3	4	5	6	7	8	9	10	11	12	13	14	15	16	16½	17	17½	18
39	2	3	4	5	6	7	8	9	10	11	12	13	14	15	16	17	17½	18	18½
40	2	3	4	5	6	7	8	9	10	11	12	13	14	15	16	17	18	18½	19
41	2	3	4	5	6	7	8	9	10	11	12	13	14	15	16	17	18	19	19½
42	2½	3½	4½	5½	6½	7½	8½	9½	10½	11½	12½	13½	14½	15½	16½	17½	18½	19½	20½
43	3	4	5	6	7	8	9	10	11	12	13	14	15	16	17	18	19	20	21
44	3	4½	5½	6½	7½	8½	9½	10½	11½	12½	13½	14½	15½	16½	17½	18½	19½	20½	21½
45	3	4½	6	7	8	9	10	11	12	13	14	15	16	17	18	19	20	21	22
46	3	4½	6	7½	8½	9½	10½	11½	12½	13½	14½	15½	16½	17½	18½	19½	20½	21½	22½
47	3	4½	6	7½	9	10	11	12	13	14	15	16	17	18	19	20	21	22	23
48	3	4½	6	7½	9	10½	11½	12½	13½	14½	15½	16½	17½	18½	19½	20½	21½	22½	23½
49	3	4½	6	7½	9	10½	12	13	14	15	16	17	18	19	20	21	22	23	24
50	3	4½	6	7½	9	10½	12	13½	14½	15½	16½	17½	18½	19½	20½	21½	22½	23½	24½
51	3	4½	6	7½	9	10½	12	13½	15	16	17	18	19	20	21	22	23	24	25
52	3	4½	6	7½	9	10½	12	13½	15	16½	17½	18½	19½	20½	21½	22½	23½	24½	25½
53	3	4½	6	7½	9	10½	12	13½	15	16½	18	19	20	21	22	23	24	25	26
54	3	4½	6	7½	9	10½	12	13½	15	16½	18	19½	20½	21½	22½	23½	24½	25½	26½
55	3	4½	6	7½	9	10½	12	13½	15	16½	18	19½	21	22	23	24	25	26	27
56	3	4½	6	7½	9	10½	12	13½	15	16½	18	19½	21	22½	23½	24½	25½	26½	27½
57	3	4½	6	7½	9	10½	12	13½	15	16½	18	19½	21	22½	24	25	26	27	28
58	3	4½	6	7½	9	10½	12	13½	15	16½	18	19½	21	22½	24	25½	26½	27½	28½
59	3	4½	6	7½	9	10½	12	13½	15	16½	18	19½	21	22½	24	25½	27	28	29
60	3	4½	6	7½	9	10½	12	13½	15	16½	18	19½	21	22½	24	25½	27	28½	29½
61+	3	4½	6	7½	9	10½	12	13½	15	16½	18	19½	21	22½	24	25½	27	28½	30

Table 14: Statutory Notice Periods

Period of continuous employment (years)	Minimum period of notice (weeks)
Less than 2 years (but more than 1 month)	1
At least 2 but less than 3	2
At least 3 but less than 4	3
At least 4 but less than 5	4
At least 5 but less than 6	5
At least 6 but less than 7	6
At least 7 but less than 8	7
At least 8 but less than 9	8
At least 9 but less than 10	9
At least 10 but less than 11	10
At least 11 but less than 12	11
12 years or more	12

Statutory Rates

Table 15: National Minimum and Living Wage Rates

Year	Living wage for adults aged 25 and over[1]	National Minimum Wage for workers between the ages of 21 and 24[2]	Development Rate (for 18 to 20 year olds)	16-17 year olds rate	Apprentice rate[3]
01/04/2018 to 31/03/2019	£7.83	£7.38	£5.90	£4.20	£3.70
01/04/2019 to 31/03/2020	£8.21	£7.70	£6.15	£4.35	£3.90
01/04/2020 to 31/03/2021	£8.72	£8.20	£6.45	£4.55	£4.15
01/04/2021 to 31/03/2022	£8.91	£8.36	£6.56	£4.62	£4.30
01/10/2022 to 31/03/2023	£9.50	£9.18	£6.83	£4.81	£4.81
01/04/2023 to 31/03/2024	£10.42	£10.18	£7.49	£5.28	£5.28

[1] The living wage applies to anyone **aged 23 and over** from 1 April 2021.

[2] From 1 April 2021, this rate applies to anyone **aged 21 to 22** inclusive.

[3] This rate is for apprentices under 19 or those in their first year. For anyone over the age of 19, and past their first year, the rate is applicable to the age.

Table 16: Statutory maternity, paternity, adoption, shared parental, parental bereavement and sick pay rates

Date	Statutory Maternity Pay (SMP) (payable for up to 39 weeks)	Ordinary Statutory Paternity Pay (OSPP) (payable for up to 2 weeks)	Statutory Adoption Pay (SAP) (payable for up to 39 weeks)	Statutory Shared Parental Pay (ShPP) (for parents of children due or adopted on or after 5 April 2015) (remaining weeks up to 39)	Statutory Parental Bereavement Pay (for employed parents who lose a child on or after 6 April 2020) (payable for up to 2 weeks)	Statutory Sick Pay (SSP)
06/04/2021 to 05/04/2022	90% of average weekly gross pay for first 6 weeks; and then £151.97 or 90% of average gross weekly earnings (whichever is lower) for the next 33 weeks	£151.97 or 90% of average gross weekly earnings (whichever is lower)	90% of average weekly gross pay for first 6 weeks; and then £151.97 or 90% of average gross weekly earnings (whichever is lower) for the next 33 weeks	£151.97 or 90% of average gross weekly earnings (whichever is lower)	£151.97 or 90% of average gross weekly earnings (whichever is lower)	£96.35 per week
06/04/2022 to 05/04/2023	90% of average weekly gross pay for first 6 weeks; and then £156.66 or 90% of average gross weekly earnings (whichever is lower) for the next 33 weeks	£156.66 or 90% of average gross weekly earnings (whichever is lower)	90% of average weekly gross pay for first 6 weeks; and then £156.66 or 90% of average gross weekly earnings (whichever is lower) for the next 33 weeks	£156.66 or 90% of average gross weekly earnings (whichever is lower)	£156.66 or 90% of average gross weekly earnings (whichever is lower)	£99.35 per week
06/04/2023 to 05/04/2024	90% of average weekly gross pay for first 6 weeks; and then £172.48 or 90% of average gross weekly earnings (whichever is lower) for the next 33 weeks	£172.48 or 90% of average gross weekly earnings (whichever is lower)	90% of average weekly gross pay for first 6 weeks; and then £172.48 or 90% of average gross weekly earnings (whichever is lower) for the next 33 weeks	£172.48 or 90% of average gross weekly earnings (whichever is lower)	£172.48 or 90% of average gross weekly earnings (whichever is lower)	£109.40 per week

Legislation

Table 17: List of abbreviated statutes and statutory instruments	
AWR 2010	Agency Workers Regulations 2010
CA 2020	Coronavirus Act 2020
CAR 2004	Civil Aviation (Working Time) Regulations 2004
CCBR 2007	Companies (Cross-Border Mergers) Regulations 2007
CEC 1975	Colleges of Education (Compensation) Regulations 1975
COMAH 1999	Control of Major Accident Hazards Regulations 1999
CRA(TU)PE 2014	Collective Redundancies and Transfer of Undertakings (Protection of Employment) (Amendment) Regulations 2014
EA 2002	Employment Act 2002
EA 2010	Equality Act 2010
EA 2016	Enterprise Act 2016
EAA 1973	Employment Agencies Act 1973
ECSR 2006	European Cooperative Society (Involvement of Employees) Regulations 2006
EE(RB)R 2003	Employment Equality (Religion or Belief) Regulations 2003
EE(SO)R 2003	Employment Equality (Sexual Orientation) Regulations 2003
EJOs 1994	Employment Tribunals Extension of Jurisdiction (England and Wales) Order 1994(13); and Employment Tribunals Extension of Jurisdiction (Scotland) Order 1994
EOR 2009	Ecclesiastical Offices (Terms of Service) Regulations 2009
ELLR 2009	European Public Limited-Liability Company (Employee Involvement) (Great Britain) Regulations 2009
EPA 1970	Equal Pay Act 1970
EP(RJAIS) Regs 1996	Employment Protection (Recoupment of Jobseeker's Allowance and Income Support) Regulations 1996
ERA 1996	Employment Rights Act 1996
ERelA 1999	Employment Relations Act 1999
ERR 2013	Enterprise and Regulatory Reform Act 2013
EST (PR) Regs 2010	Employee Study and Training (Procedural Requirements) Regulations 2010
EST (ECR) Regulations 2010	Employee Study and Training (Eligibility, Complaints and Remedies) Regulations 2010
ETA 1996	Employment Tribunals Act 1996
ET(I) Order 2013	Employment Tribunals (Interest) Order (Amendment) Order 2013
ET(IADC) Regs 2013	Employment Tribunals (Interest on Awards in Discrimination Cases)(Amendment) Regulations 2013
ETZH C (R) Regs 2015	Exclusivity Terms in Zero Hours Contracts (Redress) Regulations 2015
FA 2017	Finance Act 2017
FTE(PLFT) Regs 2002	Fixed Term Employees (Prevention of less favourable treatment) Regulations 2002
FVR 2004	Fishing Vessels (Working Time: Sea-fishermen) Regulations 2004
FW(PR) Regs 2002	Flexible Working (Procedural Requirements) Regulations 2002
FW(ECR) Regs 2002	Flexible Working (Eligibility, Complaints and Remedies) Regulations 2002
HSCE 1996	Health and Safety (Consultation with Employees) Regulations 1996
HSWA 1974	Health and Safety at Work etc Act 1974
ICE Regs 2004	Information and Consultation of Employees Regulations 2004
ICR 2004	Information and Consultation of Employees Regulations 2004
ITA 1982	Industrial Training Act 1982
IT(IADC) Regs 1996	Industrial Tribunals (Interest on Awards in Discrimination Cases) Regulations 1996
MSR 2003	Merchant Shipping (Working Time: Inland Waterways) Regulations 2003
NMWA 1998	National Minimum Wage Act 1998
OPPS Regs 2006	The Occupational and Personal Pension Schemes (Consultation by Employers and Miscellaneous Amendment) Regulations 2006
OPS(CO)R 1996	Occupational Pension Schemes (Contracting-Out) Regulations 1996

Legislation

Table 17: List of abbreviated statutes and statutory instruments

OPS(DI)R 1996	Occupational Pensions Schemes (Disclosure of Information) Regulations 1996
PSA 1993	Pension Schemes Act 1993
PTW(PLFT) Regs 2000	Part Time Workers (Prevention of less favourable treatment) Regulations 2000
PWER Regs 2016	The Posted Workers (Enforcement of Employment Rights) Regulations 2016
REACHER 2008	REACH Enforcement Regulations 2008
RTR 2005	Road Transport (Working Time) Regulations 2005
SBEE 2015	Small Business, Enterprise and Employment Act 2015
TICE 1999	Transnational Information and Consultation of Employees Regulations 1999
TULR(C)A 1992	Trade Union and Labour Relations (Consolidation) Act 1992
TUPE Regs 2006	The Transfer of Undertakings (Protection of Employment) Regulations 2006
WTR 1998	Working Time Regulations 1998

Table 18: Limitation periods and requisite minimum qualifying periods for claims

Claim	Limitation period (maximum length of time that can elapse for claim to be brought to ET)	Length of service required before a claim can be brought to ET
Discrimination (ss13, 15, 16, 18, 19, 21, 26, 27 EA 2010)	3 months (or 6 months if relating to armed forces service) (s123 EA 2010)	None
Right of union member not to be unjustifiably disciplined (s64 TULR(C)A)	3 months (s66 TULR(C)A)	None
Right of union member to compensation if declared to be unjustifiably disciplined (s67 TULR(C)A)	6 months, but not before 4 weeks (s67(3) TULR(C)A)	None
Right of union member not to suffer deduction of unauthorised or excessive subscriptions (s68 TULR(C)A)	3 months (s68A(1) TULR(C)A)	None
Right of union member not to suffer deduction of contributions to a political fund (s86 TULR(C)A)	3 months (s87(2) TULR(C)A)	None
Right of union member if employer has failed to comply with their right not to suffer deduction of contributions to a political fund (s87(5) TULR(C)A)	6 months but not before 4 weeks (s87(6) TULR(C)A)	None
Refusal of employment on grounds related to trade union membership (s137 TULR(C)A)	3 months (s139(1) TULR(C)A)	None
Right not to be offered inducements relating to union membership or activities (s145A TULR(C)A)	3 months (s145C TULR(C)A)	None
Right not to be offered inducements relating to collective bargaining (s145B TULR(C)A)	3 months (s145C TULR(C)A)	None
Protection from detriment (not dismissal) relating to union membership or activities (s146 TULR(C)A)	3 months (s147(1) TULR(C)A)	None
Time off for union duties (s168 TULR(C)A)	3 months (s171 TULR(C)A)	None
Time off for union learning representatives (s168A TULR(C)A)	3 months (s171 TULR(C)A)	None
Payment for time off for union duties and union learning reps (s169 TULR(C)A)	3 months (s171 TULR(C)A)	None
Time off for union activities (s170 TULR(C)A)	3 months (s171 TULR(C)A)	None
Right not to be excluded or expelled from union (s174 TULR(C)A)	6 months (s175 TULR(C)A)	None

Table 18: Limitation periods and requisite minimum qualifying periods for claims

Claim	Limitation period (maximum length of time that can elapse for claim to be brought to ET)	Length of service required before a claim can be brought to ET
Right to compensation if excluded or expelled from union (s176(2) TULR(C)A)	6 months (but not before 4 weeks) (s176(3) TULR(C)A)	None
Redundancy - right to be consulted (s188 TULR(C)A)	3 months (s189(5) TULR(C)A)	None
Redundancy - right to election of employee reps (s188A TULR(C)A)	3 months (s189(5) TULR(C)A)	None
Redundancy - right to be paid during protected period (s190 TULR(C)A)	3 months (s192(3) TULR(C)A)	None
Right to written statement of particulars (s1(1) ERA), or change in particulars (s4(1) ERA), or itemised pay statement (s8(1) ERA)	During employment or within 3 months of termination (s11(4) ERA)	1 month (s198 ERA) (none in the case of itemised statement)
Right not to suffer unauthorised deductions (normal) (s13(1) ERA), (retail) (s18(1)), not to make payments to employer (normal) (s15(1)), (retail) (s21(1))	3 months (s23 ERA)	None
Right to guarantee payments (s28(1) ERA)	3 months (s34(2) ERA)	1 month (s29 ERA)
Right not to suffer detriment (ss43M, 44, 45, 45A, 46, 47, 47A, 47B, 47C, 47D, 47E, 47F ERA; Reg 4 Exclusivity Terms in Zero Hours Contracts (Redress) Regulations 2015)	3 months (s48(3) ERA; Reg 3 Exclusivity Terms in Zero Hours Contracts (Redress) Regulations 2015 The time limit may be extended under the Exclusivity Terms Act in certain circumstances	None, except: 26 weeks in the case of Ordinary Adoption Leave (pre-5 April 2015 only), Additional Adoption Leave (pre-5 April 2015 only), Ordinary Paternity Leave (birth), Additional Paternity Leave (birth) (pre-5 April 2015 only), Paternity Leave (adoption), Shared Parental Leave; 1 year in the case of Parental Leave (reg 13 Maternity and Parental Leave etc Regs 1999)
Time off for public duties (s50(1) ERA)	3 months (s51(2) ERA)	None
Time off on redundancy to look for work or arrange training (s52(1) ERA) and payment for time off on redundancy to look for work or arrange training (ss53(1) and 53(4) ERA)	3 months (s54(2) ERA)	2 years (s52(2) ERA)
Time off for ante-natal care (s55(1) ERA) and payment for this time off (s56(1) ERA)	3 months (s57(2) ERA)	None
Time off for dependants (s57A ERA)	3 months (s57B(2) ERA)	None
Time off for pension scheme trustees (s58(1) ERA) and payment for this time off (s59(1) ERA)	3 months (s60(2) ERA)	None
Time off for employee representatives (s61(1) ERA) and payment for this time off (s62(1) ERA)	3 months (s63(2) ERA)	None
Time off for young person for study or training (s63A ERA) and payment for this time off (s63B ERA)	3 months (s63C(2) ERA)	None
Time off for study or training (s63D ERA)	3 months (s63I(5) ERA)	26 weeks (s63D(a) ERA)
Payment for suspension on medical grounds (s64(1) ERA) or maternity grounds (s68 ERA)	3 months (s70(2) ERA)	1 month (s65(1) ERA)
Offer of alternative work when suspended on maternity grounds (s67 ERA)	3 months (s70(5) ERA)	None
Right to request flexible working (s80F ERA)	3 months (s80H(5) ERA)	26 weeks (reg 13 Flexible Working (Eligibility etc) Regs 2002
Right of employee to minimum notice period (s86 ERA)	6 years under contract	1 month (s86 ERA 1996)

Table 18: Limitation periods and requisite minimum qualifying periods for claims

Claim	Limitation period (maximum length of time that can elapse for claim to be brought to ET)	Length of service required before a claim can be brought to ET
Right to written reasons for dismissal (s92(1) ERA)	3 months (s93(3) ERA)	1 year (s92(3) ERA)
Unfair dismissal (s94(1) ERA)	3 months (s111(2) ERA) The time limit may be extended in certain circumstances for claims under Reg 2 Exclusivity Terms in Zero Hours Contracts (Redress) Regulations 2015	1 year where period of continuous service started prior to 6 April 2012; 2 years where period of continuous service started on or after 6 April 2012. There is no qualifying period if the principal reasons for dismissal relates to: ERA ss98B; 99; 100 (1); 101; 101A(1); 102; 103; 103A; 104; s104A; 104B; 104C; 104E; 104F; 105; TULR(C)A Sch A1 para 161; ss238A; 152-153; ICE Reg 30 TICE Reg 28; OPPS 2006; Reg 7 PRW Regs; Reg 6 FTE Regs; s12 ERelA 1999; Sch 6 para 13(5) Exclusivity Terms in Zero Hours Contracts (Redress) Regulations 2015 Reg 2
Right to redundancy payment (s135(1) ERA)	6 months (s164 ERA)	2 years (s155 ERA)
Insolvency claim to Secretary of State (s182 ERA)	3 months (s188(2) ERA)	None
Time off for health and safety reps 1996 and payment for time off (Reg 7 HSC Regs)	3 months (Sch 2 HSC Regs 1996)	None
Claims under the Working Time Regulations (Regs 10, 11, 12, 13, 14, 16, 24, 24A, 25, 27, 27A WTR)	3 months (Reg 30(2) WTR)	None
Right to National Minimum Wage (s1(1) NMWA 1998)	3 months (s23(2) ERA) or 6 years under contract	None
Right to access to records in relation to (s10 NMWA)	3 months (s11 NMWA)	None
Right not to suffer detriment for asserting rights in connection with (s23 NMWA)	3 months (s24(2) NMWA)	None
Right to be accompanied at a grievance or disciplinary meeting (s10 ERelA 1999) and right not to suffer detriment in connection with this right (s12 ERelA)	3 months (s11(2) and s12(2) ERelA)	None
Time off for works body member and right to payment during this time off (Regs 25 and 26 TICE 1999)	3 months (Reg 27(2) TICE)	None
Part-time worker discrimination (Regs 5 and 7(2) PTW Regs 2000)	3 months (Reg 8(2) PTW Regs)	None
Fixed term worker discrimination (Regs 3 and 6(2) FTE Regs 2002)	3 months (Reg 7(2) FTE)	None

Table 18: Limitation periods and requisite minimum qualifying periods for claims

Claim	Limitation period (maximum length of time that can elapse for claim to be brought to ET)	Length of service required before a claim can be brought to ET
Right to be accompanied at, or postponement of, flexible working meeting (Reg 14(2) and 14(4) FW(PR) Regs 2002)	3 months (Reg 15(2) FW(PR) Regs)	None
Time off for employee reps (reg 27 ICE Regs 2004) and payment for time off (Reg 28 ICE)	3 months (Reg 29(2) ICE)	None
Right to be informed and /or consulted over TUPE (Reg 13 TUPE 2006) and right to election of employee reps (Reg 14 TUPE)	3 months (Reg 15(12) TUPE)	None
Time off for employee reps (Sch paragraph 2 OPPS Regs 2006) and payment for time off (Sch paragraph 3 OPPS)	3 months (Schedule paragraph 4(2) OPPS)	None
Right not to suffer detriment in connection with employee reps (Schedule paragraph 7 OPPS)	3 months (Schedule paragraph 8(2) OPPS)	None
Breach of Sex Equality Clause (s66 EA 2010) or Maternity Equality Clause (s73 EA 2010)	6 months (or 9 months if relating to armed forces service) (s129 EA 2010)	None
Right to be accompanied to a meeting concerning study and training (Reg 16 EST (PR) Regs 2010)	3 months (Reg 17(2) EST (PR) Regs)	None

Table 19: Matters to which the prescribed element is attributable

See Schedule to Employment Protection (Recoupment of Jobseeker's Allowance and Income Support) Regulations 1996.

Payment	Proceedings	Matter to which prescribed element is attributable
Guarantee payments under section 28.	Complaint under section 34.	Any amount found to be due to the employee and ordered to be paid under section 34(3) for a period before the conclusion of the tribunal proceedings.
Payments under any collective agreement having regard to which the appropriate Minister has made an exemption order under section 35.	Complaint under section 35(4).	Any amount found to be due to the employee and ordered to be paid under section 34(3), as applied by section 35(4), for a period before the conclusion of the tribunal proceedings.
Payments of remuneration in respect of a period of suspension on medical grounds under section 64 and section 108(2).	Complaint under section 70.	Any amount found to be due to the employee and ordered to be paid under section 70(3) for a period before the conclusion of the tribunal proceedings.
Payments of remuneration in respect of a period of suspension on maternity grounds under section 68.	Complaint under section 70.	Any amount found to be due to the employee and ordered to be paid under section 70(3) for a period before the conclusion of the tribunal proceedings.
Payments under an order for reinstatement under section 114(1).	Complaint of unfair dismissal under section 111(1).	Any amount ordered to be paid under section 114(2)(a) in respect of arrears of pay for a period before the conclusion of the tribunal proceedings.
Payments under an order for re-engagement under section 117(8).	Complaint of unfair dismissal under section 111(1).	Any amount ordered to be paid under section 115(2)(d) in respect of arrears of pay for a period before the conclusion of the tribunal proceedings.
Payments under an award of compensation for unfair dismissal in cases falling under section 112(4) (cases where no order for reinstatement or re-engagement has been made).	Complaint of unfair dismissal under section 111(1).	Any amount ordered to be paid and calculated under section 123 in respect of compensation for loss of wages for a period before the conclusion of the tribunal proceedings.
Payments under an award of compensation for unfair dismissal under section 117(3) where reinstatement order not complied with.	Proceedings in respect of non-compliance with order.	Any amount ordered to be paid and calculated under section 123 in respect of compensation for loss of wages for a period before the conclusion of the tribunal proceedings.

Table 19: Matters to which the prescribed element is attributable

See Schedule to Employment Protection (Recoupment of Jobseeker's Allowance and Income Support) Regulations 1996.

Payment	Proceedings	Matter to which prescribed element is attributable
Payments under an award of compensation for unfair dismissal under section 117(3) where re-engagement order not complied with.	Proceedings in respect of non-compliance with order.	Any amount ordered to be paid and calculated under section 123 in respect of compensation for loss of wages for a period before the conclusion of the tribunal proceedings.
Payments under an interim order for reinstatement under section 163(4) of the 1992 Act.	Proceedings on an application for an order for interim relief under section 161(1) of the 1992 Act.	Any amount found to be due to the complainant and ordered to be paid in respect of arrears of pay for the period between the date of termination of employment and the conclusion of the tribunal proceedings.
Payments under an interim order for re-engagement under section 163(5)(a) of the 1992 Act.	Proceedings on an application for an order for interim relief under section 161(1) of the 1992 Act.	Any amount found to be due to the complainant and ordered to be paid in respect of arrears of pay for the period between the date of termination of employment and the conclusion of the tribunal proceedings.
Payments under an order for the continuation of a contract of employment under section 163(5)(b) of the 1992 Act where employee reasonably refuses re-engagement.	Proceedings on an application for an order for interim relief under section 161(1) of the 1992 Act.	Any amount found to be due to the complainant and ordered to be paid in respect of arrears of pay for the period between the date of termination of employment and the conclusion of the tribunal proceedings.
Payments under an order for the continuation of a contract of employment under section 163(6) of the 1992 Act where employer fails to attend or is unwilling to reinstate or re-engage.	Proceedings on an application for an order for interim relief under section 161(1) of the 1992 Act.	Any amount found to be due to the complainant and ordered to be paid in respect of arrears of pay for the period between the date of termination of employment and the conclusion of the tribunal proceedings.
Payments under an order for the continuation of a contract of employment under sections 166(1) and (2) of the 1992 Act where reinstatement or re-engagement order not complied with.	Proceedings in respect of non-compliance with order.	Any amount ordered to be paid to the employee by way of compensation under section 166(1)(b) of the 1992 Act for loss of wages for the period between the date of termination of employment and the conclusion of the tribunal proceedings.
Payments under an order for compensation under sections 166(3)–(5) of the 1992 Act where order for the continuation of contract of employment not complied with.	Proceedings in respect of non-compliance with order.	Any amount ordered to be paid to the employee by way of compensation under section 166(3)–(4) of the 1992 Act for loss of wages for the period between the date of termination of employment and the conclusion of the tribunal proceedings.
Payments under an order under section 192(3) of the 1992 Act on employer's default in respect of remuneration due to employee under protective award.	Complaint under section 192(1) of the 1992 Act.	Any amount ordered to be paid to the employee in respect of so much of the relevant protected period as falls before the date of the conclusion of the tribunal proceedings.

Pensions

Table 20: State pension age for women born on or before 5 December 1953

For women born	Date State Pension age reached
On or before 5 April 1950	Age 60
6 April 1950 to 5 May 1950	6 May 2010
6 May 1950 to 5 June 1950	6 July 2010
6 June 1950 to 5 July 1950	6 September 2010
6 July 1950 to 5 August 1950	6 November 2010

Pensions

Table 20: State pension age for women born on or before 5 December 1953	
For women born	**Date State Pension age reached**
6 August 1950 to 5 September 1950	6 January 2011
6 September 1950 to 5 October 1950	6 March 2011
6 October 1950 to 5 November 1950	6 May 2011
6 November 1950 to 5 December 1950	6 July 2011
6 December 1950 to 5 January 1951	6 September 2011
6 January 1951 to 5 February 1951	6 November 2011
6 February 1951 to 5 March 1951	6 January 2012
6 March 1951 to 5 April 1951	6 March 2012
6 April 1951 to 5 May 1951	6 May 2012
6 May 1951 to 5 June 1951	6 July 2012
6 June 1951 to 5 July 1951	6 September 2012
6 July 1951 to 5 August 1951	6 November 2012
6 August 1951 to 5 September 1951	6 January 2013
6 September 1951 to 5 October 1951	6 March 2013
6 October 1951 to 5 November 1951	6 May 2013
6 November 1951 to 5 December 1951	6 July 2013
6 December 1951 to 5 January 1952	6 September 2013
6 January 1952 to 5 February 1952	6 November 2013
6 February 1952 to 5 March 1952	6 January 2014
6 March 1952 to 5 April 1952	6 March 2014
6 April 1952 to 5 May 1952	6 May 2014
6 May 1952 to 5 June 1952	6 July 2014
6 June 1952 to 5 July 1952	6 September 2014
6 July 1952 to 5 August 1952	6 November 2014
6 August 1952 to 5 September 1952	6 January 2015
6 September 1952 to 5 October 1952	6 March 2015
6 October 1952 to 5 November 1952	6 May 2015
6 November 1952 to 5 December 1952	6 July 2015
6 December 1952 to 5 January 1953	6 September 2015
6 January 1953 to 5 February 1953	6 November 2015
6 February 1953 to 5 March 1953	6 January 2016
6 March 1953 to 5 April 1953	6 March 2016
6 April 1953 to 5 May 1953	6 July 2016
6 May 1953 to 5 June 1953	6 November 2016
6 June 1953 to 5 July 1953	6 March 2017
6 July 1953 to 5 August 1953	6 July 2017
6 August 1953 to 5 September 1953	6 November 2017
6 September 1953 to 5 October 1953	6 March 2018
6 October 1953 to 5 November 1953	6 July 2018
6 November 1953 to 5 December 1953	6 November 2018

Table 21: State pension age for men and women born after 5 December 1953

For men and women born	Date State Pension age reached
6 December 1953 to 5 January 1954	6 March 2019
6 January 1954 to 5 February 1954	6 May 2019
6 February 1954 to 5 March 1954	6 July 2019
6 March 1954 to 5 April 1954	6 September 2019
6 April 1954 to 5 May 1954	6 November 2019
6 May 1954 to 5 June 1954	6 January 2020
6 June 1954 to 5 July 1954	6 March 2020
6 July 1954 to 5 August 1954	6 May 2020
6 August 1954 to 5 September 1954	6 July 2020
6 September 1954 to 5 October 1954	6 September 2020
6 October 1954 to 5 April 1960	66th birthday
6 April 1960 to 5 May 1960	Age 66 and 1 month
6 May 1960 to 5 June 1960	Age 66 and 2 months
6 June 1960 to 5 July 1960	Age 66 and 3 months
6 July 1960 to 5 August 1960	Age 66 and 4 months
6 August 1960 to 5 September 1960	Age 66 and 5 months
6 September 1960 to 5 October 1960	Age 66 and 6 months
6 October to 5 November 1960	Age 66 and 7 months
6 November 1960 to 5 December 1960	Age 66 and 8 months
6 December 1960 to 5 January 1961	Age 66 and 9 months
6 January 1961 to 5 February 1961	Age 66 and 10 months
6 February 1961 to 5 March 1961	Age 66 and 11 months
6 March 1961 to 5 April 1977	67th birthday
6 April 1977 and 5 May 1977	6 May 2044
6 May 1977 and 5 June 1977	6 July 2044
6 June 1977 and 5 July 1977	6 September 2044
6 July 1977 and 5 August 1977	6 November 2044
6 August 1977 and 5 September 1977	6 January 2045
6 September 1977 and 5 October 1977	6 March 2045
6 October 1977 and 5 November 1977	6 May 2045
6 November 1977 and 5 December 1977	6 July 2045
6 December 1977 and 5 January 1978	6 September 2045
6 January 1978 and 5 February 1978	6 November 2045
6 February 1978 and 5 March 1978	6 January 2046
6 March 1978 and 5 April 1978	6 March 2046
On or after 6 April 1978	68th birthday

Table 22: State pension

	Weekly pension		Number of qualifying years	
	2022/23	2023/24	For full pension	For some pension
Women born before 6 April 1950	£141.85	£156.20	39	10
Women born after 5 April 1950 and before 6 April 1953	£141.85	£156.20	30	1
Women born after 5 April 1953	£185.15	£203.85	35	10
Men born before 6 April 1945	£141.85	£156.20	44	11
Men born after 5 April 1945 and before 6 April 1951	£141.85	£156.20	30	1
Men born after 5 April 1951	£185.15	£203.85	35	10

Table 23: Auto-enrolment rates

Date	Employer minimum contribution	Employee minimum contribution	Total minimum contribution
Before 5 April 2018	1%	1%	2%
6 April 2018 – 5 April 2019	2%	3%	5%
6 April 2019 onwards	3%	5%	8%

Table 24: Auto-enrolment earnings thresholds

Annual earnings	6 April 2021 - 5 April 2022	6 April 2022 - 5 April 2023	6 April 2023 - 5 April 2024
Lower level of qualifying earnings	£6,240	£6,240	£6,240
Earnings trigger for automatic enrolment	£10,000	£10,000	£10,000
Upper level of qualifying earnings	£50,000	£50,270	£50,270

Ogden Tables: 8ᵗʰ edition

The 8th edition of the Ogden Tables was published in July 2020 and are primarily used to assess lump sum damages for personal injury awards but they can also be used to calculate pension loss in certain cases for defined benefit pension schemes. (See Principles For Compensating Pension Loss which was revised in March 2021). All of the Ogden Tables have been summarised to provide only the relevant discount rates, and some (Ogden Tables 3 to 34 which are Tables 26 to 37 below) have been interpolated to provide multipliers in between the ages of 50 and 55 etc.

Ogden Tables 1 and 2
These tables contain the multipliers for men and women, for different discount rates, which are used to calculate life long loss. Table 25 below lists the multipliers for a discount rate of 0% which tells you a person's life expectancy. For example, a woman age 35 would be expected to live a further 54.61 years. This table should be used when the multiplier must be apportioned for variable periods of pension loss (see the example of Rosa in the Principles For Compensating Pension Loss).

Ogden Tables 3 to 18
These tables contain the multipliers for men and women for loss of **earnings** to pension age (or earlier death), for different discount rates. Tables 34 to 37 list the multipliers for discount rates of -0.25% (England & Wales) and -0.75% (Scotland). There is NO 2 year adjustment for loss of earnings.

Ogden Tables 19 to 34
These tables contain the multipliers for men and women for loss of **pension** to death (based on life expectancy projections). Tables 26 to 33 list the multipliers for discount rates of -0.25% (England & Wales) and -0.75% (Scotland), with and without the 2 year adjustment.

Ogden Table 35
This table contains discounting factors for term certain (i.e. factors to discount a sum which has been received early). A positive discount rate assumes that any capital sum paid will be decreased in anticipation of the sum earning interest. A negative discount rate on the other hand assumes that money invested will shrink compared to price inflation, not grow, and so its application will increase the overall sum. Table 38 has reproduced Ogden Table 35 with discount rates of -0.25% (England & Wales) and -0.75% (Scotland).

Ogden Table 36
In cases where pecuniary loss is to be valued for a fixed period, the multipliers in Ogden Table 36 may be used. These make no allowance for mortality or any other contingency but assume that regular frequent payments (e.g. weekly or monthly) will continue throughout the period. For example, if the monthly loss is to continue for 5 years at a discount rate of -0.25%, the correct multiplier will be 5.03. Table 39 has reproduced Ogden Table 36 with discount rates of -0.25% (England & Wales) and -0.75% (Scotland).

Table 25: 8th edition Ogden multipliers for pecuniary loss

This table is a combination of Ogden Tables 1 and 2 with a discount rate of 0%. It shows the life expectancy of men and women which is required when the multiplier must be apportioned for variable periods of pension loss.

Age at date of claim	Multiplier for pecuniary loss for life		Age at date of claim	Multiplier for pecuniary loss for life	
	Men	Women		Men	Women
16	70.76	73.53	59	25.70	28.11
17	69.66	72.44	60	24.76	27.14
18	68.56	71.35	61	23.84	26.18
19	67.46	70.26	62	22.93	25.22
20	66.36	69.17	63	22.02	24.27
21	65.27	68.09	64	21.13	23.34
22	64.17	67.00	65	20.25	22.41
23	63.08	65.91	66	19.39	21.49
24	61.99	64.83	67	18.54	20.58
25	60.90	63.74	68	17.70	19.68
26	59.81	62.65	69	16.88	18.80
27	58.72	61.57	70	16.07	17.92
28	57.63	60.48	71	15.27	17.06
29	56.55	59.40	72	14.49	16.21
30	55.46	58.32	73	13.73	15.38
31	54.38	57.24	74	12.98	14.57
32	53.31	56.16	75	12.25	13.77
33	52.23	55.09	76	11.54	13.00
34	51.16	54.01	77	10.85	12.24
35	50.09	52.94	78	10.19	11.50
36	49.02	51.87	79	9.54	10.79
37	47.96	50.80	80	8.92	10.10
38	46.90	49.73	81	8.33	9.43
39	45.85	48.67	82	7.76	8.79
40	44.80	47.61	83	7.22	8.17
41	43.75	46.55	84	6.70	7.58
42	42.71	45.49	85	6.21	7.01
43	41.68	44.44	86	5.75	6.48
44	40.65	43.39	87	5.32	5.97
45	39.62	42.34	88	4.91	5.49
46	38.59	41.29	89	4.53	5.05
47	37.57	40.25	90	4.18	4.64
48	36.55	39.21	91	3.85	4.26
49	35.54	38.17	92	3.55	3.92
50	34.53	37.14	93	3.27	3.61
51	33.52	36.12	94	3.01	3.32
52	32.52	35.09	95	2.78	3.06
53	31.52	34.08	96	2.57	2.82
54	30.53	33.07	97	2.37	2.60
55	29.55	32.06	98	2.19	2.39
56	28.57	31.06	99	2.03	2.20
57	27.60	30.07	100	1.88	2.03
58	26.64	29.08			

Table 26: 8th edition Ogden multipliers, loss of PENSION, MEN, discount rate: −0.25%, 2 YEAR ADJUSTMENT

Age	Loss of pension from age																									
	52	53	54	55	56	57	58	59	60	61	62	63	64	65	66	67	68	69	70	71	72	73	74	75	76	77
18	42.52	41.47	40.42	39.36	38.29	37.22	36.18	35.12	34.06	33.00	31.92	30.88	29.84	28.79	27.73	26.67	25.65	24.62	23.55	22.55	21.50	20.52	19.53	18.53	17.52	16.50
19	42.29	41.25	40.19	39.14	38.08	37.00	35.96	34.91	33.86	32.79	31.72	30.69	29.64	28.60	27.55	26.48	25.47	24.45	23.38	22.38	21.33	20.36	19.37	18.37	17.37	16.36
20	42.06	41.02	39.97	38.92	37.85	36.79	35.75	34.70	33.65	32.59	31.52	30.49	29.45	28.41	27.35	26.30	25.29	24.27	23.21	22.21	21.17	20.19	19.21	18.22	17.22	16.21
21	41.83	40.80	39.75	38.70	37.64	36.57	35.54	34.50	33.45	32.38	31.32	30.30	29.26	28.22	27.17	26.11	25.11	24.10	23.03	22.04	21.00	20.04	19.06	18.07	17.07	16.06
22	41.60	40.57	39.53	38.49	37.42	36.36	35.33	34.29	33.24	32.19	31.12	30.10	29.07	28.04	26.98	25.93	24.93	23.92	22.86	21.88	20.84	19.87	18.90	17.92	16.92	15.92
23	41.38	40.35	39.31	38.27	37.22	36.15	35.12	34.09	33.04	31.99	30.93	29.91	28.88	27.85	26.81	25.75	24.75	23.75	22.69	21.72	20.68	19.72	18.75	17.77	16.79	15.78
24	41.17	40.13	39.09	38.06	37.00	35.95	34.92	33.88	32.84	31.79	30.74	29.72	28.69	27.67	26.62	25.58	24.58	23.58	22.53	21.55	20.53	19.56	18.60	17.62	16.63	15.65
25	40.94	39.92	38.88	37.84	36.80	35.74	34.72	33.68	32.65	31.60	30.54	29.54	28.51	27.48	26.45	25.40	24.41	23.41	22.36	21.39	20.36	19.42	18.44	17.47	16.50	15.50
26	40.73	39.70	38.68	37.63	36.58	35.54	34.51	33.49	32.45	31.41	30.36	29.34	28.33	27.30	26.26	25.23	24.24	23.24	22.20	21.23	20.21	19.25	18.30	17.33	16.35	15.37
27	40.51	39.49	38.46	37.43	36.38	35.33	34.32	33.29	32.26	31.21	30.17	29.16	28.14	27.13	26.09	25.05	24.07	23.08	22.03	21.06	20.05	19.10	18.14	17.19	16.21	15.23
28	40.30	39.28	38.25	37.22	36.19	35.13	34.11	33.10	32.06	31.03	29.98	28.98	27.96	26.95	25.92	24.88	23.90	22.91	21.87	20.91	19.89	18.95	18.00	17.04	16.07	15.09
29	40.09	39.07	38.04	37.02	35.98	34.94	33.92	32.89	31.87	30.84	29.80	28.79	27.78	26.77	25.75	24.72	23.73	22.74	21.71	20.75	19.74	18.80	17.85	16.89	15.93	14.96
30	39.88	38.87	37.84	36.81	35.78	34.74	33.73	32.71	31.68	30.65	29.61	28.62	27.60	26.59	25.57	24.55	23.57	22.58	21.55	20.59	19.59	18.65	17.70	16.75	15.79	14.82
31	39.66	38.66	37.64	36.61	35.57	34.54	33.54	32.52	31.49	30.46	29.43	28.43	27.43	26.42	25.39	24.37	23.41	22.43	21.39	20.43	19.43	18.51	17.56	16.61	15.65	14.68
32	39.46	38.45	37.44	36.42	35.38	34.34	33.34	32.33	31.32	30.28	29.24	28.26	27.25	26.25	25.23	24.20	23.23	22.27	21.23	20.28	19.28	18.35	17.42	16.48	15.51	14.55
33	39.26	38.25	37.23	36.22	35.19	34.15	33.15	32.14	31.13	30.11	29.07	28.07	27.08	26.08	25.06	24.04	23.07	22.10	21.08	20.14	19.13	18.21	17.27	16.34	15.39	14.42
34	39.06	38.06	37.04	36.02	35.00	33.97	32.96	31.96	30.94	29.92	28.90	27.91	26.91	25.91	24.90	23.88	22.92	21.94	20.93	19.98	18.99	18.06	17.14	16.20	15.25	14.30
35	38.87	37.86	36.86	35.84	34.80	33.78	32.79	31.78	30.76	29.74	28.72	27.74	26.74	25.74	24.73	23.72	22.76	21.79	20.78	19.83	18.84	17.93	17.00	16.06	15.12	14.17
36	38.67	37.68	36.66	35.65	34.63	33.59	32.60	31.60	30.59	29.57	28.54	27.57	26.58	25.58	24.58	23.56	22.60	21.64	20.62	19.69	18.69	17.78	16.86	15.93	14.99	14.04
37	38.48	37.48	36.48	35.47	34.45	33.42	32.42	31.42	30.42	29.41	28.38	27.39	26.41	25.42	24.41	23.41	22.45	21.49	20.48	19.54	18.56	17.64	16.72	15.80	14.87	13.92
38	38.30	37.30	36.30	35.29	34.27	33.25	32.25	31.25	30.25	29.23	28.22	27.24	26.25	25.26	24.26	23.25	22.30	21.34	20.33	19.39	18.42	17.51	16.59	15.67	14.73	13.80
39	38.11	37.12	36.12	35.11	34.09	33.07	32.09	31.08	30.08	29.07	28.05	27.08	26.09	25.10	24.10	23.10	22.15	21.20	20.18	19.26	18.27	17.38	16.46	15.53	14.61	13.67
40	37.94	36.94	35.95	34.94	33.93	32.90	31.92	30.93	29.92	28.91	27.89	26.92	25.94	24.95	23.96	22.95	22.01	21.05	20.05	19.12	18.14	17.24	16.33	15.42	14.48	13.55
41	37.76	36.78	35.78	34.77	33.76	32.74	31.75	30.76	29.76	28.75	27.74	26.76	25.79	24.81	23.80	22.81	21.86	20.91	19.91	18.99	18.01	17.11	16.20	15.29	14.37	13.43
42	37.60	36.61	35.62	34.61	33.60	32.58	31.60	30.60	29.61	28.60	27.58	26.62	25.64	24.66	23.67	22.66	21.73	20.77	19.77	18.85	17.88	16.98	16.08	15.17	14.24	13.32
43	37.44	36.45	35.45	34.45	33.45	32.42	31.44	30.45	29.46	28.45	27.44	26.47	25.50	24.51	23.53	22.53	21.58	20.64	19.64	18.72	17.75	16.86	15.96	15.04	14.13	13.20
44	37.28	36.30	35.30	34.30	33.29	32.28	31.29	30.30	29.31	28.31	27.30	26.33	25.35	24.37	23.39	22.40	21.45	20.50	19.52	18.60	17.63	16.73	15.84	14.93	14.01	13.10
45	37.13	36.14	35.15	34.15	33.14	32.13	31.15	30.16	29.17	28.16	27.16	26.19	25.22	24.24	23.25	22.26	21.33	20.38	19.39	18.47	17.51	16.62	15.71	14.81	13.91	12.98
46	36.98	36.00	35.01	34.01	33.00	31.99	31.01	30.02	29.02	28.03	27.02	26.06	25.09	24.10	23.12	22.13	21.19	20.26	19.26	18.35	17.39	16.50	15.61	14.70	13.79	12.88
47	36.85	35.86	34.87	33.87	32.86	31.85	30.87	29.89	28.90	27.89	26.89	25.92	24.96	23.98	22.99	22.01	21.07	20.13	19.14	18.23	17.27	16.39	15.49	14.59	13.68	12.77
48	36.71	35.73	34.73	33.73	32.74	31.72	30.74	29.76	28.76	27.77	26.76	25.80	24.83	23.85	22.88	21.88	20.95	20.01	19.02	18.12	17.15	16.27	15.38	14.48	13.58	12.66

Table 26: 8th edition Ogden multipliers, loss of PENSION, MEN, discount rate: −0.25%, 2 YEAR ADJUSTMENT

Loss of pension from age

Age	52	53	54	55	56	57	58	59	60	61	62	63	64	65	66	67	68	69	70	71	72	73	74	75	76	77
49	36.59	35.60	34.61	33.61	32.60	31.60	30.61	29.63	28.64	27.64	26.64	25.67	24.71	23.73	22.75	21.77	20.83	19.90	18.92	18.00	17.05	16.16	15.27	14.38	13.47	12.57
50	36.46	35.48	34.49	33.49	32.48	31.47	30.50	29.51	28.52	27.53	26.52	25.56	24.59	23.61	22.64	21.65	20.72	19.78	18.80	17.89	16.93	16.06	15.17	14.28	13.37	12.46
51	36.35	35.36	34.37	33.37	32.37	31.36	30.38	29.40	28.40	27.41	26.41	25.44	24.48	23.50	22.52	21.54	20.61	19.68	18.69	17.79	16.83	15.95	15.07	14.17	13.28	12.37
52	36.24	35.26	34.26	33.27	32.26	31.25	30.27	29.28	28.30	27.30	26.30	25.34	24.37	23.40	22.42	21.43	20.50	19.57	18.59	17.68	16.73	15.85	14.96	14.08	13.18	12.28
53		35.16	34.17	33.16	32.16	31.15	30.17	29.19	28.19	27.20	26.19	25.24	24.27	23.29	22.32	21.33	20.40	19.47	18.49	17.59	16.63	15.75	14.87	13.98	13.09	12.19
54			34.07	33.07	32.06	31.05	30.08	29.09	28.10	27.09	26.10	25.13	24.17	23.20	22.22	21.24	20.31	19.37	18.39	17.48	16.54	15.66	14.78	13.89	12.99	12.10
55				32.99	31.98	30.96	29.99	29.01	28.01	27.02	26.00	25.05	24.08	23.11	22.13	21.14	20.22	19.28	18.30	17.40	16.44	15.57	14.69	13.80	12.91	12.01
56					31.90	30.89	29.91	28.92	27.93	26.93	25.93	24.96	24.00	23.02	22.04	21.06	20.13	19.20	18.22	17.31	16.36	15.48	14.61	13.73	12.83	11.93
57						30.82	29.85	28.86	27.86	26.86	25.85	24.90	23.92	22.95	21.97	20.98	20.06	19.12	18.13	17.23	16.28	15.41	14.52	13.64	12.76	11.85
58							29.79	28.81	27.80	26.79	25.79	24.83	23.87	22.88	21.90	20.91	19.98	19.05	18.07	17.16	16.21	15.34	14.46	13.57	12.68	11.79
59								28.76	27.76	26.75	25.73	24.78	23.81	22.83	21.84	20.85	19.92	18.99	17.99	17.09	16.14	15.27	14.39	13.50	12.61	11.71
60									27.74	26.72	25.70	24.73	23.77	22.79	21.80	20.80	19.87	18.94	17.94	17.04	16.08	15.21	14.33	13.45	12.55	11.65
61										26.71	25.68	24.71	23.74	22.76	21.77	20.77	19.83	18.90	17.90	17.00	16.04	15.16	14.28	13.40	12.50	11.60
62											25.68	24.71	23.73	22.74	21.75	20.75	19.81	18.86	17.87	16.97	16.00	15.12	14.24	13.35	12.46	11.56
63												24.72	23.73	22.74	21.75	20.74	19.80	18.85	17.85	16.95	15.98	15.09	14.20	13.31	12.42	11.52
64													23.76	22.76	21.76	20.75	19.80	18.85	17.85	16.93	15.97	15.08	14.18	13.29	12.39	11.49
65														22.80	21.78	20.77	19.82	18.86	17.86	16.93	15.96	15.08	14.18	13.27	12.37	11.47
66															21.84	20.81	19.86	18.90	17.88	16.95	15.97	15.08	14.18	13.27	12.36	11.45
67																20.88	19.92	18.95	17.92	16.99	16.00	15.10	14.19	13.29	12.37	11.45
68																	20.00	19.02	17.99	17.05	16.05	15.14	14.23	13.31	12.39	11.47
69																		19.12	18.08	17.12	16.12	15.20	14.28	13.35	12.42	11.50
70																			18.19	17.23	16.21	15.28	14.35	13.41	12.48	11.54
71																				17.36	16.34	15.38	14.44	13.49	12.55	11.61
72																					16.48	15.53	14.55	13.60	12.64	11.69
73																						15.68	14.71	13.73	12.76	11.79
74																							14.89	13.90	12.90	11.92
75																								14.09	13.08	12.07
76																									13.30	12.27
77																										12.50

Table 27: 8th edition Ogden multipliers, loss of PENSION, WOMEN, discount rate: −0.25%, 2 YEAR ADJUSTMENT

Loss of pension from age

Age	52	53	54	55	56	57	58	59	60	61	62	63	64	65	66	67	68	69	70	71	72	73	74	75	76	77
18	45.64	44.59	43.52	42.45	41.37	40.27	39.22	38.14	37.06	35.98	34.88	33.82	32.76	31.68	30.60	29.50	28.45	27.39	26.29	25.24	24.16	23.13	22.09	21.04	19.99	18.91
19	45.43	44.36	43.30	42.23	41.15	40.07	39.00	37.94	36.86	35.78	34.70	33.63	32.57	31.49	30.41	29.33	28.27	27.22	26.12	25.08	24.00	22.97	21.94	20.88	19.83	18.78
20	45.20	44.15	43.08	42.02	40.94	39.86	38.80	37.73	36.67	35.58	34.50	33.45	32.37	31.31	30.23	29.14	28.10	27.04	25.95	24.91	23.84	22.81	21.78	20.74	19.68	18.63
21	44.98	43.93	42.87	41.80	40.73	39.65	38.60	37.54	36.46	35.39	34.30	33.25	32.20	31.12	30.06	28.97	27.92	26.88	25.78	24.75	23.67	22.66	21.63	20.58	19.55	18.48
22	44.76	43.71	42.65	41.60	40.52	39.45	38.39	37.33	36.27	35.19	34.12	33.06	32.01	30.95	29.86	28.80	27.75	26.70	25.62	24.58	23.52	22.49	21.47	20.44	19.39	18.35
23	44.54	43.49	42.44	41.38	40.32	39.24	38.19	37.13	36.07	35.01	33.92	32.88	31.82	30.76	29.70	28.61	27.58	26.53	25.45	24.43	23.35	22.34	21.31	20.29	19.26	18.20
24	44.33	43.28	42.22	41.17	40.10	39.04	37.99	36.93	35.87	34.80	33.74	32.69	31.64	30.57	29.52	28.45	27.40	26.37	25.29	24.26	23.20	22.18	21.17	20.14	19.10	18.07
25	44.11	43.07	42.02	40.96	39.90	38.83	37.79	36.74	35.68	34.61	33.54	32.51	31.45	30.40	29.33	28.27	27.24	26.19	25.12	24.10	23.04	22.03	21.01	19.99	18.96	17.92
26	43.89	42.85	41.81	40.75	39.69	38.63	37.59	36.54	35.48	34.42	33.35	32.31	31.28	30.22	29.16	28.09	27.07	26.04	24.96	23.94	22.88	21.88	20.87	19.85	18.82	17.78
27	43.67	42.64	41.60	40.55	39.49	38.42	37.39	36.34	35.29	34.23	33.16	32.13	31.09	30.04	28.98	27.92	26.89	25.87	24.79	23.78	22.72	21.72	20.72	19.70	18.68	17.64
28	43.46	42.42	41.39	40.34	39.29	38.23	37.18	36.15	35.10	34.04	32.98	31.94	30.91	29.86	28.81	27.75	26.73	25.70	24.63	23.63	22.57	21.57	20.57	19.56	18.54	17.51
29	43.25	42.22	41.17	40.13	39.09	38.03	37.00	35.95	34.91	33.85	32.79	31.76	30.72	29.68	28.64	27.58	26.56	25.53	24.47	23.47	22.42	21.42	20.42	19.41	18.40	17.37
30	43.04	42.01	40.97	39.93	38.88	37.83	36.80	35.76	34.71	33.67	32.61	31.58	30.55	29.51	28.46	27.41	26.40	25.37	24.31	23.31	22.27	21.28	20.27	19.26	18.26	17.24
31	42.83	41.80	40.77	39.73	38.68	37.63	36.61	35.57	34.53	33.48	32.43	31.40	30.37	29.33	28.29	27.24	26.23	25.21	24.15	23.14	22.11	21.13	20.13	19.13	18.11	17.10
32	42.62	41.60	40.57	39.53	38.48	37.43	36.41	35.38	34.35	33.29	32.24	31.23	30.20	29.16	28.12	27.07	26.06	25.05	23.99	22.99	21.95	20.98	19.99	18.99	17.98	16.96
33	42.41	41.39	40.37	39.33	38.29	37.24	36.22	35.19	34.16	33.12	32.06	31.04	30.03	28.99	27.95	26.90	25.90	24.89	23.83	22.84	21.80	20.82	19.84	18.84	17.84	16.83
34	42.21	41.19	40.17	39.14	38.10	37.05	36.03	35.00	33.98	32.93	31.89	30.87	29.85	28.82	27.79	26.74	25.74	24.73	23.68	22.69	21.66	20.68	19.69	18.71	17.70	16.70
35	42.01	40.99	39.97	38.94	37.91	36.86	35.84	34.82	33.79	32.76	31.71	30.70	29.68	28.65	27.62	26.58	25.58	24.57	23.52	22.54	21.51	20.54	19.55	18.57	17.57	16.56
36	41.82	40.80	39.78	38.75	37.72	36.68	35.66	34.64	33.62	32.57	31.54	30.53	29.51	28.48	27.46	26.42	25.42	24.42	23.37	22.39	21.36	20.39	19.42	18.43	17.44	16.44
37	41.62	40.61	39.59	38.56	37.53	36.49	35.48	34.46	33.43	32.41	31.36	30.36	29.34	28.32	27.29	26.26	25.27	24.26	23.22	22.24	21.22	20.25	19.28	18.29	17.30	16.31
38	41.43	40.42	39.40	38.38	37.35	36.31	35.30	34.28	33.26	32.23	31.20	30.18	29.18	28.16	27.13	26.10	25.11	24.11	23.07	22.09	21.08	20.11	19.14	18.16	17.17	16.18
39	41.23	40.23	39.21	38.20	37.17	36.13	35.12	34.11	33.09	32.06	31.02	30.03	28.99	27.99	26.97	25.94	24.96	23.96	22.92	21.95	20.93	19.98	19.00	18.02	17.05	16.05
40	41.05	40.04	39.03	38.01	36.99	35.96	34.95	33.93	32.91	31.89	30.86	29.85	28.86	27.83	26.81	25.79	24.80	23.81	22.78	21.80	20.79	19.83	18.87	17.90	16.91	15.93
41	40.86	39.86	38.85	37.84	36.80	35.78	34.78	33.77	32.75	31.72	30.69	29.70	28.69	27.68	26.66	25.63	24.66	23.66	22.63	21.66	20.65	19.70	18.73	17.77	16.79	15.80
42	40.68	39.68	38.67	37.65	36.64	35.60	34.61	33.60	32.58	31.56	30.53	29.53	28.54	27.52	26.51	25.48	24.50	23.52	22.49	21.52	20.51	19.56	18.60	17.64	16.66	15.68
43	40.50	39.50	38.50	37.49	36.46	35.44	34.43	33.43	32.43	31.40	30.37	29.38	28.38	27.37	26.36	25.34	24.36	23.37	22.35	21.38	20.38	19.43	18.47	17.51	16.54	15.56
44	40.33	39.33	38.32	37.31	36.30	35.27	34.28	33.26	32.26	31.25	30.22	29.22	28.23	27.22	26.21	25.19	24.22	23.23	22.21	21.25	20.24	19.30	18.34	17.39	16.41	15.44
45	40.16	39.16	38.16	37.15	36.13	35.11	34.11	33.12	32.10	31.08	30.07	29.08	28.08	27.07	26.07	25.05	24.07	23.10	22.08	21.11	20.12	19.17	18.22	17.26	16.30	15.32
46	39.99	39.00	38.00	36.99	35.97	34.95	33.96	32.95	31.95	30.93	29.91	28.93	27.93	26.93	25.92	24.91	23.94	22.96	21.94	20.98	19.98	19.05	18.09	17.14	16.17	15.21
47	39.83	38.83	37.84	36.83	35.82	34.79	33.80	32.81	31.80	30.79	29.76	28.78	27.79	26.79	25.79	24.77	23.80	22.83	21.81	20.85	19.86	18.91	17.98	17.02	16.06	15.09
48	39.67	38.68	37.68	36.68	35.67	34.65	33.65	32.65	31.65	30.64	29.63	28.63	27.65	26.66	25.64	24.64	23.67	22.69	21.68	20.73	19.73	18.80	17.85	16.90	15.94	14.98

Table 27: 8th edition Ogden multipliers, loss of PENSION, WOMEN, discount rate: −0.25%, 2 YEAR ADJUSTMENT

Loss of pension from age

Age	52	53	54	55	56	57	58	59	60	61	62	63	64	65	66	67	68	69	70	71	72	73	74	75	76	77
49	39.52	38.53	37.53	36.52	35.52	34.50	33.51	32.51	31.51	30.50	29.48	28.51	27.51	26.51	25.52	24.50	23.54	22.57	21.55	20.60	19.61	18.67	17.74	16.78	15.83	14.87
50	39.37	38.38	37.39	36.39	35.37	34.36	33.37	32.37	31.37	30.36	29.35	28.36	27.38	26.38	25.38	24.38	23.41	22.44	21.43	20.48	19.49	18.56	17.62	16.67	15.72	14.76
51	39.22	38.24	37.25	36.24	35.24	34.21	33.23	32.24	31.24	30.23	29.21	28.24	27.25	26.26	25.26	24.25	23.29	22.32	21.30	20.36	19.37	18.44	17.51	16.56	15.61	14.65
52	39.09	38.10	37.11	36.11	35.10	34.09	33.09	32.11	31.11	30.10	29.09	28.11	27.13	26.13	25.13	24.13	23.17	22.20	21.19	20.25	19.26	18.33	17.39	16.45	15.51	14.55
53		37.98	36.98	35.98	34.98	33.96	32.98	31.98	30.98	29.98	28.96	27.99	27.00	26.01	25.02	24.01	23.05	22.09	21.08	20.13	19.15	18.22	17.29	16.35	15.40	14.45
54			36.87	35.86	34.85	33.84	32.86	31.87	30.86	29.86	28.85	27.87	26.89	25.90	24.90	23.90	22.94	21.98	20.97	20.02	19.04	18.12	17.19	16.24	15.30	14.35
55				35.75	34.74	33.72	32.75	31.76	30.76	29.75	28.73	27.77	26.78	25.80	24.79	23.79	22.84	21.87	20.86	19.92	18.93	18.02	17.09	16.15	15.20	14.25
56					34.64	33.62	32.64	31.66	30.65	29.65	28.63	27.65	26.68	25.68	24.70	23.69	22.73	21.77	20.76	19.83	18.84	17.91	16.99	16.05	15.12	14.16
57						33.53	32.55	31.55	30.56	29.55	28.54	27.56	26.58	25.60	24.59	23.60	22.64	21.67	20.67	19.73	18.75	17.83	16.89	15.97	15.02	14.08
58							32.46	31.47	30.47	29.47	28.45	27.48	26.49	25.50	24.51	23.50	22.56	21.59	20.58	19.64	18.66	17.74	16.82	15.88	14.94	13.99
59								31.40	30.40	29.38	28.38	27.40	26.42	25.43	24.43	23.43	22.47	21.51	20.51	19.56	18.58	17.66	16.73	15.80	14.86	13.92
60									30.33	29.32	28.30	27.34	26.35	25.35	24.36	23.35	22.40	21.43	20.43	19.49	18.50	17.58	16.66	15.73	14.79	13.84
61										29.27	28.25	27.27	26.30	25.29	24.29	23.29	22.33	21.37	20.37	19.42	18.44	17.51	16.59	15.65	14.72	13.78
62											28.20	27.23	26.24	25.25	24.24	23.23	22.28	21.31	20.30	19.36	18.38	17.46	16.52	15.59	14.65	13.71
63												27.19	26.21	25.21	24.21	23.19	22.23	21.27	20.26	19.32	18.33	17.40	16.48	15.54	14.60	13.65
64													26.18	25.18	24.18	23.17	22.20	21.23	20.22	19.28	18.29	17.36	16.43	15.49	14.55	13.60
65														25.17	24.16	23.15	22.18	21.20	20.19	19.24	18.26	17.33	16.39	15.45	14.51	13.56
66															24.16	23.14	22.17	21.20	20.18	19.22	18.23	17.30	16.37	15.42	14.48	13.53
67																23.15	22.18	21.20	20.17	19.21	18.22	17.29	16.35	15.40	14.45	13.50
68																	22.20	21.22	20.18	19.23	18.22	17.29	16.34	15.39	14.44	13.48
69																		21.25	20.21	19.25	18.24	17.29	16.35	15.40	14.44	13.48
70																			20.26	19.29	18.27	17.33	16.37	15.42	14.45	13.48
71																				19.36	18.33	17.37	16.42	15.44	14.48	13.51
72																					18.41	17.45	16.47	15.50	14.52	13.55
73																						17.54	16.56	15.58	14.59	13.59
74																							16.67	15.68	14.68	13.68
75																								15.81	14.79	13.78
76																									14.94	13.91
77																										14.07

Table 28: 8th edition Ogden multipliers, loss of PENSION, MEN, discount rate: −0.25%, NO 2 YEAR ADJUSTMENT

Loss of pension from age

Age	50	51	52	53	54	55	56	57	58	59	60	61	62	63	64	65	66	67	68	69	70	71	72	73	74	75
16	42.52	41.47	40.42	39.36	38.29	37.22	36.18	35.12	34.06	33.00	31.92	30.88	29.84	28.79	27.73	26.67	25.65	24.62	23.55	22.55	21.50	20.52	19.53	18.53	17.52	16.50
17	42.29	41.25	40.19	39.14	38.08	37.00	35.96	34.91	33.86	32.79	31.72	30.69	29.64	28.60	27.55	26.48	25.47	24.45	23.38	22.38	21.33	20.36	19.37	18.37	17.37	16.36
18	42.06	41.02	39.97	38.92	37.85	36.79	35.75	34.70	33.65	32.59	31.52	30.49	29.45	28.41	27.35	26.30	25.29	24.27	23.21	22.21	21.17	20.19	19.21	18.22	17.22	16.21
19	41.83	40.80	39.75	38.70	37.64	36.57	35.54	34.50	33.45	32.38	31.32	30.30	29.26	28.22	27.17	26.11	25.11	24.10	23.03	22.04	21.00	20.04	19.06	18.07	17.07	16.06
20	41.60	40.57	39.53	38.49	37.42	36.36	35.33	34.29	33.24	32.19	31.12	30.10	29.07	28.04	26.98	25.93	24.93	23.92	22.86	21.88	20.84	19.87	18.90	17.92	16.92	15.92
21	41.38	40.35	39.31	38.27	37.22	36.15	35.12	34.09	33.04	31.99	30.93	29.91	28.88	27.85	26.81	25.75	24.75	23.75	22.69	21.72	20.68	19.72	18.75	17.77	16.79	15.78
22	41.17	40.13	39.09	38.06	37.00	35.95	34.92	33.88	32.84	31.79	30.74	29.72	28.69	27.67	26.62	25.58	24.58	23.58	22.53	21.55	20.53	19.56	18.60	17.62	16.63	15.65
23	40.94	39.92	38.88	37.84	36.80	35.74	34.72	33.68	32.65	31.60	30.54	29.54	28.51	27.48	26.45	25.40	24.41	23.41	22.36	21.39	20.36	19.42	18.44	17.47	16.50	15.50
24	40.73	39.70	38.68	37.63	36.58	35.54	34.51	33.49	32.45	31.41	30.36	29.34	28.33	27.30	26.26	25.23	24.24	23.24	22.20	21.23	20.21	19.25	18.30	17.33	16.35	15.37
25	40.51	39.49	38.46	37.43	36.38	35.33	34.32	33.29	32.26	31.21	30.17	29.16	28.14	27.13	26.09	25.05	24.07	23.08	22.03	21.06	20.05	19.10	18.14	17.19	16.21	15.23
26	40.30	39.28	38.25	37.22	36.19	35.13	34.11	33.10	32.06	31.03	29.98	28.98	27.96	26.95	25.92	24.88	23.90	22.91	21.87	20.91	19.89	18.95	18.00	17.04	16.07	15.09
27	40.09	39.07	38.04	37.02	35.98	34.94	33.92	32.89	31.87	30.84	29.80	28.79	27.78	26.77	25.75	24.72	23.73	22.74	21.71	20.75	19.74	18.80	17.85	16.89	15.93	14.96
28	39.88	38.87	37.84	36.81	35.78	34.74	33.73	32.71	31.68	30.65	29.61	28.62	27.60	26.59	25.57	24.55	23.57	22.58	21.55	20.59	19.59	18.65	17.70	16.75	15.79	14.82
29	39.66	38.66	37.64	36.61	35.57	34.54	33.54	32.52	31.49	30.46	29.43	28.43	27.43	26.42	25.39	24.37	23.41	22.43	21.39	20.43	19.43	18.51	17.56	16.61	15.65	14.68
30	39.46	38.45	37.44	36.42	35.38	34.34	33.34	32.33	31.32	30.28	29.24	28.26	27.25	26.25	25.23	24.20	23.23	22.27	21.23	20.28	19.28	18.35	17.42	16.48	15.51	14.55
31	39.26	38.25	37.23	36.22	35.19	34.15	33.15	32.14	31.13	30.11	29.07	28.07	27.08	26.08	25.06	24.04	23.07	22.10	21.08	20.14	19.13	18.21	17.27	16.34	15.39	14.42
32	39.06	38.06	37.04	36.02	35.00	33.97	32.96	31.96	30.94	29.92	28.90	27.91	26.91	25.91	24.90	23.88	22.92	21.87	20.93	19.98	18.99	18.06	17.14	16.20	15.25	14.30
33	38.87	37.86	36.86	35.84	34.80	33.78	32.79	31.78	30.76	29.74	28.72	27.74	26.74	25.74	24.73	23.72	22.76	21.79	20.78	19.83	18.84	17.93	17.00	16.06	15.12	14.17
34	38.67	37.68	36.66	35.65	34.63	33.59	32.60	31.60	30.59	29.57	28.54	27.57	26.58	25.58	24.58	23.56	22.60	21.64	20.62	19.69	18.69	17.78	16.86	15.93	14.99	14.04
35	38.48	37.48	36.48	35.47	34.45	33.42	32.42	31.42	30.42	29.41	28.38	27.39	26.41	25.42	24.41	23.41	22.45	21.49	20.48	19.54	18.56	17.64	16.72	15.80	14.87	13.92
36	38.30	37.30	36.30	35.29	34.27	33.25	32.25	31.25	30.25	29.23	28.22	27.24	26.25	25.26	24.26	23.25	22.30	21.34	20.33	19.39	18.42	17.51	16.59	15.67	14.73	13.80
37	38.11	37.12	36.12	35.11	34.09	33.07	32.09	31.08	30.08	29.07	28.05	27.08	26.09	25.10	24.10	23.10	22.15	21.20	20.18	19.26	18.27	17.38	16.46	15.53	14.61	13.67
38	37.94	36.94	35.95	34.94	33.93	32.90	31.92	30.93	29.92	28.91	27.89	26.92	25.94	24.95	23.96	22.95	22.01	21.05	20.05	19.12	18.14	17.24	16.33	15.42	14.48	13.55
39	37.76	36.78	35.78	34.77	33.76	32.74	31.75	30.76	29.76	28.75	27.74	26.76	25.79	24.81	23.80	22.81	21.86	20.91	19.91	18.99	18.01	17.11	16.20	15.29	14.37	13.43
40	37.60	36.61	35.62	34.61	33.60	32.58	31.60	30.60	29.61	28.60	27.58	26.62	25.64	24.66	23.67	22.66	21.73	20.77	19.77	18.85	17.88	16.98	16.08	15.17	14.24	13.32
41	37.44	36.45	35.45	34.45	33.45	32.42	31.44	30.45	29.46	28.45	27.44	26.47	25.50	24.51	23.53	22.53	21.58	20.64	19.64	18.72	17.75	16.86	15.96	15.04	14.13	13.20
42	37.28	36.30	35.30	34.30	33.29	32.28	31.29	30.30	29.31	28.31	27.30	26.33	25.35	24.37	23.39	22.40	21.45	20.50	19.52	18.60	17.63	16.73	15.84	14.93	14.01	13.10
43	37.13	36.14	35.15	34.15	33.14	32.13	31.15	30.16	29.17	28.16	27.16	26.19	25.22	24.24	23.25	22.26	21.33	20.38	19.39	18.47	17.51	16.62	15.71	14.81	13.91	12.98
44	36.98	36.00	35.01	34.01	33.00	31.99	31.01	30.02	29.02	28.03	27.02	26.06	25.09	24.10	23.12	22.13	21.19	20.26	19.26	18.35	17.39	16.50	15.61	14.70	13.79	12.88
45	36.85	35.86	34.87	33.87	32.86	31.85	30.87	29.89	28.90	27.89	26.89	25.92	24.96	23.98	22.99	22.01	21.07	20.13	19.14	18.23	17.27	16.39	15.49	14.59	13.68	12.77
46	36.71	35.73	34.73	33.73	32.74	31.72	30.74	29.76	28.76	27.77	26.76	25.80	24.83	23.85	22.88	21.88	20.95	20.01	19.02	18.12	17.15	16.27	15.38	14.48	13.58	12.66

Table 28: 8th edition Ogden multipliers, loss of PENSION, MEN, discount rate: −0.25%, NO 2 YEAR ADJUSTMENT

Loss of pension from age

Age	50	51	52	53	54	55	56	57	58	59	60	61	62	63	64	65	66	67	68	69	70	71	72	73	74	75
47	36.59	35.60	34.61	33.61	32.60	31.60	30.61	29.63	28.64	27.64	26.64	25.67	24.71	23.73	22.75	21.77	20.83	19.90	18.92	18.00	17.05	16.16	15.27	14.38	13.47	12.57
48	36.46	35.48	34.49	33.49	32.48	31.47	30.50	29.51	28.52	27.53	26.52	25.56	24.59	23.61	22.64	21.65	20.72	19.78	18.80	17.89	16.93	16.06	15.17	14.28	13.37	12.46
49	36.35	35.36	34.37	33.37	32.37	31.36	30.38	29.40	28.40	27.41	26.41	25.44	24.48	23.50	22.52	21.54	20.61	19.68	18.69	17.79	16.83	15.95	15.07	14.17	13.28	12.37
50	36.24	35.26	34.26	33.27	32.26	31.25	30.27	29.28	28.30	27.30	26.30	25.34	24.37	23.40	22.42	21.43	20.50	19.57	18.59	17.68	16.73	15.85	14.96	14.08	13.18	12.28
51		35.16	34.17	33.16	32.16	31.15	30.17	29.19	28.19	27.20	26.19	25.24	24.27	23.29	22.32	21.33	20.40	19.47	18.49	17.59	16.63	15.75	14.87	13.98	13.09	12.19
52			34.07	33.07	32.06	31.05	30.08	29.09	28.10	27.09	26.10	25.13	24.17	23.20	22.22	21.24	20.31	19.37	18.39	17.48	16.54	15.66	14.78	13.89	12.99	12.10
53				32.99	31.98	30.96	29.99	29.01	28.01	27.02	26.00	25.05	24.08	23.11	22.13	21.14	20.22	19.28	18.30	17.40	16.44	15.57	14.69	13.80	12.91	12.01
54					31.90	30.89	29.91	28.92	27.93	26.93	25.93	24.96	24.00	23.02	22.04	21.06	20.13	19.20	18.22	17.31	16.36	15.48	14.61	13.73	12.83	11.93
55						30.82	29.85	28.86	27.86	26.86	25.85	24.90	23.92	22.95	21.97	20.98	20.06	19.12	18.13	17.23	16.28	15.41	14.52	13.64	12.76	11.85
56							29.79	28.81	27.80	26.79	25.79	24.83	23.87	22.88	21.90	20.91	19.98	19.05	18.07	17.16	16.21	15.34	14.46	13.57	12.68	11.79
57								28.76	27.76	26.75	25.73	24.78	23.81	22.83	21.84	20.85	19.92	18.99	17.99	17.09	16.14	15.27	14.39	13.50	12.61	11.71
58									27.74	26.72	25.70	24.73	23.77	22.79	21.80	20.80	19.87	18.94	17.94	17.04	16.08	15.21	14.33	13.45	12.55	11.65
59										26.71	25.68	24.71	23.74	22.76	21.77	20.77	19.83	18.90	17.90	17.00	16.04	15.16	14.28	13.40	12.50	11.60
60											25.68	24.71	23.73	22.74	21.75	20.75	19.81	18.86	17.87	16.97	16.00	15.12	14.24	13.35	12.46	11.56
61												24.72	23.73	22.74	21.75	20.74	19.80	18.85	17.85	16.95	15.98	15.09	14.20	13.31	12.42	11.52
62													23.76	22.76	21.76	20.75	19.80	18.85	17.85	16.93	15.97	15.08	14.18	13.29	12.39	11.49
63														22.80	21.78	20.77	19.82	18.86	17.86	16.93	15.96	15.08	14.18	13.27	12.37	11.47
64															21.84	20.81	19.86	18.90	17.88	16.95	15.97	15.08	14.18	13.27	12.36	11.45
65																20.88	19.92	18.95	17.92	16.99	16.00	15.10	14.19	13.29	12.37	11.45
66																	20.00	19.02	17.99	17.05	16.05	15.14	14.23	13.31	12.39	11.47
67																		19.12	18.08	17.12	16.12	15.20	14.28	13.35	12.42	11.50
68																			18.19	17.23	16.21	15.28	14.35	13.41	12.48	11.54
69																				17.36	16.34	15.38	14.44	13.49	12.55	11.61
70																					16.48	15.53	14.55	13.60	12.64	11.69
71																						15.68	14.71	13.73	12.76	11.79
72																							14.89	13.90	12.90	11.92
73																								14.09	13.08	12.07
74																									13.30	12.27
75																										12.50

Table 29: 8th edition Ogden multipliers, loss of PENSION, WOMEN, discount rate: −0.25%, NO 2 YEAR ADJUSTMENT

Age	Loss of pension from age																									
	50	51	52	53	54	55	56	57	58	59	60	61	62	63	64	65	66	67	68	69	70	71	72	73	74	75
16	45.64	44.59	43.52	42.45	41.37	40.27	39.22	38.14	37.06	35.98	34.88	33.82	32.76	31.68	30.60	29.50	28.45	27.39	26.29	25.24	24.16	23.13	22.09	21.04	19.99	18.91
17	45.43	44.36	43.30	42.23	41.15	40.07	39.00	37.94	36.86	35.78	34.70	33.63	32.57	31.49	30.41	29.33	28.27	27.22	26.12	25.08	24.00	22.97	21.94	20.88	19.83	18.78
18	45.20	44.15	43.08	42.02	40.94	39.86	38.80	37.73	36.67	35.58	34.50	33.45	32.37	31.31	30.23	29.14	28.10	27.04	25.95	24.91	23.84	22.81	21.78	20.74	19.68	18.63
19	44.98	43.93	42.87	41.80	40.73	39.65	38.60	37.54	36.46	35.39	34.30	33.25	32.20	31.12	30.06	28.97	27.92	26.88	25.78	24.75	23.67	22.66	21.63	20.58	19.55	18.48
20	44.76	43.71	42.65	41.60	40.52	39.45	38.39	37.33	36.27	35.19	34.12	33.06	32.01	30.95	29.86	28.80	27.75	26.70	25.62	24.58	23.52	22.49	21.47	20.44	19.39	18.35
21	44.54	43.49	42.44	41.38	40.32	39.24	38.19	37.13	36.07	35.01	33.92	32.88	31.82	30.76	29.70	28.61	27.58	26.53	25.45	24.43	23.35	22.34	21.31	20.29	19.26	18.20
22	44.33	43.28	42.22	41.17	40.10	39.04	37.99	36.93	35.87	34.80	33.74	32.69	31.64	30.57	29.52	28.45	27.40	26.37	25.29	24.26	23.20	22.18	21.17	20.14	19.10	18.07
23	44.11	43.07	42.02	40.96	39.90	38.83	37.79	36.74	35.68	34.61	33.54	32.51	31.45	30.40	29.33	28.27	27.24	26.19	25.12	24.10	23.04	22.03	21.01	19.99	18.96	17.92
24	43.89	42.85	41.81	40.75	39.69	38.63	37.59	36.54	35.48	34.42	33.35	32.31	31.28	30.22	29.16	28.09	27.07	26.04	24.96	23.94	22.88	21.88	20.87	19.85	18.82	17.78
25	43.67	42.64	41.60	40.55	39.49	38.42	37.39	36.34	35.29	34.23	33.16	32.13	31.09	30.04	28.98	27.92	26.89	25.87	24.79	23.78	22.72	21.72	20.72	19.70	18.68	17.64
26	43.46	42.42	41.39	40.34	39.29	38.23	37.18	36.15	35.10	34.04	32.98	31.94	30.91	29.86	28.81	27.75	26.73	25.70	24.63	23.63	22.57	21.57	20.57	19.56	18.54	17.51
27	43.25	42.22	41.17	40.13	39.09	38.03	37.00	35.95	34.91	33.85	32.79	31.76	30.72	29.68	28.64	27.58	26.56	25.53	24.47	23.47	22.42	21.42	20.42	19.41	18.40	17.37
28	43.04	42.01	40.97	39.93	38.88	37.83	36.80	35.76	34.71	33.67	32.61	31.58	30.55	29.51	28.46	27.41	26.40	25.37	24.31	23.31	22.27	21.28	20.27	19.26	18.26	17.24
29	42.83	41.80	40.77	39.73	38.68	37.63	36.61	35.57	34.53	33.48	32.43	31.40	30.37	29.33	28.29	27.24	26.23	25.21	24.15	23.14	22.11	21.13	20.13	19.13	18.11	17.10
30	42.62	41.60	40.57	39.53	38.48	37.43	36.41	35.38	34.35	33.29	32.24	31.23	30.20	29.16	28.12	27.07	26.06	25.05	23.99	22.99	21.95	20.98	19.99	18.99	17.98	16.96
31	42.41	41.39	40.37	39.33	38.29	37.24	36.22	35.19	34.16	33.12	32.06	31.04	30.03	28.99	27.95	26.90	25.90	24.89	23.83	22.84	21.80	20.82	19.84	18.84	17.84	16.83
32	42.21	41.19	40.17	39.14	38.10	37.05	36.03	35.00	33.98	32.93	31.89	30.87	29.85	28.82	27.79	26.74	25.74	24.73	23.68	22.69	21.66	20.68	19.69	18.71	17.70	16.70
33	42.01	40.99	39.97	38.94	37.91	36.86	35.84	34.82	33.79	32.76	31.71	30.70	29.68	28.65	27.62	26.58	25.58	24.57	23.52	22.54	21.51	20.54	19.55	18.57	17.57	16.56
34	41.82	40.80	39.78	38.75	37.72	36.68	35.66	34.64	33.62	32.57	31.54	30.53	29.51	28.48	27.46	26.42	25.42	24.42	23.37	22.39	21.36	20.39	19.42	18.43	17.44	16.44
35	41.62	40.61	39.59	38.56	37.53	36.49	35.48	34.46	33.43	32.41	31.36	30.36	29.34	28.32	27.29	26.26	25.27	24.26	23.22	22.24	21.22	20.25	19.28	18.29	17.30	16.31
36	41.43	40.42	39.40	38.38	37.35	36.31	35.30	34.28	33.26	32.23	31.20	30.18	29.16	28.16	27.13	26.10	25.11	24.11	23.07	22.09	21.08	20.11	19.14	18.16	17.17	16.18
37	41.23	40.23	39.21	38.20	37.17	36.13	35.12	34.11	33.09	32.06	31.02	30.03	29.01	27.99	26.97	25.94	24.96	23.96	22.92	21.95	20.93	19.98	19.00	18.02	17.05	16.05
38	41.05	40.04	39.03	38.01	36.99	35.96	34.95	33.93	32.91	31.89	30.86	29.85	28.86	27.83	26.81	25.79	24.80	23.81	22.78	21.80	20.79	19.83	18.87	17.90	16.91	15.93
39	40.86	39.86	38.85	37.84	36.80	35.78	34.78	33.77	32.75	31.72	30.69	29.70	28.69	27.68	26.66	25.63	24.66	23.66	22.63	21.66	20.65	19.70	18.73	17.77	16.79	15.80
40	40.68	39.68	38.67	37.65	36.64	35.60	34.61	33.60	32.58	31.56	30.53	29.53	28.54	27.52	26.51	25.48	24.50	23.52	22.49	21.52	20.51	19.56	18.60	17.64	16.66	15.68
41	40.50	39.50	38.50	37.49	36.46	35.44	34.43	33.43	32.43	31.40	30.37	29.38	28.38	27.37	26.36	25.34	24.36	23.37	22.35	21.38	20.38	19.43	18.47	17.51	16.54	15.56
42	40.33	39.33	38.32	37.31	36.30	35.27	34.28	33.26	32.26	31.25	30.22	29.22	28.23	27.22	26.21	25.19	24.22	23.23	22.21	21.25	20.24	19.30	18.34	17.39	16.41	15.44
43	40.16	39.16	38.16	37.15	36.13	35.11	34.11	33.12	32.10	31.08	30.07	29.08	28.08	27.07	26.07	25.05	24.07	23.10	22.08	21.11	20.12	19.17	18.22	17.26	16.30	15.32
44	39.99	39.00	38.00	36.99	35.97	34.95	33.96	32.95	31.95	30.93	29.91	28.93	27.93	26.93	25.92	24.91	23.94	22.96	21.94	20.98	19.98	19.05	18.09	17.14	16.17	15.21
45	39.83	38.83	37.84	36.83	35.82	34.79	33.80	32.81	31.80	30.79	29.76	28.78	27.79	26.79	25.79	24.77	23.80	22.83	21.81	20.85	19.86	18.91	17.98	17.02	16.06	15.09
46	39.67	38.68	37.68	36.68	35.67	34.65	33.65	32.65	31.65	30.64	29.63	28.63	27.65	26.66	25.64	24.64	23.67	22.69	21.68	20.73	19.73	18.80	17.85	16.90	15.94	14.98

Tables

Table 29: 8th edition Ogden multipliers, loss of PENSION, WOMEN, discount rate: −0.25%, NO 2 YEAR ADJUSTMENT

Loss of pension from age

Age	50	51	52	53	54	55	56	57	58	59	60	61	62	63	64	65	66	67	68	69	70	71	72	73	74	75
47	39.52	38.53	37.53	36.52	35.52	34.50	33.51	32.51	31.51	30.50	29.48	28.51	27.51	26.51	25.52	24.50	23.54	22.57	21.55	20.60	19.61	18.67	17.74	16.78	15.83	14.87
48	39.37	38.38	37.39	36.39	35.37	34.36	33.37	32.37	31.37	30.36	29.35	28.36	27.38	26.38	25.38	24.38	23.41	22.44	21.43	20.48	19.49	18.56	17.62	16.67	15.72	14.76
49	39.22	38.24	37.25	36.24	35.24	34.21	33.23	32.24	31.24	30.23	29.21	28.24	27.25	26.26	25.26	24.25	23.29	22.32	21.30	20.36	19.37	18.44	17.51	16.56	15.61	14.65
50	39.09	38.10	37.11	36.11	35.10	34.09	33.09	32.11	31.11	30.10	29.09	28.11	27.13	26.13	25.13	24.13	23.17	22.20	21.19	20.25	19.26	18.33	17.39	16.45	15.51	14.55
51		37.98	36.98	35.98	34.98	33.96	32.98	31.98	30.98	29.98	28.96	27.99	27.00	26.01	25.02	24.01	23.05	22.09	21.08	20.13	19.15	18.22	17.29	16.35	15.40	14.45
52			36.87	35.86	34.85	33.84	32.86	31.87	30.86	29.86	28.85	27.87	26.89	25.90	24.90	23.90	22.94	21.98	20.97	20.02	19.04	18.12	17.19	16.24	15.30	14.35
53				35.75	34.74	33.72	32.75	31.76	30.76	29.75	28.73	27.77	26.78	25.80	24.79	23.79	22.84	21.87	20.86	19.92	18.93	18.02	17.09	16.15	15.20	14.25
54					34.64	33.62	32.64	31.66	30.65	29.65	28.63	27.65	26.68	25.68	24.70	23.69	22.73	21.77	20.76	19.83	18.84	17.91	16.99	16.05	15.12	14.16
55						33.53	32.55	31.55	30.56	29.55	28.54	27.56	26.58	25.60	24.59	23.60	22.64	21.67	20.67	19.73	18.75	17.83	16.89	15.97	15.02	14.08
56							32.46	31.47	30.47	29.47	28.45	27.48	26.49	25.50	24.51	23.50	22.56	21.59	20.58	19.64	18.66	17.74	16.82	15.88	14.94	13.99
57								31.40	30.40	29.38	28.38	27.40	26.42	25.43	24.43	23.43	22.47	21.51	20.51	19.56	18.58	17.66	16.73	15.80	14.86	13.92
58									30.33	29.32	28.30	27.34	26.35	25.35	24.36	23.35	22.40	21.43	20.43	19.49	18.50	17.58	16.66	15.73	14.79	13.84
59										29.27	28.25	27.27	26.30	25.29	24.29	23.29	22.33	21.37	20.37	19.42	18.44	17.51	16.59	15.65	14.72	13.78
60											28.20	27.23	26.24	25.25	24.24	23.23	22.28	21.31	20.30	19.36	18.38	17.46	16.52	15.59	14.65	13.71
61												27.19	26.21	25.21	24.21	23.19	22.23	21.27	20.26	19.32	18.33	17.40	16.48	15.54	14.60	13.65
62													26.18	25.18	24.18	23.17	22.20	21.23	20.22	19.28	18.29	17.36	16.43	15.49	14.55	13.60
63														25.17	24.16	23.15	22.18	21.20	20.19	19.24	18.26	17.33	16.39	15.45	14.51	13.56
64															24.16	23.14	22.17	21.20	20.18	19.22	18.23	17.30	16.37	15.42	14.48	13.53
65																23.15	22.18	21.20	20.17	19.21	18.22	17.29	16.35	15.40	14.45	13.50
66																	22.20	21.22	20.18	19.23	18.22	17.29	16.34	15.39	14.44	13.48
67																		21.25	20.21	19.25	18.24	17.29	16.35	15.40	14.44	13.48
68																			20.26	19.29	18.27	17.33	16.37	15.42	14.45	13.48
69																				19.36	18.33	17.37	16.42	15.44	14.48	13.51
70																					18.41	17.45	16.47	15.50	14.52	13.55
71																						17.54	16.56	15.58	14.59	13.59
72																							16.67	15.68	14.68	13.68
73																								15.81	14.79	13.78
74																									14.94	13.91
75																										14.07

Table 30: 8th edition Ogden multipliers, loss of PENSION, MEN, discount rate: –0.75%, 2 YEAR ADJUSTMENT

Loss of pension from age

Age	52	53	54	55	56	57	58	59	60	61	62	63	64	65	66	67	68	69	70	71	72	73	74	75	76	77
18	56.21	55.00	53.75	52.48	51.18	49.85	48.60	47.33	46.02	44.69	43.32	42.05	40.75	39.43	38.07	36.68	35.41	34.09	32.67	31.39	29.99	28.73	27.43	26.10	24.74	23.35
19	55.62	54.40	53.17	51.91	50.62	49.30	48.06	46.79	45.50	44.18	42.83	41.56	40.27	38.96	37.62	36.24	34.97	33.67	32.26	30.99	29.61	28.35	27.06	25.75	24.40	23.03
20	55.03	53.83	52.59	51.35	50.06	48.76	47.53	46.27	44.99	43.68	42.34	41.09	39.80	38.50	37.16	35.81	34.54	33.26	31.86	30.60	29.23	27.98	26.70	25.40	24.07	22.71
21	54.44	53.25	52.04	50.79	49.52	48.22	47.00	45.76	44.48	43.18	41.85	40.61	39.34	38.05	36.72	35.37	34.13	32.85	31.46	30.20	28.85	27.62	26.35	25.06	23.73	22.39
22	53.86	52.68	51.48	50.24	48.98	47.69	46.48	45.24	43.98	42.69	41.37	40.14	38.88	37.60	36.29	34.94	33.70	32.44	31.06	29.83	28.47	27.25	26.00	24.73	23.41	22.07
23	53.30	52.12	50.92	49.70	48.45	47.17	45.96	44.74	43.49	42.21	40.90	39.67	38.43	37.16	35.85	34.53	33.29	32.04	30.68	29.46	28.12	26.89	25.66	24.39	23.10	21.77
24	52.74	51.57	50.37	49.16	47.93	46.66	45.46	44.24	43.00	41.73	40.44	39.22	37.98	36.71	35.43	34.11	32.89	31.64	30.30	29.07	27.76	26.55	25.31	24.06	22.77	21.47
25	52.18	51.03	49.84	48.63	47.40	46.15	44.96	43.75	42.51	41.26	39.97	38.77	37.54	36.28	35.00	33.70	32.49	31.25	29.91	28.71	27.39	26.21	24.98	23.73	22.47	21.16
26	51.63	50.48	49.31	48.11	46.88	45.64	44.47	43.27	42.03	40.79	39.52	38.32	37.10	35.85	34.59	33.29	32.09	30.87	29.54	28.34	27.04	25.85	24.66	23.42	22.15	20.87
27	51.09	49.95	48.78	47.60	46.38	45.14	43.97	42.79	41.57	40.32	39.06	37.88	36.67	35.44	34.17	32.89	31.70	30.49	29.16	27.98	26.69	25.52	24.32	23.10	21.85	20.57
28	50.55	49.42	48.26	47.08	45.88	44.65	43.49	42.31	41.10	39.88	38.61	37.44	36.24	35.01	33.77	32.49	31.31	30.11	28.80	27.63	26.34	25.18	24.00	22.78	21.55	20.28
29	50.02	48.90	47.75	46.58	45.38	44.17	43.02	41.84	40.64	39.42	38.18	37.01	35.82	34.61	33.36	32.10	30.93	29.74	28.44	27.28	26.01	24.85	23.67	22.47	21.25	20.00
30	49.50	48.38	47.25	46.08	44.89	43.68	42.55	41.38	40.19	38.98	37.74	36.59	35.40	34.19	32.97	31.71	30.55	29.37	28.08	26.93	25.67	24.53	23.36	22.17	20.95	19.71
31	48.98	47.88	46.74	45.59	44.41	43.21	42.08	40.93	39.75	38.54	37.31	36.16	34.99	33.80	32.57	31.33	30.18	29.01	27.73	26.59	25.34	24.21	23.05	21.87	20.66	19.43
32	48.47	47.37	46.25	45.10	43.94	42.74	41.62	40.47	39.30	38.11	36.89	35.75	34.59	33.40	32.19	30.95	29.81	28.65	27.38	26.25	25.01	23.89	22.75	21.58	20.38	19.15
33	47.97	46.88	45.76	44.63	43.46	42.29	41.17	40.03	38.87	37.68	36.48	35.34	34.19	33.03	31.80	30.59	29.45	28.30	27.05	25.92	24.69	23.58	22.44	21.28	20.10	18.89
34	47.47	46.39	45.29	44.16	43.00	41.82	40.73	39.59	38.44	37.26	36.06	34.95	33.80	32.62	31.44	30.21	29.10	27.95	26.70	25.59	24.37	23.27	22.15	21.00	19.82	18.62
35	46.99	45.91	44.82	43.69	42.55	41.38	40.28	39.17	38.02	36.85	35.66	34.54	33.42	32.25	31.06	29.86	28.74	27.61	26.37	25.27	24.06	22.97	21.85	20.71	19.55	18.36
36	46.51	45.44	44.35	43.24	42.10	40.94	39.85	38.74	37.61	36.44	35.26	34.16	33.03	31.88	30.71	29.50	28.40	27.28	26.04	24.95	23.75	22.67	21.56	20.44	19.28	18.10
37	46.04	44.98	43.90	42.79	41.67	40.51	39.43	38.32	37.19	36.05	34.87	33.77	32.66	31.51	30.35	29.16	28.06	26.94	25.72	24.64	23.45	22.38	21.28	20.16	19.02	17.85
38	45.58	44.52	43.45	42.35	41.23	40.09	39.01	37.91	36.80	35.65	34.49	33.40	32.29	31.15	30.00	28.82	27.73	26.62	25.41	24.33	23.15	22.09	21.00	19.89	18.75	17.60
39	45.12	44.08	43.01	41.92	40.81	39.67	38.61	37.51	36.40	35.27	34.11	33.03	31.92	30.80	29.65	28.48	27.41	26.30	25.10	24.03	22.86	21.80	20.73	19.63	18.50	17.35
40	44.68	43.64	42.58	41.49	40.39	39.26	38.20	37.12	36.01	34.88	33.74	32.67	31.57	30.45	29.32	28.15	27.08	25.99	24.79	23.73	22.57	21.53	20.46	19.36	18.25	17.11
41	44.24	43.21	42.16	41.09	39.98	38.86	37.81	36.73	35.64	34.51	33.37	32.31	31.23	30.12	28.97	27.83	26.76	25.68	24.50	23.44	22.29	21.25	20.19	19.11	18.00	16.88
42	43.81	42.79	41.74	40.67	39.59	38.46	37.42	36.35	35.27	34.15	33.01	31.96	30.88	29.78	28.66	27.50	26.46	25.37	24.20	23.16	22.01	20.98	19.93	18.86	17.77	16.64
43	43.40	42.38	41.34	40.28	39.19	38.09	37.04	35.98	34.90	33.80	32.67	31.61	30.55	29.45	28.34	27.20	26.14	25.09	23.92	22.88	21.75	20.72	19.68	18.61	17.52	16.42
44	42.99	41.98	40.94	39.89	38.81	37.71	36.68	35.62	34.55	33.44	32.33	31.28	30.21	29.13	28.02	26.90	25.85	24.79	23.64	22.60	21.48	20.47	19.43	18.37	17.29	16.19
45	42.59	41.58	40.56	39.51	38.44	37.34	36.31	35.27	34.19	33.11	31.99	30.96	29.90	28.82	27.72	26.59	25.57	24.51	23.36	22.34	21.21	20.21	19.19	18.13	17.07	15.97
46	42.20	41.20	40.18	39.13	38.07	36.99	35.96	34.92	33.86	32.77	31.67	30.63	29.59	28.51	27.42	26.31	25.27	24.23	23.09	22.08	20.97	19.96	18.94	17.90	16.84	15.76
47	41.82	40.82	39.81	38.77	37.71	36.64	35.62	34.58	33.52	32.45	31.35	30.32	29.27	28.21	27.13	26.02	25.00	23.95	22.83	21.82	20.72	19.73	18.71	17.68	16.62	15.55
48	41.45	40.46	39.45	38.42	37.37	36.29	35.28	34.25	33.20	32.13	31.04	30.02	28.98	27.92	26.84	25.74	24.73	23.69	22.57	21.56	20.47	19.49	18.49	17.45	16.41	15.34

Table 30: 8th edition Ogden multipliers, loss of PENSION, MEN, discount rate: −0.75%, 2 YEAR ADJUSTMENT

Loss of pension from age

Age	52	53	54	55	56	57	58	59	60	61	62	63	64	65	66	67	68	69	70	71	72	73	74	75	76	77
49	41.09	40.10	39.10	38.07	37.03	35.96	34.95	33.93	32.89	31.82	30.73	29.72	28.69	27.63	26.56	25.47	24.46	23.43	22.32	21.32	20.23	19.25	18.26	17.24	16.20	15.14
50	40.74	39.76	38.75	37.73	36.70	35.64	34.63	33.61	32.57	31.52	30.44	29.42	28.40	27.35	26.29	25.20	24.20	23.18	22.07	21.08	20.00	19.02	18.03	17.02	16.00	14.95
51	40.40	39.42	38.42	37.41	36.37	35.32	34.33	33.31	32.27	31.22	30.15	29.15	28.12	27.08	26.02	24.94	23.94	22.93	21.83	20.84	19.77	18.81	17.82	16.82	15.79	14.76
52	40.06	39.10	38.10	37.09	36.06	35.01	34.02	33.01	31.98	30.93	29.86	28.87	27.85	26.81	25.76	24.69	23.70	22.69	21.59	20.61	19.55	18.59	17.61	16.61	15.60	14.56
53		38.77	37.79	36.78	35.75	34.71	33.73	32.72	31.70	30.66	29.59	28.60	27.59	26.56	25.51	24.44	23.46	22.45	21.36	20.39	19.33	18.38	17.41	16.42	15.41	14.38
54			37.49	36.49	35.46	34.42	33.44	32.45	31.43	30.38	29.33	28.34	27.33	26.31	25.26	24.20	23.22	22.23	21.14	20.18	19.12	18.17	17.21	16.22	15.22	14.20
55				36.20	35.18	34.14	33.17	32.18	31.16	30.13	29.07	28.09	27.09	26.07	25.03	23.97	23.00	22.01	20.93	19.96	18.92	17.98	17.02	16.04	15.04	14.03
56					34.92	33.88	32.91	31.92	30.91	29.88	28.83	27.85	26.86	25.84	24.80	23.75	22.78	21.79	20.72	19.77	18.72	17.79	16.83	15.86	14.87	13.86
57						33.63	32.67	31.68	30.67	29.65	28.60	27.63	26.63	25.62	24.59	23.54	22.58	21.59	20.52	19.58	18.54	17.60	16.66	15.69	14.71	13.70
58							32.44	31.46	30.45	29.42	28.38	27.42	26.43	25.42	24.39	23.34	22.38	21.40	20.34	19.38	18.36	17.44	16.49	15.52	14.54	13.55
59								31.25	30.24	29.22	28.17	27.21	26.23	25.22	24.20	23.15	22.20	21.22	20.16	19.22	18.18	17.27	16.33	15.37	14.39	13.40
60									30.05	29.03	27.99	27.02	26.05	25.05	24.02	22.98	22.02	21.06	19.99	19.05	18.03	17.10	16.18	15.23	14.26	13.26
61										28.86	27.82	26.86	25.88	24.88	23.86	22.82	21.87	20.90	19.84	18.91	17.88	16.97	16.03	15.08	14.12	13.14
62											27.67	26.71	25.73	24.73	23.72	22.68	21.73	20.76	19.71	18.77	17.75	16.83	15.90	14.95	13.99	13.02
63												26.58	25.60	24.60	23.59	22.55	21.60	20.63	19.58	18.65	17.63	16.71	15.78	14.84	13.88	12.90
64													25.49	24.50	23.47	22.44	21.49	20.52	19.47	18.53	17.52	16.61	15.68	14.74	13.77	12.80
65														24.41	23.39	22.34	21.40	20.43	19.38	18.44	17.42	16.51	15.59	14.64	13.69	12.71
66															23.32	22.28	21.32	20.36	19.31	18.37	17.35	16.43	15.51	14.56	13.61	12.64
67																22.23	21.28	20.30	19.25	18.32	17.29	16.37	15.44	14.50	13.54	12.57
68																	21.25	20.28	19.22	18.28	17.26	16.33	15.40	14.45	13.50	12.52
69																		20.27	19.21	18.26	17.24	16.32	15.37	14.42	13.46	12.49
70																			19.23	18.28	17.24	16.31	15.37	14.41	13.45	12.47
71																				18.32	17.28	16.33	15.39	14.43	13.45	12.47
72																					17.34	16.39	15.43	14.46	13.48	12.49
73																						16.48	15.51	14.52	13.54	12.54
74																							15.61	14.62	13.62	12.61
75																								14.75	13.74	12.71
76																									13.88	12.85
77																										13.02

Table 31: 8th edition Ogden multipliers, loss of PENSION, WOMEN, discount rate: −0.75%, 2 YEAR ADJUSTMENT

Loss of pension from age

Age	52	53	54	55	56	57	58	59	60	61	62	63	64	65	66	67	68	69	70	71	72	73	74	75	76	77
18	60.62	59.38	58.12	56.83	55.51	54.17	52.90	51.59	50.26	48.91	47.53	46.23	44.88	43.53	42.14	40.73	39.41	38.04	36.58	35.25	33.81	32.48	31.10	29.71	28.29	26.84
19	60.01	58.78	57.52	56.24	54.94	53.61	52.34	51.05	49.73	48.39	47.02	45.72	44.40	43.05	41.68	40.27	38.95	37.61	36.17	34.83	33.41	32.08	30.73	29.35	27.94	26.50
20	59.41	58.19	56.94	55.67	54.37	53.05	51.80	50.51	49.21	47.87	46.51	45.23	43.91	42.58	41.21	39.82	38.51	37.18	35.74	34.43	33.01	31.70	30.35	28.99	27.59	26.16
21	58.81	57.60	56.36	55.09	53.81	52.50	51.25	49.99	48.69	47.36	46.01	44.73	43.44	42.11	40.75	39.37	38.07	36.75	35.33	34.02	32.62	31.31	29.99	28.63	27.24	25.83
22	58.21	57.01	55.79	54.54	53.25	51.95	50.72	49.45	48.17	46.86	45.52	44.25	42.95	41.64	40.30	38.93	37.64	36.33	34.92	33.63	32.23	30.94	29.61	28.27	26.90	25.50
23	57.63	56.43	55.22	53.97	52.71	51.41	50.18	48.94	47.66	46.36	45.03	43.77	42.49	41.18	39.85	38.49	37.21	35.91	34.51	33.23	31.85	30.56	29.26	27.92	26.56	25.17
24	57.05	55.86	54.65	53.42	52.16	50.89	49.66	48.42	47.15	45.86	44.55	43.30	42.02	40.72	39.40	38.06	36.79	35.50	34.12	32.84	31.47	30.20	28.90	27.57	26.22	24.85
25	56.47	55.30	54.09	52.87	51.63	50.35	49.15	47.91	46.65	45.37	44.06	42.83	41.56	40.28	38.96	37.62	36.37	35.09	33.71	32.45	31.09	29.83	28.55	27.23	25.89	24.52
26	55.90	54.73	53.55	52.33	51.09	49.83	48.63	47.41	46.15	44.89	43.59	42.36	41.11	39.83	38.53	37.20	35.95	34.69	33.32	32.07	30.72	29.47	28.19	26.89	25.57	24.21
27	55.34	54.18	52.99	51.79	50.56	49.31	48.12	46.90	45.67	44.40	43.12	41.90	40.65	39.39	38.09	36.78	35.54	34.28	32.93	31.69	30.35	29.11	27.85	26.56	25.24	23.90
28	54.78	53.63	52.45	51.26	50.04	48.79	47.62	46.41	45.18	43.93	42.65	41.44	40.21	38.95	37.67	36.36	35.14	33.88	32.54	31.32	29.99	28.76	27.50	26.22	24.92	23.59
29	54.22	53.09	51.92	50.73	49.52	48.29	47.11	45.92	44.70	43.45	42.19	40.99	39.77	38.52	37.24	35.95	34.73	33.50	32.16	30.94	29.63	28.41	27.17	25.90	24.60	23.28
30	53.67	52.54	51.39	50.22	49.00	47.78	46.62	45.43	44.23	42.99	41.73	40.54	39.33	38.09	36.83	35.54	34.34	33.10	31.78	30.57	29.27	28.07	26.83	25.57	24.29	22.98
31	53.13	52.01	50.87	49.70	48.51	47.28	46.13	44.96	43.75	42.53	41.28	40.10	38.90	37.67	36.42	35.14	33.94	32.73	31.41	30.21	28.91	27.72	26.50	25.25	23.98	22.68
32	52.60	51.48	50.35	49.19	48.00	46.80	45.65	44.48	43.29	42.07	40.84	39.66	38.47	37.25	36.01	34.74	33.56	32.35	31.05	29.85	28.57	27.38	26.17	24.94	23.67	22.39
33	52.07	50.97	49.84	48.69	47.52	46.31	45.18	44.01	42.84	41.63	40.39	39.24	38.05	36.85	35.61	34.35	33.17	31.97	30.68	29.50	28.22	27.05	25.84	24.63	23.37	22.09
34	51.56	50.45	49.34	48.19	47.03	45.84	44.71	43.56	42.38	41.19	39.96	38.81	37.64	36.43	35.22	33.96	32.80	31.60	30.32	29.16	27.89	26.72	25.53	24.31	23.08	21.81
35	51.05	49.96	48.84	47.70	46.55	45.37	44.25	43.10	41.94	40.74	39.54	38.39	37.22	36.04	34.82	33.59	32.42	31.24	29.98	28.80	27.56	26.40	25.21	24.01	22.77	21.53
36	50.53	49.46	48.35	47.22	46.07	44.90	43.79	42.66	41.50	40.32	39.11	37.98	36.82	35.64	34.44	33.20	32.06	30.88	29.62	28.47	27.22	26.08	24.91	23.71	22.49	21.24
37	50.04	48.96	47.87	46.75	45.61	44.44	43.34	42.22	41.06	39.89	38.70	37.57	36.42	35.24	34.05	32.84	31.69	30.53	29.28	28.13	26.90	25.76	24.60	23.41	22.20	20.97
38	49.55	48.48	47.39	46.29	45.14	43.99	42.89	41.78	40.64	39.47	38.29	37.17	36.02	34.87	33.67	32.47	31.34	30.18	28.94	27.80	26.58	25.45	24.29	23.13	21.92	20.70
39	49.05	48.00	46.92	45.81	44.70	43.54	42.46	41.34	40.21	39.07	37.88	36.77	35.64	34.48	33.31	32.10	30.98	29.84	28.60	27.48	26.26	25.14	24.00	22.83	21.65	20.43
40	48.58	47.52	46.46	45.36	44.24	43.11	42.02	40.92	39.80	38.65	37.49	36.38	35.26	34.11	32.93	31.75	30.63	29.50	28.28	27.15	25.95	24.84	23.71	22.55	21.36	20.17
41	48.11	47.06	45.99	44.91	43.80	42.67	41.60	40.50	39.39	38.25	37.09	36.00	34.88	33.74	32.58	31.39	30.29	29.16	27.95	26.84	25.64	24.54	23.42	22.27	21.10	19.90
42	47.64	46.61	45.55	44.46	43.37	42.24	41.18	40.09	38.98	37.85	36.70	35.61	34.51	33.37	32.23	31.05	29.95	28.83	27.62	26.53	25.34	24.24	23.13	21.99	20.84	19.65
43	47.19	46.15	45.11	44.03	42.93	41.82	40.76	39.69	38.59	37.46	36.32	35.24	34.14	33.02	31.87	30.71	29.62	28.50	27.31	26.22	25.04	23.96	22.85	21.72	20.57	19.40
44	46.73	45.72	44.67	43.60	42.52	41.40	40.36	39.28	38.19	37.08	35.94	34.87	33.78	32.66	31.53	30.37	29.29	28.19	27.00	25.92	24.75	23.67	22.58	21.45	20.31	19.15
45	46.29	45.27	44.25	43.18	42.10	41.00	39.95	38.90	37.81	36.70	35.57	34.51	33.43	32.32	31.19	30.04	28.97	27.88	26.69	25.61	24.46	23.39	22.30	21.19	20.06	18.90
46	45.86	44.85	43.81	42.77	41.70	40.60	39.57	38.50	37.43	36.33	35.21	34.15	33.08	31.98	30.86	29.71	28.65	27.56	26.39	25.33	24.17	23.12	22.03	20.94	19.81	18.66
47	45.43	44.43	43.41	42.36	41.30	40.21	39.18	38.13	37.06	35.97	34.85	33.81	32.73	31.64	30.54	29.40	28.33	27.26	26.10	25.05	23.90	22.84	21.78	20.68	19.57	18.43
48	45.02	44.02	43.00	41.96	40.90	39.83	38.80	37.76	36.70	35.61	34.51	33.46	32.40	31.32	30.21	29.09	28.04	26.96	25.81	24.75	23.63	22.58	21.51	20.43	19.32	18.20

Tables

Table 31: 8th edition Ogden multipliers, loss of PENSION, WOMEN, discount rate: –0.75%, 2 YEAR ADJUSTMENT

Loss of pension from age

Age	52	53	54	55	56	57	58	59	60	61	62	63	64	65	66	67	68	69	70	71	72	73	74	75	76	77
49	44.60	43.62	42.60	41.58	40.52	39.44	38.44	37.39	36.34	35.26	34.16	33.13	32.07	31.00	29.90	28.78	27.74	26.67	25.52	24.48	23.35	22.32	21.26	20.19	19.09	17.96
50	44.21	43.22	42.22	41.19	40.15	39.08	38.07	37.05	35.99	34.92	33.83	32.80	31.75	30.67	29.59	28.48	27.44	26.39	25.25	24.21	23.09	22.06	21.02	19.95	18.86	17.75
51	43.82	42.84	41.84	40.83	39.77	38.72	37.72	36.69	35.65	34.58	33.50	32.48	31.44	30.38	29.28	28.19	27.16	26.11	24.98	23.94	22.83	21.81	20.77	19.71	18.63	17.53
52	43.43	42.47	41.47	40.46	39.43	38.36	37.37	36.36	35.32	34.26	33.17	32.16	31.13	30.07	29.00	27.89	26.88	25.83	24.70	23.69	22.58	21.56	20.53	19.48	18.41	17.31
53		42.10	41.12	40.11	39.08	38.03	37.03	36.02	34.99	33.94	32.87	31.85	30.83	29.78	28.71	27.62	26.59	25.57	24.45	23.44	22.34	21.33	20.30	19.26	18.19	17.10
54			40.76	39.76	38.74	37.70	36.71	35.70	34.68	33.63	32.57	31.56	30.53	29.49	28.43	27.35	26.34	25.30	24.20	23.18	22.10	21.10	20.07	19.03	17.98	16.90
55				39.43	38.41	37.37	36.40	35.40	34.37	33.33	32.27	31.28	30.26	29.21	28.16	27.08	26.08	25.06	23.95	22.94	21.86	20.87	19.86	18.82	17.77	16.70
56					38.09	37.06	36.09	35.10	34.08	33.04	31.98	31.00	29.99	28.95	27.89	26.82	25.83	24.81	23.71	22.71	21.63	20.65	19.65	18.62	17.56	16.50
57						36.76	35.80	34.81	33.80	32.77	31.71	30.72	29.72	28.70	27.65	26.57	25.58	24.57	23.48	22.49	21.41	20.43	19.44	18.42	17.38	16.31
58							35.51	34.53	33.52	32.50	31.45	30.47	29.46	28.45	27.41	26.34	25.35	24.34	23.26	22.28	21.21	20.22	19.23	18.22	17.20	16.14
59								34.27	33.27	32.24	31.20	30.22	29.23	28.21	27.17	26.12	25.13	24.13	23.05	22.06	21.01	20.04	19.04	18.04	17.01	15.97
60									33.02	32.00	30.96	29.99	29.00	27.98	26.95	25.90	24.92	23.92	22.85	21.87	20.81	19.85	18.86	17.85	16.84	15.80
61										31.78	30.74	29.77	28.78	27.77	26.74	25.69	24.72	23.73	22.65	21.68	20.63	19.66	18.69	17.69	16.67	15.64
62											30.53	29.57	28.58	27.57	26.55	25.50	24.53	23.54	22.47	21.51	20.46	19.50	18.52	17.52	16.51	15.48
63												29.37	28.39	27.39	26.36	25.32	24.35	23.36	22.30	21.34	20.30	19.34	18.36	17.37	16.36	15.34
64													28.22	27.22	26.20	25.15	24.19	23.20	22.14	21.18	20.14	19.19	18.22	17.23	16.23	15.20
65														27.06	26.04	25.01	24.04	23.06	22.00	21.03	20.00	19.05	18.08	17.10	16.09	15.08
66															25.91	24.87	23.91	22.92	21.87	20.91	19.87	18.92	17.96	16.98	15.98	14.96
67																24.75	23.79	22.81	21.75	20.79	19.76	18.81	17.84	16.86	15.87	14.86
68																	23.69	22.71	21.65	20.69	19.66	18.71	17.75	16.77	15.77	14.76
69																		22.63	21.57	20.62	19.58	18.63	17.66	16.68	15.69	14.68
70																			21.51	20.55	19.52	18.57	17.60	16.62	15.62	14.61
71																				20.51	19.47	18.53	17.56	16.57	15.57	14.56
72																					19.45	18.50	17.53	16.54	15.54	14.52
73																						18.50	17.53	16.54	15.53	14.51
74																							17.55	16.55	15.54	14.52
75																								16.60	15.58	14.55
76																									15.65	14.61
77																										14.70

Table 32: 8th edition Ogden multipliers, loss of PENSION, MEN, discount rate: −0.75%, NO 2 YEAR ADJUSTMENT

Age	Loss of pension from age																									
	50	51	52	53	54	55	56	57	58	59	60	61	62	63	64	65	66	67	68	69	70	71	72	73	74	75
16	56.21	55.00	53.75	52.48	51.18	49.85	48.60	47.33	46.02	44.69	43.32	42.05	40.75	39.43	38.07	36.68	35.41	34.09	32.67	31.39	29.99	28.73	27.43	26.10	24.74	23.35
17	55.62	54.40	53.17	51.91	50.62	49.30	48.06	46.79	45.50	44.18	42.83	41.56	40.27	38.96	37.62	36.24	34.97	33.67	32.26	30.99	29.61	28.35	27.06	25.75	24.40	23.03
18	55.03	53.83	52.59	51.35	50.06	48.76	47.53	46.27	44.99	43.68	42.34	41.09	39.80	38.50	37.16	35.81	34.54	33.26	31.86	30.60	29.23	27.98	26.70	25.40	24.07	22.71
19	54.44	53.25	52.04	50.79	49.52	48.22	47.00	45.76	44.48	43.18	41.85	40.61	39.34	38.05	36.72	35.37	34.13	32.85	31.46	30.20	28.85	27.62	26.35	25.06	23.73	22.39
20	53.86	52.68	51.48	50.24	48.98	47.69	46.48	45.24	43.98	42.69	41.37	40.14	38.88	37.60	36.29	34.94	33.70	32.44	31.06	29.83	28.47	27.25	26.00	24.73	23.41	22.07
21	53.30	52.12	50.92	49.70	48.45	47.17	45.96	44.74	43.49	42.21	40.90	39.67	38.43	37.16	35.85	34.53	33.29	32.04	30.68	29.46	28.12	26.89	25.66	24.39	23.10	21.77
22	52.74	51.57	50.37	49.16	47.93	46.66	45.46	44.24	43.00	41.73	40.44	39.22	37.98	36.71	35.43	34.11	32.89	31.64	30.30	29.07	27.76	26.55	25.31	24.06	22.77	21.47
23	52.18	51.03	49.84	48.63	47.40	46.15	44.96	43.75	42.51	41.26	39.97	38.77	37.54	36.28	35.00	33.70	32.49	31.25	29.91	28.71	27.39	26.21	24.98	23.73	22.47	21.16
24	51.63	50.48	49.31	48.11	46.88	45.64	44.47	43.27	42.03	40.79	39.52	38.32	37.10	35.85	34.59	33.29	32.09	30.87	29.54	28.34	27.04	25.85	24.66	23.42	22.15	20.87
25	51.09	49.95	48.78	47.60	46.38	45.14	43.97	42.79	41.57	40.32	39.06	37.88	36.67	35.44	34.17	32.89	31.70	30.49	29.16	27.98	26.69	25.52	24.32	23.10	21.85	20.57
26	50.55	49.42	48.26	47.08	45.88	44.65	43.49	42.31	41.10	39.88	38.61	37.44	36.24	35.01	33.77	32.49	31.31	30.11	28.80	27.63	26.34	25.18	24.00	22.78	21.55	20.28
27	50.02	48.90	47.75	46.58	45.38	44.17	43.02	41.84	40.64	39.42	38.18	37.01	35.82	34.61	33.36	32.10	30.93	29.74	28.44	27.28	26.01	24.85	23.67	22.47	21.25	20.00
28	49.50	48.38	47.25	46.08	44.89	43.68	42.55	41.38	40.19	38.98	37.74	36.59	35.40	34.19	32.97	31.71	30.55	29.37	28.08	26.93	25.67	24.53	23.36	22.17	20.95	19.71
29	48.98	47.88	46.74	45.59	44.41	43.21	42.08	40.93	39.75	38.54	37.31	36.16	34.99	33.80	32.57	31.33	30.18	29.01	27.73	26.59	25.34	24.21	23.05	21.87	20.66	19.43
30	48.47	47.37	46.25	45.10	43.94	42.74	41.62	40.47	39.30	38.11	36.89	35.75	34.59	33.40	32.19	30.95	29.81	28.65	27.38	26.25	25.01	23.89	22.75	21.58	20.38	19.15
31	47.97	46.88	45.76	44.63	43.46	42.29	41.17	40.03	38.87	37.68	36.48	35.34	34.19	33.01	31.80	30.59	29.45	28.30	27.05	25.92	24.69	23.58	22.44	21.28	20.10	18.89
32	47.47	46.39	45.29	44.16	43.00	41.82	40.73	39.59	38.44	37.26	36.06	34.95	33.80	32.62	31.44	30.21	29.10	27.95	26.70	25.59	24.37	23.27	22.15	21.00	19.82	18.62
33	46.99	45.91	44.82	43.69	42.55	41.38	40.28	39.17	38.02	36.85	35.66	34.54	33.42	32.25	31.06	29.86	28.74	27.61	26.37	25.27	24.06	22.97	21.85	20.71	19.55	18.36
34	46.51	45.44	44.35	43.24	42.10	40.94	39.85	38.74	37.61	36.44	35.26	34.16	33.03	31.88	30.71	29.50	28.40	27.27	26.04	24.95	23.75	22.67	21.56	20.44	19.28	18.10
35	46.04	44.98	43.90	42.79	41.67	40.51	39.43	38.32	37.19	36.05	34.87	33.77	32.66	31.51	30.35	29.16	28.06	26.94	25.72	24.64	23.45	22.38	21.28	20.16	19.02	17.85
36	45.58	44.52	43.45	42.35	41.23	40.09	39.01	37.91	36.80	35.65	34.49	33.40	32.29	31.15	30.00	28.82	27.73	26.62	25.41	24.33	23.15	22.09	21.00	19.89	18.75	17.60
37	45.12	44.08	43.01	41.92	40.81	39.67	38.61	37.51	36.40	35.27	34.11	33.03	31.92	30.80	29.65	28.48	27.41	26.30	25.10	24.03	22.86	21.80	20.73	19.63	18.50	17.35
38	44.68	43.64	42.58	41.49	40.39	39.26	38.20	37.12	36.01	34.88	33.74	32.67	31.57	30.45	29.32	28.15	27.08	25.99	24.79	23.73	22.57	21.53	20.46	19.36	18.25	17.11
39	44.24	43.21	42.16	41.09	39.98	38.86	37.81	36.73	35.64	34.51	33.37	32.31	31.23	30.12	28.97	27.83	26.76	25.68	24.50	23.44	22.29	21.25	20.19	19.11	18.00	16.88
40	43.81	42.79	41.74	40.67	39.59	38.46	37.42	36.35	35.27	34.15	33.01	31.96	30.88	29.78	28.66	27.50	26.46	25.37	24.20	23.16	22.01	20.98	19.93	18.86	17.77	16.64
41	43.40	42.38	41.34	40.28	39.19	38.09	37.04	35.98	34.90	33.80	32.67	31.61	30.55	29.45	28.34	27.20	26.14	25.09	23.92	22.88	21.75	20.72	19.68	18.61	17.52	16.42
42	42.99	41.98	40.94	39.89	38.81	37.71	36.68	35.62	34.55	33.44	32.33	31.28	30.21	29.13	28.02	26.90	25.85	24.79	23.64	22.60	21.48	20.47	19.43	18.37	17.29	16.19
43	42.59	41.58	40.56	39.51	38.44	37.34	36.31	35.27	34.19	33.11	31.99	30.96	29.90	28.82	27.72	26.59	25.57	24.51	23.36	22.34	21.21	20.21	19.19	18.13	17.07	15.97
44	42.20	41.20	40.18	39.13	38.07	36.99	35.96	34.92	33.86	32.77	31.67	30.63	29.59	28.51	27.42	26.31	25.27	24.23	23.09	22.08	20.97	19.96	18.94	17.90	16.84	15.76
45	41.82	40.82	39.81	38.77	37.71	36.64	35.62	34.58	33.52	32.45	31.35	30.32	29.27	28.21	27.13	26.02	25.00	23.95	22.83	21.82	20.72	19.73	18.71	17.68	16.62	15.55
46	41.45	40.46	39.45	38.42	37.37	36.29	35.28	34.25	33.20	32.13	31.04	30.02	28.98	27.92	26.84	25.74	24.73	23.69	22.57	21.56	20.47	19.49	18.49	17.45	16.41	15.34

Table 32: 8th edition Ogden multipliers, loss of PENSION, MEN, discount rate: −0.75%, NO 2 YEAR ADJUSTMENT

Loss of pension from age

Age	50	51	52	53	54	55	56	57	58	59	60	61	62	63	64	65	66	67	68	69	70	71	72	73	74	75
47	41.09	40.10	39.10	38.07	37.03	35.96	34.95	33.93	32.89	31.82	30.73	29.72	28.69	27.63	26.56	25.47	24.46	23.43	22.32	21.32	20.23	19.25	18.26	17.24	16.20	15.14
48	40.74	39.76	38.75	37.73	36.70	35.64	34.63	33.61	32.57	31.52	30.44	29.42	28.40	27.35	26.29	25.20	24.20	23.18	22.07	21.08	20.00	19.02	18.03	17.02	16.00	14.95
49	40.40	39.42	38.42	37.41	36.37	35.32	34.33	33.31	32.27	31.22	30.15	29.15	28.12	27.08	26.02	24.94	23.94	22.93	21.83	20.84	19.77	18.81	17.82	16.82	15.79	14.76
50	40.06	39.10	38.10	37.09	36.06	35.01	34.02	33.01	31.98	30.93	29.86	28.87	27.85	26.81	25.76	24.69	23.70	22.69	21.59	20.61	19.55	18.59	17.61	16.61	15.60	14.56
51		38.77	37.79	36.78	35.75	34.71	33.73	32.72	31.70	30.66	29.59	28.60	27.59	26.56	25.51	24.44	23.46	22.45	21.36	20.39	19.33	18.38	17.41	16.42	15.41	14.38
52			37.49	36.49	35.46	34.42	33.44	32.45	31.43	30.38	29.33	28.34	27.33	26.31	25.26	24.20	23.22	22.23	21.14	20.18	19.12	18.17	17.21	16.22	15.22	14.20
53				36.20	35.18	34.14	33.17	32.18	31.16	30.13	29.07	28.09	27.09	26.07	25.03	23.97	23.00	22.01	20.93	19.96	18.92	17.98	17.02	16.04	15.04	14.03
54					34.92	33.88	32.91	31.92	30.91	29.88	28.83	27.85	26.86	25.84	24.80	23.75	22.78	21.79	20.72	19.77	18.72	17.79	16.83	15.86	14.87	13.86
55						33.63	32.67	31.68	30.67	29.65	28.60	27.63	26.63	25.62	24.59	23.54	22.58	21.59	20.52	19.58	18.54	17.60	16.66	15.69	14.71	13.70
56							32.44	31.46	30.45	29.42	28.38	27.42	26.43	25.42	24.39	23.34	22.38	21.40	20.34	19.38	18.36	17.44	16.49	15.52	14.54	13.55
57								31.25	30.24	29.22	28.17	27.21	26.23	25.22	24.20	23.15	22.20	21.22	20.16	19.22	18.18	17.27	16.33	15.37	14.39	13.40
58									30.05	29.03	27.99	27.02	26.05	25.05	24.02	22.98	22.02	21.06	19.99	19.05	18.03	17.10	16.18	15.23	14.26	13.26
59										28.86	27.82	26.86	25.88	24.88	23.86	22.82	21.87	20.90	19.84	18.91	17.88	16.97	16.03	15.08	14.12	13.14
60											27.67	26.71	25.73	24.73	23.72	22.68	21.73	20.76	19.71	18.77	17.75	16.83	15.90	14.95	13.99	13.02
61												26.58	25.60	24.60	23.59	22.55	21.60	20.63	19.58	18.65	17.63	16.71	15.78	14.84	13.88	12.90
62													25.49	24.50	23.47	22.44	21.49	20.52	19.47	18.53	17.52	16.61	15.68	14.74	13.77	12.80
63														24.41	23.39	22.34	21.40	20.43	19.38	18.44	17.42	16.51	15.59	14.64	13.69	12.71
64															23.32	22.28	21.32	20.36	19.31	18.37	17.35	16.43	15.51	14.56	13.61	12.64
65																22.23	21.28	20.30	19.25	18.32	17.29	16.37	15.44	14.50	13.54	12.57
66																	21.25	20.28	19.22	18.28	17.26	16.33	15.40	14.45	13.50	12.52
67																		20.27	19.21	18.26	17.24	16.32	15.37	14.42	13.46	12.49
68																			19.23	18.28	17.24	16.31	15.37	14.41	13.45	12.47
69																				18.32	17.28	16.33	15.39	14.43	13.45	12.47
70																					17.34	16.39	15.43	14.46	13.48	12.49
71																						16.48	15.51	14.52	13.54	12.54
72																							15.61	14.62	13.62	12.61
73																								14.75	13.74	12.71
74																									13.88	12.85
75																										13.02

Tables

Table 33: 8th edition Ogden multipliers, loss of PENSION, WOMEN, discount rate: −0.75%, NO 2 YEAR ADJUSTMENT

Loss of pension from age

Age	50	51	52	53	54	55	56	57	58	59	60	61	62	63	64	65	66	67	68	69	70	71	72	73	74	75
16	60.62	59.38	58.12	56.83	55.51	54.17	52.90	51.59	50.26	48.91	47.53	46.23	44.88	43.53	42.14	40.73	39.41	38.04	36.58	35.25	33.81	32.48	31.10	29.71	28.29	26.84
17	60.01	58.78	57.52	56.24	54.94	53.61	52.34	51.05	49.73	48.39	47.02	45.72	44.40	43.05	41.68	40.27	38.95	37.61	36.17	34.83	33.41	32.08	30.73	29.35	27.94	26.50
18	59.41	58.19	56.94	55.67	54.37	53.05	51.80	50.51	49.21	47.87	46.51	45.23	43.91	42.58	41.21	39.82	38.51	37.18	35.74	34.43	33.01	31.70	30.35	28.99	27.59	26.16
19	58.81	57.60	56.36	55.09	53.81	52.50	51.25	49.99	48.69	47.36	46.01	44.73	43.44	42.11	40.75	39.37	38.07	36.75	35.33	34.02	32.62	31.31	29.99	28.63	27.24	25.83
20	58.21	57.01	55.79	54.54	53.25	51.95	50.72	49.45	48.17	46.86	45.52	44.25	42.95	41.64	40.30	38.93	37.64	36.33	34.92	33.63	32.23	30.94	29.61	28.27	26.90	25.50
21	57.63	56.43	55.22	53.97	52.71	51.41	50.18	48.94	47.66	46.36	45.03	43.77	42.49	41.18	39.85	38.49	37.21	35.91	34.51	33.23	31.85	30.56	29.26	27.92	26.56	25.17
22	57.05	55.86	54.65	53.42	52.16	50.89	49.66	48.42	47.15	45.86	44.55	43.30	42.02	40.72	39.40	38.06	36.79	35.50	34.12	32.84	31.47	30.20	28.90	27.57	26.22	24.85
23	56.47	55.30	54.09	52.87	51.63	50.35	49.15	47.91	46.65	45.37	44.06	42.83	41.56	40.28	38.96	37.62	36.37	35.09	33.71	32.45	31.09	29.83	28.55	27.23	25.89	24.52
24	55.90	54.73	53.55	52.33	51.09	49.83	48.63	47.41	46.15	44.89	43.59	42.36	41.11	39.83	38.53	37.20	35.95	34.69	33.32	32.07	30.72	29.47	28.19	26.89	25.57	24.21
25	55.34	54.18	52.99	51.79	50.56	49.31	48.12	46.90	45.67	44.40	43.12	41.90	40.65	39.39	38.09	36.78	35.54	34.28	32.93	31.69	30.35	29.11	27.85	26.56	25.24	23.90
26	54.78	53.63	52.45	51.26	50.04	48.79	47.62	46.41	45.18	43.93	42.65	41.44	40.21	38.95	37.67	36.36	35.14	33.88	32.54	31.32	29.99	28.76	27.50	26.22	24.92	23.59
27	54.22	53.09	51.92	50.73	49.52	48.29	47.11	45.92	44.70	43.45	42.19	40.99	39.77	38.52	37.24	35.95	34.73	33.50	32.16	30.94	29.63	28.41	27.17	25.90	24.60	23.28
28	53.67	52.54	51.39	50.22	49.00	47.78	46.62	45.43	44.23	42.99	41.73	40.54	39.33	38.09	36.83	35.54	34.34	33.10	31.78	30.57	29.27	28.07	26.83	25.57	24.29	22.98
29	53.13	52.01	50.87	49.70	48.51	47.28	46.13	44.96	43.75	42.53	41.28	40.10	38.90	37.67	36.42	35.14	33.94	32.73	31.41	30.21	28.91	27.72	26.50	25.25	23.98	22.68
30	52.60	51.48	50.35	49.19	48.00	46.80	45.65	44.48	43.29	42.07	40.84	39.66	38.47	37.25	36.01	34.74	33.56	32.35	31.05	29.85	28.57	27.38	26.17	24.94	23.67	22.39
31	52.07	50.97	49.84	48.69	47.52	46.31	45.18	44.01	42.84	41.63	40.39	39.24	38.05	36.85	35.61	34.35	33.17	31.97	30.68	29.50	28.22	27.05	25.84	24.63	23.37	22.09
32	51.56	50.45	49.34	48.19	47.03	45.84	44.71	43.56	42.38	41.19	39.96	38.81	37.64	36.43	35.22	33.96	32.80	31.60	30.32	29.16	27.89	26.72	25.53	24.31	23.08	21.81
33	51.05	49.96	48.84	47.70	46.55	45.37	44.25	43.10	41.94	40.74	39.54	38.39	37.22	36.04	34.82	33.59	32.42	31.24	29.98	28.80	27.56	26.40	25.21	24.01	22.77	21.53
34	50.53	49.46	48.35	47.22	46.07	44.90	43.79	42.66	41.50	40.32	39.11	37.98	36.82	35.64	34.44	33.20	32.06	30.88	29.62	28.47	27.22	26.08	24.91	23.71	22.49	21.24
35	50.04	48.96	47.87	46.75	45.61	44.44	43.34	42.22	41.06	39.89	38.70	37.57	36.42	35.24	34.05	32.84	31.69	30.53	29.28	28.13	26.90	25.76	24.60	23.41	22.20	20.97
36	49.55	48.48	47.39	46.29	45.14	43.99	42.89	41.78	40.64	39.47	38.29	37.17	36.02	34.87	33.67	32.47	31.34	30.18	28.94	27.80	26.58	25.45	24.29	23.13	21.92	20.70
37	49.05	48.00	46.92	45.81	44.70	43.54	42.46	41.34	40.21	39.07	37.88	36.77	35.64	34.48	33.31	32.10	30.98	29.84	28.60	27.48	26.26	25.14	24.00	22.83	21.65	20.43
38	48.58	47.52	46.46	45.36	44.24	43.11	42.02	40.92	39.80	38.65	37.49	36.38	35.26	34.11	32.93	31.75	30.63	29.50	28.28	27.15	25.95	24.84	23.71	22.55	21.36	20.17
39	48.11	47.06	45.99	44.91	43.80	42.67	41.60	40.50	39.39	38.25	37.09	36.00	34.88	33.74	32.58	31.39	30.29	29.16	27.95	26.84	25.64	24.54	23.42	22.27	21.10	19.90
40	47.64	46.61	45.55	44.46	43.37	42.24	41.18	40.09	38.98	37.85	36.70	35.61	34.51	33.37	32.23	31.05	29.95	28.83	27.62	26.53	25.34	24.24	23.13	21.99	20.84	19.65
41	47.19	46.15	45.11	44.03	42.93	41.82	40.76	39.69	38.59	37.46	36.32	35.24	34.14	33.02	31.87	30.71	29.62	28.50	27.31	26.22	25.04	23.96	22.85	21.72	20.57	19.40
42	46.73	45.72	44.67	43.60	42.52	41.40	40.36	39.28	38.19	37.08	35.94	34.87	33.78	32.66	31.53	30.37	29.29	28.19	27.00	25.92	24.75	23.67	22.58	21.45	20.31	19.15
43	46.29	45.27	44.25	43.18	42.10	41.00	39.95	38.90	37.81	36.70	35.57	34.51	33.43	32.32	31.19	30.04	28.97	27.88	26.69	25.61	24.46	23.39	22.30	21.19	20.06	18.90
44	45.86	44.85	43.81	42.77	41.70	40.60	39.57	38.59	37.43	36.33	35.21	34.15	33.08	31.98	30.86	29.71	28.65	27.56	26.39	25.33	24.17	23.12	22.03	20.94	19.81	18.66
45	45.43	44.43	43.41	42.36	41.30	40.21	39.18	38.13	37.06	35.97	34.85	33.81	32.73	31.64	30.54	29.40	28.33	27.26	26.10	25.05	23.90	22.84	21.78	20.68	19.57	18.43
46	45.02	44.02	43.00	41.96	40.90	39.83	38.80	37.76	36.70	35.61	34.51	33.46	32.40	31.32	30.21	29.09	28.04	26.96	25.81	24.75	23.63	22.58	21.51	20.43	19.32	18.20

Tables

Table 33: 8th edition Ogden multipliers, loss of PENSION, WOMEN, discount rate: −0.75%, NO 2 YEAR ADJUSTMENT

Loss of pension from age

Age	50	51	52	53	54	55	56	57	58	59	60	61	62	63	64	65	66	67	68	69	70	71	72	73	74	75
47	44.60	43.62	42.60	41.58	40.52	39.44	38.44	37.39	36.34	35.26	34.16	33.13	32.07	31.00	29.90	28.78	27.74	26.67	25.52	24.48	23.35	22.32	21.26	20.19	19.09	17.96
48	44.21	43.22	42.22	41.19	40.15	39.08	38.07	37.05	35.99	34.92	33.83	32.80	31.75	30.67	29.59	28.48	27.44	26.39	25.25	24.21	23.09	22.06	21.02	19.95	18.86	17.75
49	43.82	42.84	41.84	40.83	39.77	38.72	37.72	36.69	35.65	34.58	33.50	32.48	31.44	30.38	29.28	28.19	27.16	26.11	24.98	23.94	22.83	21.81	20.77	19.71	18.63	17.53
50	43.43	42.47	41.47	40.46	39.43	38.36	37.37	36.36	35.32	34.26	33.17	32.16	31.13	30.07	29.00	27.89	26.88	25.83	24.70	23.69	22.58	21.56	20.53	19.48	18.41	17.31
51		42.10	41.12	40.11	39.08	38.03	37.03	36.02	34.99	33.94	32.87	31.85	30.83	29.78	28.71	27.62	26.59	25.57	24.45	23.44	22.34	21.33	20.30	19.26	18.19	17.10
52			40.76	39.76	38.74	37.70	36.71	35.70	34.68	33.63	32.57	31.56	30.53	29.49	28.43	27.35	26.34	25.30	24.20	23.18	22.10	21.10	20.07	19.03	17.98	16.90
53				39.43	38.41	37.37	36.40	35.40	34.37	33.33	32.27	31.28	30.26	29.21	28.16	27.08	26.08	25.06	23.95	22.94	21.86	20.87	19.86	18.82	17.77	16.70
54					38.09	37.06	36.09	35.10	34.08	33.04	31.98	31.00	29.99	28.95	27.89	26.82	25.83	24.81	23.71	22.71	21.63	20.65	19.65	18.62	17.56	16.50
55						36.76	35.80	34.81	33.80	32.77	31.71	30.72	29.72	28.70	27.65	26.57	25.58	24.57	23.48	22.49	21.41	20.43	19.44	18.42	17.38	16.31
56							35.51	34.53	33.52	32.50	31.45	30.47	29.46	28.45	27.41	26.34	25.35	24.34	23.26	22.28	21.21	20.22	19.23	18.22	17.20	16.14
57								34.27	33.27	32.24	31.20	30.22	29.23	28.21	27.17	26.12	25.13	24.13	23.05	22.06	21.01	20.04	19.04	18.04	17.01	15.97
58									33.02	32.00	30.96	29.99	29.00	27.98	26.95	25.90	24.92	23.92	22.85	21.87	20.81	19.85	18.86	17.85	16.84	15.80
59										31.78	30.74	29.77	28.78	27.77	26.74	25.69	24.72	23.73	22.65	21.68	20.63	19.66	18.69	17.69	16.67	15.64
60											30.53	29.57	28.58	27.57	26.55	25.50	24.53	23.54	22.47	21.51	20.46	19.50	18.52	17.52	16.51	15.48
61												29.37	28.39	27.39	26.36	25.32	24.35	23.36	22.30	21.34	20.30	19.34	18.36	17.37	16.36	15.34
62													28.22	27.22	26.20	25.15	24.19	23.20	22.14	21.18	20.14	19.19	18.22	17.23	16.23	15.20
63														27.06	26.04	25.01	24.04	23.06	22.00	21.03	20.00	19.05	18.08	17.10	16.09	15.08
64															25.91	24.87	23.91	22.92	21.87	20.91	19.87	18.92	17.96	16.98	15.98	14.96
65																24.75	23.79	22.81	21.75	20.79	19.76	18.81	17.84	16.86	15.87	14.86
66																	23.69	22.71	21.65	20.69	19.66	18.71	17.75	16.77	15.77	14.76
67																		22.63	21.57	20.62	19.58	18.63	17.66	16.68	15.69	14.68
68																			21.51	20.55	19.52	18.57	17.60	16.62	15.62	14.61
69																				20.51	19.47	18.53	17.56	16.57	15.57	14.56
70																					19.45	18.50	17.53	16.54	15.54	14.52
71																						18.50	17.53	16.54	15.53	14.51
72																							17.55	16.55	15.54	14.52
73																								16.60	15.58	14.55
74																									15.65	14.61
75																										14.70

Table 34: 8th edition Ogden multipliers, loss of EARNINGS, MEN, discount rate: −0.25%, NO 2 YEAR ADJUSTMENT

Loss of earnings to pension age

Age	50	51	52	53	54	55	56	57	58	59	60	61	62	63	64	65	66	67	68	69	70	71	72	73	74	75
16	35.18	36.24	37.30	38.36	39.42	40.48	41.54	42.60	43.66	44.72	45.78	46.83	47.89	48.94	49.99	51.03	52.08	53.11	54.15	55.17	56.20	57.21	58.22	59.22	60.21	61.20
17	34.09	35.15	36.21	37.26	38.32	39.38	40.44	41.49	42.55	43.61	44.66	45.71	46.76	47.81	48.86	49.90	50.94	51.97	53.00	54.03	55.05	56.06	57.06	58.06	59.05	60.02
18	33.01	34.06	35.12	36.17	37.23	38.28	39.34	40.39	41.44	42.50	43.55	44.60	45.65	46.69	47.73	48.77	49.81	50.84	51.86	52.88	53.90	54.91	55.91	56.90	57.88	58.86
19	31.93	32.98	34.04	35.09	36.14	37.19	38.24	39.29	40.34	41.39	42.44	43.49	44.53	45.57	46.61	47.65	48.68	49.71	50.73	51.75	52.76	53.76	54.76	55.75	56.73	57.70
20	30.86	31.91	32.96	34.01	35.05	36.10	37.15	38.20	39.25	40.29	41.34	42.38	43.42	44.46	45.50	46.53	47.56	48.58	49.60	50.61	51.62	52.62	53.62	54.60	55.58	56.54
21	29.79	30.83	31.88	32.93	33.97	35.02	36.07	37.11	38.16	39.20	40.24	41.28	42.32	43.36	44.39	45.42	46.44	47.46	48.48	49.49	50.49	51.49	52.48	53.46	54.43	55.39
22	28.72	29.77	30.81	31.85	32.90	33.94	34.98	36.03	37.07	38.11	39.15	40.18	41.22	42.25	43.28	44.31	45.33	46.35	47.36	48.36	49.36	50.36	51.34	52.32	53.29	54.24
23	27.66	28.70	29.74	30.78	31.82	32.86	33.90	34.94	35.98	37.02	38.06	39.09	40.12	41.15	42.18	43.20	44.22	45.23	46.24	47.24	48.24	49.23	50.21	51.18	52.15	53.10
24	26.60	27.64	28.67	29.71	30.75	31.79	32.83	33.86	34.90	35.93	36.97	38.00	39.03	40.05	41.08	42.10	43.11	44.12	45.13	46.13	47.12	48.11	49.08	50.05	51.01	51.96
25	25.54	26.58	27.61	28.65	29.68	30.72	31.75	32.79	33.82	34.85	35.88	36.91	37.94	38.96	39.98	41.00	42.01	43.02	44.02	45.01	46.00	46.99	47.96	48.92	49.88	50.82
26	24.48	25.52	26.55	27.58	28.62	29.65	30.68	31.71	32.74	33.77	34.80	35.83	36.85	37.87	38.89	39.90	40.91	41.91	42.91	43.90	44.89	45.87	46.84	47.80	48.75	49.69
27	23.43	24.46	25.49	26.52	27.55	28.58	29.61	30.64	31.67	32.70	33.72	34.74	35.76	36.78	37.80	38.80	39.81	40.81	41.81	42.80	43.78	44.75	45.72	46.68	47.63	48.56
28	22.38	23.41	24.44	25.47	26.49	27.52	28.55	29.58	30.60	31.62	32.65	33.67	34.68	35.70	36.71	37.71	38.72	39.71	40.71	41.69	42.67	43.64	44.61	45.56	46.50	47.44
29	21.34	22.36	23.39	24.41	25.44	26.46	27.49	28.51	29.53	30.56	31.57	32.59	33.61	34.62	35.63	36.63	37.63	38.62	39.61	40.59	41.57	42.54	43.50	44.45	45.39	46.32
30	20.29	21.32	22.34	23.36	24.39	25.41	26.43	27.45	28.47	29.49	30.51	31.52	32.53	33.54	34.55	35.55	36.54	37.53	38.52	39.50	40.47	41.44	42.39	43.34	44.27	45.20
31	19.25	20.28	21.30	22.32	23.34	24.36	25.38	26.40	27.41	28.43	29.44	30.46	31.46	32.47	33.47	34.47	35.46	36.45	37.43	38.41	39.38	40.34	41.29	42.24	43.17	44.09
32	18.22	19.24	20.26	21.27	22.29	23.31	24.33	25.34	26.36	27.37	28.38	29.39	30.40	31.40	32.40	33.40	34.39	35.37	36.35	37.32	38.29	39.25	40.20	41.14	42.06	42.98
33	17.18	18.20	19.22	20.23	21.25	22.27	23.28	24.29	25.31	26.32	27.33	28.33	29.34	30.34	31.33	32.33	33.31	34.30	35.27	36.24	37.21	38.16	39.11	40.04	40.97	41.88
34	16.15	17.17	18.18	19.20	20.21	21.23	22.24	23.25	24.26	25.27	26.28	27.28	28.28	29.28	30.27	31.26	32.25	33.23	34.20	35.17	36.13	37.08	38.02	38.95	39.87	40.78
35	15.13	16.14	17.15	18.16	19.18	20.19	21.20	22.21	23.22	24.22	25.23	26.23	27.23	28.22	29.21	30.20	31.18	32.16	33.13	34.10	35.05	36.00	36.94	37.87	38.79	39.69
36	14.10	15.11	16.12	17.13	18.14	19.15	20.16	21.17	22.18	23.18	24.18	25.18	26.18	27.17	28.16	29.15	30.12	31.10	32.07	33.03	33.98	34.93	35.86	36.79	37.70	38.60
37	13.08	14.09	15.10	16.11	17.12	18.12	19.13	20.14	21.14	22.14	23.14	24.14	25.13	26.12	27.11	28.09	29.07	30.04	31.01	31.97	32.92	33.86	34.79	35.71	36.62	37.52
38	12.06	13.07	14.08	15.08	16.09	17.10	18.10	19.11	20.11	21.11	22.11	23.10	24.09	25.08	26.07	27.05	28.02	28.99	29.95	30.91	31.86	32.80	33.73	34.64	35.55	36.45
39	11.05	12.05	13.06	14.06	15.07	16.07	17.08	18.08	19.08	20.08	21.07	22.07	23.06	24.04	25.03	26.00	26.98	27.94	28.90	29.86	30.80	31.74	32.67	33.58	34.49	35.38
40	10.03	11.04	12.04	13.05	14.05	15.05	16.06	17.06	18.05	19.05	20.05	21.04	22.03	23.01	23.99	24.97	25.94	26.90	27.86	28.81	29.75	30.69	31.61	32.52	33.43	34.31
41	9.02	10.03	11.03	12.03	13.04	14.04	15.04	16.04	17.03	18.03	19.02	20.01	21.00	21.98	22.96	23.93	24.90	25.86	26.82	27.77	28.71	29.64	30.56	31.47	32.37	33.26
42	8.02	9.02	10.02	11.02	12.02	13.02	14.02	15.02	16.02	17.01	18.00	18.99	19.97	20.96	21.93	22.90	23.87	24.83	25.78	26.73	27.67	28.60	29.52	30.42	31.32	32.20
43	7.01	8.01	9.01	10.01	11.01	12.01	13.01	14.01	15.00	15.99	16.98	17.97	18.95	19.93	20.91	21.88	22.84	23.80	24.75	25.70	26.63	27.56	28.48	29.38	30.28	31.16
44	6.01	7.01	8.01	9.01	10.01	11.00	12.00	13.00	13.99	14.98	15.97	16.96	17.94	18.92	19.89	20.86	21.82	22.78	23.73	24.67	25.60	26.53	27.44	28.35	29.24	30.11
45	5.00	6.00	7.00	8.00	9.00	10.00	10.99	11.99	12.98	13.97	14.96	15.94	16.93	17.90	18.87	19.84	20.80	21.76	22.71	23.65	24.58	25.50	26.41	27.31	28.20	29.08
46	4.00	5.00	6.00	7.00	8.00	8.99	9.99	10.98	11.97	12.96	13.95	14.94	15.92	16.89	17.86	18.83	19.79	20.74	21.69	22.63	23.56	24.48	25.39	26.29	27.17	28.05

Table 34: 8th edition Ogden multipliers, loss of EARNINGS, MEN, discount rate: −0.25%, NO 2 YEAR ADJUSTMENT

Loss of earnings to pension age

Age	50	51	52	53	54	55	56	57	58	59	60	61	62	63	64	65	66	67	68	69	70	71	72	73	74	75
47	3.00	4.00	5.00	6.00	6.99	7.99	8.99	9.98	10.97	11.96	12.95	13.93	14.91	15.88	16.85	17.82	18.78	19.73	20.67	21.61	22.54	23.46	24.37	25.26	26.15	27.02
48	2.00	3.00	4.00	5.00	5.99	6.99	7.98	8.98	9.97	10.96	11.94	12.93	13.90	14.88	15.85	16.81	17.77	18.72	19.66	20.60	21.53	22.44	23.35	24.25	25.13	26.00
49	1.00	2.00	3.00	4.00	4.99	5.99	6.98	7.98	8.97	9.96	10.94	11.92	12.90	13.88	14.84	15.81	16.76	17.71	18.66	19.59	20.52	21.43	22.34	23.23	24.11	24.98
50		1.00	2.00	3.00	3.99	4.99	5.99	6.98	7.97	8.96	9.94	10.92	11.90	12.88	13.84	14.81	15.76	16.71	17.65	18.59	19.51	20.43	21.33	22.22	23.10	23.96
51			1.00	2.00	3.00	3.99	4.99	5.98	6.97	7.96	8.95	9.93	10.91	11.88	12.85	13.81	14.76	15.71	16.65	17.59	18.51	19.42	20.33	21.22	22.09	22.95
52				1.00	2.00	3.00	3.99	4.98	5.98	6.96	7.95	8.93	9.91	10.88	11.85	12.81	13.77	14.72	15.66	16.59	17.51	18.42	19.33	20.21	21.09	21.95
53					1.00	2.00	2.99	3.99	4.98	5.97	6.96	7.94	8.92	9.89	10.86	11.82	12.77	13.72	14.66	15.60	16.52	17.43	18.33	19.22	20.09	20.95
54						1.00	2.00	2.99	3.99	4.98	5.96	6.95	7.92	8.90	9.87	10.83	11.78	12.73	13.67	14.60	15.53	16.44	17.34	18.22	19.10	19.96
55							1.00	2.00	2.99	3.98	4.97	5.95	6.93	7.91	8.88	9.84	10.80	11.75	12.69	13.62	14.54	15.45	16.35	17.24	18.11	18.97
56								1.00	2.00	2.99	3.98	4.96	5.95	6.92	7.89	8.86	9.81	10.76	11.70	12.64	13.56	14.47	15.37	16.26	17.13	17.98
57									1.00	1.99	2.99	3.97	4.96	5.93	6.91	7.87	8.83	9.78	10.73	11.66	12.58	13.49	14.39	15.28	16.15	17.01
58										1.00	1.99	2.98	3.97	4.95	5.92	6.89	7.85	8.81	9.75	10.68	11.61	12.52	13.42	14.31	15.18	16.04
59											1.00	1.99	2.98	3.96	4.94	5.91	6.88	7.83	8.78	9.71	10.64	11.56	12.46	13.35	14.22	15.08
60												1.00	1.99	2.98	3.96	4.93	5.90	6.86	7.81	8.75	9.68	10.59	11.50	12.39	13.26	14.12
61													1.00	1.99	2.97	3.95	4.92	5.89	6.84	7.78	8.71	9.63	10.54	11.44	12.31	13.17
62														1.00	1.99	2.97	3.95	4.91	5.87	6.82	7.75	8.68	9.59	10.49	11.37	12.23
63															1.00	1.99	2.97	3.94	4.90	5.86	6.80	7.73	8.64	9.54	10.43	11.29
64																1.00	1.98	2.96	3.93	4.89	5.84	6.77	7.69	8.60	9.49	10.36
65																	1.00	1.98	2.96	3.92	4.88	5.82	6.75	7.66	8.55	9.43
66																		1.00	1.98	2.95	3.92	4.86	5.80	6.72	7.62	8.50
67																			0.99	1.98	2.95	3.91	4.85	5.77	6.68	7.57
68																				0.99	1.98	2.94	3.89	4.83	5.75	6.65
69																					0.99	1.97	2.94	3.88	4.81	5.72
70																						0.99	1.97	2.93	3.87	4.79
71																							0.99	1.97	2.92	3.85
72																								0.99	1.96	2.91
73																									0.99	1.96
74																										0.99

Table 35: 8th edition Ogden multipliers, loss of EARNINGS, WOMEN, discount rate: −0.25%, NO 2 YEAR ADJUSTMENT

Loss of earnings to pension age

Age	50	51	52	53	54	55	56	57	58	59	60	61	62	63	64	65	66	67	68	69	70	71	72	73	74	75
16	35.31	36.38	37.45	38.53	39.60	40.68	41.76	42.83	43.91	44.99	46.07	47.15	48.22	49.30	50.38	51.45	52.52	53.60	54.66	55.73	56.79	57.85	58.91	59.96	61.00	62.04
17	34.22	35.29	36.36	37.43	38.51	39.58	40.65	41.73	42.80	43.88	44.95	46.03	47.10	48.18	49.25	50.32	51.39	52.46	53.53	54.59	55.65	56.70	57.75	58.80	59.84	60.87
18	33.14	34.21	35.27	36.34	37.41	38.48	39.55	40.63	41.70	42.77	43.84	44.92	45.99	47.06	48.13	49.20	50.26	51.33	52.39	53.45	54.50	55.56	56.60	57.65	58.68	59.71
19	32.06	33.12	34.19	35.26	36.32	37.39	38.46	39.53	40.60	41.67	42.74	43.81	44.87	45.94	47.01	48.07	49.14	50.20	51.26	52.31	53.37	54.41	55.46	56.50	57.53	58.56
20	30.99	32.05	33.11	34.17	35.24	36.30	37.37	38.43	39.50	40.57	41.63	42.70	43.76	44.83	45.89	46.95	48.01	49.07	50.13	51.18	52.23	53.27	54.32	55.35	56.38	57.40
21	29.91	30.97	32.03	33.09	34.15	35.21	36.28	37.34	38.40	39.47	40.53	41.59	42.66	43.72	44.78	45.84	46.89	47.95	49.00	50.05	51.10	52.14	53.18	54.21	55.23	56.25
22	28.84	29.90	30.95	32.01	33.07	34.13	35.19	36.25	37.31	38.37	39.43	40.49	41.55	42.61	43.67	44.72	45.78	46.83	47.88	48.92	49.97	51.01	52.04	53.07	54.09	55.10
23	27.77	28.83	29.88	30.94	31.99	33.05	34.11	35.16	36.22	37.28	38.34	39.40	40.45	41.51	42.56	43.61	44.66	45.71	46.76	47.80	48.84	49.88	50.91	51.93	52.95	53.96
24	26.71	27.76	28.81	29.86	30.92	31.97	33.03	34.08	35.14	36.19	37.25	38.30	39.35	40.41	41.46	42.51	43.55	44.60	45.64	46.68	47.72	48.75	49.77	50.80	51.81	52.82
25	25.65	26.70	27.74	28.79	29.84	30.90	31.95	33.00	34.05	35.10	36.16	37.21	38.26	39.31	40.36	41.40	42.45	43.49	44.53	45.56	46.60	47.62	48.65	49.66	50.67	51.68
26	24.59	25.63	26.68	27.73	28.77	29.82	30.87	31.92	32.97	34.02	35.07	36.12	37.17	38.21	39.26	40.30	41.34	42.38	43.42	44.45	45.48	46.50	47.52	48.54	49.54	50.54
27	23.53	24.57	25.62	26.66	27.71	28.75	29.80	30.85	31.89	32.94	33.99	35.03	36.08	37.12	38.16	39.20	40.24	41.28	42.31	43.34	44.36	45.39	46.40	47.41	48.42	49.41
28	22.48	23.52	24.56	25.60	26.64	27.69	28.73	29.78	30.82	31.86	32.91	33.95	34.99	36.03	37.07	38.11	39.14	40.18	41.21	42.23	43.25	44.27	45.29	46.29	47.29	48.28
29	21.43	22.47	23.50	24.54	25.58	26.63	27.67	28.71	29.75	30.79	31.83	32.87	33.91	34.95	35.98	37.02	38.05	39.08	40.11	41.13	42.15	43.16	44.17	45.18	46.17	47.16
30	20.38	21.42	22.45	23.49	24.53	25.57	26.60	27.64	28.68	29.72	30.76	31.80	32.83	33.87	34.90	35.93	36.96	37.99	39.01	40.03	41.05	42.06	43.06	44.06	45.06	46.04
31	19.34	20.37	21.40	22.44	23.47	24.51	25.55	26.58	27.62	28.65	29.69	30.72	31.76	32.79	33.82	34.85	35.87	36.90	37.92	38.94	39.95	40.96	41.96	42.95	43.94	44.92
32	18.30	19.33	20.36	21.39	22.42	23.46	24.49	25.52	26.56	27.59	28.62	29.66	30.69	31.72	32.74	33.77	34.79	35.81	36.83	37.84	38.85	39.86	40.86	41.85	42.84	43.81
33	17.26	18.29	19.32	20.35	21.38	22.41	23.44	24.47	25.50	26.53	27.56	28.59	29.62	30.65	31.67	32.69	33.71	34.73	35.75	36.76	37.76	38.76	39.76	40.75	41.73	42.71
34	16.22	17.25	18.28	19.30	20.33	21.36	22.39	23.42	24.45	25.47	26.50	27.53	28.55	29.58	30.60	31.62	32.64	33.65	34.67	35.67	36.68	37.67	38.67	39.65	40.63	41.60
35	15.19	16.22	17.24	18.26	19.29	20.32	21.34	22.37	23.40	24.42	25.45	26.47	27.49	28.52	29.54	30.55	31.57	32.58	33.59	34.59	35.59	36.59	37.58	38.56	39.54	40.50
36	14.16	15.18	16.21	17.23	18.25	19.28	20.30	21.32	22.35	23.37	24.39	25.42	26.44	27.46	28.47	29.49	30.50	31.51	32.52	33.52	34.51	35.51	36.49	37.47	38.45	39.41
37	13.14	14.15	15.18	16.20	17.22	18.24	19.26	20.28	21.30	22.33	23.35	24.37	25.38	26.40	27.41	28.43	29.44	30.44	31.45	32.44	33.44	34.43	35.41	36.39	37.36	38.32
38	12.11	13.13	14.15	15.17	16.19	17.20	18.22	19.24	20.26	21.28	22.30	23.32	24.33	25.35	26.36	27.37	28.38	29.38	30.38	31.38	32.37	33.35	34.34	35.31	36.27	37.23
39	11.09	12.11	13.12	14.14	15.16	16.17	17.19	18.21	19.23	20.24	21.26	22.27	23.29	24.30	25.31	26.32	27.32	28.32	29.32	30.31	31.30	32.29	33.26	34.23	35.20	36.15
40	10.07	11.09	12.10	13.12	14.13	15.15	16.16	17.18	18.19	19.21	20.22	21.23	22.24	23.25	24.26	25.27	26.27	27.27	28.26	29.25	30.24	31.22	32.19	33.16	34.12	35.07
41	9.06	10.07	11.08	12.09	13.11	14.12	15.13	16.15	17.16	18.17	19.19	20.20	21.20	22.21	23.22	24.22	25.22	26.22	27.21	28.20	29.18	30.16	31.13	32.09	33.05	34.00
42	8.04	9.05	10.06	11.07	12.09	13.10	14.11	15.12	16.13	17.14	18.15	19.16	20.17	21.17	22.18	23.18	24.17	25.17	26.16	27.14	28.13	29.10	30.07	31.03	31.99	32.93
43	7.03	8.04	9.05	10.06	11.07	12.08	13.09	14.10	15.11	16.12	17.12	18.13	19.14	20.14	21.14	22.14	23.13	24.12	25.11	26.10	27.07	28.05	29.01	29.97	30.92	31.87
44	6.02	7.03	8.04	9.04	10.05	11.06	12.07	13.08	14.09	15.09	16.10	17.10	18.11	19.11	20.11	21.10	22.10	23.08	24.07	25.05	26.03	27.00	27.96	28.92	29.87	30.80
45	5.01	6.02	7.03	8.03	9.04	10.05	11.05	12.06	13.07	14.07	15.08	16.08	17.08	18.08	19.08	20.07	21.06	22.05	23.03	24.01	24.98	25.95	26.91	27.87	28.81	29.75
46	4.01	5.01	6.02	7.02	8.03	9.03	10.04	11.04	12.05	13.05	14.05	15.06	16.06	17.05	18.05	19.04	20.03	21.02	22.00	22.97	23.95	24.91	25.87	26.82	27.76	28.70

Table 35: 8th edition Ogden multipliers, loss of EARNINGS, WOMEN, discount rate: −0.25%, NO 2 YEAR ADJUSTMENT

Loss of earnings to pension age

Age	50	51	52	53	54	55	56	57	58	59	60	61	62	63	64	65	66	67	68	69	70	71	72	73	74	75
47	3.00	4.01	5.01	6.01	7.02	8.02	9.03	10.03	11.03	12.04	13.04	14.04	15.04	16.03	17.02	18.02	19.00	19.99	20.97	21.94	22.91	23.87	24.83	25.78	26.72	27.65
48	2.00	3.00	4.01	5.01	6.01	7.01	8.02	9.02	10.02	11.02	12.02	13.02	14.02	15.01	16.00	16.99	17.98	18.96	19.94	20.91	21.88	22.84	23.79	24.74	25.68	26.61
49	1.00	2.00	3.00	4.00	5.01	6.01	7.01	8.01	9.01	10.01	11.01	12.01	13.00	14.00	14.99	15.97	16.96	17.94	18.92	19.89	20.85	21.81	22.76	23.71	24.64	25.57
50		1.00	2.00	3.00	4.00	5.00	6.01	7.01	8.01	9.00	10.00	11.00	11.99	12.98	13.97	14.96	15.94	16.92	17.90	18.87	19.83	20.79	21.74	22.68	23.61	24.54
51			1.00	2.00	3.00	4.00	5.00	6.00	7.00	8.00	9.00	9.99	10.98	11.97	12.96	13.95	14.93	15.91	16.88	17.85	18.81	19.77	20.72	21.66	22.59	23.51
52				1.00	2.00	3.00	4.00	5.00	6.00	7.00	7.99	8.99	9.98	10.97	11.96	12.94	13.92	14.90	15.87	16.84	17.80	18.75	19.70	20.64	21.57	22.49
53					1.00	2.00	3.00	4.00	5.00	5.99	6.99	7.98	8.97	9.96	10.95	11.93	12.91	13.89	14.86	15.83	16.79	17.74	18.69	19.62	20.55	21.47
54						1.00	2.00	3.00	4.00	4.99	5.99	6.98	7.97	8.96	9.95	10.93	11.91	12.89	13.86	14.82	15.78	16.73	17.68	18.61	19.54	20.46
55							1.00	2.00	3.00	3.99	4.99	5.98	6.97	7.96	8.95	9.93	10.91	11.89	12.86	13.82	14.78	15.73	16.67	17.61	18.53	19.45
56								1.00	2.00	3.00	3.99	4.99	5.98	6.97	7.95	8.94	9.91	10.89	11.86	12.82	13.78	14.73	15.67	16.61	17.53	18.45
57									1.00	2.00	2.99	3.99	4.98	5.97	6.96	7.94	8.92	9.89	10.86	11.83	12.79	13.74	14.68	15.61	16.54	17.45
58										1.00	2.00	2.99	3.99	4.98	5.96	6.95	7.93	8.90	9.87	10.84	11.80	12.75	13.69	14.62	15.55	16.46
59											1.00	2.00	2.99	3.98	4.97	5.96	6.94	7.91	8.88	9.85	10.81	11.76	12.70	13.64	14.56	15.47
60												1.00	2.00	2.99	3.98	4.97	5.95	6.93	7.90	8.86	9.82	10.78	11.72	12.66	13.58	14.49
61													1.00	1.99	2.99	3.98	4.96	5.94	6.91	7.88	8.84	9.80	10.74	11.68	12.60	13.52
62														1.00	1.99	2.98	3.97	4.95	5.93	6.90	7.86	8.82	9.77	10.70	11.63	12.55
63															1.00	1.99	2.98	3.97	4.95	5.92	6.88	7.84	8.79	9.73	10.66	11.58
64																1.00	1.99	2.98	3.96	4.94	5.91	6.87	7.82	8.76	9.69	10.61
65																	1.00	1.99	2.98	3.96	4.93	5.89	6.85	7.80	8.73	9.65
66																		1.00	1.99	2.97	3.95	4.92	5.88	6.83	7.77	8.69
67																			1.00	1.99	2.97	3.94	4.91	5.86	6.80	7.73
68																				1.00	1.99	2.97	3.94	4.90	5.84	6.78
69																					1.00	1.98	2.96	3.93	4.88	5.82
70																						1.00	1.98	2.95	3.92	4.86
71																							0.99	1.98	2.95	3.91
72																								0.99	1.97	2.94
73																									0.99	1.97
74																										0.99

Tables

Table 36: 8th edition Ogden multipliers, loss of EARNINGS, MEN, discount rate: −0.75%, NO 2 YEAR ADJUSTMENT

Loss of earnings to pension age

Age	50	51	52	53	54	55	56	57	58	59	60	61	62	63	64	65	66	67	68	69	70	71	72	73	74	75
16	38.40	39.66	40.92	42.20	43.48	44.76	46.06	47.36	48.66	49.97	51.29	52.61	53.93	55.26	56.59	57.93	59.27	60.60	61.94	63.28	64.62	65.95	67.29	68.62	69.94	71.26
17	37.11	38.36	39.62	40.88	42.15	43.43	44.71	46.00	47.30	48.60	49.90	51.21	52.53	53.85	55.17	56.49	57.81	59.14	60.47	61.80	63.12	64.45	65.77	67.08	68.40	69.70
18	35.84	37.08	38.33	39.58	40.84	42.11	43.38	44.66	45.95	47.24	48.53	49.83	51.13	52.44	53.75	55.06	56.38	57.69	59.01	60.32	61.64	62.95	64.26	65.57	66.87	68.16
19	34.58	35.81	37.05	38.29	39.54	40.80	42.06	43.33	44.61	45.89	47.17	48.46	49.75	51.05	52.35	53.65	54.95	56.26	57.56	58.87	60.17	61.47	62.77	64.06	65.35	66.63
20	33.33	34.55	35.78	37.01	38.25	39.50	40.76	42.01	43.28	44.55	45.82	47.10	48.39	49.67	50.96	52.25	53.54	54.84	56.13	57.42	58.72	60.01	61.29	62.57	63.85	65.12
21	32.09	33.30	34.52	35.75	36.98	38.22	39.46	40.71	41.96	43.22	44.49	45.76	47.03	48.30	49.58	50.86	52.14	53.43	54.71	55.99	57.27	58.55	59.83	61.10	62.36	63.62
22	30.86	32.06	33.27	34.49	35.71	36.94	38.17	39.41	40.66	41.91	43.16	44.42	45.68	46.95	48.22	49.49	50.76	52.03	53.30	54.57	55.84	57.11	58.38	59.63	60.89	62.13
23	29.64	30.83	32.03	33.24	34.45	35.67	36.90	38.13	39.36	40.60	41.85	43.10	44.35	45.61	46.86	48.12	49.38	50.64	51.91	53.17	54.43	55.68	56.93	58.18	59.42	60.66
24	28.43	29.61	30.80	32.00	33.21	34.42	35.63	36.85	38.08	39.31	40.54	41.78	43.03	44.27	45.52	46.77	48.02	49.27	50.52	51.77	53.02	54.26	55.51	56.74	57.97	59.19
25	27.22	28.40	29.58	30.77	31.97	33.17	34.38	35.59	36.80	38.02	39.25	40.48	41.71	42.95	44.18	45.42	46.66	47.91	49.15	50.39	51.62	52.86	54.09	55.31	56.53	57.74
26	26.03	27.20	28.37	29.55	30.74	31.93	33.13	34.33	35.54	36.75	37.97	39.19	40.41	41.63	42.86	44.09	45.32	46.55	47.78	49.01	50.24	51.46	52.68	53.90	55.10	56.30
27	24.85	26.01	27.17	28.34	29.52	30.70	31.89	33.09	34.28	35.49	36.69	37.90	39.12	40.33	41.55	42.77	43.99	45.21	46.43	47.65	48.86	50.08	51.29	52.49	53.69	54.87
28	23.67	24.82	25.98	27.14	28.31	29.49	30.67	31.85	33.04	34.23	35.43	36.63	37.83	39.04	40.25	41.46	42.67	43.88	45.09	46.30	47.50	48.70	49.90	51.10	52.28	53.46
29	22.51	23.65	24.80	25.95	27.11	28.28	29.45	30.62	31.80	32.99	34.18	35.37	36.56	37.76	38.96	40.16	41.36	42.56	43.76	44.96	46.15	47.34	48.53	49.71	50.89	52.06
30	21.35	22.49	23.63	24.77	25.92	27.08	28.24	29.41	30.58	31.76	32.93	34.12	35.30	36.49	37.68	38.87	40.06	41.25	42.44	43.63	44.81	46.00	47.17	48.35	49.51	50.67
31	20.21	21.33	22.46	23.60	24.74	25.89	27.05	28.20	29.37	30.53	31.70	32.88	34.05	35.23	36.41	37.59	38.77	39.95	41.13	42.31	43.49	44.66	45.83	46.99	48.14	49.29
32	19.07	20.19	21.31	22.44	23.58	24.72	25.86	27.01	28.16	29.32	30.48	31.65	32.81	33.98	35.15	36.33	37.50	38.67	39.84	41.01	42.17	43.34	44.49	45.65	46.79	47.92
33	17.94	19.05	20.17	21.29	22.42	23.55	24.68	25.82	26.97	28.12	29.27	30.43	31.59	32.75	33.91	35.07	36.23	37.40	38.56	39.72	40.87	42.02	43.17	44.31	45.45	46.57
34	16.82	17.93	19.03	20.15	21.26	22.39	23.52	24.65	25.79	26.93	28.07	29.22	30.37	31.52	32.67	33.83	34.98	36.13	37.29	38.44	39.58	40.72	41.86	42.99	44.12	45.23
35	15.71	16.81	17.91	19.01	20.12	21.24	22.36	23.48	24.61	25.75	26.88	28.02	29.16	30.30	31.45	32.59	33.74	34.88	36.03	37.17	38.30	39.44	40.56	41.69	42.80	43.90
36	14.61	15.70	16.79	17.89	18.99	20.10	21.21	22.33	23.45	24.57	25.70	26.83	27.97	29.10	30.24	31.37	32.51	33.64	34.78	35.91	37.04	38.16	39.28	40.39	41.50	42.59
37	13.52	14.60	15.68	16.77	17.87	18.97	20.07	21.18	22.30	23.41	24.53	25.66	26.78	27.91	29.03	30.16	31.29	32.42	33.54	34.66	35.78	36.90	38.01	39.11	40.20	41.29
38	12.43	13.51	14.59	15.67	16.76	17.85	18.95	20.05	21.15	22.26	23.37	24.49	25.61	26.72	27.84	28.96	30.08	31.20	32.32	33.43	34.54	35.65	36.75	37.84	38.92	40.00
39	11.36	12.42	13.50	14.57	15.65	16.74	17.83	18.92	20.02	21.12	22.23	23.33	24.44	25.55	26.66	27.77	28.88	29.99	31.10	32.21	33.31	34.41	35.50	36.58	37.66	38.72
40	10.29	11.35	12.41	13.48	14.56	15.64	16.72	17.81	18.90	19.99	21.09	22.19	23.29	24.39	25.49	26.60	27.70	28.80	29.90	31.00	32.09	33.18	34.26	35.34	36.41	37.46
41	9.23	10.28	11.34	12.40	13.47	14.54	15.62	16.70	17.78	18.87	19.96	21.05	22.14	23.24	24.33	25.43	26.52	27.62	28.71	29.80	30.88	31.96	33.04	34.11	35.16	36.21
42	8.18	9.23	10.28	11.33	12.39	13.46	14.53	15.60	16.68	17.76	18.84	19.92	21.01	22.10	23.19	24.27	25.36	26.45	27.53	28.61	29.69	30.76	31.83	32.89	33.94	34.98
43	7.13	8.17	9.22	10.27	11.32	12.38	13.44	14.51	15.58	16.65	17.73	18.81	19.89	20.97	22.05	23.13	24.21	25.29	26.36	27.44	28.51	29.57	30.63	31.68	32.72	33.75
44	6.10	7.13	8.17	9.21	10.26	11.31	12.37	13.43	14.49	15.56	16.63	17.70	18.77	19.85	20.92	21.99	23.07	24.14	25.21	26.27	27.33	28.39	29.44	30.48	31.52	32.54
45	5.07	6.09	7.13	8.16	9.21	10.25	11.30	12.36	13.41	14.47	15.54	16.60	17.67	18.73	19.80	20.87	21.93	23.00	24.06	25.12	26.17	27.22	28.26	29.30	30.32	31.34
46	4.04	5.06	6.09	7.12	8.16	9.20	10.24	11.29	12.34	13.40	14.45	15.51	16.57	17.63	18.69	19.75	20.81	21.87	22.92	23.97	25.02	26.06	27.10	28.12	29.14	30.15

Tables

Table 36: 8th edition Ogden multipliers, loss of EARNINGS, MEN, discount rate: −0.75%, NO 2 YEAR ADJUSTMENT

Loss of earnings to pension age

Age	50	51	52	53	54	55	56	57	58	59	60	61	62	63	64	65	66	67	68	69	70	71	72	73	74	75
47	3.02	4.04	5.06	6.09	7.12	8.15	9.19	10.23	11.28	12.33	13.38	14.43	15.48	16.54	17.59	18.64	19.70	20.75	21.79	22.84	23.88	24.91	25.94	26.96	27.97	28.97
48	2.01	3.02	4.04	5.06	6.08	7.11	8.15	9.18	10.22	11.27	12.31	13.36	14.40	15.45	16.50	17.55	18.59	19.64	20.68	21.71	22.75	23.77	24.79	25.81	26.81	27.80
49	1.00	2.01	3.02	4.04	5.06	6.08	7.11	8.14	9.17	10.21	11.25	12.29	13.33	14.37	15.42	16.46	17.50	18.53	19.57	20.60	21.63	22.65	23.66	24.66	25.66	26.64
50		1.00	2.01	3.02	4.04	5.05	6.08	7.10	8.13	9.16	10.20	11.23	12.27	13.30	14.34	15.37	16.41	17.44	18.47	19.49	20.51	21.53	22.53	23.53	24.52	25.50
51			1.00	2.01	3.02	4.03	5.05	6.07	7.10	8.12	9.15	10.18	11.21	12.24	13.27	14.30	15.33	16.36	17.38	18.40	19.41	20.42	21.42	22.41	23.39	24.36
52				1.00	2.01	3.02	4.03	5.05	6.07	7.09	8.11	9.14	10.16	11.19	12.21	13.24	14.26	15.28	16.30	17.31	18.32	19.32	20.31	21.30	22.27	23.24
53					1.00	2.01	3.02	4.03	5.04	6.06	7.08	8.10	9.12	10.14	11.16	12.18	13.20	14.21	15.22	16.23	17.23	18.23	19.22	20.20	21.16	22.12
54						1.00	2.01	3.01	4.03	5.04	6.05	7.07	8.09	9.10	10.12	11.13	12.14	13.15	14.16	15.16	16.16	17.15	18.13	19.10	20.07	21.02
55							1.00	2.01	3.01	4.02	5.03	6.04	7.06	8.07	9.08	10.09	11.10	12.10	13.11	14.10	15.09	16.08	17.06	18.02	18.98	19.93
56								1.00	2.01	3.01	4.02	5.03	6.04	7.04	8.05	9.06	10.06	11.06	12.06	13.05	14.04	15.02	15.99	16.96	17.91	18.85
57									1.00	2.00	3.01	4.01	5.02	6.02	7.03	8.03	9.03	10.03	11.02	12.01	13.00	13.97	14.94	15.90	16.85	17.78
58										1.00	2.00	3.01	4.01	5.01	6.01	7.01	8.01	9.01	10.00	10.98	11.96	12.93	13.90	14.85	15.80	16.73
59											1.00	2.00	3.00	4.00	5.00	6.00	7.00	7.99	8.98	9.96	10.94	11.91	12.87	13.82	14.76	15.68
60												1.00	2.00	3.00	4.00	4.99	5.99	6.98	7.96	8.95	9.92	10.89	11.85	12.79	13.73	14.65
61													1.00	2.00	3.00	3.99	4.99	5.97	6.96	7.94	8.91	9.88	10.83	11.78	12.72	13.64
62														1.00	2.00	2.99	3.99	4.98	5.96	6.94	7.91	8.88	9.83	10.78	11.71	12.63
63															1.00	2.00	2.99	3.98	4.96	5.94	6.92	7.88	8.84	9.78	10.71	11.63
64																1.00	1.99	2.99	3.97	4.95	5.93	6.89	7.85	8.79	9.72	10.64
65																	1.00	1.99	2.98	3.96	4.94	5.91	6.86	7.81	8.74	9.66
66																		1.00	1.99	2.98	3.95	4.92	5.88	6.83	7.77	8.69
67																			1.00	1.99	2.97	3.94	4.91	5.86	6.80	7.72
68																				1.00	1.99	2.96	3.93	4.89	5.83	6.76
69																					1.00	1.98	2.96	3.92	4.87	5.81
70																						0.99	1.98	2.95	3.91	4.85
71																							0.99	1.98	2.94	3.89
72																								0.99	1.97	2.93
73																									0.99	1.97
74																										0.99

Table 37: 8th edition Ogden multipliers, loss of EARNINGS, WOMEN, discount rate: –0.75%, NO 2 YEAR ADJUSTMENT

Loss of earnings to pension age

Age	50	51	52	53	54	55	56	57	58	59	60	61	62	63	64	65	66	67	68	69	70	71	72	73	74	75
16	38.54	39.82	41.10	42.39	43.69	44.99	46.31	47.63	48.96	50.29	51.63	52.98	54.34	55.70	57.06	58.43	59.81	61.19	62.58	63.96	65.35	66.75	68.14	69.54	70.93	72.32
17	37.26	38.52	39.80	41.08	42.37	43.66	44.97	46.28	47.59	48.92	50.25	51.59	52.93	54.28	55.64	57.00	58.36	59.73	61.10	62.48	63.86	65.24	66.62	68.01	69.39	70.77
18	35.98	37.24	38.50	39.77	41.05	42.34	43.63	44.93	46.24	47.56	48.88	50.20	51.54	52.88	54.22	55.57	56.92	58.28	59.65	61.01	62.38	63.75	65.12	66.49	67.86	69.23
19	34.72	35.97	37.22	38.48	39.75	41.03	42.31	43.60	44.90	46.20	47.52	48.83	50.16	51.48	52.82	54.16	55.50	56.85	58.20	59.55	60.91	62.27	63.63	64.99	66.34	67.70
20	33.47	34.70	35.95	37.20	38.48	39.73	41.00	42.28	43.57	44.86	46.16	47.47	48.78	50.10	51.42	52.75	54.09	55.42	56.76	58.10	59.45	60.80	62.15	63.49	64.84	66.18
21	32.22	33.45	34.69	35.93	37.20	38.44	39.70	40.97	42.25	43.53	44.82	46.12	47.42	48.73	50.04	51.36	52.68	54.01	55.34	56.67	58.00	59.34	60.68	62.01	63.35	64.68
22	30.99	32.21	33.43	34.67	35.91	37.15	38.41	39.67	40.94	42.21	43.49	44.78	46.07	47.37	48.67	49.98	51.29	52.60	53.92	55.24	56.57	57.89	59.22	60.54	61.87	63.19
23	29.76	30.97	32.19	33.41	34.64	35.88	37.13	38.38	39.64	40.90	42.17	43.45	44.73	46.02	47.31	48.61	49.91	51.21	52.52	53.83	55.14	56.46	57.77	59.08	60.40	61.71
24	28.55	29.75	30.96	32.17	33.39	34.62	35.86	37.10	38.35	39.60	40.86	42.13	43.40	44.68	45.96	47.25	48.54	49.83	51.13	52.43	53.73	55.03	56.34	57.64	58.94	60.24
25	27.34	28.53	29.73	30.94	32.15	33.37	34.59	35.83	37.07	38.31	39.56	40.82	42.08	43.35	44.62	45.90	47.18	48.46	49.75	51.04	52.33	53.62	54.91	56.20	57.49	58.78
26	26.14	27.33	28.52	29.71	30.91	32.13	33.34	34.57	35.79	37.03	38.27	39.52	40.77	42.03	43.29	44.56	45.83	47.10	48.38	49.65	50.93	52.22	53.50	54.78	56.06	57.33
27	24.96	26.13	27.31	28.50	29.69	30.89	32.10	33.31	34.53	35.76	36.99	38.23	39.47	40.72	41.97	43.23	44.49	45.75	47.02	48.28	49.55	50.82	52.09	53.36	54.63	55.90
28	23.78	24.94	26.11	27.29	28.48	29.67	30.87	32.07	33.28	34.50	35.72	36.95	38.18	39.42	40.66	41.91	43.16	44.41	45.67	46.93	48.18	49.44	50.70	51.96	53.22	54.47
29	22.61	23.76	24.93	26.10	27.27	28.46	29.64	30.84	32.04	33.25	34.46	35.68	36.90	38.13	39.37	40.60	41.84	43.08	44.33	45.58	46.83	48.08	49.33	50.57	51.82	53.06
30	21.45	22.59	23.75	24.91	26.08	27.25	28.43	29.62	30.81	32.01	33.21	34.42	35.64	36.86	38.08	39.31	40.54	41.77	43.00	44.24	45.48	46.72	47.96	49.20	50.43	51.66
31	20.30	21.44	22.58	23.73	24.89	26.06	27.23	28.41	29.59	30.78	31.98	33.18	34.38	35.59	36.80	38.02	39.24	40.46	41.69	42.92	44.15	45.38	46.60	47.83	49.06	50.28
32	19.15	20.28	21.42	22.57	23.72	24.87	26.04	27.21	28.38	29.56	30.75	31.94	33.13	34.33	35.54	36.75	37.96	39.17	40.39	41.60	42.82	44.04	45.26	46.48	47.69	48.90
33	18.02	19.14	20.27	21.41	22.55	23.70	24.85	26.01	27.18	28.35	29.53	30.71	31.90	33.09	34.28	35.48	36.68	37.89	39.09	40.30	41.51	42.72	43.93	45.14	46.34	47.54
34	16.90	18.01	19.13	20.26	21.39	22.53	23.68	24.83	25.99	27.15	28.32	29.49	30.67	31.85	33.04	34.23	35.42	36.61	37.81	39.01	40.21	41.41	42.61	43.80	45.00	46.19
35	15.78	16.89	18.00	19.12	20.25	21.38	22.52	23.66	24.81	25.96	27.12	28.29	29.45	30.63	31.80	32.98	34.17	35.35	36.54	37.73	38.92	40.11	41.30	42.48	43.67	44.85
36	14.67	15.77	16.88	17.99	19.11	20.23	21.36	22.50	23.64	24.78	25.93	27.09	28.25	29.41	30.58	31.75	32.93	34.10	35.28	36.46	37.64	38.82	40.00	41.18	42.35	43.52
37	13.58	14.67	15.76	16.87	17.98	19.09	20.21	21.34	22.47	23.61	24.75	25.90	27.05	28.21	29.37	30.53	31.69	32.86	34.03	35.20	36.37	37.54	38.71	39.88	41.04	42.20
38	12.49	13.57	14.66	15.75	16.86	17.96	19.08	20.20	21.32	22.45	23.58	24.72	25.87	27.01	28.16	29.32	30.47	31.63	32.79	33.95	35.12	36.28	37.44	38.59	39.75	40.90
39	11.40	12.48	13.56	14.65	15.74	16.84	17.95	19.06	20.18	21.30	22.42	23.55	24.69	25.83	26.97	28.12	29.26	30.41	31.56	32.72	33.87	35.02	36.17	37.32	38.47	39.61
40	10.33	11.40	12.47	13.55	14.64	15.73	16.83	17.93	19.04	20.16	21.27	22.40	23.52	24.65	25.79	26.92	28.06	29.20	30.35	31.49	32.63	33.78	34.92	36.06	37.19	38.32
41	9.26	10.33	11.39	12.47	13.55	14.63	15.72	16.82	17.92	19.02	20.13	21.25	22.37	23.49	24.61	25.74	26.87	28.01	29.14	30.27	31.41	32.54	33.68	34.81	35.93	37.05
42	8.21	9.26	10.32	11.39	12.46	13.54	14.62	15.71	16.80	17.90	19.00	20.11	21.22	22.33	23.45	24.57	25.69	26.82	27.94	29.07	30.19	31.32	32.44	33.57	34.68	35.79
43	7.16	8.20	9.26	10.32	11.38	12.45	13.53	14.61	15.69	16.78	17.88	18.98	20.08	21.19	22.30	23.41	24.52	25.64	26.76	27.87	28.99	30.11	31.22	32.34	33.44	34.55
44	6.11	7.15	8.20	9.25	10.31	11.37	12.44	13.51	14.59	15.68	16.76	17.86	18.95	20.05	21.15	22.26	23.36	24.47	25.58	26.69	27.80	28.91	30.01	31.12	32.22	33.31
45	5.08	6.11	7.15	8.20	9.25	10.30	11.36	12.43	13.50	14.58	15.66	16.74	17.83	18.92	20.02	21.11	22.21	23.31	24.41	25.51	26.61	27.72	28.81	29.91	31.00	32.08
46	4.05	5.08	6.11	7.15	8.19	9.24	10.30	11.36	12.42	13.49	14.56	15.64	16.72	17.80	18.89	19.98	21.07	22.16	23.26	24.35	25.44	26.53	27.62	28.71	29.79	30.87

Tables

Table 37: 8th edition Ogden multipliers, loss of EARNINGS, WOMEN, discount rate: −0.75%, NO 2 YEAR ADJUSTMENT

Loss of earnings to pension age

Age	50	51	52	53	54	55	56	57	58	59	60	61	62	63	64	65	66	67	68	69	70	71	72	73	74	75
47	3.03	4.05	5.07	6.11	7.14	8.19	9.23	10.29	11.35	12.41	13.47	14.54	15.62	16.69	17.77	18.85	19.94	21.02	22.11	23.19	24.28	25.36	26.45	27.52	28.60	29.67
48	2.01	3.03	4.05	5.07	6.10	7.14	8.18	9.23	10.28	11.33	12.39	13.46	14.52	15.59	16.66	17.74	18.82	19.89	20.97	22.05	23.13	24.20	25.28	26.35	27.41	28.47
49	1.00	2.01	3.03	4.05	5.07	6.10	7.14	8.18	9.22	10.27	11.32	12.38	13.44	14.50	15.57	16.63	17.70	18.77	19.84	20.91	21.99	23.05	24.12	25.18	26.24	27.29
50		1.00	2.01	3.02	4.04	5.07	6.10	7.13	8.17	9.21	10.26	11.31	12.36	13.42	14.48	15.54	16.60	17.66	18.73	19.79	20.85	21.92	22.97	24.03	25.08	26.12
51			1.00	2.01	3.02	4.04	5.07	6.09	7.13	8.16	9.20	10.25	11.29	12.34	13.39	14.45	15.50	16.56	17.62	18.68	19.73	20.79	21.84	22.89	23.93	24.97
52				1.00	2.01	3.02	4.04	5.06	6.09	7.12	8.15	9.19	10.23	11.28	12.32	13.37	14.42	15.47	16.52	17.57	18.62	19.67	20.71	21.75	22.79	23.82
53					1.00	2.01	3.02	4.04	5.06	6.08	7.11	8.15	9.18	10.22	11.26	12.30	13.34	14.39	15.43	16.48	17.52	18.56	19.60	20.63	21.66	22.68
54						1.00	2.01	3.02	4.04	5.06	6.08	7.11	8.14	9.17	10.20	11.24	12.28	13.31	14.35	15.39	16.43	17.46	18.49	19.52	20.54	21.56
55							1.00	2.01	3.02	4.03	5.05	6.07	7.10	8.13	9.15	10.19	11.22	12.25	13.28	14.31	15.35	16.37	17.40	18.42	19.44	20.45
56								1.00	2.01	3.02	4.03	5.05	6.07	7.09	8.11	9.14	10.17	11.19	12.22	13.25	14.27	15.30	16.32	17.33	18.34	19.34
57									1.00	2.01	3.02	4.03	5.04	6.06	7.08	8.10	9.12	10.15	11.17	12.19	13.21	14.23	15.24	16.25	17.26	18.25
58										1.00	2.01	3.02	4.03	5.04	6.05	7.07	8.09	9.11	10.12	11.14	12.16	13.17	14.18	15.18	16.18	17.17
59											1.00	2.01	3.01	4.02	5.03	6.05	7.06	8.07	9.09	10.10	11.11	12.12	13.12	14.12	15.12	16.10
60												1.00	2.01	3.01	4.02	5.03	6.04	7.05	8.06	9.07	10.07	11.08	12.08	13.07	14.06	15.05
61													1.00	2.00	3.01	4.02	5.02	6.03	7.04	8.04	9.04	10.04	11.04	12.03	13.02	14.00
62														1.00	2.00	3.01	4.01	5.02	6.02	7.02	8.02	9.02	10.01	11.00	11.98	12.96
63															1.00	2.00	3.00	4.01	5.01	6.01	7.01	8.00	8.99	9.98	10.96	11.93
64																1.00	2.00	3.00	4.00	5.00	6.00	6.99	7.98	8.96	9.94	10.91
65																	1.00	2.00	3.00	4.00	4.99	5.98	6.97	7.95	8.93	9.89
66																		1.00	2.00	3.00	3.99	4.98	5.97	6.95	7.92	8.89
67																			1.00	2.00	2.99	3.98	4.97	5.95	6.92	7.89
68																				1.00	1.99	2.99	3.98	4.96	5.93	6.90
69																					1.00	1.99	2.98	3.97	4.94	5.91
70																						1.00	1.99	2.98	3.96	4.93
71																							1.00	1.99	2.97	3.94
72																								1.00	1.98	2.96
73																									1.00	1.98
74																										0.99

Table 38 (8th edition Ogden Table 35): Discounting factors for term certain

Factor to discount value of multiplier for a period of deferment.

	Discount Rate				Discount Rate	
Term	−0.75%	−0.25%	Term	−0.75%	−0.25%
1	1.0076	1.0025	41	1.3616	1.1081
2	1.0152	1.0050	42	1.3719	1.1109
3	1.0228	1.0075	43	1.3823	1.1136
4	1.0306	1.0101	44	1.3927	1.1164
5	1.0384	1.0126	45	1.4032	1.1192
6	1.0462	1.0151	46	1.4138	1.1220
7	1.0541	1.0177	47	1.4245	1.1248
8	1.0621	1.0202	48	1.4353	1.1277
9	1.0701	1.0228	49	1.4461	1.1305
10	1.0782	1.0253	50	1.4570	1.1333
11	1.0863	1.0279	51	1.4681	1.1362
12	1.0945	1.0305	52	1.4792	1.1390
13	1.1028	1.0331	53	1.4903	1.1419
14	1.1112	1.0357	54	1.5016	1.1447
15	1.1195	1.0383	55	1.5129	1.1476
16	1.1280	1.0409	56	1.5244	1.1505
17	1.1365	1.0435	57	1.5359	1.1534
18	1.1451	1.0461	58	1.5475	1.1562
19	1.1538	1.0487	59	1.5592	1.1591
20	1.1625	1.0513	60	1.5710	1.1621
21	1.1713	1.0540	61	1.5828	1.1650
22	1.1801	1.0566	62	1.5948	1.1679
23	1.1890	1.0593	63	1.6069	1.1708
24	1.1980	1.0619	64	1.6190	1.1737
25	1.2071	1.0646	65	1.6312	1.1767
26	1.2162	1.0672	66	1.6436	1.1796
27	1.2254	1.0699	67	1.6560	1.1826
28	1.2347	1.0726	68	1.6685	1.1856
29	1.2440	1.0753	69	1.6811	1.1885
30	1.2534	1.0780	70	1.6938	1.1915
31	1.2629	1.0807	71	1.7066	1.1945
32	1.2724	1.0834	72	1.7195	1.1975
33	1.2820	1.0861	73	1.7325	1.2005
34	1.2917	1.0888	74	1.7456	1.2035
35	1.3015	1.0916	75	1.7588	1.2065
36	1.3113	1.0943	76	1.7721	1.2095
37	1.3212	1.0970	77	1.7855	1.2126
38	1.3312	1.0998	78	1.7990	1.2156
39	1.3413	1.1025	79	1.8125	1.2187
40	1.3514	1.1053	80	1.8262	1.2217

Table 39 (8th edition Ogden Table 36): Multipliers for pecuniary loss for term certain

Multiplier for regular frequent payments for a term certain.

	Discount Rate	
Term	**–0.75%**	**–0.25%**
1	1.00	1.00
2	2.02	2.01
3	3.03	3.01
4	4.06	4.02
5	5.10	5.03
6	6.14	6.05
7	7.19	7.06
8	8.25	8.08
9	9.31	9.10
10	10.39	10.13
11	11.47	11.15
12	12.56	12.18
13	13.66	13.21
14	14.76	14.25
15	15.88	15.29
16	17.00	16.32
17	18.14	17.37
18	19.28	18.41
19	20.43	19.46
20	21.58	20.51
21	22.75	21.56
22	23.93	22.62
23	25.11	23.67
24	26.30	24.74
25	27.51	25.80
26	28.72	26.86
27	29.94	27.93
28	31.17	29.00
29	32.41	30.08
30	33.66	31.16
31	34.92	32.23
32	36.18	33.32
33	37.46	34.40
34	38.75	35.49
35	40.04	36.58
36	41.35	37.67
37	42.67	38.77
38	43.99	39.87
39	45.33	40.97
40	46.68	42.07

	Discount Rate	
Term	**–0.75%**	**–0.25%**
41	48.03	43.18
42	49.40	44.29
43	50.78	45.40
44	52.16	46.51
45	53.56	47.63
46	54.97	48.75
47	56.39	49.88
48	57.82	51.00
49	59.26	52.13
50	60.71	53.26
51	62.17	54.40
52	63.65	55.54
53	65.13	56.68
54	66.63	57.82
55	68.14	58.97
56	69.65	60.11
57	71.18	61.27
58	72.73	62.42
59	74.28	63.58
60	75.84	64.74
61	77.42	65.90
62	79.01	67.07
63	80.61	68.24
64	82.22	69.41
65	83.85	70.59
66	85.49	71.76
67	87.14	72.95
68	88.80	74.13
69	90.47	75.32
70	92.16	76.51
71	93.86	77.70
72	95.57	78.90
73	97.30	80.10
74	99.04	81.30
75	100.79	82.50
76	102.56	83.71
77	104.33	84.92
78	106.13	86.14
79	107.93	87.35
80	109.75	88.57

APPENDIX 1: Presidential Guidance - General Case Management

This guidance was re-issued on 22 January 2018 and updated on 23 March 2018.

GUIDANCE NOTE 6

REMEDY

What is remedy?

1) After an Employment Tribunal has decided whether the claimant's claim succeeds it will consider how the successful party should be compensated. This part of the judgment is called "Remedy". Sometimes it is done immediately after the merits or liability judgment, but in long or complex cases it may be adjourned to another day.

2) The Tribunal has different powers for each different type of claim. It must calculate loss and order an appropriate remedy for each part of a successful claim. Accurate and often detailed information from both parties is needed to make correct calculations and to issue a judgment which is fair to all. Sometimes the Tribunal can only estimate the loss: for example, for how long a party may be out of work.

Different types of remedy

3) For some claims the only remedy is to order the employer/respondent to pay a sum of money: for example, wages due, holiday pay and notice pay.

4) For unfair dismissal the Tribunal may:

4.1 Order the employer to "reinstate" the dismissed employee. This is to put them back in their old job, as if they had not been dismissed; or to "re-engage" them, which is to employ them in a suitable but different job. In each case the Tribunal may order payment of lost earnings, etc.

4.2 If those orders are not sought by the claimant or are not practicable, the Tribunal may order the employer to pay compensation. This is calculated in two parts:

- a "Basic Award", which is calculated in a similar way to a statutory redundancy payment; and

- a "Compensatory Award", which is intended to compensate the employee for the financial loss suffered.

5) In claims of unlawful discrimination, the Tribunal may:

5.1 make a declaration setting out the parties' rights; and/or

5.2 order compensation to be paid by the employer and/or fellow workers who have committed discriminatory acts. If the employer can show that it has taken all reasonable steps to prevent employees from committing such acts (called the "statutory defence"), the only award which can be made is against the fellow worker, not the employer; and/or

5.3 make a recommendation, such as for the claimant's colleagues or managers to be given training to ensure that discrimination does not happen again.

Mitigation

6) All persons who have been subjected to wrongdoing are expected to do their best, within reasonable bounds, to limit the effects on them. If the Tribunal concludes that a claimant has not done so, it must reduce the compensation so that a fair sum is payable.

7) The Tribunal will expect evidence to be provided by claimants about their attempts to obtain suitable alternative work and about any earnings from alternative employment.

8) The Tribunal will expect respondents, who consider that the claimant has not tried hard enough, to provide evidence about other jobs which the claimant could have applied for.

Statement of remedy

9) The Tribunal will usually order the claimant to make a calculation showing how each amount claimed has been worked out. For example: x weeks' pay at £y per week. Sometimes this is called a "Schedule of loss" or a "Statement of remedy".

10) Tribunals are expected to calculate remedy for each different type of loss – sometimes called "Heads of loss" or "Heads of damage". Therefore the statement should show how much is claimed under each head.

11) If the claimant has received State benefits, he or she should also specify the type of benefit, the dates of receipt, the amount received and the claimant's national insurance number. (See also "Recoupment" below).

12) Typical heads of loss include;

- wages due

- pay in lieu of notice (where no notice or inadequate notice was given)

- outstanding holiday pay

- a basic award or redundancy payment

- past loss of earnings

- future loss of earnings

- loss of pension entitlements.

13) In discrimination cases, the heads of loss will also typically include:

- injury to feelings

- aggravated or exemplary damages (which are rare)

- damages for personal injury (but only when the act of discrimination is the cause of the claimant becoming ill).

14) The Tribunal will usually order the statement to be produced early in the proceedings, as it can help in settlement negotiations, when considering mediation and when assessing the length of the hearing. It should be updated near to the hearing date.

Submissions on *Polkey* and contributory fault

15) In an unfair dismissal claim, if an employee has been dismissed, but the employer has not followed a proper procedure (such as the ACAS Code), the Tribunal will follow the guidance in the case of *Polkey v AE Dayton Services Limited* and subsequent cases. The Tribunal will consider whether, if a fair procedure had been followed, the claimant might still have been fairly dismissed, either at all, or at some later time. This question is often referred to as the "*Polkey*" question or deduction.

16) There are also cases where the dismissal may be procedurally unfair, but the employee's own conduct has contributed to the position they now find themselves in. This is called "contributory conduct".

17) Where either or both of these are relevant, the Tribunal will reduce the compensation awarded by an appropriate percentage in each case. This means that there may be two reductions, which, where there has been really serious misconduct, could be as high as 100%, so that nothing would be payable.

18) Generally the Tribunal will decide these issues at the same time as it reaches its decision on the merits of the claim. Sometimes this will be done at a separate remedy hearing. The Tribunal will usually explain at the start of the hearing which of those options it will follow. If it does not, then the parties should ask for clarification of when they are expected to give evidence and to make submissions on these matters.

Injury to Feelings

19) In discrimination cases and some other detriment claims, Tribunals may award a sum of money to compensate for injury to feelings. When they do so, they must fix fair, reasonable and just compensation in the particular circumstances of the case. The Tribunal will bear in mind that compensation is designed to compensate the injured party rather than to punish the guilty one. It will also remind itself that awards should bear some relationship to those made by the courts for personal injury.

20) The Tribunal will follow guidelines first given in the case of *Vento v Chief Constable of West Yorkshire Police* and in subsequent cases. These guidelines are referred to as the "*Vento* guidelines" or the "*Vento* bands". The President of Employment Tribunals will issue from time to time separate guidance on the present value of the *Vento* bands or guidelines.

21) The Tribunal will expect claimants to explain in their statement of remedy which *Vento* band they consider their case falls in. They will also expect both parties to make submissions on this during the remedy part of the hearing.

Information needed to calculate remedy

22) This varies in each case dependent on what is being claimed. Each party should look for any relevant information which could help the Tribunal with any necessary calculations in their case. They should provide copies of this information to each other and include those copies in the hearing bundle.

23) The types of information that could be relevant include:

- the contract of employment or statement of terms & conditions with the old employer
- the date the claimant started work with that employer
- details of any pension scheme and pension contributions
- pay slips for the last 13 weeks in the old employment
- any other document showing the claimant's gross pay and net pay
- proof of any payments actually made by the old employer, such as a redundancy payment or payment in lieu of notice
- any document recording the day the claimant last actually worked
- any document explaining how many days and hours per week the claimant worked
- any document explaining how overtime was paid
- any document recording when the holiday year started
- any document recording when holiday has been taken in that year and what has been paid for those days
- any documents setting out the terms of the old employer's pension scheme
- any documents showing the claimant's attempts to find new or other work
- contract of employment and payslips for any new job with a new employer
- documents such as bank statements, if losses for bank charges are claimed
- medical reports or "Fit notes" if unable to work since dismissal
- any documents showing that jobs were or are available in the locality for which the claimant could have applied.

24) The witness statements should tell the Tribunal which parts of these documents are important and why. Providing enough information to the Tribunal at an early stage could help to promote a settlement and so avoid a hearing.

Is all loss awarded?

25) For claims such as unpaid wages, holiday pay and notice pay the Tribunal will order the difference between what should have been paid and what has actually been paid. Wages and holiday pay are usually calculated gross, but pay in lieu of notice is usually calculated net of tax and national insurance. The judgment should specify whether each payment ordered has been calculated gross or net.

26) In the case of unfair dismissal there are several limits (called statutory caps) on what can be awarded.

Grossing up

27) The rules on when tax is payable on awards made by Tribunals are too complex for inclusion here. When it is clear that the claimant will have to pay tax on the sum awarded, the Tribunal will award a higher figure, calculated so that tax can be paid and the claimant will receive the net sum which properly represents the loss. This calculation is called "grossing up".

Interest

28) There are two separate situations where interest is relevant

29) First, when a Tribunal calculates compensation for discrimination, it is obliged to consider awarding interest. If it decides to do so, it calculates interest from the date of the act of discrimination up to the date of the calculation. The exception is for interest on lost wages, where the calculation is made from the middle of that period (as that is simpler than calculating interest separately on each missing wage, but leads to a roughly similar result). The Tribunal will then include that interest in the award made.

30) In addition, interest is payable on awards for all claims if they are not paid when due. A note accompanying the

Tribunal's judgment will explain how interest has been calculated. In respect of all claims presented on or after 29 July 2013 interest is calculated from the day after the day upon which the written judgment was sent to the parties, unless payment is actually made within the first 14 days, in which case no interest is payable.

31) The Employment Tribunal plays no part in enforcing payment of the award it makes. That is done by the civil courts, who issue separate guidance on how to enforce payments.

Recoupment

32) For some claims, such as unfair dismissal, if the claimant has received certain State benefits the Tribunal is obliged to ensure that the employer responsible for causing the loss of earnings reimburses the State for the benefits paid. In those cases the Tribunal will order only part of the award to be paid to the claimant straightaway, with the rest set aside until the respondent is told by the State how much the benefits were. The respondent then pays that money to the State and anything left over to the claimant.

33) This is called "recoupment". The Tribunal should set out in the judgment whether or not recoupment applies, and if it does, how much of the award is set aside for recoupment purposes. If either party is in any doubt about recoupment, they should ask the Tribunal to explain how it affects them.

Costs

34) See the separate guidance on "Costs".

Pensions loss

35) The President of Employment Tribunals has issued separate guidance and principles on the calculation of pensions loss. See:

https://www.judiciary.uk/wp-content/uploads/2015/03/Basic-Guide-to-Compensation-for-Pension-Loss-2021.pdf

https://www.judiciary.uk/wp-content/uploads/2015/03/Principles-Third-Revision-2021.pdf.

APPENDIX 2: Sample schedule of loss

Claimant's schedule of loss – Green v XYZ Ltd

Background

Mrs Green, who was born on 14/02/1988, started work with XYZ Ltd on 24/10/2018. Her gross weekly salary was £2,500 and her net weekly salary, after the deduction of tax and employee national insurance, was £2,000. She was a member of the employer's defined benefit pension scheme, the details of which are added below. On 17/04/2022, she was dismissed summarily for gross misconduct and was given £2,000 as payment in lieu of notice. Her contractual notice period was 8 weeks. Mrs Green found part time work from 23/07/2022 until the date of the tribunal hearing, earning a net amount of £15,523 up until the date of the hearing. This arrangement was expected to continue for the next few months at least. Mrs Green was not eligible to join the pension scheme in her new job until she had worked for them for 2 years.

The date of the remedies hearing has been listed for 03/01/2023.

Mrs Green's claims

- On 28/06/2022 Mrs Green brought claims of unfair and wrongful dismissal and sex discrimination at the ET.
- She maintained it would take a year to find another equivalent permanent job and therefore was claiming future loss of earnings until 17/04/2023.
- She was entitled to a sum representing loss of statutory rights.
- Any award should be increased by 25% for the failure of the employer to comply with the Code of Practice.
- She was entitled to a sum of £850 representing untaken accrued holiday which the respondent had not paid on termination.
- She claimed a sum of £18,000 for injury to feelings and interest on this figure, from 01/01/2020 until 01/01/2022.
- Mrs Green argued that as it would take 2 years for her to become eligible to join the pension scheme in her new job she wants to be compensated for loss of pension for that time.

Pension information

- Her gross weekly pensionable pay at the date of dismissal was £2,500.
- Her employer contributed 12% of its wage bill to the private pension scheme.

Respondent's Counter Schedule of Loss – Green v XYZ Ltd

Counter arguments

- The claimant's schedule of loss does not include her expected earnings, which are estimated to be £3,000 from the date of the hearing to the date when the employer's liability ends. This needs to be recorded.
- The respondent disputes the 25% uplift for failing to follow the Code of Practice for unfair dismissal, submitting that the figure should be closer to 10%.
- The respondent submits that pension loss should be limited to the period up to the hearing date.
- The respondent also submits that the claimant was also partly responsible for her own dismissal to the extent of 10% (for both the basic and compensatory awards).
- A deduction of 2% should also be made for accelerated payment of future sums of compensation.
- The sum of £18,000 for injury to feelings is disputed – there was no discriminatory conduct on the part of the respondent.
- The compensation cap should be applied to the final figure since the dismissal of the claimant was not discriminatory.

IN THE EMPLOYMENT TRIBUNALS
CASE NO: 3452/87

BETWEEN

Green
AND
XYZ

CLAIMANT'S SCHEDULE OF LOSS

1. Details

Date of birth	14/02/1988
Date started employment	24/10/2018
Effective Date of Termination	17/04/2022
Period of continuous service (years)	3
Age at Effective Date of Termination	34
Remedy hearing date	03/01/2023
Cut-off date for future loss of earnings	17/04/2023
Contractual notice period (weeks)	8
Statutory notice period (weeks)	3
Net weekly pay at EDT	£2,000
Gross weekly pay at EDT	£2,500

2. Basic award

Number of qualifying weeks (3) x Gross weekly pay (£571.00[1])	£1,713.00
Total basic award	**£1,713.00**

3. Damages for wrongful dismissal

Loss of earnings: Damages period (8) x Net weekly pay (£2,000)	£16,000.00
Plus failure by employer to follow statutory procedures @ 25%[2]	£4,000.00[3]
Total damages	**£20,000.00**

4. Compensatory award (immediate loss)

Loss of net earnings: Number of weeks (29.3[4]) x Net weekly pay (£2,000)	£58,600.00
Plus loss of statutory rights	£350.00
Plus accrued holiday pay	£850.00
Less payment in lieu	-£2,000.00
Less earnings: (23/07/2022 to 03/01/2023)	-£15,523.00
Pension loss (loss of employer contributions)[5]	
£2,500 x 0.12 x 37.3 weeks	£11,190.00
Total compensation (immediate loss)	**£53,467.00**

---

[1] £571 was the limit on a week's pay at an EDT of 17/04/2022

[2] The ACAS uplift can also apply to damages for wrongful dismissal – see Adjustments and order of adjustments and Schedule A2 of TULR(C)A

[3] £16,000 x 0.25

[4] 29.3 weeks has been calculated by subtracting the damages period of 8 weeks from the total number of weeks between EDT and the hearing date (37.3)

[5] Following the guidance in *Principles for Calculating Pension Loss* which was updated in March 2021

5. Compensatory award (future loss)

Loss of future earnings: Number of weeks (14.9[6]) x Net weekly pay (£2,000)	£29,800.00
Future loss of pension (loss of employer contributions)	
£2,500 x 0.12 x 66.7[7] weeks	£20,010.00
Total compensation (future loss)	**£49,810.00**

6. Adjustments to total compensatory award

Failure by employer to follow statutory procedures @ 25%	£25,819.25[8]
Compensatory award before adjustments	**£103,277.00**
Total adjustments to the compensatory award	**£25,819.25**
Compensatory award after adjustments	**£129,096.25**

7. Discrimination

Injury to feelings	£18,000.00
Plus interest @ 8%[9] for 730 days	£2,880.00[10]
Discrimination award	**£20,880.00**

8. Summary totals

Basic award	£1,713.00
Wrongful dismissal	£20,000.00
Compensation award	£129,096.25
Discrimination	£20,880.00
TOTAL	**£171,689.25**
TOTAL AFTER GROSSING UP AT 40%	**£265,582.08[11]**

---

[6] Number of weeks between 03/01/2023 and 17/04/2023

[7] 104 weeks (i.e. 2 years) minus 37.3 weeks immediate loss

[8] (£53,467.00 + £49,810.00) x 0.25. Remember that accrued holiday pay which has not been paid can be classed as unlawful deductions and thus uplifted according to Schedule A2 of TULR(C)A

[9] The interest rate is 8% from 29/07/2013

[10] £18,000 x 0.08 x 730 ÷ 365

[11] (£1,713 + £20,000 + £129,096.25 + £20,880 - £850) - £30,000 (i.e. the tax free amount) = £170,839.25 - £30,000.00 = £140,839.25. Remember that the £850 holiday pay should not be grossed up since it should be paid gross by the employer. The award for injury to feelings figure is also included here because this is fully taxable for EDTs after 06/04/2018

Grossed up at 40% = £140,839.25 ÷ 0.6 = £234,732.08

Add back the £30,000.00 and £850, and the final award comes to £265,582.08

The statutory cap does not apply since the claimant is claiming that the dismissal was for discriminatory reasons (see respondent's counter schedule)

IN THE EMPLOYMENT TRIBUNALS
CASE NO: 3452/87

BETWEEN

Green
AND
XYZ

RESPONDENT'S COUNTER SCHEDULE OF LOSS

1. Details

Date of birth	14/02/1988
Date started employment	24/10/2018
Effective Date of Termination	17/04/2022
Period of continuous service (years)	3
Age at Effective Date of Termination	34
Remedy hearing date	03/01/2023
Cut-off date for future loss of earnings	17/04/2023
Contractual notice period (weeks)	8
Statutory notice period (weeks)	3
Net weekly pay at EDT	£2,000
Gross weekly pay at EDT	£2,500

2. Basic award

Number of qualifying weeks (3) x Gross weekly pay (£571.00)	£1,713.00
Less contributory fault @ 10%	-£171.30
Total basic award	**£1,541.70**

3. Damages for wrongful dismissal

Loss of earnings: Damages period (8) x Net weekly pay (£2,000)	£16,000.00
Plus failure by employer to follow statutory procedures @ 10%	£1,600.00
Total damages	**£17,600.00**

4. Compensatory award (immediate loss)

Loss of net earnings: Number of weeks (29.3) x Net weekly pay (£2,000)	£58,600.00
Plus loss of statutory rights	£350.00
Plus accrued holiday pay	£850.00
Less payment in lieu	-£2,000.00
Less earnings: (23/07/2022 to 03/01/2023)	-£15,523.00
Pension loss	
£2,500 x 0.12 x 37.3 weeks	£11,190.00
Total compensation (immediate loss)	**£53,467.00**

5. Compensatory award (future loss)

Loss of future earnings: Number of weeks (14.9) x Net weekly pay (£2,000)	£29,800.00
Less expected future earnings (04/01/2023 to 17/04/2023)	-£3,000.00
Total compensation (future loss)	**£26,800.00**

6. Adjustments to total compensatory award

Less accelerated payment	-£536.00[12]
Plus failure by employer to follow statutory procedures (ACAS uplift) @ 10%	£7,973.10[13]
Less contributory fault (compensation award) @ 10%	-£8,685.41[14]
Compensatory award before adjustments	**£80,267.00**
Total adjustments to the compensatory award	**-£1,248.31[15]**
Compensatory award after adjustments	**£79,018.69**

7. Summary totals

Basic award	£1,541.70
Wrongful dismissal	£17,600.00
Compensatory award	£79,018.69
TOTAL	**£98,160.39**
GROSSED UP AWARD AT 40%	**£142,826.98[16]**
TOTAL AWARD CAPPED AT LOWER OF GROSS ANNUAL SALARY (£130,000) AND STATUTORY CAP (£93,878)[17]	**£106,311.50[18]**

---

[12] Accelerated payment only applies to future loss. The future loss figure is £26,800 and 2% of this figure is £26,800 x 0.02 = £536

[13] Immediate loss + future loss − accelerated receipt = £53,467 + £26,800 - £536 = £79,731. The ACAS adjustment should now be applied to this figure = £79,731 x 0.1 = £7,973.10

[14] This has been calculated by first adding together the immediate loss, future loss and ACAS uplift, and deducting the sums for accelerated receipt to get £53,467 + £26,800 + £7,973.10 - £536 = £87,704.10

Next, the contributory fault deduction needs to be applied to this new figure but LESS the £850 holiday pay sum because contributory fault does not apply to holiday pay. This now becomes: (£87,704.10 - £850) x 0.1 = £8,685.41

[15] - £536 + £7,973.10 - £8,685.41 = - £1,248.31

[16] (£1,541.70 + £17,600 + 79,018.69 - £850) - £30,000 = £97,310.39 - £30,000 = £67,310.39. Remember that the £850 holiday pay should not be grossed up since it should be paid gross by the employer

Grossed up at 40% = £67,310.39 ÷ 0.6 = £112,183.98

Add back £30,000 + £850 = £143,033.98

[17] The statutory cap applicable at an EDT of 17/04/2022 is £93,878 (see Table 1). Compare this with the claimant's gross annual salary of £130,000 (i.e. £2,500 x 52) and the smaller figure, in this case £93,878, applies.

[18] First, we need to find out what just the compensatory award is after the grossing up has been done to check if that figure exceeds the statutory cap. £10,858.30 was tax free (because £30,000 - £1,541.70 - £17,600 = £10,858.30). The balance of £67,310.39 (i.e. £79,018.69 - £10,858.30 - £850) is grossed up to get £112,183.98 (i.e. £67,310.39 ÷ 0.6)

Thus the total compensatory award = £10,858.30 + £112,183.98 (excluding the holiday pay) = £123,042.28 which exceeds the lower of the statutory cap and the gross annual salary

Therefore, the total capped award is: £1,541.70 + £17,600 + £93,878 + £850 = £113,869.70. Remember that the £850 holiday pay does not count towards the compensation cap

APPENDIX 3: Calculating holiday entitlement

The calculation of holiday entitlement can be a complicated matter. The calculation ultimately depends upon the construction of the contract of employment, and where relevant the construction of the Working Time Regulations. The Working Time Regulations must themselves be interpreted consistently with the Working Time Directive where it is the four weeks of paid leave that derive from the Directive that are under consideration (see *Bear Scotland & Ors v Fulton & Ors* [2015] ICR 221). Subject to that strong note of caution, the following principles will often assist in calculating holiday entitlement.

Working 5 or more days a week

Most workers who work a 5-day week have a statutory entitlement to 28 days paid annual leave per year which amounts to 5.6 weeks.

Note that the statutory minimum is limited to 28 days - even if a worker works 6 days per week, they will still only be statutorily entitled to 28 days holiday per year (not 6 x 5.6 which is 33.6 days).

Working part-time

Part-time workers are also entitled to a statutory minimum of 5.6 weeks of paid holiday each year, although this may amount to fewer actual days of paid holiday than a full-time worker would get. For example, someone working 4 days per week will be entitled to a minimum of 4 x 5.6 weeks which comes to 22.4 days per year.

Working a fixed number of days per week

Number of days entitlement per year = number of days worked per week (up to a maximum of 5 for the statutory minimum) x number of weeks holiday entitlement (5.6 is the statutory minimum although the contract of employment may provide for more)

> *Example 1*: for a worker who works 3 days per week, and who is contractually entitled to 7 weeks holiday per year, they would be entitled to 3 x 7 days = 21 days

> *Example 2*: a worker who works 4 days a week and is contractually entitled to 35 days a year pro rata would be entitled to 4 ÷ 5 x 35 = 28 days

> *Example 3*: a worker who works 4 days per week but has no contractual right to holiday would be entitled to 4 x 5.6 = 22.4 days

Working a fixed number of hours per week

Sometimes it is easier to calculate holiday entitlement in terms of hours rather than days, especially if the worker does not work whole days. It also means it is easier to calculate how much holiday is due to a worker who leaves part way through the leave year.

> *Example 4*: a worker works 20 hours per week, and is entitled to the statutory 5.6 weeks per year.

> Holiday entitlement is 20 x 5.6 hours per year = 112 hours

Working a different number of hours per week and variable number of days per week

This will apply to many casual workers and again it is usually easier to calculate holiday entitlement in hours, with direct reference to the number of hours actually worked. Note that the WTD provides for entitlement to four weeks paid leave.

Statutory holiday entitlement only

For each hour worked, the worker accrues 0.1207 of an hour or roughly 7 minutes of holiday. The 0.1207 is the proportion of the working year that a worker is entitled to have as holiday by statute, and is worked out as:

> 5.6 ÷ (52 - 5.6) = 5.6 ÷ 46.4 = 0.1207 [The 5.6 weeks are excluded from the calculation as the worker would not be at work during those 5.6 weeks in order to accrue annual leave.]

> *Example 5*: a worker works 20 hours in a week.

> Holiday entitlement = 20 x 0.1207 = 2.41 hours, which is approximately 2 hours and 25 minutes.

Holiday entitlement in excess of statutory minimum where holiday is expressed in weeks (W)

For each hour worked, the worker is entitled to W ÷ (52 - W) of an hour.

> *Example 6*: a worker works 25 hours per week, and holiday entitlement is 6 weeks per year.
>
> Holiday entitlement per hour of work = 6 ÷ (52 - 6) = 0.1304 of an hour or about 8 minutes.

Holiday entitlement in excess of statutory minimum where holiday is expressed in days (D)

For each hour worked, the worker is entitled to D/5 ÷ (52 - D/5) of an hour (this divides days by 5 rather than 7, since the statutory formula is worked out on the basis of 5 working days).

> *Example 7*: a worker works 25 hours and holiday entitlement is 34 days per year.
>
> Holiday entitlement per hour of work = 34/5 ÷ (52 - 34/5) = 0.1504 of an hour = approximately 9 minutes

Annualised hours

The following calculations would be suitable for any worker who works a set number of hours per year. The easiest way to calculate holiday entitlement is to treat the worker as a casual worker and calculate the number of hours of holiday accrued per hour of work actually done.

For statutory holiday entitlement

Holiday in hours = hours actually worked x 0.1207

For holiday entitlement in excess of statutory minimum

Holiday in hours = hours worked x W ÷ (52 - W) where W is the number of weeks holiday the worker is entitled to according to their employment contract.

> *Example 8*: a worker works 1000 hours per year and is entitled to 8 weeks holiday per year.
>
> Holiday entitlement = 1000 x 8 ÷ (52 - 8) = 181.82 hours per year.

Compressed hours

Some workers work compressed hours; for example, they may work 40 hours compressed into 4 days instead of 5.

The easiest way in which this is calculated is by working out the number of hours' holiday that is being accrued. This avoids having to calculate the length of a day for the purposes of taking a day off.

Holiday entitlement (hours) = hours worked in a week x number of weeks of contractual holiday (or 5.6 if only statutory holiday).

Shift workers

The easiest way in which holiday entitlement can be calculated in this case is to work out the number of shifts the worker is entitled to take off. To do this calculate the proportion of the entire shift pattern (including days off) that the worker has actually worked to work out the average number of shifts worked per week, and then multiply this number of shifts by the number of weeks of annual holiday entitlement.

> *Example 9*: a worker works four 12 hour shifts in a week and then has 2 days off. He is only entitled to statutory holiday.
>
> First find out the average number of shifts worked per week. The complete shift pattern is 6 days, of which the worker works 4. So in a 7 day week they work on average: 4 ÷ (4 + 2) x 7 = 4.67 shifts.
>
> Then, annual holiday entitlement = 4.67 x 5.6 = 26.15 shifts

Entitlement if a worker starts or leaves part way through the leave year

Starters

You need to work out the proportion of the year left from the day the worker started to the end of the leave year, then multiply by the entitlement as calculated above.

> *Example 10*: leave year is from 1 January to 31 December. A worker starts on 18 September. Full years' entitlement (as calculated using the above formulae) = 28 days.
>
> First, the number of days between 18 September and 31 December, including both days = 105.
>
> Holiday entitlement for the remaining period = 28 x 105 ÷ 365 (or 366 in a leap year) = 8 days

Leavers

You need to work out the proportion of the leave year actually worked, then multiply by the entitlement as calculated above. Finally subtract any holiday actually taken.

> **Example 11**: leave year is from 1 June to 31 May. A casual worker worked a total of 600 hours and left on 24 October and had already taken 20 hours holiday. Statutory holiday entitlement applies.
>
> In this case, because holiday is being accrued for each hour worked, we don't need to work out the proportion of the leave year worked.
>
> Holiday entitlement = 600 x 0.1207 hours = 72.42 hours
>
> Holiday pay due = 72.42 - 20 = 52.42 hours
>
> **Example 12**: leave year is from 1 June to 31 May. A worker, who worked 3 days a week, left on 24 October and had already taken 4 days holiday in that leave year. Statutory holiday entitlement applies.
>
> Annual holiday entitlement = 3 x 5.6 = 16.8 days
>
> Then, number of days between 1 June and 24 October inclusive = 146 days
>
> Holiday entitlement = 16.8 x 146 ÷ 365 (366 in a leap year) = 6.72
>
> Holiday pay due = 6.72 - 4 = 2.72 days

Term time only workers

There is no specific calculation for working out the holiday entitlement for term time workers and the easiest and fairest calculations might be those used for annualised hours or casual/irregular hours .

Calculating accrued holiday pay on termination of employment

If an employee has left employment part way through a leave year, and at the effective date of termination he has taken less holiday than he is entitled to up to that date, the employer should make a payment in lieu to the employee, either according to a relevant agreement (see below) or, if no such agreement exists, then the accrued holiday is calculated according to Reg 14 WTR 1998 which then needs to be multiplied by a day's pay or an hour's pay:

(A x B) - C

where:

A is the period of leave to which the worker is entitled;

B is the proportion of the worker's leave year which expired before the termination date; and

C is the period of leave taken by the worker between the start of the leave year and the termination date.

What is a day's pay?

The calculation of a days' pay can be a complicated matter. The calculation ultimately depends upon the construction of the contract of employment, and where relevant the construction of the Working Time Regulations and ss221 to 224 ERA 1996. The Working Time Regulations must themselves be interpreted consistently with the Working Time Directive where it is the four weeks of paid leave that derive from the Directive that are under consideration, such that provisions in the ERA 1996 for calculating a days' pay cannot be relied upon at face value (see *Bear Scotland & Ors v Fulton & Ors* [2015] ICR 221). Subject to that strong note of caution, the following principles will often assist in calculating holiday entitlement.

A day's pay for the purposes of working out holiday pay is calculated according to a 'working' year rather than a full 365 day calendar year. This approach was adopted by the EAT in *Leisure Leagues UK Ltd v Macconnachie* UKEAT/940/01. It held that a year's pay should be divided by 233 because this was the number of actual days worked by the claimant in the year.

What is an hour's pay?

For workers for whom it is easier to calculate holiday entitlement in terms of hours rather than days, it will be necessary to calculate the appropriate hourly rate of pay. Where there is a straightforward hourly rate of pay with no variations or additional sums, this will be simple to establish. Otherwise, this may be calculated by identifying the total remuneration over the last 12 weeks and dividing this by the total number of hours worked over the last 12 weeks, in accordance with the calculation of a day's pay, but using hours worked instead of days.

Relevant agreement

Podlasiak v Edinburgh Woollen Mill Ltd is an ET decision where the tribunal held that a clause in the claimant's contract of employment, providing that they would receive £1 in respect of any accrued holiday pay on termination of employment, was unlawful and unenforceable. It was incompatible with the Working Time Directive, even though otherwise consistent with the wording in the WTR.